Global Tantra

AMERICAN ACADEMY OF RELIGION

RELIGION, CULTURE, AND HISTORY

SERIES EDITOR
Robert A. Yelle, Ludwig-Maximilians-Universität München

A Publication Series of
the American Academy of Religion
and
Oxford University Press

ANTI-JUDAISM IN FEMINIST RELIGIOUS WRITINGS
Katharina von Kellenbach

CROSS-CULTURAL CONVERSATION
(Initiation)
Edited by Anindita Niyogi Balslev

ON DECONSTRUCTING LIFE-WORLDS
Buddhism, Christianity, Culture
Robert Magliola

THE GREAT WHITE FLOOD
Racism in Australia
Anne Pattel-Gray

IMAG(IN)ING OTHERNESS
Filmic Visions of Living Together
Edited by S. Brent Plate and David Jasper

CULTURAL OTHERNESS
Correspondence with Richard Rorty, Second Edition
Anindita Niyogi Balslev

FEMINIST POETICS OF THE SACRED
Creative Suspicions
Edited by Frances Devlin-Glass and Lyn McCredden

PARABLES FOR OUR TIME
Rereading New Testament Scholarship after the Holocaust
Tania Oldenhage

MOSES IN AMERICA
The Cultural Uses of Biblical Narrative
Melanie Jane Wright

INTERSECTING PATHWAYS
Modern Jewish Theologians in Conversation with Christianity
Marc A. Krell

ASCETICISM AND ITS CRITICS
Historical Accounts and Comparative Perspectives
Edited by Oliver Freiberger

VIRTUOUS BODIES
The Physical Dimensions of Morality in Buddhist Ethics
Susanne Mrozik

IMAGINING THE FETUS
The Unborn in Myth, Religion, and Culture
Edited by Vanessa R. Sasson and Jane Marie Law

VICTORIAN REFORMATION
The Fight over Idolatry in the Church of England, 1840–1860
Dominic Janes

SCHLEIERMACHER ON RELIGION AND THE NATURAL ORDER
Andrew C. Dole

MUSLIMS AND OTHERS IN SACRED SPACE
Edited by Margaret Cormack

LITTLE BUDDHAS
Children and Childhoods in Buddhist Texts and Traditions
Edited by Vanessa R. Sasson

HINDU CHRISTIAN FAQIR
Modern Monks, Global Christianity, and Indian Sainthood
Timothy S. Dobe

MUSLIMS BEYOND THE ARAB WORLD
The Odyssey of ʿAjamī *and the Murīdiyya*
Fallou Ngom

LATINO AND MUSLIM IN AMERICA
Race, Religion, and the Making of a New Minority
Harold D. Morales

THE MANY FACES OF A HIMALAYAN GODDESS
Haḍimbā, Her Devotees, and Religion in Rapid Change
Ehud Halperin

MISSIONARY CALCULUS
Americans in the Making of Sunday Schools in Victorian India
Anilkumar Belvadi

DEVOTIONAL SOVEREIGNTY
Kingship and Religion in India
Caleb Simmons

ECOLOGIES OF RESONANCE IN CHRISTIAN MUSICKING
Mark Porter

GLOBAL TANTRA
Religion, Science, and Nationalism in Colonial Modernity
Julian Strube

AMERICAN ACADEMY OF RELIGION

Global Tantra

Religion, Science, and Nationalism in Colonial Modernity

JULIAN STRUBE

OXFORD
UNIVERSITY PRESS

OXFORD
UNIVERSITY PRESS

Oxford University Press is a department of the University of Oxford. It furthers the University's objective of excellence in research, scholarship, and education by publishing worldwide. Oxford is a registered trade mark of Oxford University Press in the UK and certain other countries.

Published in the United States of America by Oxford University Press
198 Madison Avenue, New York, NY 10016, United States of America.

Library of Congress Cataloging-in-Publication Data
Names: Strube, Julian, author.
Title: Global tantra : religion, science, and nationalism
in colonial modernity / Julian Strube.
Description: New York, NY, United States of America : Oxford University Press, [2022] |
Series: AAR religion culture and history |
Includes bibliographical references and index.
Identifiers: LCCN 2021035123 (print) | LCCN 2021035124 (ebook) |
ISBN 9780197627112 (hardback) | ISBN 9780197627136 (epub) |
Subjects: LCSH: Tantrism—India—History. | India—Intellectual life. |
India—Religion. | Science—India. | Political science—India.
Classification: LCC BL1283.83 .S77 2022 (print) |
LCC BL1283.83 (ebook) | DDC 294.5/514—dc23
LC record available at https://lccn.loc.gov/2021035123
LC ebook record available at https://lccn.loc.gov/2021035124

DOI: 10.1093/oso/9780197627112.001.0001

1 3 5 7 9 8 6 4 2

Printed by Integrated Books International, United States of America

إلى نور قمري، لهيب حياتي

Contents

Acknowledgments ix
Note on Transliteration xi

Introduction: Why a Global Religious History? 1
Global Tantra 1
Regional and Local Entanglements 9
Traditional Revival or Modern Reform? 12
Global Religious History 16
Esotericism and Religion in the Context of Colonial Modernity 21
Agency under Colonialism: The Case of Theosophy 28
Outline of the Chapters 33

1. The Bengali Intervention 38
The Theosophical Quest for Esoteric Truth 38
Baradakanta Majumdar's Defense of Tantrik Occultism 43
The Regional Background of Bengali Tantra 48
Baradakanta, the Theosophist 55
Where the Threads Meet: Arthur Avalon 62
Esotericism and Orientalist Scholarship 65

2. Theosophy in Bengal 69
Theosophy and the Revival of "Aryan Civilization" 69
The Notion of "Aryan" in the Tangle of Orientalism and Theosophy 73
The Ārya Samāj and the Brāhma Samāj 82
The Beginning of Theosophical Activities in Bengal 89

3. The Contested Science of Yoga 96
"Yoga Vidya" between Science and Religion 96
The Separation between Hatha and Raja Yoga 104
The First Wave of Bengali Contributions 110
The Basu Brothers 116

4. Reformism and Spiritualist Perspectives on Tantra 124
Pyarichand Mitra and Reformist Tantra 125
Kshetrapal Chakravarti: "Tantra Is Science, Tantra Is Religion" 131
Light of the East 137
Shishirkumar Ghosh and the *Hindu Spiritual Magazine* 141

5. Revivalism and Theosophy 149
Reform through the Authority of Antiquity: The *Mahānirvāṇa Tantra* 149
Struggles about the Meaning of Revival and Reform 152
Tantra as *Sanātana Dharma* 155
Theosophy among the Revivalists 158

6. Shivachandra Vidyarnava 163
The Intellectual Atmosphere at Kumarkhali 164
Vernacular Education and the Formation of a Tantric Pandit 167
Public Activities and the Sarvamaṅgalā Sabhā 170
Tantratattva: The Principles of Tantra 174
Science and *Sādhana* in *Tantratattva* 179
Heralding the Dawn of a New Kaula Age 185

7. Tantra and Nationalism 187
The Swadeshi Context 188
Awakening the Bloodthirsty Mother 192
Shashadhar Tarkachuramani's Spiritual Science 199
Pramathanath Mukhopadhyay and National Education 207

8. Arthur Avalon and Tantrik Occultism 213
Enter John Woodroffe 213
The Network behind Arthur Avalon 220
The Woodroffes and the Theosophical Society 226
The Science of Tantrik Spiritual Culture 229
Science and Education, Eastern and Western 233
Esoteric Universalism 237

9. Conclusion: What a Global Religious History Could Offer 242

Notes 253
Bibliography 295
Index 323

Acknowledgments

The completion of this book would not have been possible without the support of more people than I can name here. I am first and foremost grateful for the supervision and invaluable feedback from my *Habilitation* referees, Michael Bergunder, Hans Harder, and Adrian Hermann. The research has been enabled by funding from the German Research Foundation (DFG) at the University of Heidelberg and was facilitated in the run-up to and wake of the project by positions at the Cluster of Excellence "Asia and Europe in a Global Context" at the University of Heidelberg, as well as at the Cluster of Excellence "Religion and Politics" at the University of Münster, which provided additional funding. The finishing touches to the manuscript were added at the University of Hamburg and the University of Vienna. I am thankful for the effort put into this publication by Robert Yelle, Cynthia Read, Zara Cannon-Mohammed, Archanaa Rajapandian, and Judith Hoover, as well as for the comments by the anonymous referees who helped me to improve the original manuscript.

I have benefited from outstanding teachers who have taught me Bengali, namely Chaiti Basu, Sunanda Basu, and Mala Al-Farooq. Throughout recent years, I have also received precious help in working with Bengali sources and conducting research in West Bengal, especially by Swastik Banerjee, Saswati Mukherjee, Sulagna Mukhopadhyay, Judhajit Sarkar, and Shabnam Surita. Without them, this study would be considerably poorer. The same applies to those working in libraries, archives, and other collections that I have accessed, including the Theosophical Society in Adyar, where I especially thank Tim Boyd, Jaishree Kannan, and Prof. C. A. Shinde. I was welcomed and helped at the Bengal Theosophical Society in Kolkata, the Ramakrishna Vedanta Math, the Ramakrishna Mission Institute of Culture, the Bangiya Sahitya Parishat, the Asiatic Society in Kolkata, the Indian National Library, the West Bengal State Library, the British Library, and the Royal Asiatic Society in London. The Rev. Mother Sudha Puri of the Vedanta Centre in Cohasset, Massachusetts, and Sister Murtimata of the Ananda Ashrama, La Crescenta, California, have provided me with valuable information.

The descendants of Shivachandra Bhattacharyya Vidyarnava have received me with great hospitality, for which I am especially grateful to

Rabindranath and Dipa Bhattacharya as well as Sourav Chatterjee and Rupam Lahiri. Siddhartha Ghosh welcomed me warmly at the residence of Atalbihari Ghosh's family.

This project would have been impossible without the pioneering research of Kathleen Taylor, on whose in-depth biographical work about John Woodroffe I could base crucial parts of this book. I am very thankful for our friendly conversations and the source material that she provided me with.

Among the many colleagues, friends, and interlocutors who have accompanied me during the work on my manuscript, I would like to thank Egil Asprem, Karl Baier, Swarnabha Bala, Jayati Banerjee, Milinda Banerjee, Priyanka Basu, Joel Bordeaux, Keith Cantú, Sukla Chatterjee, Madhumita Das, Rahul Peter Das, Alokeranjan Dasgupta, Philip Deslippe, Arindam Dutt, Swarupa Gupta, Martin Hribek, Knut Jacobsen, Hans Martin Krämer, Borayin Maitreya Larios, Carola Erika Lorea, Aritra Majumdar, Yves Mühlematter, Jyotirmoy Mukherjee, Mriganka Mukhopadhyay, Suzanne Newcombe, Karen O'Brien-Kop, Dimitry Okropiridze, Russell Ó Ríagáin, Baijayanti Roy, Ferdinando Sardella, Subhabrata Sen, Sudipta Munsi, Layli Uddin, and Helmut Zander. My exchanges with them are deeply ingrained in the pages that follow. A thundering "up to irons" goes to my brother Dylan Burns. I also benefited from the wonderful working environment at Münster, where my fellow postdocs and PhD students accompanied the crucial phase of the publication, especially Francesco Gusella, Kirsten Kamphuis, Franziska Kleybolte, Haila Manteghi Amin, and Florian Neitmann. A special shoutout goes to my fellow traveler and brother Hakan Özkan.

All this would have been inconceivable without my friends and family. In addition to those who know that they are meant, I would especially like to thank my mother, Christine, as well as Rosalie Basten for her friendship and support. Above everything shines my moonlight, Liana Saif.

Vienna, August 16, 2021

Note on Transliteration

Due to the lack of a commonly accepted standardized transliteration system for Bengali, I have attempted to strike a balance between those readers who understand Bengali and those who would be distracted by an abundance of diacritics. While it would be possible to strictly adhere to the International Alphabet of Sanskrit Transliteration when romanizing Bengali, this would poorly reflect the actual spelling and pronunciation of Bengali terms. I have decided to stick closely to the Sanskritized version, but I am providing more exact romanizations in quotes, names, and titles within the bibliographical references. In the main text, widespread Sanskrit terms are romanized according to Sanskrit, not Bengali, rules.

Terms that are well established in English, such as "kundalini," "shakti," "Vaishnava," and "Hatha Yoga," are written without diacritics. In all quotes, the original diacritics will be provided, whether correct or not. Older conventions, such as á and â, have been converted to ā. While I avoided diacritics in proper names throughout the main text, I do use them for societies and titles.

Historical Bengalis will be referred to by their "first names," as is usual in Bengal, where many people share the same "last name." For instance, when I discuss Bankimchandra Chattopadhyay, the reader will find a mention not of "Mr. Chattopadhyay" but of Bankimchandra, whose first names are written together rather than separate (as in Bankim Chandra). Since it is also common to simply refer to Bankim, I will mostly use that version.

Bengali names have historically been romanized in diverse ways. Last names especially have been rendered in ways that might be confusing for the uninitiated, with Mukhopadhyay often turning into Mookerji, Mookerjee, or Mukherji, among other variants. Other examples are Chattopadhyay turning into Chatterjee and Bandyopadhyay turning into Banerjee, Bonnerji, etc. My not entirely satisfying solution is the standardization of last names in the main text according to the "original" variant (i.e., Mukhopadhyay, Chattopadhyay), while the bibliography will provide the exact names used in the original English-language publications and the more accurately romanized name for publications in Bengali. In the index, all proper names are standardized. Exceptions are names that are so famous that a standardization would be confusing, for instance, Rabindranath Tagore instead of Thakur. The names of locations are given in their nineteenth-century version, with a reference to today's name at first mention, for instance, Calcutta (now Kolkata).

Introduction

Why a Global Religious History?

Global Tantra

Today, Tantra is a widely discussed subject across the globe. It is often associated with notions such as sacred sexuality, feminine spirituality, sociopolitical and sexual liberation, or mental and bodily well-being. Countless people practice a vast spectrum of interpretations of Tantra, many of which relate to issues such as commodification, commercialization, and sensationalism.[1] What is "it," however? Most scholars would agree that there is more than one answer to this question, varying drastically in different contexts. Many have encountered Tantra in the context of prominent movements such as that of Osho or Bhagwan Rajneesh, which have cemented the subject's association with "New Age" spirituality that scholars such as David Gordon White, Gavin Flood, and André Padoux tend to assess critically.[2] There is, in short, a significant discrepancy between "popular" and "academic" perceptions of Tantra. One aim of this study is to demonstrate that these spheres are historically difficult to distinguish, without denying the major distinctions between different trajectories of the reception of Tantra.

Experts on Asian history, and Sanskrit sources in particular, rightfully highlight the vast and complicated history of what might be subsumed under the term "tantra." While there are scriptures called the *tantras*, their content is highly diverse and can hardly help to delineate a monolithic tradition or doctrine. Rather, a wide range of Tantric elements form an integral part of (South) Asian history for a period of over one thousand years; Indian culture from the village level to that of kingship cannot be understood without them.[3] The utterance of mantras or the ritual mapping of the deity on the practitioner's body (*nyāsa*); the construction of mandalas, yantras, and temples; instructions for kings; philosophical contemplation about the relationship between the individual and the universe—these and many more integral aspects of South Asian religious, social, and political life are inexorably

Global Tantra. Julian Strube, Oxford University Press. © Oxford University Press 2022.
DOI: 10.1093/oso/9780197627112.003.0001

intertwined with various Tantric scriptures and traditions.[4] Tantra plays an especially significant role in goddess-centered traditions, in those focusing on Shiva (Shaivism), and in those focusing on the impersonal female aspect, shakti (*śakti*), that pervades the world (Shaktism). This latter aspect often leads to a (qualified) nondualism, which assumes an ultimate unity of all Being and consequently embraces the material world in order to achieve liberation.

The realization of an absolute identity of everything also underlies the highly ritualized transgression of norms of caste, sex, and purity that is essential to some variants of Tantric practice; the consumption of impure substances and the central role of sexual intercourse (*maithuna*) are expressions of the futility of ultimate distinctions between pure and impure, as well as of the value of the material world for the practitioner.[5] A complex variety of yogic practice leading to the acquirement of special powers (*siddhi*) is another hallmark of Tantra that links it closely to the general subject of yoga, both historically and today. We can observe, then, that modern understandings of Tantra do have some grounding in aspects of historical Tantric traditions, such as femininity, sexuality, and yoga. Yet the commercialized and commodified "Tantric sex" that any internet search will yield usually has little to do with the practices and ideas that are presented in the *tantras*, and apt criticism has been leveled against the unreflected appropriation of these South Asian traditions. Tantra, like yoga, has been turned into a product catering to the consumer and popular cultures of "Western" countries.[6]

At the same time, specialists such as Hugh Urban have emphasized that modern understandings of Tantra were the outcome of global exchanges that are not simply determined by "Western" imagination and appropriation.[7] The Osho movement is a case in point, as it defies clear-cut categorizations into "East" and "West."[8] In fact, Urban has described it as "the first truly transnational religious movement of the modern era," and hence as an impressive example of the role of religion within the process of "globalization" after the Second World War.[9] Consequently, modern "Neo-Tantra" is framed with notions such as "postmodern spirituality," the "spiritual marketplace," the "spiritual logic of late capitalism," or "neoliberalism."[10] This postwar focus on what Tulasi Srinivas has referred to as "cultural globalization" was mainly concerned with unraveling the *contemporary* role of religion in light of multiculturalism, capitalism, and the neoliberal marketplace from anthropological, ethnographic, and sociological perspectives.[11] Srinivas, too, has stressed that it would be too simplistic to view these processes in terms of a unidirectional flow of ideas "from the West to the rest," as they reveal "a far more dynamic and multidirectional global flow of religious forms."[12] In short, there are valuable studies that demonstrate the complexities and contradictions of South Asian religious traditions, and Tantra in particular, within the process of globalization since the 1950s.

There remains, however, a glaring gap with regard to the nineteenth century, and its global dimension in particular. While Urban, for instance, has provided vital insights into the nineteenth-century history of Tantra, his research was not carried out within a global historical framework. His assessment of the Osho-Rajneesh movement as "the first truly transnational religious movement of the modern era" illustrates the blind spots arising from this, as it does not take into account another movement that is generally almost absent in Urban's and other works on Tantra: the Theosophical Society, which preceded Osho-Rajneesh by roughly a century and was very much a truly global religious movement.[13]

I hold that this combined neglect of a global perspective on the religious history of the nineteenth century and Theosophy in particular is emblematic of tendencies within religious studies in general, but also within disciplines such as global history and South Asian studies. First, although there is broad consensus about the crucial relevance of the nineteenth century for the emergence or renegotiation of terms such as "religion," "Tantra," and "Hinduism," research on their histories remains largely compartmentalized into regional, linguistic, and disciplinary fields. Second, this constitutes a major obstacle to in-depth explorations of the global connections that shaped historical understandings of our research subjects throughout the nineteenth century and up to the present day, especially as the disciplines of religious studies and South Asian studies rarely engage with global history and related fields in a more than superficial manner. A third aspect directly results from the previous two: while the importance of the subject area that might be summarized as "esotericism" is frequently acknowledged in studies of Tantra, and Indian religions more broadly, previous research has followed a Eurocentric "export model" that more or less explicitly presupposed the diffusion of a "Western esotericism" into South Asia.

These aspects place the subject of this book right at the heart of major ongoing debates about theoretical and methodological challenges revolving around Eurocentrism, orientalism, the notion of the "global," colonialism, and the emergence of "modern" understandings of religion. I here propose the approach of global religious history (*globale Religionsgeschichte*) as a fruitful way out of current deadlocks and a constructive transgression of disciplinary boundaries that, departing from the repertoire of religious studies, engages with the fields of global history and South Asian studies. Before I detail this approach, it is necessary to illustrate the entanglements among global, regional, and local contexts through which the subject at hand has emerged.

The most obviously *global* organization that is relevant for the study of modern Tantra is the Theosophical Society, which was founded in New York in 1875 and relocated its headquarters to India in 1879 in search of esoteric "Aryan wisdom." Even though the role of Theosophy for the history of Tantra since the nineteenth century was decisive and duly recognized by contemporaries, it is only briefly mentioned by Urban and other recent experts on the subject. This is partly due to the ambivalent attitude of leading Theosophists toward Tantra, but mainly to more fundamental theoretical and methodical issues, most significantly, a persistent focus on the "Western" representatives of Theosophy, such as the charismatic Helena Petrovna Blavatsky (1831–1891).

Mentioning that the "Western appropriation of Tantra had already begun in the late nineteenth century," Urban singles out Blavatsky's predominant perception of Tantra as "black magic" as fundamentally different from its later, more positive appropriation by the "Western popular imagination," when it became "identified more and more with the pursuit of sensual pleasure and erotic bliss."[14] While Urban is correct in distinguishing between the viewpoint of Blavatsky and later New Age receptions of "Tantric sex," I argue that his discussion of Theosophy could be enriched and complexified by considering three aspects. First, Theosophy and related esoteric currents such as New Thought, Christian Science, occultism, and Spiritualism were foundational for what later came to be called New Age spirituality and cannot be historically separated from it.[15] Second, Urban exclusively focuses on Blavatsky while ignoring not only the broad spectrum of different standpoints toward Tantra within the Society but especially the many thousands of Indians and other Asians who were members of and interacted with the Theosophical Society. It would be misleading to view the Theosophical engagement with Tantra simply in terms of "Western appropriation," as the evidence provided in this book will prove. Third, fully considering Theosophy would help to expand the historical contextualization of Tantra, especially with regard to the global dimension of the exchanges that shaped understandings of it prior to the period after the Second World War.

Exploring the role of Theosophy in its own right does not merely serve to unearth a marginal aspect of nineteenth-century history that might be of interest only for experts on esotericism. This becomes evident in light of a figure who was of decisive importance for the emergence of Tantra, not only as a heterogeneous set of practices and ideas across the globe but also as a reputed subject of academic study: Arthur Avalon. The publications of this pseudonymous author revolutionized academic approaches to Tantra and exerted a lasting influence on a global scale. That generations of academic scholars have by now devoted their careers to its study is largely due to these works.

It was believed for a long time that the person behind the alias was the British colonial judge John Woodroffe (1865–1936). After studying law in Oxford, he had followed his father, James Tisdall Woodroffe, the advocate-general of Bengal, to Calcutta (now Kolkata), where he began working at the High Court in 1890. In 1904, he was appointed judge, a position that he held until 1922, when he left India to teach Indian law at Oxford. The year 1913 saw the first publication by Arthur Avalon, followed by a substantial number of translations, editions, and studies of Tantric sources, and Tantra in general.[16] It did not take long before Woodroffe was identified as the driving force behind these remarkable efforts, and after a few years he began to publish several writings on Tantra and related topics under his own name. Later editions of Avalon's books were also published under Woodroffe's name.

Today, experts such as Urban and White portray Woodroffe as a "remarkable pioneer and even as the father of the modern study of the Tantras,"[17] as the "father of Tantric studies and, by extension, of the emergence of 'Tantric' practice in Europe and the United States."[18] In a way, this is true. After Tantra had been denounced as black magic, devil worship, and sexual license by missionaries, orientalists, and Indian "reformers," the Avalon publications established it as a reputable, if controversial, subject of study. These publications were hugely influential not only among academics but also in esoteric and New Age contexts that were, as Jeffrey Kripal points out, inherently intertwined with the academic study of Tantra.[19] Beginning with diverse personalities such as Heinrich Zimmer, Mircea Eliade, Jakob Wilhelm Hauer, Carl Gustav Jung, Sylvain Lévi, Paul Masson-Oursel, and Agehananda Bharati, the works of Arthur Avalon informed generations of scholars.[20] In India, they were important references for scholars such as

Shashibhusan Das Gupta and Sures Chandra Banerji. At the same time, they influenced a plethora of esoteric practitioners, including the fascistic author Julius Evola and occultists such as Israel Regardie, Gerald J. Yorke, and Kenneth Grant.[21]

While the importance of Arthur Avalon for the history of modern Tantra is beyond question, the prevalent focus on Woodroffe is not only highly misleading for an understanding of the historical developments that led to and shaped the Avalon project, but it also carries theoretical and methodological consequences that pertain to the issues of Eurocentrism and agency under colonialism. As was repeatedly admitted in the Avalon publications, a team of collaborators stood behind that name, rather than one individual. From the very beginning, Avalon thanked their "Indian friends for the aid they have given me."[22] While this suggests that the author of such statements was indeed Woodroffe, there can be no doubt that he had to rely on his partners for information and linguistic expertise.[23] As late as in 1921, he admitted that he was only in the process of learning Sanskrit, which implies that his skills were not sufficient to do the translations and editions himself.[24] In 2001, this has been elucidated in a biography by Kathleen Taylor, who was able to identify Woodroffe's most important partners, mainly the Bengali scholar Atalbihari Ghosh (1864–1936).[25] Yet Woodroffe tends to remain in the spotlight and is still shorthand for Arthur Avalon. From historical contemporaries via postwar scholarship up to the recent diverse works by Urban, White, Flood, Padoux, June McDaniel, and Andrew Sartori, we read that Woodroffe "translated" and "wrote" the Avalon publications, or was simply identical with the synonym.[26]

Clearly, the insights provided by Taylor have not been taken to their logical consequence, which would include a thorough historical contextualization of the Avalon project and an exploration of his South Asian, predominantly Bengali collaborators. In turn, although Taylor has done important work to shed light on the team effort that was Avalon, she focused on the role of Atalbihari Ghosh. Her study is a biographical one that dwells only on the larger historical context where it is directly relevant for Woodroffe. Both the diachronic and synchronic contexts of Tantra in Bengal, and certainly its global dimensions, remain largely unexplored.

Again, this lacuna is forcefully highlighted by Theosophy, since the Avalon project was the outcome of a longer development that started before Woodroffe arrived in Calcutta; the pivotal moment in the emergence of "global Tantra" can be traced to the year 1880, when learned Bengalis began to articulate their understanding of Tantra to an English-speaking audience. Their chosen interlocutors were none other than the readers of *The Theosophist*, the worldwide-distributed flagship journal of the recently founded Theosophical Society. The Bengali intellectuals challenged the predominantly negative image of Tantra. Often invoked as the most extreme example of the supposed inferiority or degeneracy of Indian culture, Tantra had become a highly contested subject in debates among Indian "reformers" and the propagators of a Hindu "orthodoxy" allegedly threatened by foreign corruptions. The "Bengali intervention" would significantly, if not entirely, transform the Theosophical perception of Tantra—and, as it was a direct predecessor to the Avalon project, it also lies at the root of the transformation of academic perceptions of Tantra.

The Bengali authors identified Tantra as a form of Indian esotericism, or "Tantrik Occultism," in the words of the initiator of the intervention, Baradakanta Majumdar. Baradakanta presented Tantrik Occultism as a "science" that he considered superior to its Western counterparts and that was linked to burning issues such as British education, Indian nationalism, the relationship between "East and West," and the meaning of "Hinduism" or *dharma*. Tantric practice and philosophy, especially the concepts of shakti and kundalini, were explicitly related to, and explained with, concepts such as magnetism and electricity and their occultist-magical employment. The Western Theosophists who had recently arrived in India were eager to learn from their Indian interlocutors, especially as their own understanding of Theosophy and Hinduism was anything but set. As will emerge in the chapters that follow, this exchange about Tantra and related subjects, most notably yoga, had ramifications that can be felt up to the present day.

For instance, it led to a rather idiosyncratic differentiation between a supposedly esoteric and noble Raja Yoga on the one hand, and an exoteric and inferior Hatha Yoga on the other. As Elizabeth De Michelis has pointed out, this differentiation would later be taken up by Swami Vivekananda through his "assimilation of Western occultism."[27] According to De Michelis, esotericism—alongside supposedly opposed subjects such as Enlightenment, modernization, and industrialization—had been "imported" into an India that "was all of a sudden faced with an intense barrage of imported new ideas."[28] One of my central arguments is, however, that the Theosophical debates about Tantra and yoga were *not* shaped by a unidirectional interpretation of Westerners or an "import" of Western esotericism, but through complex exchanges with Indians and other Asian actors. Similar to Urban's treatment of Theosophy, De Michelis's assessment is based on an exclusive focus on its Western representatives and implies a dichotomy between Western esotericism and "Indian teachings." It also implies an encounter between "Western modernity" (Enlightenment, industrialization, etc.) and "Indian tradition." The Bengali intervention and its manifold ramifications, including the Avalon project, strongly contradict this binary model.

In the Avalon publications, we observe the exact identification of Tantra with occultism and its accompanying conceptualizations of Tantric practice and philosophy that were propagated by Baradakanta and his fellow Bengalis. They were also taken up directly by Woodroffe in the writings published under his own name. This is no coincidence. Not only do we find Baradakanta among Woodroffe's collaborators, but Baradakanta, Woodroffe himself, and his two closest collaborators, Atalbihari Ghosh and Pramathanath Mukhopadhyay (1880–1973), were the disciples of the same guru, the Bengali Tantric Shivachandra Bhattacharyya Vidyarnava (1860–1913). The second major Avalon publication, *Principles of Tantra* (1914–1916), was a translation of *Tantratattva* (1893), Shivachandra's central work. Baradakanta wrote a lengthy introduction to the second volume of that translation. Avalon's first major publication, *The Tantra of the Great Liberation* (1913), was a translation of the *Mahānirvāṇa Tantra*, which served as the main authority for Shivachandra and other Bengali Tantrikas. The fundamental links between the Bengali intervention in 1880 and the publications of Avalon could hardly be more obvious.

The crucial point is that, similar to the exchange between the Bengali Tantrikas and the Theosophists, the agency behind Avalon was chiefly an Indian one.[29] It is hence imperative to take into account the Bengali network behind Avalon without isolating it from the supposedly Western sphere of Theosophy. This also means revising the strict boundaries drawn by previous scholars between the Theosophical engagement with Tantra, the works of Woodroffe, and the later New Age contexts that largely depended on them.[30] Several disagreements notwithstanding, the Avalon project was closely linked to the Theosophical Society. Most books published under the names of Avalon and Woodroffe were printed by the Theosophical publisher Ganesh & Co. in Madras. Woodroffe's wife, Ellen, was a member of the Society, and John himself published in Theosophical journals and gave lectures to Theosophists. All this stands in stark contrast to Taylor's distancing of the Avalon publications from the sphere of Theosophy.[31] It also contradicts Urban's categorical differentiation between Theosophical and post–Second World War discourses, as well as McDaniel's assessment of a "split between traditional Hindu understandings of kundalini and Western occultism."[32] The situation was vastly more complex.

Regional and Local Entanglements

An investigation of this tangle of exchanges requires a frequent "zooming in and out" from the global to the regional and local. Baradakanta and the other Bengali *Theosophist* authors hailed from the Nadiya and adjacent districts (see figure I.1), which today are shared between Bangladesh and the Indian state of West Bengal. For centuries, this region had been the center of Brahmanical learning in Bengal, with cities such as Navadvip and Krishnagar being crucial for the emergence and development of Bengali Vaishnava and Shakta currents. It was there where Chaitanya (1486–1533)

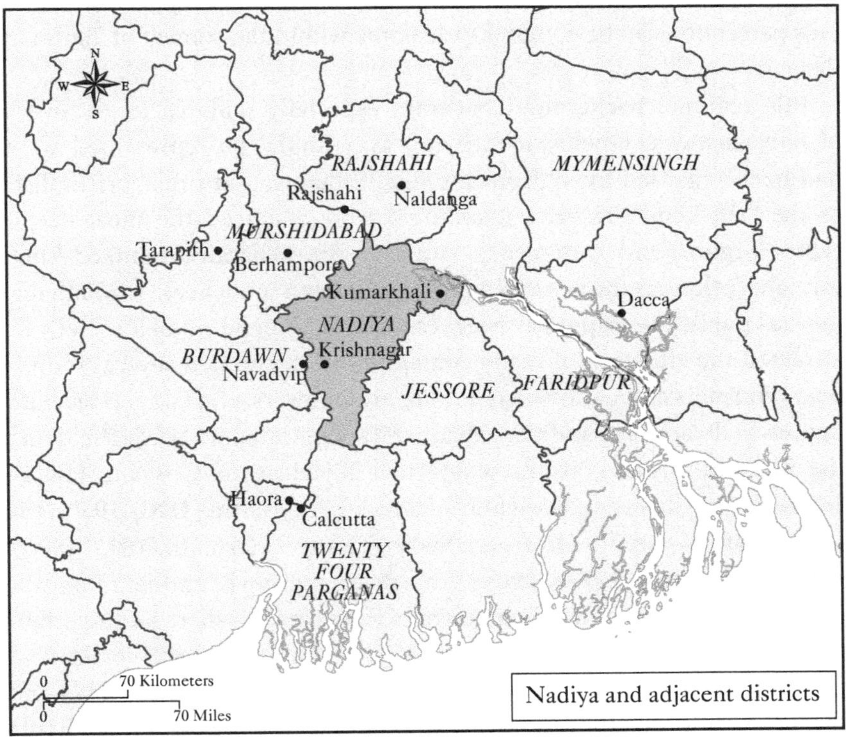

Figure I.1 Nadiya and adjacent districts.

laid the foundations of Gaudiya Vaishnavism, which witnessed significant renegotiations during the nineteenth century that will occupy us repeatedly throughout this book. Since the second half of the eighteenth century, it also saw the active promotion of Shaiva-Shakta currents under the reign of Krishnachandra Ray (1710–1782), as well as the emergence of the Shakta devotional poetry most famously epitomized by Ramprasad Sen. In contrast to other regions of India, the Tantras—which were denounced by orientalists such as Friedrich Max Müller, Horace Hayman Wilson, and others as the "most corrupted" Indian scriptures—were an integral part of Brahmanical culture in Bengal, and hence not simply opposed to an alleged orthodoxy.[33]

The arguments of the Bengali Tantrikas reflected those regional peculiarities, as they sought legitimation not only through Western scholarship and science but also through the authority of the most widely disseminated Tantric scriptures in Bengal. This played directly into the debates about the "Brahmanical orthodoxy" or "true Hinduism" that both orientalists such as Müller and the Theosophists strove to discover; in the eyes of the Bengali Tantrikas, Tantra formed the esoteric core of Vedic orthodoxy par excellence. This perception can be comprehended only within the context of Tantra in Bengal.

This regional background becomes especially tangible in the work of Shivachandra. Openly identifying as a Kaula, he represented what had been regarded by Wilson, Monier Williams, and other orientalists as the "left-hand" Tantrics (*vāmācārī*) who practiced the most despicable "orgies" and outrageous rituals.[34] Shivachandra rebuked such misconceptions as the worst symptoms of foreign influences. Through numerous publications, public speeches, and the foundation of a society, he attracted the attention of many contemporaries, counted several prominent reformers and nationalists among his followers, and cooperated with figures as diverse as pandit Shashadhar Tarkacuramani (1851–1928) and the Brahmo-turned–Vaishnava reformer Bijaykrishna Gosvami (1841–1899). Among his friends we find Akshaykumar Maitra (1861–1930), the founder of the Varendra Research Society; Kangal Harinath (1833–1896); and Lalon Fakir (c. 1772–1890).[35] This diverse group of eminent Bengalis gathered at Shivachandra's hometown of Kumarkhali, where he also established his Sarvamaṅgalā Sabhā, one of the highly successful "orthodox" Hindu societies (*sabhās*) that aimed at opposing Western influences and the propagation of the "Aryan" *sanātana dharma*, the eternal and true dharma.

This local configuration illustrates the intricacy of the historical situation that I explore in the coming chapters. Shivachandra was a pandit educated in the Bengali tradition of Navadvip and took an ostensibly anti-Western and "anti-reformist" stance. At the same time, he was associated with prominent "reformers" and had disciples and friends who had not only received a British colonial education but actively engaged with Western science, religion, and philosophy. The ambivalence of his anti-Western and anti-reformist stance becomes most obvious in light of the fact that he accepted Woodroffe as a disciple and actively supported the Avalon project, most notably the English translation of his *Tantratattva*. Considering the local context, it is also important to note that Shivachandra published in Bengali, rather than Sanskrit, whereas pandits "traditionally" tended to reject the learned use of Prakrit languages.[36] Moreover, his proximity to a figure like Bijaykrishna and the declared goal of his *sabhā* to bridge Shakta-Vaishnava divisions underscores that lines between these factions cannot easily be drawn. This also pertains to Shivachandra's focus on *bhakti*, or devotion, that was shaped by the Shakta poetry in the vein of Ramprasad and the emerging Baul poetry as represented by Lalon.

Shivachandra's efforts to create unity among Hindus—and to define what "Hindu" ought to mean—were marked by poignant polemics. In his *Tantratattva*, Shivachandra insisted that Tantra embodied the Aryan *sanātana dharma*. Invoking the authority of the Puranas, Tantras such as the *Kulārṇava Tantra*, but especially the *Mahānirvāṇa Tantra*, Shivachandra insisted that Tantra was in accordance with the Veda and prescribed the correct dharma for the Kali Yuga, the present age of darkness and decay. The failure to recognize this was attributed to the catastrophic influences of English education, which had generated a class of Western-educated Indians ignorant of their own tradition. When mastered properly, Tantric ritual practice (*sādhana*) was superior to both "Western materialistic science" and the abstract speculations of philosophy, as it was based on, and proven by, "actual experience." However, as Tantra was a secret or "esoteric" (*nigūṛh*, *gūṛha*) doctrine, it required initiation (*dīkṣā*) by a proper guru, a dire necessity in this age of corruption.[37] Like Baradakanta, his Theosophical audience, and Woodroffe, Shivachandra defined Tantra by highlighting its relationship to science and the secret character of its doctrines, and by positioning these qualities against the corrupting influences of Western modernity. These similarities are no coincidence but the outcome of developments that point far beyond Bengal's centers of learning.[38]

I will argue throughout this book that these central aspects—the claim for the "orthodoxy" of Tantra, criticism of English education, and a polemical stance against "reformism" and "modernity"—reflected the globally entangled Bengali discourses that I trace back to the second half of the nineteenth century. This argument runs contrary to the assumption that the work of Woodroffe and Avalon resulted from a Western gaze, that it should be viewed as a unidirectional act of appropriation, as is suggested in White's statement that "*Tantra* was enough of a Brahmanic religious fashion in early 20th-century Bengal to excite the imagination of the [*sic*] Sir John Woodroffe."[39] The conceptualization of Tantra in the work of Avalon and Woodroffe was not simply the outcome of the imagination of a Westerner; neither was it a "Brahmanic religious fashion." It must be viewed against a deeper historical background.

An exploration of that background requires relating the local and regional contexts from Kumarkhali via Nadiya and Bengal to the global connections that emerge through an exploration of Theosophy and its manifold links to orientalist scholarship, colonialism, and broader debates about the meaning and relationship of religion, science, and philosophy. Shivachandra is an important nodal point for this investigation. Although he has so far not been the subject of dedicated historical inquiry, his importance has not escaped previous scholars. Sartori has discussed the work of Pramathanath Mukhopadhyay within the framework of global intellectual history and recognized the importance of Shivachandra in this regard.[40] The guru, however, was discussed only in light of the Avalon project. His own activities and the historical context in which they unfolded remain unexplored.

Traditional Revival or Modern Reform?

Shivachandra's polemics against Western influences and misguided reformers might give the impression that he represented a "traditional" form of Tantra that clashed with colonial "modernity." However, my investigation of his efforts, as well as of the Avalon project and the Bengali intervention, reveals a much more complicated situation that demands careful historical contextualization. The need for this becomes apparent in McDaniel's study of "Bengali Shakta Tantra," which heavily relies on the *Principles of Tantra* translation.[41] Although such categories are absent in said work, McDaniel compartmentalizes Bengali Shakta Tantra into folk/tribal, tantric/yogic, and bhakti Shaktism.[42] The category of tantric/yogic Shaktism is further differentiated into folk/popular and classical/scholastic, the latter of which, according to McDaniel, is represented by both Shivachandra and Woodroffe.[43] Surprisingly, McDaniel does not address the links between the two men, and Woodroffe appears as the author and translator behind Avalon. It is, however, precisely those links, including the Bengali intervention and the historical context within which it unfolded, that complicate the perception of both Shivachandra and Woodroffe as the propagators of a "traditional," "classical," or "scholastic" form of "Hindu understandings" of Tantra. Not only do both men defy the categories proposed by McDaniel. That the Bengali intervention, Shivachandra's activities, and the Avalon project largely revolved around an ostensible rejection of modernity and reformism that went hand in hand with a proclamation of Hindu orthodoxy already highlights their embeddedness in the modern colonial context. This demonstrates the importance of exploring the *nineteenth-century* context of Shivachandra's activities rather than tracing the "origins" of "tantric/yogic Shaktism" to the sixth to ninth centuries.[44] By consequence, it is vital to question historiographical distinctions between tradition and modernity, which, as Richard Weiss has argued, tend to "reinforce dichotomies between Western modernity and Indian tradition, emphasizing the role of the West in Hindu innovation, and consigning expressions of Hinduism that were largely untouched by Western ideas to the realm of static tradition."[45]

Thus, the example of Shivachandra leads us straight to the core of ongoing debates about the formation of religious identities in the nineteenth century, and those related to Hinduism in particular. The historical sources that will be scrutinized throughout this book abound not only with the rejection of modernity but also with calls to "revive" a supposedly lost (Aryan) wisdom, science, or social principles (*dharma*). Many scholars have argued that boundaries between the notions of revival and reform cannot easily be drawn. To be sure, the motive of a revival or "renaissance" after a period of decay was omnipresent throughout the nineteenth century—not least, as Brian Hatcher points out, because it served colonial narratives about precolonial anarchy and the benefits of a Pax Britannica.[46] Yet the idea that revivalism or the notion of a Hindu Renaissance is useful for analytically grasping these historical developments has come under fire for decades.[47] Tapan Raychaudhuri has famously rejected the notion of revivalism for two reasons. First, he argued that prominent revivalists such as Bhudev Mukhopadhyay, Bankimchandra Chattopadhyay, and Vivekananda projected an ideal that was determined by nationalist sentiment and the influence of European thought rather than ancient sources. And second, he asserted that the term was misleading because "it is difficult to revive something that is far from dead."[48] Amiya P. Sen has countered these points by arguing that, similar to using "Renaissance" to describe that Italian era, the term "revivalism" does not necessarily imply a total break with the past but a contemporary consciousness of stepping into a new age.[49]

While this might very well be the case, Hatcher argued that the Renaissance paradigm is based on the prioritization of English-educated Indians, most notably the Bengali middle class known as *bhadralok*, and that it is hence focused primarily on English-language sources and their often nationalistic outlook.[50] When viewed through such a lens, Hinduism in the colonial period becomes almost identical with the activities of actors who sought to "purge" a "tradition" of colonially shaped notions of the "non-modern."[51] In line with this argument, Lucian Wong and Ferdinando Sardella have recently emphasized that the Renaissance model not only focuses on Western values and restricts its analytical lens to English-language texts, but it also suggests a uniform and unilinear development and posits a "a dramatically impoverished picture of the colonial Hindu landscape."[52] It is hence necessary to consider religious currents beyond the well-known host of figures and currents associated with the Renaissance model, which still remain "conspicuously neglected."[53] The circle around Shivachandra offers such insights, especially as it can be viewed as a burning glass of the many ambiguities and contradictions that revolve around the notions of revival and reform.

Recently, Hatcher has argued for altogether abandoning "reform" as an analytical category, since the notion of "the modern religious reform movement is too closely structured in terms of judgments about true and false religion; it presupposes a guiding narrative about modernity that makes it difficult for us to think anew about developments taking place during the early colonial moment."[54] Although I do not follow Hatcher in dismissing "reform" as an analytical lens, I subscribe to his central argument that we should think of "modern Hinduism as emerging—rather than divorcing itself—from premodern modes of innovation."[55] Instead of viewing the language of revival and renaissance in terms of a break with the past or the dawning of a new age, it is then necessary to also consider the early colonial period from roughly 1750 to 1850 as a "crucial moment of transition."[56] Here, too, Shivachandra represents an exceptionally impressive and instructive nodal point between the traditions of Brahmanical learning in Bengal and colonial modernity.

Similar to what Abhishek Ghosh has demonstrated with regard to the complicated relationship between Bengali Vaishnavism, Brahmoism, and Tantric sexo-yogical practices, negotiations of "modern Hinduism" must be viewed against the diachronic background of precolonial developments and factional polemics.[57] Against this background, I argue that "reform" can indeed be misleading as a second-order analytical category, but that it must serve as a subject of historical analysis in its own right—not because it encompasses a specific meaning but because the very contestation of its meanings by historical actors points to central aspects of the colonial period.

Certainly, Western understandings of "modernity" have had a disruptive effect on South Asian society, but they were always subject to reinterpretation and negotiation. As Gyan Prakash has argued, modern Indian identity has been significantly constituted by "science's cultural authority as the legitimating sign of rationality and progress," which was perceived as part of the colonial "civilizing mission."[58] This supposed liberation through domination from superstition, irrationalism, and backwardness, however, was "a profoundly contradictory enterprise" that impelled Western-educated Indians to reinterpret precolonial traditions and cast them in the language of the Western scientific discourse. Nationalism arose through claims to the revival of ancient scientific traditions as the heritage of the nation: "To be a nation was to be endowed with science, which had become the touchstone of rationality."[59]

These debates about modernity, nationalism, and science were not a one-way road. Indians actively participated in shaping contested understandings of modernity, including allegedly "traditional" pandits who, like Shivachandra and his associates, did not inhabit a self-contained and isolated sphere.[60] Recent studies by Joel Bordeaux and Joshua Ehrlich have underlined that the region of and around Nadiya was a vivid, intellectually fluid sphere that was marked by interactions with Islam, dynamics between Shaivas and Vaishnavas, and exchanges with European intellectuals.[61] The idea of a traditional, classical learning preserved by scholastic pandits that was confronted with Western modernity demands complication. An exploration of Shivachandra and his associates can make a forceful contribution to this debate, as it reveals crucial links between the tradition of learning at Navadvip via Hindu revivalism and its ostensive opposition to reform, to the Theosophical Society and the Avalon project.

I approach revivalism and reform, then, as historical notions that must be situated within a specific historical context, not in terms of the resuscitation of an "authentic," pure ancient tradition, but as a contentious and fluid renegotiation of the very meaning of "tradition" in the context of nascent nationalism and societal transformations within the colonial framework. It should be pointed out that this phenomenon was not restricted to the Indian context. It formed part of a global discourse that can also be observed in Europe, where national identities were not rarely crafted upon imagined Germanic or Celtic pasts. Peter van der Veer has highlighted the parallel emergence of religious and social reform movements in both Britain and India, which in some ways were not only interlinked but mutually dependent.[62] Contrary to earlier perceptions of modernity and its supposed secularizing effects, religion played a crucial role in the negotiation of political and social identities across the globe. As Tony Ballantyne has argued, this went hand in hand with an increasing systematization of religion and ongoing clashes around religion's meaning, its significance, and its place in public life. Lower social strata, including colonized people, participated in that process, in which "cross-cultural engagement" played a significant role.[63] As will be seen, a plethora of new religious movements, including New Thought, Transcendentalism, and Christian Science, frequently entered dialogue with Indian actors, and movements like "muscular Christianity" had a profound impact on Indian interpretations of Tantra and yoga as a means for national revival.[64]

Global Religious History

An investigation of that tangled context faces a range of considerable theoretical and methodological challenges that now require a detailed exposition of my approach before we dive into the sources in the first chapter. Global religious history is largely positioned within religious studies, although it actively engages with global history, the regional expertise of South Asian studies, and, in this particular case, with the field of "Western esotericism." Its theoretical repertoire is largely informed by a critical engagement with postcolonial perspectives, while its historiographical method is genealogical.

This latter aspect entails the necessity to focus on the late nineteenth and early twentieth centuries to understand the debates about Tantra. Bearing in mind Hatcher's argument about modern Hinduism as emerging, rather than divorcing itself, from premodern developments, I strongly advocate research that diachronically relates the colonial to the precolonial period.[65] However, as Michael Bergunder has emphasized, "precolonial" can only denote the time directly before the nineteenth century, rather than vaguely indicating thousand-year-old Indian traditions, the continuity of which is often simply presupposed.[66] We have seen how crucially different this approach is from previous assessments, for instance, of Shivachandra's *Tantratattva*. The genealogical perspective of global religious history tries to avoid implicit assumptions of ancient and immutable Indian traditions and views them instead as living and dynamic subjects within ongoing negotiations of the meanings of Hinduism and religion more broadly.

There is now wide consensus within religious studies that present-day understandings of religion were shaped decisively in the second half of the nineteenth century.[67] Differing interpretations of that circumstance notwithstanding, scholars of religion are well aware that non-Christian actors have, during that time, controversially positioned their own traditions toward the notion of religion. Accordingly, increased attention is being paid to the (re) conceptualization of religion by such non-Christian and "non-Western" actors. Karénina Kollmar-Paulenz has underlined the need for taking into account global historical perspectives within religious studies to advance a decentralized historiography and engage in interregional and transcultural comparison that pays specific attention to often ambivalent formations of identities in a global setting.[68]

Yet we have seen that previous scholarship on the global dimensions of Tantra has focused on developments after the Second World War. Sociological and anthropological approaches were highly fruitful in discussing "Neo-Tantra" in the context of multiculturalism and capitalism, but they failed to grasp the nineteenth-century historical developments that shaped the later reception of Tantra. Generally, there is relatively little reflection within religious studies on how to write a global history that focuses on the notion of religion, especially since the discipline's engagement with global history has so far been rather tangential. In turn, religion is often acknowledged to be of paramount importance by global historians, who, however, rarely engage with the discipline dedicated to it, religious studies.[69] Thus, the terms "global" and "religion" have scarcely enjoyed critical reflection from one another's governing disciplines: just as the question of what is "global" is only rarely subject to scrutiny in the study of religion, the problem of "religion" is usually given short shrift in global history. This is unfortunate, as both disciplines are occupied with the problem that the meaning of their main subject is quite unclear—they derive some of their strengths and substance precisely from the need to constantly reflect and debate their approaches.[70]

What does it mean, then, to write a "global" history? Where can boundaries between the local, the regional, and the global be drawn? In other words, when and where does history become global in terms of geographical and chronological dimensions? The inquirer is likely to receive different answers from different global historians. Bruce Mazlish, for instance, advocates a "new global history" that explicitly focuses on "the present-day process of globalization,"[71] while acknowledging "its antecedents and earlier forms."[72] In contrast, Pamela Crossley has proposed a longue durée perspective that departs from the earliest evidence of human activity.[73] Such an approach often has a strong comparative thrust, as is the case with Patrick Manning's "world history," which is conceptualized as an occupation with "the story of connections within the global human community." This world history, too, is explicitly positioned within a long development of historiographical attempts to write histories of humanity, while it emphasizes the new dimensions and audiences that have emerged during the past two centuries.[74]

Such contrasting approaches call attention to the importance of making clear what the "global" in "global religious history" is supposed to signify, without attempting to fixate a specific meaning or delegitimizing other perspectives on it. Most representatives of global history have adopted an epistemic modesty and tolerance for disparate approaches, such as Dominic Sachsenmaier, who has stressed the "necessary impossibility of defining global history."[75] In a similar vein, Manning understands it as "a framework for disciplinary studies, parallel in a sense to the framework of area studies."[76] Roland Wenzlhuemer has stressed that global history "should not be viewed as a solution to fundamental challenges of historiography—its methods as well as its goals for knowledge production—, but as a problematization and critical (self-)reflection that ideally provides partial solutions. It is hence primarily a *perspective*."[77] This openness only accentuates the need to specify which tools from the repertoire of global history I am employing within the framework of global religious history.

A central, arguably *the* central, concern of global historical approaches is to overcome Eurocentric perspectives and to tell, speaking with Crossley, "a story without a center."[78] In the editorial of the first issue of the *Journal of Global History*, Patrick O'Brien asserted that disciplinary boundaries must be overcome, as well as established chronologies and textual traditions for the construction of national histories.[79] These ambitions might appear so high that they can hardly be met.[80] Yet they have yielded a plethora of tools that can be effectively put into practice. Harald Fischer-Tiné, for instance, has promoted a combination of perspectives from South Asian studies and global history that "marries" micro- with macro-perspectives on historical developments.[81] When complemented with the ambitions of global history, the micro-perspectives typical of area studies can efficiently lead to new insights into the relation between contexts that have previously been viewed in isolation—the subject of this book is a strong case in point. Global history, then, does not necessarily mean macro-history, as micro-perspectives are tremendously useful in understanding broader developments.[82] Instead of writing histories spanning all regions across the globe—if such a thing should be possible—global historians might very well be concerned with understanding regionally contingent worldviews within their respective contexts, as Andrea Komlosy puts it.[83] Therefore, the aim of global religious history consists not in writing a history of religion on planet Earth but in shedding light on the global connections between different regional and local contexts in order to understand historical developments within those contexts, depending on the concrete subject under scrutiny.

It is important to clarify that the implication of the term "global" in "global religious history" is not meant to signify "universal" or "planetary."[84] On the contrary, it implies an awareness of global interconnections and structural conditions, focusing on interactions, mobility, and fluidity.[85] Highlighting these *entanglements* does not mean that "everything is connected," in the words of Sebastian Conrad, and neither to the same degree, in the same way, and at any time. An entangled history is tendentially fragmentary rather than holistic, investigating concrete problems and connections instead of postulating world-historical totalities or attempting to write a history of the entire planet.[86] The notion of entanglement helps to grasp what has been described by Ballantyne as a dynamic, complex, and shifting assemblage of connections.[87] Accordingly, I understand the notion of entanglement as describing a metaphorical tangle of connections that can rarely be investigated in its totality. Rather, the researcher must single out or follow specific connections in order to carry out a feasible analysis and eventually craft a comprehensible narrative that results from the interpretation of a disorderly, often contradictory and ambiguous tangle.[88]

Wenzlhuemer has rightfully expressed his concern that the notion of *global connections* is now so widely in use that it has become a kind of "terminological passepartout."[89] It often remains largely obscure what exactly differentiates global from regional, local, and other connections. In fact, there can be no categorical answer to this problem, as the notion of global connections should first and foremost be understood as a guiding principle that demands consistent contextualization within an ensemble of factors, even if that sometimes means that their role is marginal or null.[90] In this sense, *connections* can be viewed as *global* when they are considered within the process of the detachment of social interactions from spatial proximity, that is, when connections can be discerned over long distances and across entirely different boundaries.[91] This is certainly the case with the exchanges about Tantra that are the subject of this book.

Global connections might be grasped through an analysis of very different aspects, such as technological or economic infrastructures. My operationalization of global religious history, however, focuses on *historical actors* and their *agency*. I understand historical actors as acting human beings who, in the sum of their actions, shape history. This is agency, which is determined by capacities and boundaries.[92] From such a perspective, global connections emerge out of the actions, or the potential for actions, of people. It is through historical actors that different threads meet and exert their effects. They are the nodal points of global connections, give them substance, and make them powerful. At the same time, the relevance of global connections, the shift of spatial relations, becomes manifest in those very actors and determines their boundaries. An actor-centered investigation of a historical event thus turns into an analytical prism that makes visible the full spectrum of patterns of global connections and creates a sensibility for the many overlapping layers of meaning of the events and their contexts.[93]

This perspective also lends substance to the "intercultural transfer," to take up an expression by Karl Baier, that has shaped Theosophical approaches to yoga and Tantra.[94] *Cultures* should not be understood as fixed entities that simply engage in exchanges with another. Klaus Hock has argued that they can be approached as *contact zones* that are subject to constant change and do not revolve around stable centers.[95] Investigating the formation of religious identities within a global context, then, requires careful contextualization, which can depart from a local or regional context, or even focus on it. But, as Adrian Hermann demonstrated with regard to the concept of European religious history, it must take into account the global entanglements that defy geographical and cultural boundaries.[96] It is historical actors who both form and transgress such boundaries and who are the agents interacting with each other in contact zones, creating and depending on connections.

Esotericism and Religion in the Context of Colonial Modernity

Global religious history consciously adopts these perspectives because they are virtually absent from previous research on Theosophy and Tantra. In fact, Theosophy is a striking case in point for the need to tackle the compartmentalization of scholarship into regional foci, as well as the prevalent neglect of global approaches. Within classic works focusing on South Asia, the relevance of Theosophy for the question of "Hindu revivalism" and nationalism has often been recognized, however without examining the movement in its own right. Tapan Raychaudhuri and Amiya P. Sen, for instance, highlighted its relevance without admittedly focusing on it.[97] Recent studies note the importance of Theosophy for their subjects, although they do not examine it in detail.[98] There is hence widespread awareness of Theosophy's relevance for modern South Asian history but no in-depth engagement with it. Similar can be said about Theosophy's role in the emergence of modern understandings of religion: although Bergunder has demonstrated the interdependence of nineteenth-century debates about esotericism and religion to the degree that he speaks of their "twin birth," only few scholars, such as Wolfgang Eßbach and Helmut Zander, take note of Theosophy's role within these debates.[99] This is especially relevant because Theosophy and other esoteric currents formed an integral part, not least of the discipline of religious studies itself.[100]

In turn, although the Theosophical Society was arguably one of the most influential actors within global exchanges about religion, science, and philosophy, it is almost absent in studies of global history. It appears only as an afterthought in Christopher Bayly's *Birth of the Modern World*, where the Theosophists are mentioned as "adepts of a self-consciously global and intellectual tradition."[101] Jürgen Osterhammel acknowledges the "particular impact" of the Society but eventually regards it, in a somewhat clichéd fashion, as the expression of a widespread "irrationalism polemically counterposed to the Western faith in reason."[102] Recently, Conrad highlighted Theosophy as "the prototype of a transnationally active religion," but his discussion remains cursory.[103] It is thus curious that Theosophy's importance for global exchanges in the nineteenth century is widely recognized, but that the movement is usually mentioned only in passing, and without references to the rich scholarship dedicated to it.

That scholarship, on the other hand, is largely produced within the field of "Western esotericism" and, as one might suspect, does not approach its subject from a global perspective. Not least because of its "Western" demarcation, it is theoretically and methodologically ill-equipped to deal with the subject at hand. Its focus rests on European and North American Theosophists, rather than on those Indians and other "non-Westerners" who joined, interacted with, and shaped the Society.[104] In the comprehensive *Handbook of the Theosophical Current*, edited by Olav Hammer and Mikael Rothstein in 2013, "non-Western" and generally nonwhite actors are practically absent.[105] Nicholas Goodrick-Clarke's contribution to that volume dismisses them altogether: "For all its Asian costume and fabulous intermediaries, modern Theosophy retains its Western Hermetic motive, logic, and end."[106] A recent volume by Tim Rudbøg and Erik Reenberg Sand discusses "imaginations of the East" within the early Theosophical Society without taking into account "non-Western" perspectives.[107] Among notable exceptions to such approaches is the work of Baier, who stresses that the history of South Asian Theosophists remains to be written,[108] and a recent study by Julie Chajes acknowledges the global context in which Theosophy emerged.[109] Only one volume, however, edited by Hans Martin Krämer and myself, focuses on "non-Western" Theosophists in their own right.[110] To be sure, there is now wide agreement that "non-Western" actors within Theosophy should receive scholarly attention.[111] Yet this will be possible only if the field's Western demarcation and its heavy ideological baggage is abolished or at least thoroughly revised, as I have argued in some detail elsewhere.[112]

The first step of a global religious history must therefore be to bridge the divisions in scholarship with regard to esotericism in particular, and religion more generally. It bears emphasizing that the relationship between religion and esotericism ought to be investigated much more vigorously than has been the case so far. As Bergunder has pointed out, esotericism had "a significant influence in a global religious discourse" that went "beyond a synchronous esoteric network and points far beyond it."[113] An investigation of the history of esotericism must consequently be concerned with putting its subject into a larger historical context.

In the nineteenth century, the notion of *science* was central to formations of religious identities. As mentioned earlier, Hindu reform movements began to define "Hinduism" against the background of "the development of discrete, mutually exclusive religious identities."[114] Their efforts to prove the superiority of Hinduism were almost always marked by an insistence on its "scientific" character.[115] Esoteric movements have played a major role in attempts to overcome the dichotomy between religion and science, striving to "reunite" or "synthesize" the two. Or, more accurately, it was the dichotomization of religion and science that defined the emergence of esoteric movements in the first place.[116] Esotericism can thus be viewed, at least to a large extent, as a "transgression of boundaries" between religion and science.[117] In "striking parallel" to the case of religion, this concern "was a global endeavour right from the start" and had a significant influence on understandings of Buddhism, Hinduism, Islam, and Christianity.[118] Similarly, Nile Green has pointed out that medicine and science became important authorities for religious concepts throughout the nineteenth century and were crucial for the emergence of what he termed the "global occult."[119] Technological and economic innovations, as well as the new means of communication and mobility they entailed, established increasingly closer global connections: "The occult thus emerged at the auspicious conjunction of colonialism, technology, transportation, consumerism, and globalization." Contrary to Osterhammel's assessment, it was not simply the expression of an anti-Western irrationalism but must be viewed as "a characteristically modern religious form."[120]

Esotericism thus stands at the center of controversial negotiations of the meanings of religion and science, demonstrating how these notions were inherently intertwined during the nineteenth century and gave shape to national and religious identities. This links esotericism immediately to the question of *modernity* itself.[121] The repertoire of global history is especially useful for approaching this ambivalent and fuzzy notion, as it explicitly focuses "on the global conditions and interactions through which the modern world emerged."[122] Most actors who the reader will encounter in this book offer impressive insights into these conditions and interactions, as they shared an insistence on science and rationality, even and especially when they, like Shivachandra or Woodroffe, took a polemical stance against "modernism." Dwelling on this issue is relevant because "modernization" was directly linked by Shivachandra and Woodroffe to "Westernization," and hence to the diffusion of Western knowledge. Yet, as Conrad has shown, even when "non-Western" actors invoked "Western" standards of social and cultural change, they participated in the constant negotiation of those standards rather than passively accepting them.[123]

How, then, can we grasp historical understandings of modernity and relate them to ongoing theoretical debates? I would like to highlight two aspects that are crucial for this question. First, it should be stressed that the connections and exchanges that shaped understandings of modernity emerged out of diachronic developments. The issue of *when* we can speak of global connections is vigorously discussed among global historians, who predominantly focus on the modern period.[124] The widespread consensus is that "global connections are preceded by conditions and that it is essential to thoroughly understand these conditions before [scholars] can hope to understand the connections themselves. Exchange, in other words, may be a surface phenomenon that gives evidence of the basic structural transformations that made the exchange possible in the first place."[125] Grasping these transformations in the case of India requires careful historical contextualization and consideration of the fact that, as Sanjay Subrahmanyam has pointed out with respect to the precolonial period, Europeans "conceived India not in some purely predetermined terms, but through their dealings with local interlocutors."[126]

This leads us to the second point. Many historians and scholars of religion would agree with Shalini Randeria that forms of modernity have developed not in separation but as part of an entangled, shared history.[127] According to Elaine Fisher, modernity should be perceived as a transregional phenomenon that emerged through global exchanges between multiple regions.[128] This decentralized perspective of entanglement should not be confused with the idea of the emergence of multiple, distinct modernities.[129] It would also be misleading to regard modernity as a process of homogenization, as it went hand in hand with rejections, conflicts, and controversial negotiations. "Non-Western" actors participated in these processes, which should not be regarded as a unilateral diffusion of European knowledge. Insisting that "modernity has a global history," van der Veer highlighted that Indians were not passive recipients of concepts such as modernity, religion, or the secular, but that they "were actively involved in shaping them."[130] This is an important aspect, as global history is sometimes accused of an overemphasis on similarities and convergences, resulting not only in the superficial talk of ubiquitous connections and globality but also in narratives of global homogenization.[131] Some historians, including van der Veer, have consequently distanced themselves from specific forms of global history because of their supposed tendencies to assume a "world-systemic teleology" and to neglect that "the story of increasing integration and unification obscures the coexisting tale of increasing disintegration and disunity along ethnic and religious lines that we find everywhere."[132] Global religious history is well prepared to consider such nuances and apparent contradictions, as it takes into account the ruptures, discontinuities, and dislocations that defy any teleological understanding of history and a narrow focus on Western actors.

To achieve this, global religious history explicitly takes into account non-Anglophone sources and their respective local or regional contexts. The fruitfulness of such a "zooming in and out" has been conceptualized and demonstrated similarly by a range of scholars, including Adrian Hermann's expansion of "European" into "global religious history," Thomas A. Tweed's notion of the "translocative" character of "occult Buddhism," and Milinda Banerjee's "transversal" approach.[133] Considering the various levels of local, regional, and global contexts will be important throughout this book to demonstrate the entanglements that shaped and informed debates about Tantra, esotericism, science, religion, and national identity.

A genealogical approach to these entanglements is especially rewarding for the present topic because it helps to avoid the ideological trappings of Eurocentric diffusionist models as they manifest in the "Western" demarcation of esotericism. A genealogy always, even if implicitly, retains a focus on the present that requires the historian to reflect on her or his own positionality, including individual bias and ideological assumptions.[134] In the words of Talal Asad, a genealogy can be seen as "a way of working back from our present to the contingencies that have come together to give us our certainties."[135] By consistently asking what connections exist between today's global use of esotericism and European history, it avoids (crypto-)essentialist quarrels about origins and authenticity.[136] Global religious history departs from the matter of fact that, in the words of Dipesh Chakrabarty, European knowledge is "now everybody's heritage."[137] Through colonialism and imperialism, it has undeniably spread across the globe through vastly asymmetric power relations,[138] but this does not mean that "it" was clearly defined and fixed to begin with, and that it remained "Western" in the process. The crucial point is to acknowledge that the meanings of the "twins" of religion and esotericism have been radically transformed, or outright emerged, during the peak period of colonialism, which means that this transformation or emergence did happen, inevitably, within a global context.

In order to grasp this development, global religious history is supported by an epistemology that is substantially informed by the work of Ernesto Laclau.[139] This work revolves around the formation of social and political identities, but it can be effectively applied to religion and esotericism to analyze the complex and fluid ways in which knowledge is discursively produced and transformed.[140] The participants in discourses about contested notions such as religion are constantly concerned with fixating a "true" meaning, while a permanent fixation is, in reality, always impossible.[141] Epistemologically, "religion" or "esotericism" are hence *empty signifiers*, which means *not* that they are devoid of meaning but that this meaning is continuously renegotiated and historically contingent. Attempts at fixating this meaning are understood as historical processes and social practices,[142] which opens them up to scholarly scrutiny. Since scholars are part of that practice, they too must be the object of such inquiries.[143] In other words, scholarship must itself be the subject of genealogical inquiry.

This is also relevant because knowledge about India has largely been produced by Western scholars, or scholars who were educated and worked in the West. Not least, this raises the issue of whether global history, or at least the questions it raises, is in itself "focused around the orbit of western historical writing," in the words of John-Paul Ghobrial, and that it is not clear whether scholars from "non-Western" regions are interested in the same questions about "the global."[144] Milinda Banerjee has aptly pointed out the need to reflect on the underpinnings of global historical approaches, specifically their sometimes universalizing tendencies.[145] From a religious studies perspective, that circumstance also relates to the issue of religious comparativism. Bergunder has argued that comparative endeavors have often worked with a prototype that was based on a Western model. When religion and dharma are compared, for instance, the *tertium comparationis* implicitly remains a Western understanding of religion and hence perpetuates regionalized notions of origin.[146] Again, the solution cannot be a retreat to applying "Western" terms only to "Western" contexts, and vice versa. Claims of an unsurmountable incommensurability of Western and "other" concepts would not only result in a parochialism that lends itself to political instrumentalization; they would also, as argued differently by Bergunder and Christoph Kleine, constitute an intellectual surrender of religious studies, whose foundations have always included comparativism.[147] The resolution proposed by global religious history is a radical and consistent historicization that departs from present-day understandings and reconstructs their genealogies backward in time.

Since the period in question was shaped by colonialism, it is necessary to consider the issue of knowledge production and ponder the imbalance of resources between various regions across the globe, not only historically but also today. Knowledge is here understood as the product of negotiation and difference, which is always ambivalent.[148] Yet I do not view this difference as incommensurable, and I would emphatically refrain from framing it exclusively in terms of colonial oppression, if that means eclipsing the role of the colonized by an overemphasis on power and oppression. The object of comprehending these negotiations should be to explain them as historical processes that inform our present perspectives. Poststructuralist and postcolonial approaches have contributed significantly to this insight, but Homi Bhabha stressed as early as 1994 that "if the interest in postmodernism is limited to a celebration of the fragmentation of the 'grand narratives' of postenlightenment rationalism then, for all its intellectual excitement, it remains a profoundly parochial enterprise."[149]

This also means that the outcome of such an approach must not be the vilification or rejection of (supposedly) Western values et cetera, and neither must it result in cultural relativism. Nor does it imply that there is no such thing as "the West" as a historically contingent identity marker that had and has very real effects.[150] In the words of Chakrabarty, the goal is "to write into the history of modernity the ambivalences, contradictions, the use of force, and the tragedies and ironies that attend it."[151] It follows that the history of colonialism and imperialism is more complex than a unilateral act of appropriation. European or Western identities, too, even within the colonial framework characterized by power asymmetries, have formed through a complex dependency on and interactions with the perceived other.[152]

Such a perspective also offers a way out of debates within religious studies. Scholars such as Timothy Fitzgerald and Russell McCutcheon have argued that the use of the notion of religion outside of Europe entails a Eurocentric bias.[153] Fitzgerald has rightly pointed out the power asymmetries determining exchanges under colonialism,[154] but he is also representative of the viewpoint that studying Hinduism as religion constitutes an act of epistemic violence.[155] From the perspective of global religious history, however, this reproduces the claims of cultural incommensurability and the very Eurocentrism that historical scholarship must complicate: religion was not simply a Western export; its meanings were negotiated—in both Europe and South Asia—through global exchanges. Surely the inhabitants of colonial India had to react to extreme power asymmetries, but not only did they participate in global debates about the meaning of religion, they *actively* and significantly shaped them. This underlines the need for a critical approach to Eurocentrism in scholarship, as it is still sometimes expressed in the alleged diffusion of European achievements culminating in modernity.[156] Today it is widely acknowledged that it would be mistaken to assume a unidirectional diffusion of "the Western concept of religion" into the rest of the world.[157] Yet striking a balance between awareness of colonial power structures and the agency of colonized people demands careful historical contextualization backed up by theoretical-methodological reflection. This would also help to put religious studies in more fruitful dialogue with postcolonial studies, which, as Robert Yelle has pointed out, have paid relatively little attention to "the religious dimension of colonialism."[158]

Perspectives from global history have been a valuable corrective to some tendencies solely focusing on the hegemonic role of European colonialism.[159] A particularly important point is that "positive Western exceptionalism" sometimes found its mirror image in postcolonial notions of cultural imperialism that "are essentially diffusionist and take the European origins of modernity for granted."[160] As Fischer-Tiné and Susanne Gehrmann argue, strict lines between colonizer and colonized only "hinder our ability to grasp both the specific agency of historical actors as well as the heterogeneous and changing character of colonial cultures."[161] Global historians highlight the circumstance that the spatialization and regionalization that still serve as the foundations of academic disciplines call for recognition as historical constructs and concomitant critical self-reflection.[162]

Agency under Colonialism: The Case of Theosophy

Theosophy is an outstanding example of how a substantiated global perspective can lead to radically different insights into these intricate developments. In recent years, Theosophy played a central role in debates about the notion of "Western esotericism" and its relation to broader issues of global history, (post)colonialism, and comparativism. Several attempts have been made to address the theoretical-methodological shortcomings and ideological ramifications of its "Western" demarcation.[163] This elicited what I refer to as the "diffusionist reaction."[164] In a recent article, Wouter Hanegraaff describes the "globalization of esotericism" as a diffusion of "Western esotericism" into a world populated by passive recipients. Asserting that "originally European esoteric or occultist ideas and practices have now spread all over the globe," Hanegraaff holds that there have been "mutations" of those ideas that "traveled back to the West, only to be (mis)understood there as the 'authentic' voices of non-Western spiritualities." In this model, "non-Western" reactions to European ideas are merely inauthentic "mutations" produced by

"Westernized" individuals. Consequently, Hanegraaff insists on an investigation of the "globalization of *Western* (!) esotericism."[165]

This model is misleading for a number of reasons, among which I would like to single out a more historical and a more theoretical one.[166] First, the category of "Western esotericism" is itself a polemical identity marker that, as I have demonstrated elsewhere, was employed by nineteenth-century occultists who rejected the "Eastern" orientation of the recently founded Theosophical Society in the 1880s.[167] In France, it was the Theosophical Society that had stimulated the emergence of occultist orders at the same time, and prominent French occultists such as Papus (i.e., Gérard Encausse, 1865–1916) coined the notion of *ésotérisme occidental* precisely as a polemical counterpart to the "aberrations" of Theosophy. A similar development took place in what has been termed the "Hermetic reaction" in English-speaking nations.[168] Evidently, the notion of "Western esotericism" emerged as a reaction to global developments, and hence within a global context. That it is nowadays used as the demarcation of an academic field of study raises a number of problems, not only because it is a polemical "insider" concept but also because its very context of emergence highlights its global dimension.[169]

This leads us to the second reason pertaining to broader theoretical and methodological questions revolving around the idea of European diffusionism. As Chakrabarty has argued, the idea of "first in Europe, then elsewhere" lies at the heart of the assumption that "non-Western" societies must always be passive recipients of European knowledge.[170] One result of this assumption is that scholars of "Western esotericism" do not engage with any "non-Western" sources or scholarship devoted to them. This is not the result of ill intent, but it must be viewed as the "result of a much more complex theoretical condition under which historical knowledge is produced."[171] Although many disciplines have reflected on this issue in the past decades, the study of esotericism remains largely unaffected by this. The idea prevails that esotericism has emerged in the West and then spread to the Rest.

Dwelling on the case of Western esotericism is especially instructive for ongoing discussions about how scholars should deal with the issues of colonialism and orientalism. The many contradictions and ambiguities resulting from these issues manifest forcefully in the context of Theosophy. In contrast to most other Westerners, the Theosophists did indeed look up to India as the origin of ancient esoteric wisdom. At the same time, this admiration for "the East" was rooted in the orientalist ideas that operated within, and often served to legitimize, colonialism. Often they were more or less implicitly reproduced by the Theosophists. This repeatedly erupted in open conflicts, both among Western Theosophists and between them and their Indian interlocutors. In the 1890s, a dispute between Annie Besant and William Quan Judge revolved around the Theosophical leaders' relationship to their Indian partners and informants. While Judge proclaimed the superiority of "Western occultism," Besant defended its "Eastern" variant.[172] This conflict was one factor that contributed to a widespread disillusion among Indian Theosophists, and sometimes to open criticism of the racial dynamics within the Society.[173]

Another factor was the debunking of the so-called Mahatma letters in the middle of the 1880s. The Theosophical leaders had significantly based their authority on instructions that they allegedly received from hidden Indian "adepts," referred to as the Mahatmas or Masters. When a report by the Society for Psychical Research—a Spiritualist organization with a high reputation among prominent academic scholars—concluded that the Mahatma letters were forgeries, this plunged the Theosophical Society into a deep crisis.[174] It also laid bare one of the most ambivalent aspects of Theosophical knowledge production and its relation to Indians, as it now appeared that the leaders were presenting their own ideas as those of Eastern initiates.

Not least because of the hugely ambiguous Theosophical race doctrine, racial stereotypes and racial hierarchies were by no means absent from the Society.[175] Christopher Partridge has argued that the orientalism of Theosophists, however benevolent in intention, "happened within the context of Western political dominance and colonial expansionism."[176] While the specifics of orientalist attitudes among Theosophists might be subject to debate, "in the final analysis it was Orientalism and functioned, as all Orientalism does, as a form of colonialism."[177] Partridge's argument is an important one, but it tends to obscure the complexity of the relationship between Western and "non-Western" Theosophists in ways similar to its other extreme, the notion of "positive orientalism" that is widespread in "Western esotericism."[178] Surely a distinction can and should be made between outright malicious and derogatory forms of orientalism and the romantic admiration for "India" that characterized Theosophy. Yet "positive" images of "Orientals" as spiritual bearers of ancient wisdom are inexorably intertwined with notions of being effeminate, static, childlike, degenerate, and so on. As Sanjay Subrahmanyam has cautioned, criticism of postcolonial perspectives focusing on the oppressive structures of orientalism should not lead to naïve perceptions of "good Orientalists."[179] In the case of Theosophy, it is impossible to strictly differentiate, as Isaac Lubelsky does, between a somehow harmless "racial discourse" and more dangerous "racial politics."[180] This is so not only because the two are inextricably linked but also because Theosophy was, as Mark Bevir has shown, a highly political endeavor despite its ostensive apolitical stance.[181]

Gauri Viswanathan has focused on these tensions in some detail and interpreted the role of the Theosophical Mahatmas as a form of "ventriloquism" that appropriated (allegedly) Indian voices to effectively spread and legitimize the ideas of the Westerners behind them. At least to a large degree, this "ordinary business of occultism" was a mirror image of colonial administration.[182] While this certainly highlights very relevant aspects that every historian of Theosophy should be mindful of, Viswanathan too tends to overemphasize the colonial-oppressive structures within Theosophy, while neglecting the exceptional agency that it offered to Indian members. This becomes perhaps most clear in light of the fact that Viswanathan, like other historians of Theosophy, focuses only on white, Western Theosophists and Anglophone sources without paying any close attention to "non-Western" Theosophists. Surely it is difficult to view Theosophy in more complex ways from such an angle.

In order to paint a more comprehensive picture, it is imperative to take into full account the Indians who were members or interlocutors of Theosophy. Although the colonial framework in which they moved was certainly an unequal one, Theosophy provided the colonized with an agency that was arguably unique. This is another aspect of Theosophical orientalism, which, as Baier has pointed out, stimulated a vivid exchange of ideas and mutual associations of traditions, for instance of fringe sciences and yogic practices. It also entailed the striving for direct contact with Indians, a fact that the latter, as we will see in the following chapters, explicitly noted when they highlighted differences between the attitudes of colonial administrators and orientalist scholars on the one hand, and Theosophists on the other. Baier, then, concludes that "Theosophical orientalism" was not based on a "static juxtaposition of East and West but instead established a community of intercultural learners."[183]

These Theosophical "welcome structures" had concrete and significant sociopolitical ramifications. Van der Veer has highlighted that Theosophy, as well as Spiritualism, "played a significant role in the development of radical, anticolonial politics both in Britain and India."[184] Similarly, Green remarked that the "global occult" created "new forms of sociability that, in their more radical and transgressive expressions, overturned familiar hierarchies of empire, race, and gender." He noted, however, that occultists did abuse "the social power that their claims of mastery over hidden forces undoubtedly afforded them" and that even "progressive occultisms were involved in co-opting the cultural heritage of the colonial world."[185] Again, it becomes apparent that for all its romantic admiration for India, Theosophy was a decidedly political movement that was deeply enmeshed in the context of colonialism and must be approached as such. If scholars of esotericism are eager to point out its modernity,[186] they must come to terms with its colonial context.

This directly pertains to the question of the language of esotericism, both with regard to its use by historical actors and within present-day scholarship. Hanegraaff, for instance, has insisted that an investigation of esotericism outside "the West" would constitute a "terminological imperialism if we now tried to project this terminology on to the rest of the world."[187] Indeed, some Indian scholars, such as Ashis Nandy and Vinay Lal, have criticized global history for being a masked imperialistic project.[188] In the words of Fischer-Tiné, these critics "stress the uniqueness and incommensurability of South Asia and its past, rather than its embeddedness in broader global structures or processes."[189] This is exactly what global history wants to overcome, a goal that can be achieved only if all participants in global exchanges are investigated in their own right. Surely the solution to the historical fact of colonial conquest and oppression cannot be a retreat to "indigenous" historiographies, as this would blatantly reproduce the strict binaries that non-Eurocentric scholarship should complicate and unravel. This is where a genealogical perspective proves to be specifically helpful: it is a matter of fact that "non-Western" actors have used the language of esotericism to describe their practices and ideas since it emerged in the nineteenth century. As in the case of religion, esotericism *was and is* used globally, and quarrels about its "Western specificity" arise only when one insists on its origins in Europe and links this claim with one of ownership, the prerequisite for export.[190] In this light, warnings of "terminological imperialism" are manifestly self-contradictory.

Reflecting on the act of *translation* is thus crucial for proposing a resolution to the politically connoted conflict between "indigenous" and "global" approaches. Lydia Liu has argued that translation should not be viewed as the production of equivalents in two different languages, but that the equivalence of two terms becomes possible and is, in fact, *produced* in a specific historical context. This is not simply the outcome of either innovation within "indigenous tradition" or foreign impact; neither is it a rupture between tradition and modernity, but a product of cross-cultural interpretation.[191] Instead of assuming the incommensurability between languages, but also instead of assuming the complete translatability of concepts, Liu proposes to understand translation as a historical pragmatic practice.[192] An investigation of that translingual practice, then, focuses on the *conditions* for the possibility of translation.[193]

Liu's perspective helps to explain the "global circulatory networks of translated knowledge" that were shaped by different actors despite the power asymmetries inherent in the colonial context.[194] What can be observed in the following chapters is not a meeting of Eastern and Western religion or esotericism. Rather, different understandings of religion and/or esotericism were *produced* and *constantly negotiated* through global exchanges throughout the nineteenth century. Theosophy provided an exceptional structural basis for such exchanges, as it actively sought contact with "non-Western" people and created a platform that, as in the case of the Bengali intervention, opened up global lines of communication.

Outline of the Chapters

Tracing the work of Arthur Avalon back to Shivachandra's efforts and the exchange in the *Theosophist* reveals a network of individuals with vastly different backgrounds, including the Bengali authors, their Theosophical interlocutors, Woodroffe, and the members of Shivachandra's society. The main goal of this book is to shed light on the Bengali context in which the project of Arthur Avalon emerged, rather than focusing on the project itself or Woodroffe as an individual. To this end, the book will depart from the global exchanges that manifest in the *Theosophist* debate, circling closer and closer into the regional and local contexts connected to it, before finally contextualizing the emergence of Arthur Avalon against that background. As I have identified the Bengali intervention as a pivotal moment in the global propagation of positive understandings of Tantra, the first chapter will open up the frame of this book by introducing three of the main strands that meet in the nodal point of the *Theosophist* exchange: the emergence of the Theosophical Society and its relocation to India, the regional background of Bengali Tantra, and an outlook on the Avalon project and its implication for

Indological and South Asianist scholarship until today. The main protagonist and guiding thread of this overview is Baradakanta.

Chapter 2 details the entrance of Theosophy into the Indian intellectual landscape. I demonstrate how core ideas of Theosophists and Bengali actors were shaped by a shared global background, which prepared the structures of exchange that facilitated an influential and lasting encounter. This background was marked by social reformism and the notion of "Aryan" in relation to the search for the origin of religion. Focusing on diverse engagements between Theosophy and members of the Ārya and Brāhma Samaj, I provide examples of disagreement and skepticism, but also of the widespread opinion that Theosophists radically differed from other Westerners because of their self-proclaimed willingness to learn from Indians. When the Theosophical Society was established in Bengal in 1882, Blavatsky and her de facto co-leader Henry Steel Olcott were enthusiastically welcomed by the Calcutta intelligentsia. This enthusiasm was fueled by the Theosophists' ostentatious denunciation of English education and their reverence for the "science" of the ancient Aryan rishis.

At the core of that science stood yoga. Chapter 3 demonstrates that perceptions of yoga as an occult science prepared the setting for the entry of the Bengali authors in the 1880s. The Theosophical conceptualization of yoga was highly ambivalent, as it attempted to map yoga on occultist concepts, idiosyncratically differentiating between Hatha and Raja Yoga. However, this process was mutual and significantly determined by Indian viewpoints. Baradakanta claimed the superiority of Indian occult science over Western mesmerism, and several Indians, including Dayananda, turned their backs on the Theosophists not least because of disagreements about understandings of yoga. The crucial point is that the Theosophists' conceptualization of yoga was not fixed but subject to controversies among learned Indians. It is in that context that the Bengali intervention introduced Tantric elements into Theosophical understandings of yoga. Following Dayananda, Theosophists tended to look down on Hatha Yoga as gross and exoteric and praised Raja Yoga as subtle and esoteric. A rejection of Tantra as "black magic" used to go hand in hand with the rejection of Hatha Yoga, but Baradakanta and other Bengali authors established concepts such as kundalini, chakras, and related Tantric elements as an integral part of Theosophical understandings of yoga. The controversies revolving around these interpretations allow for instructive insights into the ambiguous power dynamics between Western Theosophists and their Indian partners, as well as into the problems of translating and comparing notions such as occultism, occult sciences, and yoga.

The Theosophists and their interlocutors were driven by a wish to "revive" the Aryan wisdom that should form the basis of a new age. Yet they also promoted decidedly "reformist" ideas that highlight the necessity to explore the meanings of the notions of reform and revival. In chapter 4, the emergence of Spiritualism in Bengal will help to flesh out the role of Tantra in social reformist programs that were characteristic of Bengali Spiritualists, as elsewhere across the globe. I will discuss prominent figures such as Pyarichand Mitra and Shishirkumar Ghosh, who extensively and creatively engaged with Theosophy, Spiritualism, New Thought, and Transcendentalism. This serves to demonstrate that Theosophy was indeed a main factor in these exchanges, but that Bengali intellectuals maintained global correspondences beyond Theosophy and that they engaged with the respective ideas independently and actively. It will become obvious that Tantra played a key role in these processes and that its discussion within Spiritualist contexts allows for instructive contrasts with Bengali Theosophists such as Baradakanta.

Chapter 5 will further illustrate that demarcations between reformism and revivalism are anything but clear, and indeed often are more misleading than helpful. The focus will rest on the ambiguous role of Theosophy within "Hindu revivalism," as contemporaries perceived the Society as part of the "revivalist" camp, while it clearly harbored "typically reformist" ideas. First, I will open up a diachronic perspective on this ambiguity by discussing the *Mahānirvāṇa Tantra* and its reception since the eighteenth century. This will provide insights into why Tantra played such a prominent role in the debates about revival and reform: it was central to the debates about *sanātana dharma* and related struggles about Hindu identity. So-called orthodox efforts were usually decisively marked by reformist agendas, while reformists often shared the same notions of *sanātana dharma* and a revival of Aryan civilization. What emerges is the deep involvement of the Theosophical Society in these debates, which had developed since the early colonial period.

Chapter 6 will further zoom into the local Bengali context and explore the thought and activities of Shivachandra, which were shaped by the intellectual atmosphere of his hometown, Kumarkhali, and the famous Baul circle around Kangal Harinath. Taken out of school by his father because of the supposedly negative influence of English education, Shivachandra was educated at Navadvip, Benares, and Calcutta. His rejection of English education and defense of what he regarded as orthodoxy led him to the foundation of the Sarvamaṅgalā Sabhā. The society proclaimed opposition to Western material science (*jaṛabijñān*), promotion of the "eternal Vedic dharma" (*sanātan vaidik dharma*), and a struggle against "the propaganda of Western materialist capitalists" (*pāścātyer dhanatāntrik'diger annadās'kuler apapracār*). Shivachandra's *Tantratattva* was essential to these efforts and is hence examined particularly with regard to his understanding of Tantra as *sanātana dharma*, as well as to the conceptualization of *sādhana* in relation to science.

Nationalist tendencies emerge as an outstanding feature of these contexts. Hence chapter 7 explores the activities of Shivachandra and his associates in the context of the Swadeshi movement and the relationship between science, education, and nationalism more generally. It also turns to the writings of Shashadhar, and his concept of a "spiritual science" (*adhyātmabijñān*) in particular, in order to demonstrate that Bengali debates about the relationship between religion and science paralleled, and were inherently intertwined with, debates that could also be observed in the Theosophical context as well as in the writings of Avalon. Another direct link to the latter will be explored through one of Woodroffe's closest partners and another disciple of Shivachandra: Pramathanath Mukhopadhyay, the later Swami Pratyagatmananda Saraswati. Special attention will be paid to his concept of "national education" and the role of Tantra for the regeneration and eventual emancipation of India.

Chapter 8 surveys how the aspects discussed in the previous chapters resurfaced in the writings of Avalon and informed Woodroffe's understanding of Tantra. The latter's relationship to Shivachandra and the broader personal network behind Avalon will be inspected in some detail, also with regard to the role of Theosophy and the colonial elite in Calcutta. On that basis, I analyze the Avalon and Woodroffe writings by first foregrounding the relationship between religion and science, and how the notions of occultism and esotericism were employed to transgress what was perceived as the destructive division between them. Second, I show that Woodroffe's adamant advocacy of national education and an awakening of India's shakti directly mirrored the ideas of his Bengali associates. Third, these notions were closely linked to universalist approaches to religion, as they presumed the existence of the same esoteric doctrine at the core of every great tradition—a perception that was linked to Catholicism by Bengali Tantrikas before Woodroffe would state similar ideas.

In sum, these chapters will reveal a complex picture of fascinating exchanges that defy clear boundaries. What will emerge, most fundamentally, is the historiographical need to relate global, regional, and local developments in order to understand the multidirectional, unstable, and ever-changing negotiations that shaped different modern understandings of Tantra, and by extension of the meaning and role of religion in modernity.

1

The Bengali Intervention

Grasping the complexity of the events that unfolded since the year 1880 requires an assessment of three contexts that shall be singled out for the sake of analysis: first, the activities and central motives of the Theosophical Society, as they manifest in an emerging debate about the meaning of yoga and Tantra in relation to the notion of esotericism. Here, the focus will rest on the major voice of the Bengali intervention, Baradakanta Majumdar. Second, following his lead, I am going to have a look at the regional background of Bengali Tantra that informed Baradakanta's thought. It follows, third, an overview of how the threads that can be singled out within the Bengali intervention met in the later project of Arthur Avalon. This will allow for a final reflection on the "esoteric" language that remains widespread within Indological and South Asian studies.

The Theosophical Quest for Esoteric Truth

The Theosophical Society is an outstanding example of a global organization that facilitated, stimulated, and initiated the debates about Tantra that will be scrutinized in what follows. It was established in New York in 1875 under the leadership of the illustrious Helena Blavatsky, Henry Steel Olcott (1832–1907), and William Quan Judge (1851–1896).[1] In February 1879, the leading members of this highly diverse and transnational society moved to Bombay (now Mumbai) in search for the "Aryan wisdom" they hoped to discover in India. Theosophy had emerged largely out of Spiritualism—the occupation with "spirit phenomena" through "mediums" and experiments that was highly popular since the middle of the century—and its opposition to what was perceived as the materialist and egoistic aberrations of contemporary society. Theosophists, however, increasingly began to polemically distance themselves from Spiritualists, whom they regarded as dabblers ignorant of the occult forces that governed spirit phenomena. Rather, they stressed the need for "initiation" into the esoteric wisdom that was guarded by the

DOI: 10.1093/oso/9780197627112.003.0002

"adepts" of Kabbalah, Hermetism, Rosicrucianism, Freemasonry, and other subjects that may be grouped together as "esotericism."[2] Magic, alchemy, and astrology were perceived as "sciences" that only the initiated could penetrate. This initiation required both personal qualification and an expertise in the relevant "tradition."

It is for that reason that the Theosophists embarked on their journey to India: to receive initiation by those enigmatic adepts who had preserved through the ages the ancient "Aryan" science at the root of all true Tradition. In doing so, they were informed by orientalist perceptions of India as a locus of magic, occult (yogic) powers, and primitive beliefs—except they turned these notions on their head by viewing them in a favorable light, as remedies to the aberrant materialism of the West.[3] This enthusiasm for Indian wisdom and the eagerness to receive instruction from learned Indians was largely responsible for the huge interest and sympathy toward Theosophy on the part of many Indians who appreciated the vast difference between the Theosophical stance and that of most colonial administrators, orientalists, and missionaries.

After entering a short-lived alliance with Dayananda Sarasvati's Ārya Samāj, the Theosophists relocated their headquarters to Adyar near Madras (now Chennai) at the end of 1882. The Theosophical Society was rapidly established as a major religious, cultural, and political force in India. In 1917, its president Annie Besant was elected president of the Indian National Congress, and Theosophy exerted a significant influence on the thought of prominent Indians such as Mahatma Gandhi.[4] It is not a surprise, then, that John Nicol Farquhar devoted the longest chapter in his well-known *Modern Religious Movements in India* (1915) to Theosophy.[5]

When the Theosophists first set foot in India in February 1879, they became deeply enmeshed in South Asian debates that attempted to position notions such as *dharma* toward "religion," and to differentiate "genuine" religion from "fake" or "unauthentic" religion.[6] It would be a mistake to assume that the Theosophists entered India and then "exerted influence." On the contrary, they were confronted by an overwhelming diversity of Indian interests. The Bengali intervention is an impressive instance of how the Theosophists were approached by a group of authors who aimed at actively transforming their perception of a specific subject. It cannot be stressed enough that their intervention was not simply directed at Western perceptions of Tantra, but was first and foremost against the alleged ignorance of contemporary reformers. These particularly included the members of the Ārya Samāj, whose leader, Dayananda Sarasvati (1824–1883), insisted on the sole authority of the Vedas, while vehemently rejecting the Tantras as the worst aberration of Indian traditions.

The relationship between the Vedas and the Tantras had long been contested on the subcontinent, and in the nineteenth century it played a significant role in debates about the "true" meaning of religion, and Hinduism in particular. At first, the Theosophists' sympathies and alliances were with Dayananda and other critics of Tantra. In May 1877, they had renamed their society The Theosophical Society of the Arya Samaj of India. Although this partnership did not last long, it predated the Theosophists' arrival in India and significantly shaped their initial approach. The Bengali intervention thus came at a time when Theosophical ideas about "true Hinduism" were still very much determined by perspectives such as Dayananda's.

The crucial point to bear in mind is that it was anything but clear what "Theosophy" was all about. During its first years, the Society was struggling to define its identity against other esoteric movements. The Theosophists' wish to distance themselves from Spiritualism, in particular, manifested in frequent polemics, for instance in the same issue of the *Theosophist* that sparked the exchange about Tantra.[7] This was not merely a question of branding but the result of fundamental differences. Spiritualism had emerged at the beginning of the nineteenth century in a radical social reformist context and had turned into an immensely popular movement since the end of the 1840s.[8] In the 1850s, the French Catholic socialist Alphonse-Louis Constant (1810–1875) adopted the pseudonym Éliphas Lévi and developed the notion of *occultisme* in a number of writings that must be counted among the main influences on Blavatsky and other Theosophists. Lévi's stance was marked by a sharp opposition to the Spiritualists, whom he accused of lack of initiation and, hence, perilous ignorance.[9] Insistence on initiation would remain a crucial point of difference between the allegedly ignorant Spiritualists on one hand, and Theosophists and occultists on the other. Yet boundaries between such groups were extremely porous, both on personal and doctrinal levels. Most of them shared an emphasis on scientific and rational explanations of religious phenomena, while opposing scientific materialism and atheism.

Spiritualists and occultists maintained that the workings of magic could be explained through an occult force, as the proponents of animal magnetism or mesmerism had claimed since the decades around 1800. From such a viewpoint, magic was elevated to the status of an ancient science whose methods were only recently understood by its modern counterpart. Many scholars held that magnetism explained many religious phenomena and practices. Soon, the focus of such inquiries was "the East." As Baier has demonstrated, orientalist perceptions of Indian yogic practices were influenced by mesmerist theories from an early point on.[10] Prominently, Abraham Hyacinthe Anquetil-Duperron linked the notion of *prāṇa* with magnetism in his *Oupnek'hat*, the Latin translation of the Persian rendering of the Upanishads (1657) that had been published in 1801/1802.

Far from being the pastime of esoteric outsiders, such ideas formed an integral part of contemporary orientalist, medical, and scientific discourses. They were also an essential ingredient to the socialist and "progressive" Catholic circles in which the writings of Lévi emerged, thus providing a direct link to later Theosophical teachings.[11] Instead of declining throughout the century, occupations with occult natural forces peaked in the decades around 1900.[12] From the perspective of esotericists, magic was regarded as superstition and heresy only by those who failed to understand its true operations. At the same time, Theosophists were eager to distance themselves from what they regarded as actual superstition. Their encounter with Tantra is thus an instructive example of how the legitimacy of a practice was negotiated in light of its alleged scientific value.

Although Theosophists and other esotericists criticized what they held to be the materialist excesses of modern science, they eagerly engaged with contemporary scientific theories, for instance those advanced by Thomas Henry Huxley (1825–1895), Ernst Haeckel (1834–1919), and Herbert Spencer (1820–1903).[13] As Egil Asprem has elucidated in some detail, Theosophy's relationship with contemporary science was complicated but highly fertile, as it not only formed a prominent nodal point for debates about religion and science but also attracted a number of world-leading scientists.[14] One outstanding example of this intricate relationship between cutting-edge science and esotericism is Alfred Russel Wallace (1823–1913), who had developed the biological theory of evolution parallel to Darwin and became an enthusiastic Spiritualist.[15] He was convinced that "Spiritualism is an experimental science, and affords the only sure foundation for a true philosophy and a pure religion."[16] For all its ambivalence, the relationship between the field of esotericism and contemporary science was characterized by entanglements, not only opposition. As Kocku von Stuckrad has highlighted, Theosophical ideas constituted a "mixture of religious and scientific thought" that reflected contemporary scientific tendencies, and "Theosophists had a lively dialogue with leading philologists and scholars of religion and so popularized academic theories and knowledge."[17]

That many Western Theosophists were convinced that India was the treasure trove of ancient Aryan wisdom was due to the widespread assumption of a common Aryan root of the Vedic Indian and the European "races." Orientalists and other scholars of religion, such as Müller, had turned to "the East," and India in particular, in order to discover the origins of religion, and hence its "true" or "pure" essence.[18] Through the enthusiastic engagement of its proponents with such theories, Theosophy became deeply entangled with the scholarship on religion that gave rise to the discipline of religious studies.[19] In the words of Jason Josephson-Storm, Theosophy can be viewed as "a historical doppelgänger" of religious studies, "a parallel movement, that drew from nearly the same social sphere, shared many intellectual objectives and political coordinates, and for a time was more successful in recruiting members and placing different religions in dialogue."[20]

Tantra played a prominent role in the many debates resulting from these endeavors, as it was regarded by many orientalists as an example of "non-Aryan" influences on the supposed Aryan conquerors of ancient India.[21] Baradakanta and other defenders of Tantra begged to differ: it was precisely through the study of Tantra that the esoteric core of Aryan civilization could be accessed, and hence the essence of all great traditions that derived from it. The central point is that the notion of an ancient Aryan civilization as the primordial root of "true religion" informed nineteenth-century understandings of religion, and that both the Theosophical newcomers and their Indian partners shared the conviction that it had to be revived in order to save humanity from both gross materialism and misguided superstition.

It is against this background that the unfolding debate about Tantra in the *Theosophist* must be viewed. Crucial for an understanding of the Theosophical reception of Tantra is the widespread contemporary assertion that "pure" Hinduism or "Brahmanism" was exclusively Vedic. This was maintained not only by Dayananda but also by orientalists such as Müller, who ranks among the major influences on Theosophical ideas about the history of religion. The last quarter of the nineteenth century saw an increased focus on the role of the Tantras within Hinduism, and consequently the emergence of "Tantrism" as an abstract category.[22] Apart from a plethora of adverse accounts by missionaries and orientalists, some scholars, such as Henry Thomas Colebrooke, had acknowledged that "the Tantras form a branch of literature highly esteemed, though at present much neglected."[23] The Bengali historian Rajendralal Mitra even stressed that the "Tantras constitute the life and soul of the modern system of Hinduism."[24] Still, the consensus among European orientalists can be exemplified by the stance of Monier Williams, who stated that the "Puranas and Tantras are the true exponents of these two last and most corrupt phases of popular Hinduism."[25] Linked to "mysticism" and "magic," their importance and complexity were not denied, but "Tāntrism, or Śāktism," was believed to be "Hindūism arrived at its last and worst stage of medieval development."[26]

In short, the role of Tantra in Indian history was the subject of ongoing controversies. These peaked just at the time when the Theosophists settled in Bombay (now Mumbai) and relocated their headquarters to Adyar near Madras (now Chennai) at the end of 1882. The Bengali intervention directly related to these broader debates and that the nineteenth century saw a rapid increase in discussions about the meaning of Tantra, especially in Bengal.[27] Within these discussions, Baradakanta and other Bengalis defended Tantra, not only as being in full accordance with the Vedas but as the appropriate mode of Vedic dharma for the Kali Yuga. The Bengali authors introduced a global readership to Tantra and its related doctrines and practices, such as Kundalini Yoga—the essence of "Tantrik Occultism," the term employed by Baradakanta to make that point.

Baradakanta Majumdar's Defense of Tantrik Occultism

It all started when the January 1880 issue of the *Theosophist* printed an article by a pseudonymous "Truth Seeker" inquiring about the nature of "Yoga Philosophy." As Baier has shown, this contribution not only marked the beginning of a transformation of the discourse about Tantra, but it was also a watershed moment in the history of modern yoga and meditation.[28] Possibly for the first time, learned Indians began to provide information about practices such as Kundalini Yoga and chakras to a large worldwide readership, paving the path for a wide and manifold reception that has had ramifications up to the present day. The framing of this exchange was, to a great extent, the practice and philosophy of yoga. The Truth Seeker opened the conversation with a reference to a series of papers in the *Dublin University Magazine* from October 1853 until January 1854 titled "The Dream of Ravan." Discussing the depiction of the mystical experience of a yogi, the article mentioned "that most mystic of all mystic books, the *Dnyaneshvari*"—that is, the *Jñāneśvarī*, the famous thirteenth-century commentary on the *Bhagavadgītā* in the Nath tradition.[29]

The Truth Seeker was interested in the ascent of a "Power"—identified in a footnote as kundalini and understood as "World Mother" and "electricity personified"—as well as in the control of the "vital breath."[30] This process was likened to "that described in the *Oupnekhat*." Therein, according to the article, the drawing up of the "lower air" was described as rising through the bodily regions and eventually up "to the sixth region, which is the interior of the nose, between the eyelids, there retain it, it is become the breath of the universal soul." This achievement would be followed by a "meditation on the great One," whose "universal voice" would make itself heard to the ecstatic who would finally "become God." The Truth Seeker asked the correspondents of the *Theosophist* for further information:

> It would be a great boon to Theosophists if Dayānand Saraswati Swāmi would give to the world a translation of this work, and also of Patanjali's *Yoga Sastra*, of which in English we know only the imperfect summaries of Ward and Thompson. . . . We Western Theosophists earnestly desire information as to all the best modes of soul-emancipation and will-culture, and turn to the East for Light.[31]

The Truth Seeker framed this account with both a comparison to the mystical experience described in Thomas Vaughan's *Anima magica abscondita* (1650) and the reference to occultist "soul-emancipation and will-culture" just quoted. Apparently, he attempted to make sense of what he learned in European esoteric terms, while reaching out to "the East" for its true meaning. This successfully invited Indians to join the conversation. In this case, their participation allows for an understanding not only of the similarities between the ideas of Theosophists and Indian reformers but also of the differences and rivalries among the latter. This becomes evident in the fact that it was not Dayananda who replied to the Truth Seeker's request, but Bengalis who had quite a different opinion about the subject at hand. The ensuing debates were concerned not simply with the discussion of yogic techniques but with the assertion of a specific Bengali identity that was largely based on Tantra. It was right under an "Indian Patriot's Prayer" that the February issue of the *Theosophist* printed a note by "a Bengali friend":

> The Swami Dayānund was in error when he condemned the *Tantras.* He has evidently seen the *black* Tantra and rejected all in disgust. But the Tantras alone contain all that has been discovered regarding the mysteries of our nature. They contain more than the Veds, Patanjali, Sankhya and other ancient works on Yoga philosophy. In Tantra alone there are hundreds of essays on Yoga, black and white magic, &c., &c. Unfortunately it is written in Bengali character or I would send it for your Library. The Dnaneshwari referred to in the January number of your magazine is a Tantric work.[32]

Impressed by this note, Olcott and Blavatsky wondered if "no one in Bengal care[s] enough for truth and science to send us English translations of the more valuable portions of this curious work." The ensuing debate would profoundly affect the ways in which Tantra and yoga were perceived, since Indian reformers like Dayananda had linked Tantra to the superstition and degeneracy allegedly responsible for the desperate state of India.[33] Beginning in the first issue of the *Theosophist*, Dayananda had published an autobiographical essay, whose second part appeared in December 1879 and was referred to by the "Bengali friend." Dayananda told the story of how he had been introduced to "the Tantras":

> But no sooner had I opened them, than my eye fell upon such an amount of incredible obscenities, mistranslations, misinterpretations of text and absurdity, that I felt perfectly horrified. In this Ritual I found that incest was permitted with mothers, daughters, and sisters (of the Shoemaker's caste), as well as among the *Pariahs* or the outcastes,—and worship was performed in a perfectly nude state. . . . By actually reading the whole contents of the *Tantrās* [*sic*] I fully assured myself of the craft and viciousness of the authors of this disgusting literature which is regarded as RELIGIOUS![34]

The image presented here was familiar from missionary accounts, which is underlined by the fact that Dayananda also tended to adopt missionary vocabulary in his attacks on Tantra. In his major work, the *Satyārth Prakāś* (*The Light of the Meaning of Truth*), he launched scathing attacks not only against Christianity and Islam but also against Tantra: "Now look at the trickery of these stupid *popes* that whatever is considered to be highly sinful and opposed to the *Veda* is regarded as virtuous by the *Vama Margis*."[35] This characterization of Tantra as debauchery and perversity, its opposition to the Vedas, and its categorization as *vāma mārga*—which would be translated as "left-hand path"—formed a most important frame of reference for Theosophists.

It was as early as April 1880 that Baradakanta's different portrayal of Tantra was published. The swiftness of this response, dated February 11, 1880, demonstrates the effectiveness with which the *Theosophist* functioned as a platform of exchange, connecting a global readership with the heartland of Tantric Bengal. Writing from Rajshahi, which is close to Nadiya, Baradakanta directly responded to the *Theosophist* article. He started his discussion of "Tantric Philosophy" by expressing his frustration about the bad reputation of Tantra: "It is deeply to be regretted that the Tantras have not found favour with some scholars and truth-seekers of this country." The problem, he explained, was not simply that these scriptures were written in Bengali script, but "[t]he Tantriks like the Freemasons and Rosicrucians studiously hide their books and secrets from the outside world." In order to "disabuse the minds of the Tantra-haters of their misconception," Baradakanta wanted to offer an introduction to the noble philosophy of the Tantras.[36]

He explained that Brahma, Vishnu, and Shiva were the personifications of the "great One," rather than independent entities, and that this realization was to be achieved through "Samadhi Yoga." The kundalini was regarded as the force behind that process, which must be seen not as an exercise in superstition but as a thoroughly scientific matter: "Modern science also teaches us that heat, light, electricity, magnetism, &c., are but the modifications of one great force."[37] The central function of this yogic process was the conjuncture of the individual *jīva*, which Baradakanta translated as "mind," and *ātmā*, the "soul." As he explained, most people were not capable of such a "fearless investigation of truth":

> The majority of the people getting no such education and addicting themselves to mundane pursuits, are not in a position to appreciate or realize the abstract God. Thrown into the whirlpool of action, tempted by passions and interest, beset by enemies and untoward circumstances, goaded by hope and ambition, struck down by fear and despair, frail man is capable of doing the greatest mischief to himself and to his fellow-brethren. The bond of religion is, therefore, of the highest importance to ensure peace and security. And what religion can the average man appreciate? Certainly not the highest theosophy.[38]

Baradakanta went on to explain that, to "suit the capacity of such men the sages expounded a system of easily tangible faith founded on the attributes and actions of the Deity." It was precisely this differentiation between a religion of the few and a religion of the masses that eventually made the latter "descend to idolatry." This narrative is crucial for an understanding of the unfolding interpretation of Tantra, as well as for the development of a common language used by the Bengali Tantrikas and their Theosophical interlocutors. Authors such as Baradakanta expressly compared Tantra with Spiritualism, magnetism, occultism, and Rosicrucianism to identify not only shared modes of scientific inquiry but also the esoteric concealment of teachings that were inaccessible to "the average man." This point was also stressed in Baradakanta's "Glimpse of Tantrik Occultism" from July 1880. Therein he explained that the author of a Tantric work "has used figurative language throughout the work which renders it valueless, except to such as have the key to the allegories."[39] The promise of such a key did not fail to make an impression on the readership of the *Theosophist*, especially since Baradakanta explicitly invoked the "Aryan philosophy," offering a synthesis of religion and science: "To the modern scientist the land of mystery is sealed with seven seals. His instruments and machines, his scalpel and retort serve him ill to solve the grand problem of existence. Is there no hope then? Are there no means by which the occultism of nature may be revealed to man? Aryan philosophy says there are."[40] Rather than portraying Tantra as black magic or debauchery, Baradakanta defined it as a science that was superior to its modern (that is, Western) counterpart, by virtue of its foundation on ancient Aryan wisdom. Baradakanta's notion of Tantrik Occultism thus invoked a shared struggle against what was perceived as a misguided scientific materialism that had to be overcome by a "synthesis of religion, science, and philosophy"—the subtitle of Blavatsky's famous *Secret Doctrine* from 1888. In Baradakanta's article "Tantric Philosophy," we learn, "The Tantras are an invaluable treasure, embracing besides religion and theology, law and medicine, cosmology, yoga, spiritualism, rules regarding the elementaries and almost all the branches of transcendental philosophy."[41] In December 1880, Baradakanta stressed that "[t]he occult sciences of India are the monuments of her ancient greatness."[42] In fact, in this and other contributions, he made it clear that "Indian occultism" was decidedly superior to "Western mesmerism," which, according to him, "is yet in its infancy; and it is hoped that with the help of Indian occultism it will fast gain the position which other sciences now occupy."[43] Baradakanta and numerous other Indians were convinced that it was the Theosophists who could learn from them, rather than vice versa.

The Bengali intervention directly related to the Theosophical conceptualization of yoga, which was hotly contested within the same issue of the *Theosophist*. It was largely due to this intervention that elements from Kundalini Yoga became an integral part of the Theosophical approach to yoga, especially the teachings about the chakras and the yogic ascent through them leading to enlightenment. Yet while the Theosophical perception of Tantra was considerably transformed, and elements of it were adopted especially with regard to yoga, it was still considered dangerous and never fully embraced in public.[44] Most Theosophists adhered to what they believed to be the "Brahmanical orthodoxy" hostile to Tantra.

The Regional Background of Bengali Tantra

The idea that "Brahmanical orthodoxy" should be opposed to Tantra stands in stark contrast to the Bengali authors' viewpoint, which was marked by traditions characteristic of Bengal and its centers of learning, Navadvip and Krishnagar. This region was home to several famed pandits, including Chandrakanta Tarkalankar (1836–1910) from Mymensingh, Shashadhar Tarkachuramani from Faridpur, and of course Shivachandra Vidyarnava from Nadiya.[45] However, those who propagated Tantra as being in harmony with the Vedic *sanātana dharma* faced a serious challenge: what is now known as Bengal lay, according to various "classical" Indian sources, outside the region called *āryāvarta* and hence outside the sphere of what was regarded as Aryan Brahmanical culture. The diffusion of Brahmanical culture in that region can only be attested from the Gupta period in the fourth and fifth centuries.[46] Although Bengal had become a prominent center of Brahmanical learning by the late fifth century, the diffusion of this learning accelerated only throughout the following centuries.

This period, from the sixth century to the establishment of the first South Asian sultanates in the thirteenth century, coincides with what Alexis Sanderson has termed the "Shaiva Age," when Shaiva Tantric traditions increasingly dominated the religious and philosophical landscape.[47] This would explain why the diffusion of Brahmanical culture in Bengal was inherently intertwined with Shaiva-Shakta traditions.[48] It is important to take this circumstance into full account, as it puts the idea into perspective that

Arthur Avalon had established a form of "deodorized" or "cosmeticized" Tantra, in which transgressive elements were abstracted, philosophized, or semanticized.[49] Significantly, this notion was borrowed from Sanderson's work, which dealt with considerably older material and shows that such "deodorizing" had already occurred long before the nineteenth century.[50] What can be encountered in nineteenth-century Bengal, then, is not the cosmeticizing of an antinomian underground, but rather the renegotiation of an integral part of regional tradition.[51] For centuries, the Tantras had been incorporated into the Brahmanical study of dharma (*dharmaśāstra*) and the learned interpretation of the Vedas (*smṛti*). Because of its prominence, several nineteenth- and twentieth-century scholars were even convinced that Tantra was a genuinely, or at least predominantly, Bengali tradition.[52]

Since the eighteenth century, the region had seen the promotion of Shaiva-Shakta traditions at the court of Krishnachandra in Krishnagar, the city where Baradakanta received his education. Krishnachandra was one of six zamindars (landlords) who had received new political freedoms since the takeover of the Mughal ruler Alivardi Khan in 1740.[53] Five of those zamindars were Hindus who regarded themselves as local rajas and were eager to legitimize their kingship on the basis of Brahmanical tradition.[54] By focusing on "upper-caste" Shaiva-Shakta traditions, Krishnachandra sought to reinforce the Brahmanical social and ritual order and reaffirm his kingship in distinction to the Mughal authority.[55] The resulting focus on goddess worship and Shakta traditions, which stood in stark contrast to developments in other parts of India, preconfigured much of the intellectual landscape in which nineteenth-century debates about Tantra would play out. The reign of Krishnachandra was so influential that some regard it as a separate period, the *kṛṣṇacandrīya yug*.[56] The prominence today of festivals like Durga Puja and the assertion that Kali is Bengal's patron deity is largely due to the zamindar's promotion of Shakta traditions, which were later embraced by the *bhadralok* (the English-educated colonial middle class) and became "inextricably embedded in the idea of Bengali culture."[57]

The reasons for the eminence of Tantra in Bengal are the subject of ongoing research. In his analysis of the first Brahmanical texts in Bengal, the *upapurāṇas* (minor Puranas) that were composed between the eighth and thirteenth centuries, Kunal Chakrabarti has argued that these writings were instrumental in absorbing local traditions, including goddess worship and elements from the Tantras.[58] Pandits were careful to make a distinction between the Tantras and the Vedas, but they reconciled them in a way that is fundamental to nineteenth-century disputes. The *Devī Bhāgavata* might be regarded as representative of this strategy; similar to the great commentator of the *Manusmṛti*, Kullukabhatta, it differentiated between Vedic and Tantric knowledge. Yet it was declared that, as long as the Tantra does not contradict the Veda, "it should certainly be regarded as authoritative."[59] The decision about whether that was the case or not was thus effectively left to the interpretation of the pandits. This allowed for a flexibility that firmly integrated the Tantras into the canon of Bengali Brahmanical culture. For instance, the Bengal Puranas have prescribed the use of Tantric mantras, and they have adopted concepts such as the six chakras (*ṣaṭcakra*). At the same time, they rejected those *vāmācāra* aspects that violated the "caste" order (*varṇāśramadharma*). They did relax some social codes, however, for instance by allowing members of the Shudra caste to listen to the Puranas and admitting women to some ritual practices. Contrary to what one might imagine in the light of modern polemics, Tantric rites in Bengal were not "stigmatized or hidden" but "normative," similar to Shaiva Siddhanta and Shri Vidya in the South of India.[60]

As the most significant center of Brahmanical learning in Bengal, Navadvip was a main stage where these developments played out. The city neighbors Krishnagar on the opposite bank of the Hugli River, approximately halfway between Calcutta and Berhampore. Jonardon Ganeri has shown how Navadvip emerged as a philosophical hotspot in the seventeenth century, when India was in "intellectual overdrive."[61] Renowned for its learning since the sixteenth century, it became the region's focal point of Sanskrit studies under Krishnachandra's reign.[62] It was famous as the birthplace of Chaitanya, but also for its scholars of New Logic (*navya nyāya*), *dharmaśāstra*, astronomy, Tantra, and Vedanta.[63] New Logic, whose founder, Ragunatha Shiromani, was born in Navadvip, first flowered under the sultanate of Husayn Shah and witnessed a second flourishing under the Mughal reign of Akbar, Jahangir, and Shah Jahan. The final period of systematic patronage brought out Brahmanical scholars, who cooperated with the British beginning in 1772 in the Anglo-Hindu legal system's adaptation of *dharmaśāstra*.[64]

Navadvip pandits made a significant contribution to *smṛti* while embracing Tantric sources and goddess worship.[65] In the early colonial period, this so-called Oxford of Bengal was frequented by the most prominent English orientalists, who worked closely with the local pandits and their most famous patron, Krishnachandra.[66] One of the court's most respected *smārtas* (scholars of *smṛti*), Gopal Nyayalankar, was responsible for assembling a team of pandits to compile a legal handbook for Warren Hastings, called *Vivādārṇavasetu* (*A Bridge over Troubled Waters of Litigation*). In Nathaniel Brassey Halhed's translation, it became the famous *Code of Gentoo Laws* (1776).[67] Gopal then assisted William Carey in the translation of the Bible into Sanskrit. Another pandit with ties to Krishnachandra's court was Jagannath Tarkapanchanan, who allegedly taught Sanskrit to William Jones and compiled a legal handbook for him that would later become Colebrooke's *Digest of Hindu Law on Contracts and Successions*.[68] Obviously, Navadvip was far from being an intellectually isolated sphere. English scholars had engaged in an active exchange with pandits since the eighteenth century, and it is probable that they "significantly furthered both the reputation of the [Navadvip] pundits and their primary patron."[69]

Gopal also promoted the teachings of the sixteenth-century Navadvip scholar Raghunandan Bhattacharya, drawing on the Tantras and New Logic to shape a distinctive "Bengali School" of thought.[70] As indicated earlier, the integration of Tantric ideas into an analysis of dharma, especially through the Puranas, had been established among pandits in Bengal who were occupied with *smṛti*.[71] Building on that tradition, Raghunandan incorporated a wide range of Tantras into his teaching, in some instances relaxing Brahmanical restrictions of caste and sex during ritual.[72] Among his main references was the *Śāradātilaka*, written by Lakshmanadeshika in the eleventh or twelfth century and famously commented on by Raghavabhatta in the fifteenth century.[73] It is an erudite and voluminous digest of instructions for worship (*upāsanā*), focusing on mantras (*mantraśāstra*), the construction of yantras, and regulations for initiation (*dīkṣā*). It also contains a discussion of yogic practice, including the awakening of the kundalini and elements from Hatha Yoga.[74] It was partially based on the *Prapañcasāra*, which was attributed to Adi Shankara. Both texts aligned themselves with Samkhya philosophy and the Brahmanical *smārta* tradition.[75]

Yet references to the authority of the Tantras remained selective and even restrictive. For instance, Raghunandan rejected even the symbolic substitution of alcohol in ritual practice, which was an integral element of Tantric worship.[76] At the same time, he relied on Tantric writings to discuss other elements of worship, such as the specific repetition of mantras (*japa*) or the ritual mapping of the divinity on the practitioner's body (*nyāsa*).[77] He also accepted the *ṣaṭcakra* system and regarded the rising of the kundalini as essential for worship, quoting even from Kaula texts such as the *Yoginī*

Tantra.[78] Some reservations about the violation of Brahmanical rules of purity notwithstanding, this attests to the "extreme popularity" of the Tantras,[79] which were "widely studied and regarded as authoritative by *smārtas*."[80]

The Bengali intervention must be viewed within this context of Bengali Brahmanical Sanskritic culture, which explains the authors' frequent insistence that Tantra lay at the heart of what they regarded as Hindu dharma. Prominent Tantras were among the main authorities invoked by our *Theosophist* authors. For instance, in his "Glimpse of Tantrik Occultism," Baradakanta referred to the *Ṣaṭcakranirūpaṇa* for his discussion of yoga.[81] This text from the southern transmission of Kaula Shaivism was published by Arthur Avalon as *The Serpent Power* in 1918, which became their most successful publication and shaped the global perception of Tantra like few other texts. It was authored by the Bengali pandit Purnananda Giri in the sixteenth century and is the main reference for the "six-plus-one" chakra system that comprised the six chakras (*ṣaṭcakra*) and the *sahasrāra*. While it is thus certainly correct to regard Avalon's *The Serpent Power* as the most immediate reason for the establishment of this system,[82] this was the outcome of a longer tradition in Bengal that promoted that system as the most authoritative among several others.

The peculiarities of Brahmanical culture in Bengal also explain the prominence of a "left-hand" Kaula Tantra like the *Kulārṇava*, a text that is usually dated between the eleventh and fourteenth century. Kaula elements have so much shaded into the Vedic *smṛti* tradition that they became virtually indistinguishable from it, a development that can also be observed in the South of India.[83] The *Kulārṇava* was mentioned repeatedly by the *Theosophist* authors. It functioned as a major reference and was commonly quoted by nineteenth-century reformers such as Rammohan Roy and later members of the Brāhma Samāj and other "reformist" groups like the Tattvabodhinī Sabhā.[84] The central role of texts such as the *Ṣaṭcakranirūpaṇa* and the *Kulārṇava* is one reason Kundalini Yoga featured so prominently among learned Bengalis.[85]

Later compendia were created in the nineteenth century and include, most notably, the *Prāṇatōṣiṇī*. This was a vast work by Ramatoshana Vidyalankara, a Brahman from the Rajshahi region. It was completed in 1820 and printed in 1824. The text is commonly cited as an authoritative ritual compilation (*nibandha*) and deals with the teachings of mantras (*mantraśāstra*), initiation (*dīkṣā*) and the guru-disciple relationship, and Kundalini Yoga, among other things.[86] It cites the *Mahānirvāṇa* and the *Kulārṇava*, discussing rituals from the Kaula sphere.[87] Ramatoshana was a descendant of the famous

Krishnananda Agamavagish, who is regarded by many as a classmate of Raghunandan.[88] Krishnananda is credited with establishing widespread Kali worship in Bengal by presenting her in her relatively benign Mahāvidyā form.[89] His famous compendium, the *Tantrasāra*, became the standard *nibandha* in East India and Nepal. It was instrumental in creating a synthesis of the Tantras and Brahmanical *dharmaśāstra*, and it was used accordingly by Krishnachandra and his pandits as the basis for their ritual activities.[90] The *Śāradātilaka* was prominently quoted by it.[91] Both the *Prāṇatōṣiṇī* and the *Tantrasāra* were described by contemporaries as the most commonly used compendia in Bengal.[92] It does not come as a surprise, then, that Baradakanta invoked the authority of the *Tantrasāra* when he addressed the awakening of the kundalini in the *Theosophist*.[93]

In order to fully understand the background of the Bengali intervention, it is necessary to expand the scope beyond Brahmanical Sanskritic traditions and also consider the rise of popular Shakta poetry since the eighteenth century. The movement was inspired by Vaishnava-oriented devotional (*bhakti*) poetry, as it was popularized by the tradition of Gaudiya Vaishnavism that had also emerged in Navadvip in the sixteenth century. This tradition put a strong emphasis on bhakti, which prioritized the personal devotion and intimate relationship with the divine over ritual practice. It is also marked by a strong insistence on secrecy and communicates its ideas in songs and poems through a heavily coded language that is almost incomprehensible to the outsider—a quality that can still be observed in Baul poetry.[94] The new Shakta poetry was thus a combination of heavily ritualized Shakta Tantric elements, on the one hand, and Vaishnava bhakti on the other, which led to a strong popularizing trend of Shakta Tantrism beyond the Brahmanical sphere. The most famous representative of this movement, Ramprasad Sen, eventually became the court poet at Krishnagar.[95] Another important Shakta poet, Kamalakanta Bhattacharya, is representative of the way in which Shakta Tantric and Vaishnava elements were combined.[96]

The end of the eighteenth century saw a surge in the popularity of Shakta devotional poetry, which increasingly took on a universalistic thrust, embracing Vaishnava and Muslim traditions. The ideas of the most celebrated nineteenth-century representative of this development, the great Baul Lalon Fakir, should be viewed against that background. Throughout the nineteenth century, these Bengali Vaishnava currents were substantially renegotiated and popularized within the colonial context.[97] These dynamics are essential for an understanding of the debates about Tantra, as a range of direct personal connections demonstrate. For instance, Kamalakanta's work *Sadhak-rañjan*, in which the kula-kundalini shakti is conceived in the image of Radha, was later edited by Atalbihari Ghosh. But even today, the development of devotional poetry and non-Brahmanical traditions is significant for Bengal.[98]

It is not surprising, then, that the reign of Krishnachandra is often associated with a revival of Shakta traditions and goddess worship.[99] As Joel Bordeaux has shown, it is possible to observe a plethora of new Shakta Tantric texts in Sanskrit circulate in the sixteenth and seventeenth centuries, which were then taken up by the pandits of Nadiya and eventually fed into the more devotionally oriented current led by famous figures such as Ramakrishna at the end of the nineteenth century. Yet it is difficult if not impossible to pin down a period or event that would convincingly mark a "Shakta revival" in implicit reaction to a period of decay or dormancy.[100] Instead of viewing the role of Tantra in Bengal since the eighteenth century in terms of "revival," it is more instructive to locate it within the contexts of (early) colonialism and the global exchanges unfolding within it. The Bengali intervention, Shivachandra's activities, and eventually the Avalon project must then be understood as forceful manifestations of ongoing struggles about the meaning of dharma, Tantra, and Hinduism. A similar point has recently been made by Lucian Wong and Ferdinando Sardella about Bengali Vaishnavism; they emphasize that the British colonial period witnessed a major transformation and reconfiguration of Vaishnavism in the region, "having dramatic implications for subsequent expressions and representations of the tradition."[101] As we shall see at a later point, Shivachandra's efforts to create a Shaiva-Vaishnava unity illustrate how deeply intertwined these historical developments were.

Baradakanta's insistence on the scientific virtues of Tantra reminds us how much these struggles were tied into contemporary global debates about the relationship between science and religion. The orientalist idea that ancient India was adept at employing natural forces—and hence was pioneering modern science through a lineage of ancient wisdom traditions—was consciously and actively taken up by learned Indians from a remarkably early point on. Joshua Ehrlich has discovered that none other than raja Krishnachandra emphasized the scientific virtues of ancient India by stressing, "Egipt . . . is well known to us. . . . [W]e have had an intercourse with its Inhabitants from time immemorial." This did not fail to have the desired effect on his curious European interlocutors, who found that Krishnachandra was "the most enlightened native [they] had ever met with, and his conversation remarkably free from all appearance of Superstition or Artifice."[102] This underlines how prominent and well-established theories about a shared pristine religious and scientific heritage at the root of both India and Egypt were among orientalist scholars and Indian intellectuals since at least the second half of the eighteenth century. Baradakanta's and the Theosophists' claims about a common Aryan origin of ancient initiatory cults were hence not at all as outlandish to contemporary observers as they might be to present-day readers; to the contrary, they perfectly harmonized with widely accepted scholarly paradigms.

Baradakanta, the Theosophist

The interest of Bengali Tantrikas in Theosophy was indeed so pronounced that a number of them chose to get properly involved with the Society. Among the first was Baradakanta, whose individual background demands further scrutiny. His upbringing was emblematic of an intricate mélange of Mughal and British learning that marked the simultaneous engagement of many Indian intellectuals with Western and Sanskritic teachings within a global context. He had attended the oldest college in Krishnagar, founded in 1846. First led by the famous educationist David Lester Richardson, the college would later emerge as a hotbed for freedom fighters and social reformers. In the year 1868 its records name Baradakanta as a third-grade B.A. student who was among the three most successful of his year, which secured him a senior scholarship. He and his seventeen fellow third-graders were among 106 students in total; the college had just seen its largest increase, from 83 in the previous year. Half of the eighteen third-graders came from zamindar and *talukdar* families—the old ruling elites and landowners of the Mughal Empire—as well as persons of independent income, all concerned with providing their heirs with a modern education. The rest consisted of "professional persons," government servants, and pensioners.[103]

These were the social circles where Baradakanta would move in the years after obtaining his degree. In 1876, he published *A Series of Moral and Civil Discourses for the Instruction of Young Proprietors of Land*, accompanied by a glossary of Persian words used in fiscal and forensic matters. This book was dedicated to raja Pramathabhushan Deva Ray of Naldanga in Jessore, about one hundred kilometers east of Krishnagar. Pramathabhushan had been born in 1858 and was only eleven and a half years old when his father died in

1870, leaving him as an underage raja in need of guidance. Baradakanta was among those who took up that task, opening his educational discourse with the statement that man was superior to all creatures and thus obliged to lead an exemplary life for the benefit of society.[104] This especially pertained to the life of a ruler; the attainment of knowledge (*jñān*) would lead to humbleness and guard against the dangers to society that arise when the privileged classes are ignorant.[105] Apparently, Pramathabhushan was receptive to such advice and became an ardent educationist and social reformer after coming of age in 1879. Fluent in English, a passionate sportsman, and the owner of no fewer than four motor cars, the young raja championed widow remarriage and opposed child marriage. He founded and maintained a High English School at his own cost, supported several educational and charitable projects and institutions, and subsidized the Muslim community.[106]

When Baradakanta published his first article in the *Theosophist*, he lived in the Ghoramara part of Rajshahi, a cultural center northwest of Naldanga. The city would later see the foundation of the Varendra Research Society (*barendra anusandhān samiti*), which was of major significance for the study of Tantra. Nadiya, Jessore, Rajshahi, and adjacent areas were marked by a strong Tantric tradition, which coexisted with the English education that young Bengalis received at institutions such as Krishnagar College.[107] Baradakanta's generation witnessed increased efforts to revive the "traditional" knowledge challenged by English education, not by outright rejecting the latter but by attempting to reconcile the two. The way in which Baradakanta opened the debate in the pages of the *Theosophist* is illustrative of this ambivalent process.

On August 26, 1880, about two weeks after he had penned the second part of his "Glimpse of Tantrik Occultism," Baradakanta joined the Theosophical Society. His early member number, 675, underlines his pioneering role in the Bengali initiative to influence Theosophical knowledge. The following years were marked by personal tragedy and an enhanced commitment to the Theosophical cause. In 1883, Baradakanta attempted to form a branch of the Society in Jessore but gave up the idea when his eldest son died.[108] In May of the same year, the *Theosophist* reported that he had succeeded in opening a Theosophical School at Naldanga, possibly under the auspices of the young raja:

> There are English, Bengali and Sanskrit classes up to the Matriculation standard of the Calcutta University. I have a Sunday School under my own

> tuition, where Hindu ethics are taught. I have already secured twenty boys and hope the number will be doubled in two or three weeks. My desire to impart religious training has not hitherto met with success for want of an elementay [*sic*] text book, the idea of which was communicated by me to Col. Olcott when he visited Calcutta in 1882.[109]

These endeavors illustrate the Theosophical educational project of reviving the "traditional" training that was considered lost among modern Indians. As is well known, Olcott was instrumental in creating a "Buddhist Catechism" that remains influential up to the present day, and similar attempts were made to provide Hindus with similar textbooks.[110] Indeed, one of the first initiatives of the Theosophical Society in Bengal was the creation of a school for "Hindu boys" in Calcutta. Baradakanta's role as a propagator of Tantra gains an important nuance when seen in this light: the revival of Shastric principles was a matter of educational policy that would elevate India to the role of the teacher of humanity rather than the recipient of British colonial knowledge. This is underlined by the fact that Baradakanta continued to be an educationist in the succeeding years, as several books directed at children demonstrate. These included *Bhūgol* (1898), dealing with geography; *Subhadrā* (1913), which is especially written for girls; and *Śiśurañjan granthābalī*, an illustrated series containing, inter alia, excerpts from the *Mahābhārata* (1914).[111] Posthumously, the director of public instruction for school students published Baradakanta's *Yiśukhriṣṭa*, a book telling the life of Jesus Christ that was supposed to familiarize schoolchildren with Christianity.[112] It went through at least five editions until 1946, which allows for an *ante quem* of Baradakanta's death.

Baradakanta's sustained educational efforts were inherently intertwined with his commitment to the Theosophical Society, which peaked during his collaboration on the Bengali Theosophical journal *Kalpa*. This monthly began publication in April 1893 and was first edited by Rakhalchandra Sen and Durganath Kabyaratna. The issues of May and June 1894 (*jaiṣṭha* and *āṣāṛh* 1301) reveal that the editorship had been handed over to Baradakanta and Debendranath Gosvami, another diligent Bengali Theosophist who edited several Sanskrit scriptures in Bengali. Like other Bengali Theosophical journals, *Kalpa* was dedicated to the promotion of *tattvabidyā*, the most common translation of Theosophy next to *brahmabidyā* or *dharmatattva*. The fourth issue, however, added a new designation to the journal's banner: "The Bengali Theosophical Society for the Promotion of the

Meaning of the Eternal Aryan Dharma" (*sanātan āryyadharmmapracārārtha baṅgadeśīya tattvasabhā*). A bit later, the name was once more changed to *tattva-jijñāsusabhā*, literally "The Society for the Investigation of Tattva."

These repeated name changes illustrate the struggle to translate "Theosophy" into the Bengali language. The Sanskrit terms *tattva*, *brahma*, and *dharma* are components of practically all varieties, most often in combination with *bidyā* (Skt. *vidyā*). All of these terms are highly difficult to translate into English.[113] *Bidyā* is sometimes translated as "science," but the Bengali intellectuals who are the focus of our examination usually preferred the Bengali term *bijñān* to refer to science in the "modern" sense. As a matter of fact, *bijñān* appears to have sometimes been perceived as subordinate—and indeed inferior—to *bidyā*. It emerges, then, that "Theosophy" was perceived as a means for accessing knowledge about *tattva*, Brahman, and *dharma*. Each of these terms, however, has a vastly complex history. It is therefore necessary to pay close attention to how Bengali Theosophists employed these terms, that is, what historical conditions formed the context in which their translingual practice was carried out. The self-declared purposes of the Bengal Theosophical Society stated in *Kalpa* are a good starting point:

1. To follow the path of truth [*satya*],[114] that is to do good to all mankind.
2. To seek after truth, that is to carefully discuss the eternal Aryan dharma [*sanātan āryyadharmma*].
3. To realize the truth, that is the practice of yoga [*yog'sādhana*].[115]

Clearly, Western Theosophists and their Indian interlocutors were often united in their goal to revive Aryan civilization and the Aryan conduct of life, dharma. The related notion of *sanātana dharma* had already figured prominently on the subcontinent and was believed by many to be the essence of Aryan-Indian wisdom and life conduct, which lay dormant after an age of degeneration. As will be discussed in more detail in the following chapters, it was usually employed by so-called orthodox thinkers or revivalists, and can be viewed as a prime exemplar of a supposed tradition juxtaposed to modernity. This tension can be observed throughout the pages of *Kalpa*, where modern science is persistently denounced, while at the same time the nature of ancient Aryan wisdom is portrayed as explicitly scientific.

We read in the programmatic editorial of the first issue that the era when truth lay dormant had ended and the age of the ancient rishis had returned to India. After a period of selfishness and cruelty that had destroyed the golden land of the Aryans, the sun of truth was shining brighter every day and was illuminating all corners of the earth. The dawn of this new epoch (*kalpa*) would reveal that the light of knowledge had first shone upon India, a land that was now bereft of strength, enthusiasm, and curiosity. The Vedas, Upanishads, Smritis, and Puranas contained most of the wisdom that the West has discovered only in the past two centuries. Thanks to the translations by William Jones, Cowell, Colebrooke, and Wilson, as well as the efforts by Blavatsky and Olcott, the West would now begin to realize that it still had a lot to learn from India. Hence Europe and America must help India overcome its inertia so that India could in turn show Europe and America the way out of ignorance. Only then could the secret (*gūṛha*) meaning of the scriptures (*śāstra*) of the Aryan rishis be comprehended.[116]

In fact, the editors claimed that it was thanks to the Bengal Theosophical Society that "Hindu dharma" was witnessing a revival. They also praised the efforts of their Western brothers and sisters, especially Annie Besant, whose name is spelt "Anna Bāsantī," the latter term signifying "spring" or the goddess Durga. She was even called the "spiritual Annapurna" (*ādhyātmik annapūrṇa*), referring to one of the highest peaks of the Himalayas, or "the one who is replete with nourishment," which again can be read as a reference to Durga.[117] This shows how Theosophical efforts were framed as a spring-like revival of dharma after a winter of oppression, with a Durga-like Besant leading the way.

The editors explained that, thanks to the activities of the Society, Hindus who just twenty years earlier had thought of their ancestors as uncivilized or half-civilized had now started to reconsider their opinion and decided to revive Hindu knowledge.[118] This knowledge taught the oneness of all beings and the ultimate identity of each individual with everything. In order to achieve that goal, it was necessary to communicate those teachings in a simple and comprehensible way, which underlines the educational intention behind that endeavor. The result would not be any new knowledge, new truths, or new scriptures, but the regeneration and dissemination of Aryan wisdom in India.[119] According to the Bengali Theosophists, this project required cooperation between East and West. Eventually, all sectarianism should be overcome and the oneness of the human race as the offspring of Brahman should be accepted by everyone. This doctrine of universal brotherhood stood at the core of the teachings of all "great men" (*mahāpuruṣ*), such as Krishna, Buddha, Christ, and Shankara, and was thus the essence of all religions.[120] In an adaptation of Blavatsky's *Key to Theosophy* (1889),

Baradakanta stressed that Theosophy was not a specific dharma but "the pinnacle of science" (*bijñān'śāstrer parākāṣṭhā*). This was so because the ancient Aryans were able to penetrate the mysteries governing the universe. Their insights led to the eternal truth (*sanātan satya*) that lay at the root of every religious tradition.[121]

This common root, however, was not exposed and visible to everyone. Theosophy, in fact, was always secret or "esoteric" (*tattvabidyā cirakāl'i gupta*). In Egypt as in Greece, the great teachers unveiled their most profound doctrines only to select students. In India, the same doctrines were preserved in the Upanishads, Vedas, and Puranas—the Tantrics were especially concerned with keeping their teachings secret. All lands had their "initiates," a term that is also provided in English in the text and translated as *dīkṣitagaṇ* or, as a footnote explains, "those who are initiated into the secret practice of the knowledge of Brahman" (*yāhārā brahmabidyār guptasādhane dīkṣita*).[122] Secret knowledge (*guptabidyā*) could not be acquired by merely reading textbooks, as the absolute self (*paramātmā*) could not be known by the individual self (*jībātmā*) without extensive preparation through yogic practice. In these many other instances, Baradakanta explained his ideas by references to Western thinkers ancient and contemporary, including Plato, Plotinus, and the American Theosophist Alexander Wilder (1823–1908).[123]

Theosophy was hence understood not as a new idea but as "the oldest and most universal branch of knowledge." Why, then, was there no trace of Theosophy among Westerners, who are supposedly the most evolved and sophisticated people? Because, Baradakanta clarified, history was full of people who were as sophisticated as and certainly more developed spiritually than people of the Western nations in the nineteenth century. St. Paul had already admonished the Athenians that crude materialism and slavish adherence to lifeless customs resulted in the disappearance of their spiritual "inner vision" or "introspection" (*antardṛṣṭi*). The failure of the West to counteract this tendency may be one reason Theosophy remained dormant. But the main reason was that real Theosophical knowledge is always secret (*gupta*), as it had to be guarded against those "common people" who were deceitful, selfish, and harmful.[124]

While both Indian and Western culture were thus depicted in terms of degeneration, Baradakanta established a hierarchy in which the East ranked higher than the West. Yet the authors of *Kalpa* consistently referred to Western thinkers to prove the common root of Aryan wisdom; they also praised the efforts of contemporary European scholars to study India.

It was remarked, for instance, that Paul Deussen had translated Shankara's commentary on Vedanta into German and had expressed his desire to do an English translation, in order to prove to the larger public that Kant was expressing the same thoughts as Shankara—an idea that is reminiscent of Müller's opinion.[125] It was clear, however, that it was the West who could learn from the East, and not vice versa. As Haranchandra Bandyopadhyay stressed at the eleventh annual conference of the Bengal Theosophical Society, ancient Aryan morality and science were superior to anything that could be found in modern societies.[126] Rakhalchandra Sen, the first editor of *Kalpa*, secretary of the Bengal Theosophical Society, and coordinator of the Vedic School of Bengal (*baṅgabedbidyālaẏ*), made it clear that the Aryan rishis had reached the pinnacle of glory in material, biological, psychological, and spiritual terms by following the Vedas in every aspect of their lives.[127] Accordingly, Rakhalchandra set up an Anglo-Vedic School near Ripon College in Calcutta, which was—*nota bene*—modeled after Dayananda's Anglo-Vedic college in Lahore and intended to impart Vedic knowledge in addition to English to Hindu students.[128]

Modern Western science features as both an adversary and an authority in the pages of *Kalpa*. For instance, one article reprimanded Western science for wanting to explain the physical world experimentally through the five senses, while ignoring those extrasensory powers that underlie all that is visible. This, according to the author, was "scientific superstition" and proved that the rishis had been far more wise than modern Western scientists, as they had experimentally analyzed both the physical and the metaphysical, the visible and invisible worlds.[129] As Baradakanta's intervention in the *Theosophist* has already demonstrated, magnetism and electricity were an integral part of this line of argumentation. *Kalpa* reprinted an article by Brajendranath Bandyopadhyay from the journal *Bhāratī* which traced the history of mesmerism back to the ancient Brahmans, who were adept at employing the power of animal magnetism like no others. In fact, they were responsible for spreading this "scientific" power to Greece, Egypt, and Babylon, whence it was transmitted to Europe.[130]

Interestingly, Tantra did not take as central a role as one might have expected in light of Baradakanta's investment in the subject. This might have been the case because the authors of *Kalpa* did not want to repel readers who associated Tantra with scandalous practices, and it might also have been because it was regarded as "too esoteric" to be openly discussed in a popular journal. Several mentions, however, do highlight its significance. It was claimed, for instance, that the three major "applied Hindu sciences" were medicine, astrology, and Tantra.[131] Another article reprimanded English-educated people for believing that the rishis had no idea of science, while nothing could be further from the truth; such misconceptions could only arise from a lack of understanding of Sanskrit texts.[132] Among those, the *Mahānirvāṇa Tantra* takes a prominent role, for instance in a piece about the realization, through yoga, of Brahman as the ultimate nondualistic reality.[133] One article describes shakti as the conscious power pervading and forming the material world,[134] while another even discusses the "five Ms" (*pañcamakāra*) as Tantric metaphors for the ascendance of the soul to the highest point of emancipation.[135]

Theosophy, it emerges, was perceived as an expression of *sanātana dharma*, or more precisely, as the means to revive that eternal Aryan dharma after a period of decay. The root of that dharma was in India, but it had spread all over the world and formed the core of all great teachings since the time of the ancient rishis. Because it was secret (*gupta* or *gūṛha*), only an elite of initiates could grasp its true meaning, but its revival crucially depended on a reform of education, so that the masses would be led to the realization of truth. In the process, it was the West who had to learn from the East, as the former had long descended into gross materialism and was out of touch with its Aryan roots. This especially concerned modern science, which was inferior to the wisdom of the ancient rishis. Their knowledge formed the basis for the practice of yoga, which was based on scientific methods that employed forces such as magnetism and electricity. Tantra stood at the core of that yogic-scientific practice. We can thus observe how Theosophy was absorbed in ongoing debates among Bengali intellectuals, and how it became enmeshed in struggles about the meaning of Hindu dharma, as well as the role of English education.

Where the Threads Meet: Arthur Avalon

Over twenty years later, the work of Avalon Arthur took up what these Bengali authors had initiated. However, the Avalon publications were directed not primarily at a Theosophical audience but at an academic readership, among which it was overwhelmingly positively received.[136] Not only did it make available a substantial amount of source material, but it also appeared to be more expertly informed than any earlier account of the subject. Although scholarship has moved on and Avalon's studies are largely outdated, they remain influential and still serve as important references.[137] It would be misleading, however, to assume that the Bengali intervention and the Avalon project mark two different trajectories, one esoteric and one academic. On the contrary, these spheres were deeply interconnected.

It is significant that Avalon, like the Theosophists and their Bengali partners, took a decisive stance against the perspective of European orientalists and missionaries. Beginning with *The Great Liberation* and *Principles of Tantra*, negative perceptions of Tantra were critically discussed and refuted in lengthy introductions, whose proficiency stunned contemporary scholars. The first sentence of the preface to *Principles* encapsulates Avalon's main thesis: "Mediaeval 'Hinduism' (to use a convenient, if somewhat vague, term) was, as its successor, modern Indian orthodoxy, is, largely Tāntrik."[138] This claim is remarkable, not only for its awareness of the problems related to the sweeping category of "Hinduism," but especially for the claim that "it" was largely Tantric, as was contemporary "Indian orthodoxy." This was an exact inversion of the standpoint shared by most orientalists and reformers such as Dayananda.

Time and again, Avalon reprimands orientalists and other European authors for ignoring that circumstance, for instance when he states that Horace Hayman Wilson "was doubtless a distinguished orientalist, and his work is in many respects of acknowledged value; but there are matters in his book which, from want of sympathy and knowledge, he wholly failed to understand."[139] Even worse was the ignorance and neglect of the "Tantra Shastra" among Indians. This, we read, was chiefly due to colonialism: "In the first place, in the case of India, must be reckoned the effects of English education. This, when first introduced, not merely struck at faith in all Indian Shastra, but was in a particular manner adverse to that form of it which was then current, and with which we here deal."[140] As Avalon explained, the British aversion toward Tantra was due to their Protestant bias, which rejected the ritualistic and ceremonial aspects central to Tantric worship as superstitious and idolatrous. Yelle has shown that this bias was indeed crucial for British approaches to what was considered idolatry, polytheism, and myth in India.[141] That the colonizers imposed this view on their subjects was vehemently criticized by Woodroffe in writings published under his name. He maintained that Indians were "ruled by a Western race which (subject perhaps to some common elements of 'Aryanism') is foreign to it in body, mind, custom and culture." The influence of English education left most

Indians "de-racialized and denationalized," which is why Woodroffe thought it necessary to establish an "education upon national lines."[142] The aim of such a national education was the regeneration of India's shakti, and consequently of the vigor of its inhabitants: "What India wanted at present was a *Religion of Power*."[143] Bereft of its ancient greatness, Indian culture and the "racial soul" from which it emanated lay suffocated by the power of the West. Worst of all, a "class arose, and still, to some extent, exists, which finding everything Western, to be good, neglected its own ancient heritage."[144] These Western-educated reformists, echoing the prejudices of British Protestants, posed the biggest threat to a proper understanding of the shastras.

That Woodroffe, as a member of the colonial administration, would voice such an endorsement of "national education" is remarkable in itself. It is also striking because he frequently linked this agenda to Catholicism. In his view, Catholicism and Tantra were united in a struggle against the materialistic, atheistic, or bigoted "reformism" that marked modernity—which seemed to be confirmed by the attacks on idolatry and superstition that had been leveled by Protestants against Catholics and Indians alike.[145] In a book published in 1918, Woodroffe asserted, "Even to-day there is less difference between a Catholic adherent of the old Christian tradition and a Hindu than between the so-called 'Modernism' of the west and the culture of the latter."[146] Taylor has discussed in some detail how Woodroffe's thought had been shaped by a liberal Catholic education—although he certainly would not qualify as a practicing Catholic, his "re-conversion" to Catholicism on his deathbed notwithstanding.[147] Still, the defense of Tantra was a deeply personal affair for Woodroffe, but one that he also regarded as vital for a humanity threatened by the destructive forces of modernity. In sharp contrast to other contemporary programs of "national education," including the one propagated by the Ārya Samāj, the regeneration of India was not supposed to be achieved by the eradication of supposed aberrations such as Tantra.[148] Rather, Tantra itself was conceived as the very means to that regeneration.

How central esotericism was for this idea becomes once more tangible in Baradakanta's notion of Tantrik Occultism, which is in direct continuity with the later publications by Avalon. Tantra was identified with "higher occultism" in the preface to the first volume of *Principles*,[149] or when Woodroffe praised it as "the storehouse of Indian occultism."[150] He frequently claimed that occultism was thoroughly scientific and stressed its "catholicity."[151] The proponents of occultism, which purportedly could be found in both Eastern and Western traditions, were thus on the same side in the struggle against modernity and reformism:

> Those familiar with the Western presentment of similar matters will more readily understand than others who, like the Orientalist and Missionary, as a rule know nothing of occultism and regard it as superstition. For this reason their presentment of Indian teaching is so often ignorant and absurd. The occultist, however, will understand the Indian doctrine which regards thought like mind, of which it is the operation, as a Power or Shakti; something therefore, very real and creative by which man can accomplish things for himself and others.[152]

It is quite extraordinary that Woodroffe here privileges the "occultist" perspective over that of the orientalist or missionary, implying not only a universal tradition of occultism but also an epistemology, worldview, and set of practices that was common to its Eastern and Western branches. The prominence of such assertions contradicts Taylor's statement that the works of Avalon "are in fact almost entirely free from Theosophical or any other Western occultist terminology."[153] While she is certainly right in highlighting differences between these contexts and the work of Avalon, she neglects the fact that the latter's work *does* abound with esoteric terminology and that the exchange between Theosophists and Bengali Tantrikas is directly linked to Avalon. Moreover, it must be taken into account that definitions of Tantra as secret (*nigūṛh*, *gūṛha*) and requiring initiation (*dīkṣā*) formed an essential part of regional understandings. Rather than speaking of a Western esoteric influence on the Bengali context, then, it is crucial to investigate these developments within broader networks of global exchange.

Esotericism and Orientalist Scholarship

This broader global context comprises the communications between Bengali Tantrikas and Western Theosophists, and also orientalist scholarship and its relevance for the meaning of esotericism. In fact, the esoteric language that marked the Avalon publications as well as the Bengali intervention has lastingly shaped scholarship on Tantra. Eliade, who relied heavily on the work of Avalon, understood yoga as the means to acquire "occult powers" (*siddhi*) and perform "magic": yogic texts strove to explain "any parapsychological and occult phenomenon" on those grounds.[154] This "occult" or "mystical knowledge" formed part of "the pan-Indian occult tradition" that revolved around the "occult sciences."[155] In his classic study, Shashibhusan Das Gupta defined the religious beliefs of the Nath yogis as "a wide-spread belief in occult power attained through the practice of yoga," and counted it as Indian "occultism," which was "associated with all esoteric religious systems in the Hindu, Buddhist and other religious schools."[156] Sures Chandra Banerji defined Tantric *sādhana* as "esoteric" and included "occultism" in the set of doctrines inherent in Tantra, even using Baradakanta's term "Tantrik Occultism" to relate the Brahmanas to the Tantras.[157] Teun Goudriaan explored the Tantric practices of an "esoteric yogic cult,"[158] while Sanderson frequently employed the notion of "gnostic" or "Gnosis" to describe Shaiva Tantric philosophy and practice.[159] This vocabulary is especially well established to examine the Kaulas, as in Padoux's discussion of their "esoteric gnosis."[160] According to Padoux, Tantra should be viewed as an "esoteric core" that can be understood in terms of "Gnosticism."[161] White refers to the "esoteric, secret rites" of the Kaulas and their "gnosis" (*jñāna*), suggesting "esotericism, mysticism, and secrecy" as "hallmarks of Tantra."[162] Similarly, "Gnosis" has long served as a standard term in Buddhist studies, with Edward Conze even calling himself a "gnostic."[163] Douglas Renfrew Brooks asserts that "Tantra may well be the esoteric movement par excellence in Indian religion,"[164] while Gavin Flood describes the *kula-prakriya* as an "esoteric rite" essential to the achievement of "esoteric revelation."[165] Elaine Fisher's study *Hindu Pluralism* abounds with references to Shakta "esoteric ritual practice" and "esotericism,"[166] evoking even a parallel with the "Western Hermetic tradition."[167] As a matter of fact, the use of esoteric vocabulary and comparisons with "other esoteric traditions" abound in academic scholarship beyond the sphere of esoteric practitioners.

This circumstance cannot simply be explained with the exchange between Bengali Tantrikas and Western Theosophists, which would later resurface in the Avalon publications; the use of esoteric language in studies on South Asian traditions significantly *predates* this exchange and can be traced right to the heart of orientalist scholarship. It can be encountered in *Asiatic Researches* as early as 1812, in an article by John Leyden, who cited a differentiation, directed at "infidels, unbelievers, and *Yogis*," between the Islamic *sharī'a* (law) and *haqīqa* (truth) as representing "the exoteric and esoteric doctrines of the law."[168] In 1827, Colebrooke defined the "esoteric" part of the Brahmanas as comprising the Upanishads and being "theological."[169] In the following year, Brian Houghton Hodgson explained the terms "Tantra" and "Purana" "as vaguely expressive of the distinction of esoteric and exoteric works."[170] Wilson, in turn, referred to the "*Esoteric* doctrine" of Tibetan Buddhism in 1832 and, in 1840 delivered two widely noted lectures "on the religious practices and opinions of the Hindus" upon a request from the bishop of Calcutta to offer the means for "the best refutation of Hinduism in its main systems, both exoteric, and esoteric."[171] The latter was especially highlighted in the context of Tantra.[172] Esoteric doctrines were discussed as an integral part of Buddhism and Hinduism, ranging from China to India and beyond, for instance by William Henry Sykes.[173]

These findings are highly significant because they precede the emergence of esoteric movements such as Spiritualism, occultism, and Theosophy. Indeed, the identification of Indian traditions as "esoteric" appears to have been articulated by orientalist scholars prior to people *identifying as* esotericists in Europe. This is all the more intriguing since the German term *Esoterik* first appeared in an orientalist work, the second edition of the multivolume *Urgeschichte* (1790–1793) by Johann Gottfried Eichhorn.[174] The influential orientalist Jacques Matter (1791–1864), who is known to be the first author to coin the notion of *ésotérisme* in French, was convinced that currents such as Gnosticism and Kabbalah had actually been influenced by Indian ideas—a claim that exerted a significant influence on Éliphas Lévi, the "founder" of occultism.[175]

It would be misleading to conclude that this was the result of different historical manifestations of a sui generis esotericism across the globe. Rather, we are dealing precisely with the globally entangled discourse about religion that rests in the focus of global religious history; since the "discovery of religious history" at the end of the eighteenth century,[176] individuals across the world engaged in de facto identifications of different "religious" traditions, theorizing about common origins and disparate developments of religion. We are thus dealing with a body of literature produced within a concrete historical setting, which formed the conditions for the translingual practice we can discern in our sources.

There are several reasonable ways to examine these historical identifications of Asian traditions as "esoteric." One way could be imagined through a comparison of structural similarities, most obviously with regard to secrecy and initiation.[177] Indeed, the background of Bengali learning has demonstrated the insistence on the secret (*nigūṛh*, *gūṛha*, *gupta*) character of certain teachings and practices that stands out in virtually all sources, whether in diverse Tantric scriptures, throughout Baradakanta's contributions to the *Theosophist*, or in the pages of *Kalpa*.

However, global religious history approaches such historical comparisons and translations from a genealogical perspective. This allows for the unraveling of concrete historical reasons for, say, the omnipresent insistence on secrecy. Of course, the guru-disciple relationship that is largely determined by *dīkṣā* already implies such an insistence. But it also resulted from the specific ways of "reading the past," in the words of Ganeri, that emerged in early modernity. The period since the sixteenth and seventeenth centuries saw a new genre of learned commentary that aimed at digging up the secret or hidden meaning (*gūṛhārtha*) of an ancient text.[178] These new modes of interpreting hidden meanings were directly tied into the negotiation of the relationship between the Tantras and the Vedas, and hence a constitutive part of the region's knowledge production.

Comparativism in the vein of global religious history departs from the present-day terminology, identifying the nineteenth century as a crucial period of transition and consistently working its way backward in time. Such a method systematically unravels how notions of secrecy and initiation emerged and developed historically, avoiding many of the trappings of classical comparativisms that more often than not tend to presuppose historically European understandings of religion or esotericism.[179] Global religious history, in turn, retains a focus on the historical conditions that determined the translingual practice of the identification of, for instance, Tantra with "Indian occultism." These historical conditions can be scrutinized only through careful historical contextualization, which the following chapters aim to achieve. While a diachronic investigation of these conditions and practices prior to the end of the nineteenth century remains a desideratum, we are now well equipped to shine more light on the tangle of orientalist scholarship, Theosophy, and Indian learning.

2
Theosophy in Bengal

When the founders of the Theosophical Society relocated to India, they were immediately able to productively engage with their Indian interlocutors. This is no matter of course. Why were they received so enthusiastically by numerous Indian intellectuals, and why, in the first place, could they enter dialogue so easily? In this chapter, I will discuss some of the fundamental conditions for these exchanges. They revolved around three aspects: first, the supposed discovery of an "Aryan" past shared by Europeans and Indians; second, the wish to revive that ancient Aryan civilization and, on these grounds, reform present society and humanity as a whole; and third, the claim that this would largely work on the basis of a synthesis, or restoration of the unity, of science, religion, and philosophy.

In this light, contemporary orientalist scholarship and its entanglement with Theosophy deserves special attention. The example of Friedrich Max Müller serves to illustrate that orientalist scholars and Theosophists might often have been rivals but were united, not only by crucial assumptions but also by shared goals. This extends to two of the most influential Indian reform movements, the Ārya Samāj and the Brāhma Samāj. I argue that these movements emerged against a globally entangled background that was *also* vital for the emergence of Theosophy. This common historical context was a main reason Indian reformers and Theosophists could enter dialogue so fruitfully. Rather than simply spreading "Western knowledge" to India, Theosophists became subject to Indian debates and were confronted by a plethora of competing interests.

Theosophy and the Revival of "Aryan Civilization"

A contemporary reader of the *Theosophist*'s edition of February 1880 would have encountered a mélange of subject that illustrates the manifold ways in which the Theosophical Society became enmeshed in the religious and political life of India. The reader could leaf through the pages of the journal on

Global Tantra. Julian Strube, Oxford University Press. © Oxford University Press 2022.
DOI: 10.1093/oso/9780197627112.003.0003

practically all continents, as the editors proudly pointed out that they had "subscribers in every part of India, in Ceylon, Burmah, and on the Persian Gulf. Our paper also goes to Great Britain, Germany, Hungary, Greece, Russia, Constantinople, Egypt, Australia, and North and South America." The Theosophists clearly made a point of transgressing geographical boundaries. When Blavatsky and Olcott arrived in Bombay on February 16, 1879, they quickly established relationships with Indian reform societies, most notably Dayananda's Ārya Samāj, but they were also supported by figures within the colonial establishment, including Alfred Percy Sinnett (1840–1921), editor of the *Pioneer*, the largest daily national newspaper, and Allan Octavian Hume (1829–1912), the former secretary to the government.[1] Shortly after their arrival in Bombay, the Theosophists reworked the rules and objects of their society in March and April, followed by an extensive revision after a meeting held in Benares in December. Their "plans" included:

a. To keep alive in man his spiritual intuitions.
b. To oppose and counteract—after due investigation and proof of its irrational nature—bigotry in every form, whether as an intolerant religious sectarianism or belief in miracles or anything supernatural.
c. To promote a feeling of brotherhood among nations; and assist in the international exchange of useful arts and products, by advice, information, and co-operation with all worthy individuals and associations. . . .
d. To seek to obtain knowledge of all the laws of Nature, and aid in diffusing it, thus to encourage the study of those laws least understood by modern people, and so termed the Occult Sciences.[2]

As is well known, these objectives were altered several times. A comparison between this first large revision and the second one, from February 17, 1881, reveals a change in focus and language:

1. To form the nucleus of a Universal Brotherhood of Humanity, the obvious philanthropic value of which must be beyond dispute, while the esoteric significance of a union formed on that plan, is conceived by the Founders, for reasons derived from a study of Oriental Philosophy, to be of great importance.
2. To study Aryan literature, religion and science, which the Founders believe to contain certain valuable truths and philosophical views, of which the Western world knows nothing.

3. To vindicate the importance of this inquiry and correct misrepresentations with which it has been clouded.
4. To explore the hidden mysteries of Nature, and the latent powers of Man, on which the Founders believe that Oriental Philosophy is in a position to throw light.[3]

It can be observed that the Theosophists' ambition to form an elite for the creation of a "universal brotherhood of humanity" has been moved to the fore, and that this goal was to be achieved by unveiling the hidden treasures of religion, science, and philosophy now categorized as "Aryan." This thorough revision highlights the year 1880 as exceptionally important for the Society's early orientation. Indeed, it will become evident that the discussion about Tantra that was initiated in February 1880 should be viewed as part of fundamental debates about the meaning of science and religion, as well as the meaning and origin of what was thought to be Aryan civilization.

These contexts are necessary for a full understanding of the motives behind the Theosophists' engagement with, and eventual relocation to, India. The fact that Blavatsky and Olcott had settled in India indicates one of the most significant differentiations that Theosophists sought to establish in opposition to other esotericists: if occult phenomena—the "hidden mysteries of Nature" alluded to in the Society's plans—were to be genuinely understood, let alone mastered, one must become an "initiate" into the occult knowledge required to decipher them. This initiation, and the access to that knowledge itself, could be found in "the Orient." While this notion was not particularly new, the Theosophists took the consequential step to relocate to that distant source of arcane wisdom.

It is hence not surprising to find in the *Theosophist* pieces about magnetism and mediumship in India, about Indian medicine, but also about Zoroastrianism and its relation to Theosophy, or "Buddha's religion." The Theosophists assumed that all occult knowledge originated from the same primordial source and could be harvested by unlocking the mysteries of all religious traditions. This *comparative* thrust was one of the hallmarks of Theosophy and was made explicit in the Society's objectives in 1896, which claimed to "encourage the study of comparative religion, philosophy and science."[4] This underlines that the emergence of Theosophy can be comprehended only in the context of nineteenth-century orientalist scholarship and the historical-critical study of religion. Taking this context into account allows for a recontextualization of the history of nineteenth-century esotericism; it also opens up a viewpoint on its global entanglement.

At the end of the 1870s, the Theosophists began to interact with Indian intellectuals who had participated for decades on debates about the origin, meaning, and future of religion. Since the first half of the nineteenth century, learned Indians had not only enabled orientalist scholarship through their expertise; they had actively engaged with it to negotiate the meaning of "Hinduism" and "Hindu dharma." In that regard, they were not simply the recipients of Western interpretations of Hinduism; they participated in its scholarly conceptualization and often took a critical stance toward orientalist scholarship. This formed the background for their exchange with the Theosophists, who often found themselves on the same side in their criticism of orientalists and missionaries.

Indeed, one of the most distinctive features of the Theosophical activities in India was the hostile stance taken toward Christian missionaries. As will be recalled, one of the Society's goals was "to correct misrepresentations" of Aryan culture, which were largely due to the polemics against Indian religions launched by missionaries. Here, too, the February issue of the *Theosophist* illustrates the importance of that context for the discussions about Tantra that ensued. In a sarcastic piece called "Lo! The 'Poor Missionary,'" an author calling himself Melmoth the Wanderer—a reference to a popular 1820 Gothic novel by the Irish writer Charles Maturin—ridiculed the fruitless missionary efforts carried out by "pious and meek Christians." Protestants and Catholics alike were plagued by the challenges they met in India: "free thinkers and infidels, like a swarm of wicked mosquitoes buzzing around, worry them worse than ever."[5] It goes without saying that the Theosophists saw themselves as keen members of that swarm, and Melmoth was quick to point out that a missionary journal had recently denounced the *Theosophist* as an "infidel pigmy."[6]

The political impact of Theosophy in India was by no means the accidental outcome of a purely intellectual endeavor. Quite the contrary, the *Theosophist* of February 1880 openly heralded "our duty to India" in an article that exemplifies Theosophists' self-perception as the revivalists of Aryan civilization. This self-perception was marked by an inner tension between racial stereotypes and emancipatory political tendencies within Theosophy. While the editors lamented the "process of denationalization" in India, they also acknowledged that it was "more or less inevitable whenever a strong race, full of masculine vigor, dominates the country of another race which has passed through its cycle of forceful aggressiveness and reached the stage of recuperative inertia." Admonishing the "influential Natives" who had given in to self-indulgence and were in a "supine, apathetic, unpatriotic" state, the editors raised hope for those who longed for change:

> But let it not be supposed that all patriotic fervor is dead under the cold breath of the Northern wind. Every sentence uttered by our President in his public addresses, here, at Meerut, Saharampore, Benares and Allahabad, about the dead splendor of Aryan civilization and the sacred duty to revive it by reviving Aryan philosophy, religion and science, has been greeted with unmistakeable [*sic*] enthusiasm, and young Natives have risen to propose votes of thanks, with moistened eyes, and voices trembling with emotion.[7]

That president was Henry Steel Olcott, an American and hence a "younger brother" of the Aryan family whose mission it was to remind his Indian brothers that it was high time to revive "the memory of Aryan deeds and greatness." A couple of pages later, "An Indian Patriot's Prayer" invoked this family relationship with a nod to the famous song "Bande Mātaram" by Bankimchandra Chattopadhyay: "The West calls to the East, 'Up brothers, / Up, and join us.' MOTHER, awake; thine hour is come."[8] It could hardly be more obvious how willing the Theosophists were to ally themselves with Indian nationalists and reformers, while at the same time perpetuating notions about a masculine West dominating an effeminate East that played a crucial role in the legitimization of colonial rule. These views could be expressed in more or less explicit ways, for instance when Olcott felt it necessary to add a patronizing footnote to one of Baradakanta's articles, remarking that the "fondness of the Asiatic mind for allegory and parable is well illustrated in this paper on Tantrik Occultism."[9]

The Notion of "Aryan" in the Tangle of Orientalism and Theosophy

This ambivalence is deeply inscribed into nineteenth-century orientalist scholarship, on which Theosophy depended to a large degree and with which it had a complicated relationship. Certainly, the Theosophists would not have looked to India for the revival of Aryan civilization without William Jones's famous discovery of what appeared to be an Indo-European language family.[10] This insight, which he first made public in 1786, revolutionized orientalist scholarship and led to the emergence of comparative religion, and eventually religious studies. Generations of scholars took up the task of discovering the assumed common origin of the Indo-European or Aryan languages. This task soon extended beyond the sphere of philology and was increasingly shaped by racist ideologies, a circumstance that is still posing challenges to scholarship.[11] While a wealth of linguistic and archaeological evidence does confirm links between different branches of an "Indo-European" group, there has never been direct evidence of a common origin. And while the term *ārya* has served as a self-designation on the Indian subcontinent and elsewhere for millennia, nobody knows who the ancient Aryans were or where they came from.[12]

This also entails that orientalists, learned Indians, and Theosophists often meant very different things when they used the term "Aryan."[13] Significantly, it became an integral aspect of caste relations and colonial power structures. Milinda Banerjee has noted that European scholars often interpreted caste in terms of race, perceiving differences between so-called high and low castes as immutable consequences of the Aryan conquest of India. Indian nationalist elites were often eager to accept this "idea of Aryan race ancestry," which "gave them a supposed civilizational parity with the Europeans." British colonial administrators frequently employed this interpretation of caste to claim that India needed perpetual British tutelage, since it was deeply divided in terms of race and community.[14]

While a detailed discussion of this aspect would require a dedicated study, it is important to pay close attention to Müller (1823–1900), as he was a vital reference for the Theosophists and stands out as a leading pioneer of religious studies. His relationship with Theosophy was equivocal: he was critical toward the Theosophists' approach to Indian sources, while sharing fundamental assumptions and aims with them. Indeed, he challenged them with his own alternative understanding of "theosophy." Müller's case illustrates that many Theosophical ideas that may now seem outlandish were quite plausible within, and inherently intertwined with, the context of nineteenth-century orientalist scholarship. For our concerns, it is important to shed light on three interrelated aspects: first, the idea of a shared Aryan civilization originating in India; second, the hierarchical "family relationship" resulting from that common origin; and third, the definition of the Vedas, and the Upanishads in particular, as "pure Hinduism" and, hence, the core of "true religion."

Müller's conceptualization of Aryan civilization was complex and subject to significant changes, as he gradually moved away from a racially defined understanding of history to a more universalistic, liberal theological conception of true religion. While an emphasis on the supposed different branches of Aryan civilization gave way to a focus on the search for true religion through the Upanishads, it is important to shed at least some light on the racial aspects of Müller's thought, as it clearly resurfaced in Theosophical and related discourses.[15] In his collection *Chips from a German Workshop* from 1867, which was followed by the establishment of his chair of comparative philology at Oxford in 1868, Müller explained that modern English was directly linked to ancient Sanskrit, "so its thoughts and feelings contain in reality the first roots and germs of that intellectual growth which by an unbroken chain connects our own generation with the ancestors of the Aryan race." He stressed, "We are by nature Aryan, Indo-European, not Semitic: our spiritual kith and kin are to be found in India."[16] This explicit racial connotation was reaffirmed in Müller's *Introduction to the Science of Religion*, wherein he discussed the "separation of the Aryan race" responsible for the multiplicity of its descendants.[17] Published in 1873, this *Introduction*—along with publications such as *Lectures on the Origin and Growth of Religion as Illustrated by the Religions of India*—ranks among the orientalist works that have informed the emphasis on Aryan civilization in the Theosophical Society's aims, which, as will be recalled, becomes tangible in the different "plans" from 1879 and 1881.

Although Müller shifted his focus from race to philology, he continued to insist on the common root of Indo-European languages, which he thought had differentiated into seven branches: the Hindus, Persians, Greeks, Romans, Celts, Teutons, and Slavs. This process was still termed "the great *Aryan Separation*."[18] Müller professed that the study of ancient Indian literature would open "the first chapter in the life of Aryan humanity."[19] In 1882, he gave a lecture series to candidates for the Indian Civil Service at Cambridge, titled *India, What Can It Teach Us?* Therein he proclaimed the need for an appreciation for India and a "liberal education" that would enable modern Europeans to recognize their origin: "We all come from the East."[20] The ancient Vedic literature

> can teach us lessons which nothing else can teach, as to the origin of our own language, the first formation of our own concepts, and the true natural germs of all that is comprehended under the name of civilisation, at least

> the civilisation of the Aryan race, that race to which we and all the greatest nations of the world—the Hindus, the Persians, the Greeks, the Romans, the Slaves, the Celts, and last, not least, the Teutons, belong.[21]

What Müller had in mind was part of a larger project of understanding the European past, a project that was deeply interwoven with colonialism, as becomes evident in his lecturing to future colonial administrators. Significantly, he envisioned an avant-garde of scholars heralding this project. He declared that there must always be "an aristocracy of those who know," advancing deep into Aryan history. This aristocracy was open "to all who have a feeling for the past, an interest in the genealogy of our thoughts, and a reverence for the ancestry of our intellect, who are in fact historians in the true sense of the word, i.e. inquirers into that which is past, but not lost."[22]

For all his admiration for the Indian origin of that Aryan civilization, Müller established a clear hierarchy among its modern members. In his *Chips*, he argued that "there exists no literary relic that carries us back to a more primitive, or, if you like, more childlike state in the history of man than the Veda."[23] Fifteen years later, when he lectured on the question of what India can teach Europeans, he emphasized that Vedic literature should not be regarded as something strange but as a glimpse into the "childhood of our race."[24] In a word, India's past was pristine and pure, but it marked a less developed step in Aryan civilization, with the modern West representing a virile, mature stage—a claim that Müller liked to illustrate with a comparison between the Vedas and Kant's *Kritik der reinen Vernunft*. For instance, Müller wrote, "[Although] the Hindus were deficient in many of those manly virtues and practical achievements which we value most, I wished to point out that there was another sphere of intellectual activity in which the Hindus excelled—the meditative and transcendent—and that here we might learn from them some lessons of life which we ourselves are but too apt to ignore or to despise."[25] This shows how the study of ancient Indian literature was thought to be relevant for an understanding of the roots of European civilization; moreover, it would only benefit those interested in "meditative and transcendent" aspects of intellectual activity. Indians were thus perceived as childlike, lacking virility and rationality. Not surprisingly, then, it was only the study of *ancient* Indian thought that seemed important to Müller, which explains why he was never interested in visiting the region.[26] From such a viewpoint, present-day India had remained static and childlike for millennia, shortcomings that appeared to be confirmed by the subordinate status of Indians under colonial rule.

Müller's efforts were shaped by the desire to apply a Protestant historical-critical method for the recovery of an eclipsed Indo-Aryan past and demonstrate its relevance for the present. His extensive editorial efforts, most famously the *Sacred Books of the East* that were inaugurated in 1879 with the Upanishads, highlight his wish to restore a pristine *Urtext* and focus his understanding of Hinduism on Sanskrit scriptural sources. In the process, and especially after his Gifford Lectures, Müller's emphasis on Aryan civilization gave way to his efforts to discover true religion through the study of ancient Eastern sources. While the idea of a shared Indo-Aryan past still informed the scope of that search, Müller now concentrated on his thesis that pure Hinduism was Vedic and that the study of the Upanishads and Advaita Vedanta would allow access to a pristine *ur*-religion. For our purpose, the crucial point is that the Tantras had no place in this scheme, as they were regarded as the worst result of the degeneracy from the pure Vedic religion.

Müller's viewpoint decisively informed the Theosophists' opinion on Tantra and seemed to confirm the polemics of Dayananda. At the same time, Müller is a prime example of the troubled relationship between Theosophy and orientalist scholarship. While a Theosophist like Blavatsky heavily relied on his studies, she referenced him by dismissively referring to "the Orientalists," implying that such academic scholars had only a distorted and incomplete understanding of true religion.[27] As is often the case, such vehement rejections are due to proximity rather than distance. Josephson-Storm has pointed out that Müller went as far as to consciously try to appropriate the meaning of "theosophy" for his project of comparative religion.[28] Müller obviously recognized the Theosophists as direct competitors to his comparative religious program, which also arose from the fact that the Theosophists had swiftly taken up their own editorial activity and extensive collaboration with learned Indians. In a letter to the Gujarati reformer Behramji Malabari (1853–1912) from October 24, 1888, Müller lauded the Theosophical publishing efforts, however not without expressing his concerns:

> But it seems to me, considering the higher objects of the Theosophical Society, that you ought to publish a complete and correct edition of the *Upanishads*. The *Upanishads* are, after all, the most important portion of the *Vedas*, for philosophical purposes, and if the Theosophical Society

means to do any real good, it must take its stand on the *Upanishads*, and *on nothing else.*[29]

Müller here seemed to approve of the objects of the Theosophists, although he cautioned against any "pollution" of Vedic truth by what he regarded as the amateurish and questionable tendencies of the Society. He did not simply dismiss the Theosophists, however, and made personal acquaintance with Olcott in the same year of 1888. In the following years, he corresponded with him in a friendly if controversial manner.[30] Eventually, he decided to openly challenge the Theosophists and their very understanding of "theosophy." In 1893, he published a volume with the remarkable title *Theosophy, or Psychological Religion*,[31] in whose preface he sought to dissociate himself from the Society:

> I ought, perhaps, to explain why, to the title of *Psychological Religion*, originally chosen for this my final course of Gifford Lectures, I have added that of *Theosophy*. It seemed to me that this venerable name, so well known among early Christian thinkers, as expressing the highest knowledge of God within the reach of the human mind, has of late been so greatly misappropriated that it was high time to restore it to its proper function. It should be known once for all that one may call oneself a theosophist, without being suspected of believing in spirit-rappings, table-turnings, or any other occult sciences and black arts.[32]

Not surprisingly, Müller repeatedly insisted on the relevance of theosophy for Christianity, to the degree that he also spoke of "Theosophy or Mystic Christianity."[33] In a central passage of the book, Müller further explained his understanding:

> If I use the name of Psychological Religion in order to comprehend under it all attempts at discovering the true relation between the soul and God, it is because other names, such as *Theosophic*, *Psychic*, or *Mystic*, have been so much misused that they are sure to convey a false impression. *Theosophic* conveys the idea of wild speculations on the hidden nature of God; *Psychic* reminds us of trances, visions, and ghosts; *Mystic* leaves the impression of something vague, nebulous, and secret, while to the student of Psychological Religion the true relation of the two souls, the human soul and the divine, is, or ought to be, as clear as the most perfect logical

> syllogism. I shall not be able to avoid these names altogether, because the most prominent representatives of Theosophy and mystic religion have prided themselves on these names, and they are very appropriate, if only clearly defined.[34]

While these statements might appear as the distancing of a detached, sober scholar from an extravagant contemporary movement, a closer look at Müller's *alternative* program of theosophy demonstrates that there were more similarities between his approach and that of the Theosophists than he might have been ready to admit. His lecture could hardly be viewed as an abstract scholarly essay; rather, it was the exposition of his vision of a true religion of humanity. At its core stood the assumption that India, as the oldest representative of Aryan civilization, had elaborated a theosophy that predated, and historically informed, that of later Christians. Müller claimed that in most of the religions of the ancient world, the relation between the soul and God had been represented as a "return of the soul to God." This return had been envisioned in very different ways, for instance as a return of the soul to God after death and as the knowledge of the unity of the divine and the human.[35] But it appeared clear to Müller that he could rely on the Vedas as the "most important, if not our only authority."[36] Their teachings culminated in the Upanishads and the doctrine of "Tat tvam asi," or "Thou art that." This proclamation of the fundamental identity between the individual and God had allegedly been expressed in both Greece and India:

> The expression Thou art that, means Thine Âtman, thy soul, thy self is the Brahman, or, as we can also express it, the last result, the highest object discovered by Physical Religion is the same as the last result, the highest subject discovered by Anthropological Religion; or, in other words, the subject and object of all being and all knowing are one and the same. This is the gist of what I call *Psychological Religion*, or Theosophy, the highest summit of thought which the human mind has reached, which has found different expressions in different religions and philosophies, but nowhere such a clear and powerful realisation as in the ancient Upanishads of India.[37]

Müller's final goal, then, was to unveil the origins of this primordial theosophy and its manifestations in different traditions. Given his Protestant standpoint, he surely disliked the ostensibly anti-Christian attitude of at least some of the leading Theosophists. However, his conception of theosophy was, essentially, not that dissimilar to the goal of the Theosophists, not least because he heralded the role of "an aristocracy of those who know" as the leader of humanity into a brighter future. To be sure, the philological and otherwise academic competence of his rivals was not comparable, but it would appear that their rivalry was due less to radical professional or ideological differences than to institutional power claims. That his relationship with the Theosophists was not marked by outright hostility can be exemplified by a letter he wrote to Olcott on March 22, 1893. After praising Paul Deussen's recent lecture about Vedanta in Bombay, Müller wrote a passage that is worth quoting at length:

> That is a true account of Vedāntism and of Theosophy, that is what you and your friends have been looking for, that is what you will find, only far more developed, in my last volume of Gifford Lectures, entitled *Theosophy or Psychological Religion*. You should now try to persuade your friends in India to make a new start, i.e. to return to their ancient philosophy in all its purity. I have not forgotten your telling me once that a new religion in order to grow must be *manured*.[38] I do not believe in that. I trust to the pure rain of heaven, and to the light and warmth of the sun, that is, to the vivifying power of truth. Everything else is of evil, particularly in India, where people are so much inclined to believe in what seems miraculous, and not in what is natural. If I have spoken and written against you, I should have done just the same against myself and my best friends, when I saw that they were seeking for the truth but were going on a wrong road to find it. You can do much good in India if you will treat the Hindus, not as children, but as men. Wait till you get my *Theosophy*, and then tell me whether that is not what you really wanted for India and for Europe also.
>
> Once more, you can do a great deal of good if you will help the people in India to discover and recover the treasure of truth in their old Brahma-sophy.[39]

Müller's wish to restore an uncorrupted *ur*-religion becomes clearly tangible here. It is also evident that he wanted to win over his Theosophical interlocutor to his own cause: he was open to joining forces. On April 25 and May 11, Olcott responded by inquiring whether Müller would believe that there is no esoteric interpretation of the Sanskrit Shastras, and to counter Müller's admonition not "to destroy all the good he had done in helping to revive Sanskrit, by pandering to the superstitious credulity of the Hindus, and telling them about phenomena that are impossible, and Mahatmas who do not exist." In his response from June 10, Müller expressed his pleasure to receive these letters, as well as his awareness of the pains of the friends of Blavatsky, who had recently passed away. Still, he insisted that Blavatsky's work equaled "a lowering of a beautiful religion."[40] He also affirmed that there was nothing esoteric in Buddhism, and that Brahmanism, while containing "much more of that esoteric teaching," did profess no such thing as the esoteric interpretation of the Shastras: "The Sāstras have but one meaning, and all who had been properly prepared by education had access to them."[41] As he did several years earlier, Müller again called upon Olcott to change the Society's course:

> You can really do a good work if you can persuade the people in India, whether Buddhists or Brahmans, to study their own religion in a reverent spirit, to keep what is good, and discard openly what is effete, antiquated and objectionable. If all religions would do that, we should soon have but *one* religion. . . . My *Sacred Books of the East* have opened people's eyes in many places.[42]

Müller's repeated attempts at conversion are remarkable. They demonstrate a fundamental appreciation of the Theosophists' work in India, which again suggests that Müller believed he shared some principal goals with his rivals. A bit later, he even wrote, "You can help to forward or retard the good work that has to be done in India. If I can be of any use, I am always willing to help."[43] There were certainly radical disagreements and differences between Müller and Olcott, but those pertained less to the aims of Theosophy or Psychological Religion and more to diverging ideas about how to achieve them.

A central parallel between Müller and a Theosophist like Olcott can be drawn in light of their attitude toward India and Indians. Although Müller admonished Olcott to treat the "Hindus, not as children, but as men," the previous quotes abundantly show that he was far from doing so himself. Constantly referring to Indians as superstitious, credulous, and childlike, he portrayed them as people to be educated rather than accepted as equals. There seems to have been no or little awareness of such contradictions; quite the opposite. Both Müller and Olcott were convinced that they were doing something empowering: they deemed their revival of true religion an invigorating, liberating endeavor. It was, however, not Indians but *they* who "revived Sanskrit," defined true Hinduism, resurrected Aryan civilization, and explained the one true (and esoteric) meaning of the Shastras. Although Müller and Olcott were the "younger brothers" in the Aryan family, it was their elders in India who remained childlike and wanting instruction.[44] This is the mentality that has already become evident in "Our Duty to India" from the February 1880 of the *Theosophist* quoted earlier.

However, the relationship between Theosophists and orientalists and their Indian interlocutors was not as clear-cut as one might think after reading such passages. As will be shown in what follows, it was precisely the Theosophical claim to revive Aryan civilization and awaken their supposedly apathetic brothers from an idle slumber that formed the common ground of a fruitful exchange with Indian intellectuals, some of whom readily joined the Society and engaged in defining "Brahma-sophy" or, as the reader might recall, *brahmabidyā*. Indeed, contemporary Indians observed a radical difference between the Theosophists and orientalist scholars: while the latter generally showed little interest in engaging with Indians "on the ground" and refrained from taking a political, or even anticolonial stance, the Theosophists did all of these things, enthusiastically. Not only did they encourage Indians from all walks of life to join their society, but they relocated their headquarters to India—in stark contrast to Müller, who never traveled there. Upon their arrival, the exchange between the Theosophists and their Indian interlocutors was significantly motivated by a "reformist" thrust that is essential for an understanding of the success of Theosophy in India.

The Ārya Samāj and the Brāhma Samāj

The *Theosophist* of February 1880 especially lauded Rammohan Roy and Dayananda for their efforts to bring about an Aryan revival, the latter being eulogized next to Blavatsky in a pair of sonnets.[45] As will be recalled, Dayananda's Ārya Samāj had been created in the same year as the Theosophical Society, and in May 1878 the two societies became affiliated. In 1878, the Theosophists established direct contact with Dayananda, who in the eyes of Blavatsky was one of the initiates of a Himalayan adept guarding ancient Aryan teachings.[46] At that time, Dayananda ranked among the most influential so-called Hindu reformers. Unlike other reformers, the Advaitin had not received an English education and was therefore perceived by the Theosophists as an especially "authentic" voice. His understanding of *ārya* certainly differed from that of the Theosophists and orientalists, but the fact that he heralded the return to a Hindu "golden age" resonated well with the preconceptions of Western contemporaries.[47] Even though his relationship with the Theosophists broke in March 1882 and ended in public quarrels, his views exerted an exceptional influence in the early years of the Theosophical Society. Perhaps most notable was his insistence that modern discoveries of science and philosophy had already been made by Aryan sages millennia earlier and were only awaiting their restoration, leading to a reconciliation of science and religious truth.[48]

At the time of the Theosophists' arrival in India, the Aryas were rapidly expanding in North India and developed into arguably the most influential reform movement until well into the twentieth century; when India became independent in 1947, it counted almost two million members.[49] In his early days, Dayananda's thought had been significantly shaped by his interactions with Brahmos.[50] However, he accused them of departing from Vedic teachings, factionalism, excessive love of English, and a neglect of the ancient rishis who were eclipsed by the Brahmo admiration for Jesus, Moses, Mohammed, Nanak, and Chaitanya. At the same time, he conceived *ārya* culture in the nationalist terms that were emphatically shared by his Brahmo friends.[51] While the doctrinal positions and organizational structure of his Ārya Samāj differed radically from the Brahmos', he employed similar propagandistic techniques to counter Christian missionary activities, assert a specific Hindu identity, and protest colonial educational and cultural policy.[52]

Dayananda had rejected the term "Hinduism" as a foreign imposition and instead insisted on the term *ārya* to signify his wish to restore the purity of India. He and his followers aggressively denounced what they perceived as idolatry, superstition, and irrationality. This position resembled that of orientalists such as Müller, and it similarly went hand in hand with a rejection of Tantra. At the same time, Aryas criticized the rigidity of the caste system, advocated the improvement of women's position in society, and championed public education—typically "reformist" ideas.[53] Many observers perceived the Ārya Samāj as a "Protestant" movement that stressed rationality, science, monotheism, and individual responsibility. At the same time, the Aryas professed the exclusive authority and infallibility of the Vedas, and they defended practices such as the veneration of cows precisely on the grounds of their supposed scientific and rational nature.[54] Their proclamation of a return to Vedic authenticity—typically "revivalist"—was very attractive for Indians who had received a Western education.[55] The movement was also popular among disadvantaged castes, since Dayananda redefined the caste order (*varṇāśramadharma*) so that it was determined by personal achievement rather than birth. Social status could thus be raised by "self-improvement." In theory, every Hindu could be welcomed into the Arya family, and it became practically possible to "convert" to Hinduism. Through a reinterpretation of the *śuddhi* ritual, even "lower" castes could be "purified."[56] As Fischer-Tiné has explored in detail, Aryas made a substantial contribution to the rise of nationalist sentiment in India, not least by the promotion of Hindi as a national language, a historiography glorifying the golden Hindu past, and an influential cultural conceptualization of Aryanism.[57]

The emergence of such a "cultural Aryan-ness," to use an expression by Swarupa Gupta, was essential for the notion of a Hindu nation that circled around the term *samāj*, which, as in English, can also refer to "society" at large. "Aryan" was reconfigured as a culturally inclusive concept that functioned as a unifying framework transcending caste and sectarian differences. The reference to a golden past was, hence, not only a historiographical discourse but also an ideal that informed concrete social practices.[58] These aspects illustrate why the Aryas were an obvious ally for the Theosophists. They shared the notion of an ancient Aryan civilization and the revival of a golden age when science and religion went hand in hand. Both groups were concerned with social and educational reform that focused on a restoration of Aryan wisdom, laying the foundation for a reinvigorated Indian nation. Finally, they were united in their opposition to Christian missionaries, colonial administrators, and the alleged ignorance of orientalist scholars.

The spectacular yet short-lived alliance between the Aryas and the Theosophists often tends to eclipse the significantly deeper, longer, and more complex relationship between the Theosophical Society and the different factions of the Brāhma Samāj. As has been indicated, the Brāhma Samāj was older than the Ārya Samāj, and its emergence within a Bengali context warrants closer scrutiny for the concerns of this study. While mostly restricted to a quantitively small group of Western-educated Bengalis, the Brāhma Samāj was by far one of the most influential movements in the modern history of India. It also is an outstanding example of the global dimension of the debates about the meaning of Hinduism. Many Brahmos were critical of the more nationalistic tendencies of their contemporaries, and they rejected the rigid Vedic focus of their Arya competitors. Yet Aryanness was an integral part of Brahmo discussions, although it tended to have a universalist drift that becomes plausible against the background of the Samāj's globally entangled context of emergence.

The most direct roots of the Brahmos reach back to the Calcutta Unitarian Committee, which had been founded by Rammohan, Dvarkanath Tagore, and the former Scottish Baptist missionary William Adam in 1823. Rammohan had already aroused the curiosity of Unitarians in 1820, when he published his famous *Precepts of Jesus*, a compilation of the ethical teachings of Christ.[59] This and other writings, most notably a series of tracts titled *Brahmunical Magazine*, caused controversy among North American and European Unitarians because of their universalistic tendency. They sparked an exchange with Bengali intellectuals that would reach its peak during the second half of the nineteenth century.[60] The universalistic, rationalistic direction of Rammohan's thought had been shaped by his Persian education and was further complexified by his eager engagement with orientalist scholarship and Western philosophy.[61] Rammohan was convinced that Upanishadic Vedanta contained the essence of Vedic truth and thus the key to purging Hinduism of its supposed superstitious, irrational, and idolatrous aberrations. These reform-minded ideas were instrumental in coining the modern perception of Hinduism, with Vedanta as its underlying philosophy and the *Bhagavadgītā* as a central scripture.[62] In fact, Rammohan is considered the first writer to employ the term "Hindooism."[63] His engagement with Unitarians laid the foundations for a rich and lasting exchange between the United States, Europe, and India. Carl T. Jackson has argued that Unitarianism consequently played a larger role in the reception of "oriental religions" in nineteenth-century America than any other religious movement.[64]

The emergence of Brahmoism can be comprehended only when viewed within a tangle of global exchanges. As David Kopf has pointed out, liberal Unitarianism slowly emerged out of the parallel experiences of like-minded individuals in Boston, Bristol, and Calcutta.[65] The parallels in Rammohan's and Müller's view on the Upanishads illustrate that these experiences resulted from the shared context of debates revolving around the meaning of religion, science, and philosophy. Rammohan's case highlights that Indian viewpoints in those debates were not simply "influenced by" orientalist or generally Western ideas. Hatcher has recently highlighted Rammohan's indebtedness to precolonial education that contradicts the present-day perception of him as predominantly "modern" and "reformist."[66] Not only, then, has this "non-Western," precolonial dimension of his thought to be taken account, but also the fact that he actively inspired his Western interlocutors. This becomes evident in Rammohan's relationship with Unitarianism. He took the initiative by engaging with it against the background of his Persian-Bengali education and was largely responsible for stimulating among Unitarians an interest in the study of other religions and the striving for religious universalism. In fact, the first convert to Unitarianism in India was the Scottish Baptist William Adam, and this conversion was motivated by none other than Rammohan.[67] The latter's influence on Transcendentalists such as Emerson and Thoreau, among many others, is well-known but deserves further scrutiny taking into account the Indian context in its own right.[68]

Brahmos, Unitarians, and Transcendentalists, as diverse as their adherents may have been, generally shared a belief in progress, a synthesis of science and religion, social reform, and eventually the creation of a universal religion of mankind.[69] This final goal sparked a vast Unitarian and Transcendentalist project of comparative religion that intensified in the second half of the century.[70] Müller was well aware of these developments, regarded Rammohan as the founder of comparative religion, and corresponded with leading Brahmos.[71] Similar to his advances toward the Theosophists, he wanted to win the Brahmos for his cause to discover and revive the true religion of humanity.

In 1828, Rammohan founded the Brāhma Sabhā to promote his ideas and attract like-minded individuals. However, the society lay dormant after Rammohan's unexpected death during his visit to Unitarian friends in Bristol in 1833. It is important to note that this marked a certain rupture in the reception of his ideas, as it took a number of years before the Brahmos reemerged as an influential movement. However, this rupture did not mean the end of reformist tendencies. A case in point is the group known as Young Bengal, which had formed at the Hindu College in Calcutta around the freethinker and poet Henry Louis Vivian Derozio (1809–1831). The "Derozians" avidly read philosophers such as Voltaire, Locke, and Adam Smith, enthusiastically engaged with Western scientific discourse, and violated socioreligious norms by demonstratively consuming beef and alcohol. They contributed to the emergence of an Indian national spirit along the lines of a rationalistic, and sometimes atheistic, reformism that took aim at "idolatry" and the alleged corruptions of the "priesthood."[72] In 1828, Derozio founded the Academic Association, which served as a hub for controversial debates about those subjects. The movement lived on after Derozio's death in 1831 and saw the foundation of another organization in 1838, the Society for the Acquisition of General Knowledge (*jñānopārjikā sabhā*), which tackled issues such as social reform, the position of women, patriotism, and education.[73] When it faded in 1843, it counted around two hundred members. The adherents of Young Bengal soon lost their fiery enthusiasm but lived on to be vocal proponents of reform.

The resurrection of the Brāhma Samāj coincided with the diffusion of Young Bengal. It was largely the work of Debendranath Tagore (1817–1905), the son of Dvarkanath and father of several eminent intellectuals, including Rabindranath Tagore. In 1839, Debendranath founded the Tattvabodhinī Sabhā (Truth-Seeker Society), whose principles, although less occupied with Christianity, paralleled those of Rammohan and put emphasis on the promotion of ultimate truth (*tattva*) based on the Upanishads.[74] In 1843, Debendranath made an effort to resurrect the Brāhma Samāj by associating it with his Sabhā, a move that successfully institutionalized it as an integral part of the Bengali intellectual landscape.[75] Brahmos were ardent propagators of what Hatcher has termed "bourgeois Hinduism," a mix of Vedantic spirituality, rationalistic monotheism, religious universalism, public education, and social reform, including widow remarriage and the prohibition of child marriage.[76]

In 1855, their active collaboration with Unitarians was revitalized when Charles Dall (1816–1886) began his mission in Calcutta that would go on for over three decades and contribute to a close-knit network of Bengali, American, and British intellectuals. Unitarianism became an integral part of the reformist landscape of Bengal; a contemporary observer from East Bengal lamented in the 1850s that most of "Young Bengal" had "no religion," but that some "are deists after Hume and Gibbon; a few, we believe, are Unitarian Christians on principle, but unbaptized; many are Vedantists [i.e., Brahmos]."[77] Despite their small size, these intellectual circles, not least through their engagement with Western ideas and their development of missionary activities, exerted a decisive and lasting influence on Indian culture.

Among those who most enthusiastically embraced Unitarianism was Keshabchandra Sen (1838–1884), who had formed an enduring friendship with Dall in 1855.[78] In 1857, he joined the Brāhma Samāj and contributed to an emerging friction between the older and the younger generation of Brahmos. In protest of Keshab's praise of Christianity, the celebrated scholar and secular reformer Ishvarchandra Vidyasagar (1820–1891) left the Tattvabodhinī Sabhā in 1859, sending shockwaves through the Brahmo milieu. More schisms followed, especially in 1866, when Keshab established the Brāhma Samāj of India (*bhāratbarṣīya brāhma samāj*) in opposition to the Ādi ("original") Brāhma Samāj that was now under the leadership of

Rajnarayan Basu (1826–1899), who succeeded Debendranath.[79] The following years until 1872 marked the peak of Keshab's enthusiasm for the Unitarian social gospel, and after a journey to England in 1870 he established the Indian Reform Association to promote "the social and moral reformation of the Natives of India."[80] He was also in close contact with members of the social reformist Free Religious Association, which had grown out of Unitarianism in 1867 and strove for the creation of a scientific religion on the basis of religious comparativism.[81] Keshab also exerted an influence on Dayananda, who stayed at Calcutta from 1872 to 1873. Dayananda adopted several methods of propaganda—and, not least, the organizational format of the Samāj—from Keshab and other Brahmos.[82]

In the following years, Keshab's thought was increasingly influenced by Bijaykrishna Gosvami, the famed Vaishnava reformer who at that time was still active as a Brahmo. In 1874, this led to the detachment of the Samadarśī (liberal) Party, which in 1876 became the Indian Association and, a decade later, initiated the formation of the Indian National Congress. This faction also created, in 1878, the Sādhāraṇ (universal) Brāhma Samāj, whose leader, Shivanath Shastri (1847–1919), gathered intellectuals who were concerned not so much with the Unitarian-influenced gospel in the vein of Keshab as with the social reformism of Unitarianism.[83]

These breakaways notwithstanding, in 1879 Keshab formed the Nababidhān, or New Dispensation Church, which propagated a universal religion headed by Keshab as prophet. After his death in 1884, a split occurred between the group's Vaishnava- and Christian-oriented members, the latter led by Pratapchandra Majumdar (1840–1905), who would later be invited by Unitarians to become a member of the Advisory Council and Selection Committee for the Parliament of the World's Religions in 1893 and develop an extensive missionary activity in the United States.[84] Müller observed these developments with great interest and even enthusiasm. In March 1879, he expressed his "full faith" in Keshab during the establishment of his New Dispensation Church.[85] In his comprehensive correspondence with Pratapchandra, Müller suggested that the Brahmos join the Church of England and insisted that they refer to themselves as "Christian Brahmos, or Christian Aryas."[86] This underlines how firmly established and globally entangled the striving for a universal religion of humanity was among factions such as the Unitarians, the orientalist Müller, and Indian reformers.[87] It also shows how intermingled and contested terms such as "Vedanta" and

"Arya" were, and how difficult it is to make distinctions between reformist and revivalist tendencies.

It is obvious that the Theosophists entered a complex intellectual landscape marked by heterogenous and rival ideas. That landscape had developed against the background of a tangle of exchanges among Indian, European, and American intellectuals. The parallels in the broad spectrum of Aryas, Brahmos, Unitarians, Transcendentalists, Spiritualist, and Theosophist are striking: a criticism of materialism and what they perceived as orthodox religion; a synthesis of science and religion; the wish for a universal religion as the foundation for a universal brotherhood of humanity; and social reform. We also find very similar historical narratives that revolve around a perennial wisdom tradition that would form the core of a future religion of humanity.[88]

It is important to highlight, with John A. Stevens, that Unitarianism and Brahmoism had drawn on a long history of shared traditions, including Theosophy, Spiritualism, mesmerism, and Freemasonry: "It was not simply the case that Unitarianism influenced Brahmoism, or vice versa."[89] The mid-1850s saw the emergence of occultism in France and the stellar success of Spiritualism in Europe and the United States, but also an intense Unitarian-Brahmo interaction that played out in the same field of religious social reformism. It does not come as a surprise, then, that Theosophists, Brahmos, and other reformers engaged in diverse and fruitful exchanges; they could enter dialogue so effectively because their ideas had been shaped by the same historical developments.[90]

The Beginning of Theosophical Activities in Bengal

The Theosophical Society took institutional root in Bengal in March 1882, when Olcott established its first branch at Berhampore before continuing to Calcutta.[91] Theosophy had aroused curiosity among the Calcutta intelligentsia in the preceding years, and some of its most prominent members had joined the Society before Olcott's arrival. These included the author, Spiritualist, and Young Bengal member Pyarichand Mitra (1814–1883), who had been the president of the Society for the Acquisition of General Knowledge. Noteworthy for our concerns are the journalist Vaishnava reformer and later Swadeshi activist Shishirkumar Ghosh (1840–1911), as well as raja Shyamashankar Ray (1837–1893), the influential zamindar who was a member of the executive council of the Indian Association. Theosophy was obviously attractive to the Western-educated intellectual elite. At the time of Olcott's tour of Bengal, the factions predominantly relevant to this study were the Sādhāraṇ Brāhma Samāj under Shivanath Shastri, the more conservative Ādi Brāhma Samāj under Rajnarayan Basu, and Keshab's prophetic Nababidhān. In what follows, it will become clear how an initial skepticism toward Theosophy soon gave way to vivid interactions between Bengalis and the Society.

An instructive example of the interplay of these different contexts is the well-known journalist and nationalist Narendranath Sen (1843–1911), a cousin of Keshab. He was from a famous learned family—his father was the lexicographer Ramkamal Sen—and was trained as an attorney, a vocation that he took up at the age of nineteen. In 1861, he was involved in the creation of the *Indian Mirror*, a newspaper he edited most of the time, other intermittent editors including Keshab and Pratapchandra. Narendranath became the paper's sole proprietor in 1879. Under his direction, it became the first daily English-language newspaper produced by Indians. It functioned as a Brahmo mouthpiece and always contained a section reporting on their activities. Through Keshab, it also became affiliated with the Nababidhān. Narendranath established himself as one of the most vocal defenders of the nationalist cause and would align himself with the moderate faction throughout the Swadeshi years.

The *Indian Mirror* illustrates how the skepticism expressed by many Indians toward the Theosophists would give way to appreciation and even enthusiasm within the first few years after the Society's arrival in Bombay. As early as February 1879, the *Indian Mirror* observed the strange newcomers favorably but with caution. On March 9, the paper's Sunday edition, which was edited by Keshab's younger brother Krishnabihari Sen, remarked, "That a number of Europeans and Americans should come to India with the express object of studying the Vedas at the feet of Pundit Dayanand Saraswati is an event of rare importance in the social history of the country."[92] On May 11, however, it still seemed unclear what the Theosophists were all about:

> We mean the creed of the Theosophist. What is it that they do believe? Besides vague yearnings after something—"a new school of Aryan Philosophy," if you like—there is nothing positive or definite which Col. Olcott tells us. His exhortation to young India is excellent; his denunciation of the growing scepticism quite up to the mark. But we are not told what

> young India is to do, besides reading the Vedas and expounding the secrets of nature. He spoke of reform, but the exact nature of it he did not specify.[93]

It was stressed repeatedly that the Theosophists should visit Calcutta so that the curiosity of their Bengali observers could be satisfied. Clearly, there was a great deal of uncertainty about the Theosophists' views and aims, but appreciation of their proclaimed intentions eventually outweighed the reservations of some Brahmos. On March 30, an article expressed this sentiment with striking words:

> We are not so sure about the justness or soundness of the views held by the members of the Theosophical Society; but when they said that they had come to learn and not to teach, there was surely something very touching and attractive in all that they said about their mission. The members, though belonging to superior races, have proclaimed themselves our brethren in every sense of the term, and there can evidently be no question of race-antagonism to mar the pleasant re-unions which must necessarily follow such a declaration. The members of the Theosophical Society have done what no Englishmen have ever thought of doing during their more than a century and-a-half's administration of this country: they have dared openly to mix with us as equals. Here is something to be grateful for.[94]

The Brahmo reactions in the *Indian Mirror* illustrate how starkly the Theosophical stance was contrasted by many Indians with that of colonial administrators, orientalists, and missionaries. The Theosophical proclamation of a shared Aryan past that had to be revived resonated strongly in the intellectual landscape that was populated by Brahmos and like-minded reformers. In contrast to the Aryas, Brahmo factions did not enter into an official alliance with the Theosophical Society,[95] but numerous Brahmos became actively involved and entered leading positions in the Society from an early point onward.

It was on March 19, 1882, that Olcott finally paid his first visit to Calcutta, arriving from Berhampore. After staying for a few days with his friend Col. William Gordon and Gordon's wife, Alice, Olcott was invited to stay at the guest house of Yatindramohan Tagore (1831–1908), the wealthiest zamindar at that time.[96] Olcott was immediately welcomed by the cultural elite of Bengal. A reception was held on April 1, where Pyarichand Mitra read out a letter declaring Olcott "a Hindu" in "spiritual conception."[97] On April 5,

Olcott gave a public lecture at the Calcutta Town Hall, which was presided over by Pyarichand and wherein he proclaimed Theosophy as "the scientific basis of religion."[98] He opened the lecture with an appraisal of prominent members of the Bengali intelligentsia who had "addressed open[ly] the most burning questions in religion and politics," including Keshab, the Indian Association cofounder and later freedom fighter Surendranath Bandyopadhyay, Shivanath Shastri, and Pratapchandra Majumdar: "a sense of personal inferiority to those great masters of rhetoric and logic oppresses and warns me."[99] Sarcastically, Olcott went on to describe the Western-educated Bengali "Babu," who, after reading his Spencer and Mill and putting on Western clothes and habits, was turning into a B.A., a "Bad Aryan." Instead, Olcott wished to provide an answer to the question to what "young India" should turn: to the wisdom of the "Aryan *Rishis*."[100]

The lecture is a good illustration of Olcott's ability to navigate the milieu that he was addressing: "You listen in surprise to hear a white man speak, as, hitherto, you have only heard your orthodox Hindus speak."[101] Olcott skillfully praised both the achievements of modern Western education and the glorious past of India by propagating the revival of an ancient civilization that lay at the roots of both. He explained that his fascination with "Aryan philosophy" had arisen from his occupation with psychology and mesmerism in the United States, and how the contact with the Mahatmas gave him "a motive to live for, an end to strive after. That motive was to gain the Aryan wisdom; that end to work for its dissemination."[102] After initial struggles, the Theosophists' relocation to India was finally coming to fruition: "Our appeals to you to remember the glories of Aryavarta and strive to revive them, have not fallen upon deaf ears."[103] The central goal was now to prove the scientific basis of Hinduism by means of "Yoga Vidya," the ancient science which was not only confirmed by modern Western research but also paralleled the "Mysticism among the European nations."[104] This is why, Olcott maintained, critics of occultism were misguided by sheer ignorance: "Of one thing such people are most certainly ignorant, and that is of the *spirit of the nineteenth century*. The day of blind faith has gone by, never, I hope, to return."[105] In this light, Olcott could herald Theosophy as the synthesis of Aryan wisdom and modern science, which aimed at the revival of ancient knowledge, not in contrast to but precisely in the spirit of modernity. This idea did not fail to enthuse the audience. Within one year, three thousand prints of the lecture were sold.[106]

Blavatsky arrived at Calcutta on the following day, April 6, and the Bengal Theosophical Society was formally inaugurated at the guest house of Yatindramohan.[107] Narendranath Sen immediately signed up as a member, together with another prominent Bengali who would become one of the most renowned Indian Theosophists, Mohinimohan Chattopadhyay (1858–1936).[108] Within the following days, several celebrated personalities joined the Society, including Yatindramohan and his younger brother, the musicologist Saurindramohan Tagore (1840–1914). Another famous member of the Tagore family was Dvijendranath (1840–1926), son of Debendranath and eldest brother of Rabindranath, who had been the secretary of the Ādi Brāhma Samāj and the Hindu Mela of 1867, which is often regarded as the first organized proclamation of Hindu nationhood.[109] This impressive assembly of Calcutta's crème de la crème also included several women, among them Debendranath's daughter and Rabindranath's sister, the famous author, artist, and social activist Svarnakumari Devi (1855–1932). Within one year, the Ladies' Theosophical Society was established.[110] After some shuffling, Pyarichand was appointed president of the Bengal Theosophical Society, Shyamashankar and Dvijendranath vice presidents. Narendranath held the offices of secretary and treasurer before becoming president in 1883.[111] Meetings of the new branch were first held at the offices of the *Indian Mirror*, before relocating to its own building.

Within the first year, Theosophical activities in Bengal flourished. From around 50 members at the end of 1882, membership in the Calcutta branch had increased to 130, which made it the largest next to the Ceylon branch. An additional twenty-five branches had been established in the region.[112] Among the foremost concerns of Theosophists was the establishment of schools, and a Sunday school opened in Calcutta on March 11, 1883. It had first taken care of seventeen students and was responsible for forty-two "Hindu boys" two months later. During the first-anniversary meeting of the Bengal Theosophical Society, held on May 21 in the Calcutta Town Hall, Narendranath highlighted the achievements of Theosophy that revolved around the synthesis of science and religion, as well as the proclamation of the ideal of brotherhood: "Modern science, such as it is, is mere child's play compared with the science which has discovered and illustrated the latent powers of man. And it is Theosophy which is a preparation for the study of that science, and, indeed, the science itself." After quoting Milton and Shakespeare to demonstrate humankind's long occupation with the spirit world, Narendranath explained that "India is the wonder-land on earth, as the cradle of the occult sciences; and Great Britain should be proud of possessing this country as a part of her great Empire. And yet Englishmen do not take the least trouble or interest in studying the ancient literature and philosophy of the Hindus."[113] Narendranath was convinced that, in fact, Englishmen were now less informed than in the early days of the Royal Asiatic Society, and Theosophy was the remedy to this neglect of Indian culture: "The best feature of Theosophy is that it inculcates the spirit of Universal Brotherhood among men, as forming part of the Universal Life." It would thus lead to the realization that all beings are creatures of God, irrespective of race, creed, or caste. This especially applied to those who belonged to the same family: "The Hindus represent the older Branch of the great Aryan stock; and our European brethren should look upon us as filled with the same blood, though marked by a different color, and retaining much of the primitive habits and customs which were once common to both."[114]

Narendranath had already emphasized these points at the seventh-anniversary meeting of the Theosophical Society in Bombay on November 27, 1882. There, he had explained the reasons for his support for the Theosophists: "Europeans by birth, they are Hindus at heart,—better Hindus than many of us, I should say." They had come to India "*not to teach us anything new*, but simply to tell us to seek wisdom at our very doors, in our own Eastern books of antiquity which we have hitherto totally neglected,—wisdom much higher than is to be met with in any other part of the known world."[115] He stressed that a purely English education had done more harm than good in India, and that a combination of both Western and Eastern education was the solution at hand: "Oriental studies are essentially necessary to keep up our national spirit, and to produce in us a larger and more abiding love of our country. Patriotism has become a lip-patriotism in India, because, as I believe, of the shameful neglect of the study of our own *Shastras*."[116] Narendranath was cautious, however, not to protest against the colonial rule per se: "It is a happy thing for us all that we are having our training, as a subject-people, under the British rule."[117] He did not call for a revolt against colonialism but for an uplifting of national spirit that he expressed, at the same time, in terms that reflected orientalist and colonial perceptions of India:

> We, the present generation of Aryans, have lost all those noble traits in our character which distinguished our forefathers, and raised them so much above all other nations as still to excite the admiration of the rest of the

> world. We are wanting in those very qualities which contribute to exalt a people. It is my belief bordering upon conviction that Theosophy will supply them all; and it is, therefore, only that I have given my adhesion to the Theosophical movement in India. . . . What better science can Modern India in particular, or the world in general, have, or wish for? Our so-called patriots and reformers in India are only groping in the dark.[118]

Hardly could it be more obvious which points made Theosophy most attractive for the learned Bengalis who so enthusiastically received Olcott in Calcutta: first, the allusion to a common Aryan past and the acknowledgment that its sources were to be found in India; second, the recognition of Indians as seemingly equal partners in the conversation about how to revive that past; third, the consistently critical attitude toward the colonial government, orientalists, and missionaries; and fourth, the social reformist proclamation of a synthesis of religion and science, based on a combination of the best of modern Western science and ancient Aryan wisdom, and thus incorporating at the same time a notion of orthodoxy that Olcott emphasized in his Calcutta speech. These ingredients fueled the national sentiment among Indians and the debates surrounding the meaning of Hinduism—not as an outside influence but as a resonance within an environment that had been shaped by a global historical background. As Varuni Bhatia has argued, bhadralok were portrayed by many contemporaries as Westernized and deracinated, while on the other hand they posed the most serious challenge to colonialism.[119] Precisely because they were not the *passive* recipients of Western education, they developed strategies and ideologies of emancipation and independence that can be comprehended only when viewed in their own right. Theosophy, then, could become a platform for social reform, artistic exchange, and scholarly projects that created new possibilities under the unequal circumstances of colonialism.

3

The Contested Science of Yoga

When Olcott gave his lecture in the Calcutta Town Hall about Theosophy as the "scientific basis of religion," he highlighted "Yoga Vidya" as the crucial means for proving the scientific basis of Hinduism and as a practice that paralleled mysticism and occultism in the West. In his speech to the seventh-anniversary meeting of the Theosophical Society in the same year, 1882, Narendranath Sen struck a similar tone: "The third object of the Society is enquiry into the mysterious powers of nature. We call it 'Yoga Vidya'; others call it Occult Science."[1] It emerges that, on one hand, yoga was perceived as the expression of a universal tradition of esoteric practices, while at the same time it represented a particularly Indian form of occult science. This perception was largely informed by orientalist scholarship, but the Theosophists were eager to engage with South Asian interlocutors to gain access to this supposed occult science. Its meaning, however, was fiercely contested. One outcome was the separation between Hatha and Raja Yoga, which originated in Indian quarrels and was mapped on Theosophical differentiations between legitimate forms of occult practice. In order to understand the disputed meanings of Tantra and their relation to science and nationalism, it is important to now scrutinize this historical background.

"Yoga Vidya" between Science and Religion

In recent decades, a wealth of studies has explored modern forms of yoga as the outcome of complex interactions between Westerners and Indians. Elizabeth De Michelis, in her groundbreaking study of what she has termed "Modern Postural Yoga," has highlighted the "esoteric myopia" in previous scholarship, which resulted in neglect of the role of esotericism in modern and contemporary Hinduism.[2] Indeed, the parallel study by Joseph S. Alter, *Yoga in Modern India,* still juxtaposed "occult" and "scientific" varieties in the emergence of modern yoga,[3] although De Michelis demonstrated that these forms were virtually indistinguishable from another and that the "occult"

Global Tantra. Julian Strube, Oxford University Press. © Oxford University Press 2022.
DOI: 10.1093/oso/9780197627112.003.0004

interpretations of yoga chronologically predated and often informed later, supposedly more "mainstream" varieties.

It is widely accepted that the crucial moment in the transmission of "yoga" to the West was the publication of Vivekananda's *Raja Yoga* in 1896, following his appearance in 1893 at the Parliament of the World's Religions in Chicago. De Michelis has argued that Vivekananda was the first Indian to popularize a yoga system in the West after Henry David Thoreau had vaguely expressed, in 1849, his conviction to be a yogi.[4] Mark Singleton, who provided many insights into the emergence of posture-based yoga systems in the Anglophone context, underlined the importance of Vivekananda.[5] De Michelis highlighted that Vivekananda was influenced by Theosophical and other "Western esoteric" ideas, to the extent that she referred to his ideas as "Neo-Vedantic occultism."[6] According to De Michelis, mesmerism, "harmonial religion" (the socialist-spiritualist reformism popular in the United States),[7] and the ideas of thinkers such as Swedenborg had been "imported" to India, where Western-educated milieus became pervaded by esotericism. It is against that background that *Raja Yoga* should be understood, according to De Michelis, as Vivekananda blended "Neo-Vedantic esotericism and avant-garde American occultism. Thus Neo-Vedantic ideology became an integral part of Western occultism and, conversely, Western occultist ideas were integrated into Neo-Vedanta. These ideas were then transmitted back to India."[8]

While both De Michelis and Singleton addressed the importance of mesmerism and Spiritualism for the emergence of yoga since the beginning of the nineteenth century, and while both acknowledged the important role played by the Theosophists in that regard,[9] their investigation of these contexts remained cursory. In contrast, Baier has extensively explored the relevance of mesmerism, Spiritualism, and occultism, but also the relevance of Christian contemplative and meditational traditions. He demonstrated that these were combined in the Theosophical and New Thought reception of yoga, which laid the foundations on which Vivekananda and other authors, such as Sri Aurobindo, would develop their ideas.[10] However, Baier did not investigate any Indian context in its own right.

While there has been growing awareness of the role of esotericism for the emergence of modern yoga, studies have focused on Anglophone sources, which were contextualized against a Western background.[11] Yet in order to fully grasp the Theosophical debate about yoga, it is necessary to shed light on the Indians who were an integral part of it, as well as on the backgrounds against which they articulated their ideas.[12] As the previous chapters have demonstrated, it is too simplistic to understand these interactions in terms of a meeting between a Western esotericism and its analogues in India. Instead of identifying such traditions typologically, as De Michelis has done on the basis of Antoine Faivre's approach,[13] they should be understood as the outcomes of a globally entangled historical development. Indians could engage in a fruitful exchange precisely because their conceptual worlds were already interlinked.

The Theosophical occupation with yoga can be observed as early as in the first issue of the *Theosophist*, in a multipart article titled "Yoga Vidya" that was published from October 1879 until January 1880, in parallel with the emerging Bengali intervention. Therein, an anonymous Theosophist discussed yoga in direct correlation with mesmerism and Spiritualism, referencing Franz Anton Mesmer, Karl von Reichenbach, and Edward Bulwer-Lytton, along with the *Śrīmad Bhāgavata* (i.e., the *Bhāgavata Purāṇa*) and the first English translation of the *Yoga Sūtra*. We learn from the article that yoga was an age-old system of self-discipline that aimed at the development of willpower. It would thus be important for present-day psychologists but especially for Spiritualists: the attainment of *siddhis* through yogic practices should be regarded as the development of "psychic faculties" rather than supposed "superhuman faculties," an argument that reflected the occultist emphasis on the mastery of natural rather than supernatural forces.[14] The value of yoga lay in understanding and mastering phenomena that only the ignorant would misunderstand as supernatural or even demonic.

This latter point was highlighted by the juxtaposition of the theories of Roger Gougenot des Mousseaux (1805–1876) with those of William Crookes (1832–1919). The former had been one of the most ardent critics of Éliphas Lévi, the pioneer of occultism, and other authors who thought that occult natural forces rather than demonic deceptions were behind the Spiritualist phenomena so popular in the second half of the nineteenth century.[15] According to the author of "Yoga Vidya," the superstitious accusations of that "Heathen-hating, Pope-adoring bigot" were remote from the sober scientific investigation of Crookes, a member of the Society for Psychical Research.[16] Once again, it is evident that Theosophists approached yoga through the lens of mesmerism, Spiritualism, and occultism, regarding it as a means to overcome the narrowmindedness of both scientific materialism and religious dogmatism.

In doing so, they were informed by a well-established and widely acknowledged body of scholarship that had related mesmerism and animal magnetism to Indian practices.[17] I have already pointed out that such a relation can be found as early as in Anquetil-Duperron's *Oupnek'hat*. One of the leading pioneers of mesmerism, the Marquis de Puységur (1751–1825), had stressed the role of the magnetizer's "will" (*volonté*) and thus highlighted the need for the cultivation of the practitioner's individual capabilities. It was largely due to the therapist's will that a "magnetic sleep" could be induced in a patient, leading to "somnambulistic" states that reached their climax in ecstatic experiences. Reported experiences included the perception of bodily energy flows along the nerve plexuses. Magnetism became linked to magical practices and often served as their "scientific" explanation. It was also widely regarded as a means to communicating with the spirit world and developing clairvoyance, for instance in the famous works of Johann Heinrich Jung-Stilling (1740–1817) and Justinus Kerner (1786–1862). Soon, animal magnetism was regarded as lying at the root of universal religious experience and became linked to theories about the common origin of myths and religion in "the East."[18] Such authors followed an openly religious agenda and often had close ties to Freemasonry, Swedenborgianism, or Rosicrucianism. Mesmerism was thus controversially transformed from a therapeutic-medical theory into an integral part of nineteenth-century religious discourse. This development was significant for the emergence of modern magical currents, such as French Martinism at the end of the eighteenth century.[19]

Numerous influential authors took up such ideas, for instance Joseph Görres (1776–1848), who discussed occult forces or substances in the context of meditation. Joseph Ennemoser (1787–1854) held that wisdom about magnetism was particularly developed in "the East" and discussed Indian magic in relation to the meditational practices of the Brahmans. Similar to widely read scholars such as Carl Alexander Ferdinand Kluge (1782–1844), Ennemoser developed a veritable "magnetic historiography" that sought to explain magic scientifically.[20] In his *Untersuchungen über den Lebensmagnetismus und das Hellsehen* from 1821, Johann Carl Passavant (1790–1857) studied travel accounts about fakirs, Sufis, and yogis ("Djogis," "Jauguis"), relating their practices to magic, somnambulism, clairvoyance, ecstasy, meditation, contemplation, or Kabbalah. Against this background, techniques of "self-magnetisation" and the control of occult forces through mesmeric magic became a prominent subject of discussion. By the middle of the nineteenth century, a famous theologian like Henri Lacordaire (1802–1861) could even claim in his *Conférences de Notre-Dame*, which attracted tens of thousands, that Jesus Christ himself had performed miracles through his mastery of occult forces.[21]

Such theories were well established among orientalist and philological scholars. The supposed connections to India were notably elaborated in the work of Karl Joseph Windischmann (1775–1839).[22] A professor of philosophy in Bonn who was also member of the medical faculty, he had specialized in magnetism both from a historical and a practical perspective. In his unfinished *Philosophie im Fortgang der Weltgeschichte* (1827–1834), he argued that "the magnetic life of the soul" was the "principle of Indian thought" and interpreted Brahmanical doctrines through the lens of animal magnetism. He drew extensive parallels between somnambulism and Indian meditational and yogic practices. Supposedly, Brahmanical practices were determined by "Joga," a method of contemplation leading to ecstasy and finally to the unification with God. Since such "magical" practices formed the foundation of Indian thought, they could be regarded as the crucial link to Western practices of magic and mesmerism, a case that Windischmann made by, among other things, identifying prana with the magnetic fluid.

Such comparisons were often explained by far-reaching claims about historical influences and common roots, for instance in the highly influential work of Matter. In his *Essai historique sur l'école d'Alexandrie* (1820), *Histoire critique du gnosticisme* (1828), and *Histoire de l'école d'Alexandrie* (1840), he advanced the thesis that the *ésotérisme* allegedly typical of ancient Pythagoreanism and the School of Alexandria existed "throughout antiquity, from China to Gallia," and that "the Greek doctrine is simply that of India, altered and materialized through its passage via Egypt."[23] Matter surmised that the Gnostics, but also the kabbalists, had received Indian "and perhaps even Chinese" ideas.[24] Gnosticism, Kabbalah, and "Indian teachings" could consequently be viewed as parts of a shared esoteric tradition.[25] Matter was concerned with more than elucidating the milieu in which Christianity emerged; his quest was for the "true" religious tradition, and his gaze was directed beyond the Mediterranean to the distant lands of India and China. Moreover, his interest was not merely historical, as he believed that the struggle between esoteric and exoteric traditions had continued ever since. In the view of Matter, who had close ties to high-degree Freemasonry, the "mystical" currents rooted in ancient esotericism contained the key to true religion.[26]

Before the middle of the nineteenth century, mesmerism and orientalist scholarship had therefore developed diverse historiographies and a complex language of contemplative bodily experience that formed a matrix for the later reception of South Asian yogic and meditational practices.[27] I showed in the first chapter that prominent Indians like Krishnachandra actively engaged with the related theories as early as the late eighteenth century—roughly one hundred years before the founding of the Theosophical Society. The Theosophical interest in yoga largely resulted from this long-standing association between yoga, occult forces, magic, and an underlying ancient wisdom tradition. The notion of *siddhi* was central to this association and features prominently in Indological scholarship, not only historically but up to the present day. Monier Williams, for instance, defined the "acquisition of magical powers" (*siddhi*) as a central aim of "left-hand worshippers" (*vāmācāri*) and remarked, "As to the Yantras these are mystical diagrams generally combinations of triangular figures, like the inverted triangles of the Freemasons supposed to possess occult powers." He concluded that "it will justly be inferred that the Tantras are generally mere manuals of mysticism, magic, and superstition of the worst and most silly kind."[28] This illustrates how the identification of *siddhi* with occult powers or magic unfolded against a polemically charged background that was shaped by debates about the legitimacy of religious practices.

Since the beginning of the nineteenth century, numerous authors have stressed mesmerism's similarity with Neo-Platonic and Hermetic concepts of the World Soul and correspondences or analogies between the bodily microcosm and the universal macrocosm. Such comparisons abound in Theosophical discussions of yoga, as well as in the writings of Avalon and Woodroffe. In the introduction to *The Great Liberation*, a subchapter is devoted to "correspondence between macrocosm and microcosm," where the Hermetic maxim "As above, so below" is related to the Tantras. The same reference reappears in *The Serpent Power* and is taken up frequently in other writings.[29] Similarly, Baradakanta explained in his introduction to the second volume of *Principles of Tantra*, "The microcosm is in miniature what the macrocosm is."[30] As I detailed in chapter 1, the same parallel is often drawn by recent scholars, for instance by Goudriaan[31] and by Padoux, who discussed the "correspondence between microcosm and macrocosm" and "a gnosis based on micro-macrocosmic correlations"[32] Such comparisons among Tantric, Gnostic, Hermetic, Masonic, and other (supposedly) esoteric currents were not drawn up by the Theosophists, but they were rooted and widely accepted in orientalist scholarship.

At the same time, Theosophical understandings of yoga were not simply the outcome of Western orientalist imagination; they were shaped and informed by South Asian actors. Dayananda played a crucial role in this regard, at least in the beginning. Curious about Dayananda's opinion on "Yoga Vidya," Blavatsky and Olcott met with him in Meerut in Uttar Pradesh on August 30, 1880.[33] According to the notes of that meeting, Dayananda confirmed that yoga was no superstition but a "true science" that was "based upon a knowledge of the laws of Nature." The Theosophists were naturally interested whether there were any living "real Yogis who can at will produce the wonderful phenomena described in Aryan books."[34] Dayananda confirmed their existence, but emphasized their small number and reclusiveness. He was ready to answer questions about their abilities, which he explained as their willpower and control of natural forces. Interestingly, he also confirmed that "certain phenomena heretofore produced by Madame Blavatsky in the presence of witnesses, such as the causing of a shower of roses to fall in a room at Benares last year," were, in fact, "phenomena of Yoga."[35]

Acknowledging the Theosophical mastery of occultism as based on the same science as yoga, Dayananda seems to have initially welcomed Blavatsky and Olcott as allies for the revival of Aryan civilization. Even after their rupture, Olcott lauded him as "one of the most distinctly Aryan personages of the time, a man of large erudition, an experienced ascetic, a powerful orator, and an intense patriot."[36] Yet the breakup between the Ārya Samāj and the Theosophical Society was the outcome of a mutual skepticism from early on. After a long discussion on the final day of their visit, Olcott and Dayananda "agreed that neither should be responsible for the views of the other: the two Societies to be allies, yet independent."[37] This distancing was not an isolated incidence. Any enthusiasm about the strange newcomers' interest in Aryan culture notwithstanding, even those Indian observers who were sympathetic toward the Theosophical cause expressed a healthy reservation. Some months after the meeting in Meerut, the *Indian Mirror* commented:

> If Colonel Olcott and his co-laborers succeed in rendering the occult sciences once more popular in Europe, they will earn the thanks of every true lover of knowledge. We are curious, however, to know whether that gentleman will consent to submit to the rules which the practice of *Yoga*

requires. European *Yogis* and *Yoginis* will not be the least interesting feature of the progressive nineteenth century.[38]

Apart from the evident skepticism in this quote, it also shows the widespread acceptance of the assumption that yoga was an occult science whose analogues had once been practiced in Europe. A bit more than a year later, the *Indian Mirror* suggested, "Occult phenomena form, perhaps, the very groundwork of the Indian systems of religion. The state of *yoga* is supposed to be favorable to all sorts of supernatural manifestations, and the man once plunged in contemplation, sees forms and figures not observed with the eyes wide open." It also stressed that occultism

> belongs to the region of physical and mental sciences; it can he explained by laws, though what those laws are has not been discovered yet. . . . Those eminent European thinkers, whose attention has been directed to it by the wonderful phenomena of spiritualism, are not aware of the existence of a vast mass of literature on the subject existing in India at the present day.[39]

However, the article's judgment was not entirely positive, as occultism and supernaturalism were indeed regarded as subjects of scientific research—but *not* of religion. The Brahmo author was thus "a little bemused" to learn that the Theosophists had supposedly assumed that Keshab had himself practiced yoga and possessed occult powers. The author denounced such claims because the "world will survive supernaturalism of all sorts, and the only miracles which will be believed in are those which result from the extraordinary moral forces and strong resolves of the human will, directed by injunctions from the Divine spirit above."[40] This theistic refutation of yoga, understood as occultism and supernaturalism, was met with a sharp reply by Blavatsky in the *Theosophist* of March 1881, wherein she disputed that any Theosophist had ever regarded Keshab as a yogi but also, more importantly, that Theosophists utterly rejected any kind of belief in miracles and supernaturalism.[41]

The *Indian Mirror* article, which was printed right next to an update on Brahmo educational activities penned by Charles Dall, demonstrates that yoga and occultism had become firmly linked in the view of educated Indians who were interacting with the Theosophical Society. However, the interpretation of yoga as existing between the poles of science and religion was highly contested. The idiosyncratic Theosophical approach to yoga unavoidably led to numerous disagreements, including the controversy with Dayananda. This interpretation developed through an ambivalent interaction with diverse learned Indians. The fact that the "spiritual" expectations of enthusiastic American and European Theosophists could be met with the theistic rationalism of an Indian Brahmo is a compelling indicator of these intricacies.

The Separation between Hatha and Raja Yoga

In their quest for "true" yoga, the Theosophists quickly established their own methods for distinguishing it from false, aberrant practices. This differentiation was mapped onto existing quarrels among both Western esotericists and Indians; somewhat analogous to the division between Spiritualism and occultism, yoga became separated into Hatha and Raja Yoga. This was not simply made up by Theosophists; it emerged out of an exchange with Indian informants, most importantly Dayananda. In his statements about "Yoga Vidya," he had drawn a sharp distinction between what he referred to as Hatha Yoga and Raja Yoga, the first leading to "physical results," the second to "spiritual powers."[42] According to Dayananda, the hardships and ordeals of Hatha Yoga—for instance "the swinging of one's body from a tree, head downwards, at a little distance from five burning fires"—were a prerequisite for the mental exercises of Raja Yoga, which could be practiced only after the body had been subjected to the will. The idea was taken up by Olcott and became an integral part of Theosophical discourses about yoga.[43] This was a hallmark in the reception of yoga and meditation that would remain highly influential during the ensuing decades.[44]

The Theosophical view of Hatha Yoga as a mere preparation for the more noble Raja Yoga would soon give way to an outright rejection of the former as a superficial and even harmful practice. This was a significant departure from earlier yogic sources from the subcontinent, which indeed knew different kinds of yoga, including the Hatha and Raja varieties, but without categorically regarding them as opposed systems.[45] The association of Hatha Yoga with Tantric elements, however, as it featured prominently in the Nath tradition, will have contributed to the negative perception of it.[46] The Theosophical resignification of yoga is reflected in the commentary to the serial publication of Navinchandra Paul's *Treatise on the Yoga Philosophy* that appeared in the *Theosophist* between September 1880 and April 1882, in direct proximity to the Bengali intervention. Paul had graduated from the Bengal Medical College in Calcutta in 1841 and originally published his treatise in 1850, to explain the effects of yoga in the light of modern medicine.[47] The Theosophical discovery of that publication brought unprecedented attention to it, but also substantially reframed it. This becomes evident in the introduction to the *Theosophist* series, which stressed that the author was not in every case "succeeding in making himself or his facts clearly understood," which is why the editors accompanied the text with numerous commentaries: "And this with the double object in view of silencing at once the malicious accusation that our Society is no better than a school of 'magic,' the word being used to signify ridiculous superstition and belief in *supernaturalism* and of preventing our readers from receiving wrong impressions in general."[48] It was further pointed out that Paul's treatise related mainly to the practice of Hatha rather than Raja Yoga, which meant a "great difference." The commentary ended with the explanation that ascetic practices, not only in India but also among Christians throughout the ages, would be vindicated by an investigation of yoga, which rested on "scientific principles." Although most of the "fakirs, gosseins, bayraguis and others of the mendicant order" of present-day India "may be and undoubtedly are worthless and idle vagabonds," they were still unknowingly imitating ancient truths. These originated in Patanjali's "Yoga Vidya" and relied on occult laws that were nowadays termed hypnotism or self-mesmerization.[49] It can be observed how yoga became related to occultist concepts that rejected the notion of "supernaturalism" by stressing the scientific nature of its effects. This, however, was only related to "spiritual," mental exercises rather than the torturing physical exercises supposedly prescribed by Hatha Yoga.

Obviously, the Theosophical discussion of yoga was anything but straightforward. On one hand, the 1880s saw a rapid increase in influence by Indians and the diverse traditions they represented. On the other hand, this influence was submitted to far-reaching idiosyncratic interpretations by Theosophical leaders. This can be exemplified by the Theosophical discourse about pranayama. Blavatsky had referred to this practice in her famous *Isis Unveiled* from 1877 as part of a "psychological science," but she did not display any in-depth knowledge of Indian primary sources.[50] In the 1880s, this would change drastically. An important step was *Occult Science: The Science of Breath*, first published in 1884 by Ram Prasad, the president of the Meerut Theosophical Society, who had become a member on December 24, 1882. Between 1887 and 1889, it was published as "Nature's Finer Forces" in the *Theosophist*, followed by an 1890 edition titled *The Science of Breath and the Philosophy of the Tattvas*. It was widely received within the Theosophical Society and beyond, for instance in the Hermetic Order of the Golden Dawn in Britain.[51] As a result, pranayama was rejected as a harmful hatha-yogic practice by Blavatsky, but at the same time it was widely received by Theosophists and other esotericists, fueling controversies about the legitimacy of "practical occultism": while groups such as the Golden Dawn emphasized the practice of ritual magic, Blavatsky stressed the spiritual and metaphysical character of Theosophy.[52]

The meaning of yoga and Tantra was directly linked to these debates, but it was also contested within Indian contexts, as the writings of Shri Sabhapati Swami help to illustrate.[53] Born around 1828 in the Madras Presidency, Sabhapati Swami was educated at a Scottish Protestant missionary school and probably first worked at a government job, marrying the daughter of a textile merchant.[54] He embarked on several extensive travels through South Asia and reportedly became a disciple of the Tamil Vedashreni Chidambara Swamigal, who had published on Vedanta and yoga as early as in 1855. In 1880, Sabhapati Swami published *Om: A Treatise on Vedantic Raj Yoga*. The text was announced in the *Theosophist* in April 1880, when Baradakanta's series on Tantra was still being published. In the previous month, "An Admirer" had given a eulogy of the "Madras Yogi."[55] *Om* focused on Kundalini Yoga and presented a twelve-chakra system, six of which were located in the head. It saw several editions in subsequent years and a German translation in 1909. Indeed, it can be regarded as the first yoga manual, as it predates the better known one by Ram Prasad, which is sometimes referred to as the first of its kind.[56]

Olcott referred to Sabhapati Swami's *Raj Yoga* in his speech to the Bengal Theosophical Society in April 1882, explaining that "mesmerism—a modern European discovery of an old Asiatic science—*is the key to the mystical phenomena of the Hindu Sastras*" and contained the hidden truth of Aryan philosophy.[57] At that time, yogic and Tantric terminology had become firmly established in Theosophical discourse.[58] This is reflected in the writings of Blavatsky, who adopted the terminology of chakras in the *Theosophist* in August 1882, when she pondered the possible mesmeric effects between the utterances of mantras. She maintained that "Western occultists and the adept Brahmans agreed all in teaching that sound emanated from the Astral Light, or *Akasa*, in its purest essence." The "Hindu occultist, or devotee, when practising Raja Yoga," would hear the same sounds emanate "from his own

Moola Adharam—the first of the series of six centres of force in the human body," that would be "fed at the inexhaustible source of the *seventh*," a reference to the "thousand-petalled lotus" (*sahasrāra*) that was located above the practitioner's head. The yogic adept would need to master control of the elemental forces of nature through channels within her or his body (the *nāḍīs*) by the practice of Raja Yoga. This Blavatsky contrasted sharply with the more detestable kind of yoga known as Hatha: "The practice of blindly 'transferring' and 'receiving'—is that of sorcerers, whether they are so consciously or unconsciously. Moreover, the ignorant practice of Hatha-Yoga leads one invariably into that undesirable acquisition. The Hatha-Yogi either becomes a sorcerer, or learns practically *nothing*; or more frequently yet, kills himself by such an injudicious practice."[59] It is interesting to observe how Blavatsky interpreted the practice of Raja Yoga by occultist theories, most notably the Astral Light that was first popularized by Éliphas Lévi.[60] At the same time, her charges against the "passive" practitioners of Hatha Yoga mirrored typical occultist and Theosophical polemics against Spiritualists. One can thus trace how European, North American, and Indian discourses about yoga were merging, not only on the level of terminology but also on that of theoretical, "scientific" explanations and polemical demarcations. While Dayananda lectured in Bombay's Framji Cowasjee Hall in March 1882 about the "humbuggery" of the Theosophists, they elaborated their own understanding of "Yoga Vidya."[61] There is little doubt that the Theosophical interpretation of yoga through the lens of mesmerism and occultism was one of the reasons for the rupture with Dayananda, who denounced his former partners as atheists and charlatans in a pamphlet reproducing his Bombay lecture:

> When the Swami had a talk with Madame Blavatsky on "yoga," at Meerut, Madame asserted that she practised *yoga* as taught in the *Yoga* and the Sankhya Shastra. On the Swami's desiring her to explain the methods of the yoga recommended by the Shastras, no answer whatever was forthcoming. In other words, it is only *mesmerism* or the juggler's art which they can practice.[62]

This eminent opposition to the mesmeric approach to yoga prevented neither other Indians nor the Theosophical leaders from elaborating the identification of occultist with yogic practices. For instance, Olcott increasingly linked the chakras to the occultist technique of "astral projection," as he saw it taught in Sabhapati Swami's *Vedantic Raj Yoga*. Astral projection was a central concept in nineteenth-century occultism. While early Theosophical texts discussed it with reference to mesmeric and ascetic practices, the use of incense or drugs, and techniques like magic mirrors, as described by earlier occultists, the shift to Kundalini Yoga for achieving astral projection is an important step in the esoteric reception of yoga.[63]

Olcott's further discussion of yoga helps to exemplify the ambivalent interplay between the activities of Indian authors, the more indirect reception of Indian sources, and their interpretation through the lens of occultist and Spiritualist concepts. In 1882, Olcott wrote an introduction to a translation of Patanjali's *Yoga Sūtra*, which was published by the Indian Theosophist and editor of Baradakanta, Tukaram Tatya (1836–1898), under the title *The Yoga Philosophy*. The book was a combination of the partial translations that had been published by James R. Ballantyne in 1852–1853 and Govindaram Shastri in the journal *Pandit*.[64] It was thus the first complete edition of the *Yoga Sūtra*, before Rajendralal Mitra published the first full coherent translation under the auspices of the Asiatic Society of Bengal in 1883.[65] The first edition of Tatya's *Yoga Philosophy*, numbering only five hundred copies, sold very quickly. In 1885, a second edition was printed with a revised introduction and was distributed worldwide.[66] In his introduction from 1882, Olcott clearly identified yoga as "self-mesmerization" and as an exercise in willpower, the highest stage of which, *samādhi*, he linked to astral projection.[67] Significantly, Olcott discussed the concentration on the "vital centres" as part of that method, referring to Sabhapati's *Om* from 1880 and describing illustrations that depicted the chakras within the body. Olcott also wrote that he had received further explanations in a personal conversation with Sabhapati.[68]

In the second edition, from 1885, Olcott still identified yoga with self-mesmerization and maintained the concentration on the "vital centres," but he removed the references to Sabhapati in the main text and added a polemical footnote explaining that the process described by Sabhapati "is far from the system of Rāja Yoga. From his treatment of the subject, it is clear that it is a part of Hatha Yoga." Accordingly, the reference to the drawing in Sabhapati's *Om* was replaced with one to the *Śiva Saṁhitā*, a text to which we will return later.[69] The reason for these changes can be found in the increasing rejection of Hatha Yoga, which was expressed even in the review of *The Yoga Philosophy* that appeared in the *Theosophist* of December 1882. The edition is recommended solely to "students of psychology," while readers are cautioned against its practical aspects: "[W]e do not recommend Yoga, especially Hatha-Yoga practice to amateurs, nor even to would-be proficients after they have passed the age of boyhood or girlhood at which, under ancient usage, they came under the care of the venerated Adept Guru."[70] This remark was clearly directed at Indian readers and can be understood as an attempt to establish the authority of Theosophical understandings of yoga over those of Indian gurus.[71]

The rejection of Hatha Yoga in favor of Raja Yoga also reflected rivalries among Indian members of the Theosophical Society. A good example is the intervention by Damodar K. Mavalankar (1857–1885), one of the earliest Indian members of the Society, who exerted far-reaching influence on its leaders. Born in Ahmedabad in 1857, he had met Blavatsky and Olcott in 1879 and became an important voice in Theosophical discourse. In a review of the second edition of Sabhapati's book in the *Theosophist* of March 1884, he strongly denounced the physical exercises described therein, including the practice of postures, or asanas. The book, now titled *The Philosophy and Science of Vedantic Raja Yoga* and edited by Srishchandra Basu, had to be viewed as "a parable": "it is purposely veiled, like so many other treatises of Occultism—in short an allegory." It thus posed a grave danger to the uninformed reader because "the author has adopted the technical terms of *Hatha Yoga,* which will disclose the real *Raja Yoga* system, only when esoterically interpreted." This was exemplified by the notion of the subjugation of the "twelve kingdoms, beginning with the lowest one, which is situated in the *Kundalee*."[72] Mavalankar stressed that this had to be interpreted as the conquering of the imperfections of the flesh rather than a physical process. He thus drove a wedge between an exoteric Hatha Yoga that would cause harm to the uninitiated and the "real" Raja Yoga esoterically hidden behind it.

Mavalankar's polemic demonstrates that the quarrels about the legitimacy of yoga were not separated into a Western Theosophist and an Indian camp, but that the situation was considerably more complex. The Theosophical discourse about yoga was not only shaped by polemics between Western Theosophists, occultists, and Spiritualists but also by polemics between different authors and movements from India. In that context, Tantra emerged as a hotly debated subject that would be radically transformed by the intervention of Baradakanta and a range of other Bengali authors who now demand our attention.

The First Wave of Bengali Contributions

While the debates about yoga were first shaped, more or less directly, by actors such as Dayananda, Sabhapati Swami, and Mavalankar, the year 1882 saw an influx of Bengali voices that contributed to the shift of focus to Tantra. This was probably a partial consequence of Baradakanta's intervention, but it was also most likely due to the successful establishment of Theosophy in Bengal since March of that year. In June 1882, Kaliprasanna Mukhopadhyay initiated a wave of articles by his discussion in "The Tantric and Puranic Ideas of the Deity." Kaliprasanna had joined the Theosophical Society on June 28, 1881. At that time, he lived in Bankipore, a neighborhood of Patna in today's Bihar, where he had studied engineering and published a book on that subject in 1873.[73] A report in the *Path* from 1887 referred to him as a "government executive engineer."[74] He was elected president of the Rajshahi Harmony Theosophical Society on the day of its founding, April 1, 1883.[75] Kaliprasanna also appears as secretary of the earliest and one of the most active branches in Bengal, the Adhi Bhoutic Theosophical Society in Berhampore, which was led by Navinkrishna Bandyopadhyay. Together with Dinanath Gangopadhyay (Ganguly) and others, Navinkrishna was one of the most hard-working Theosophists in the early years of the Society in India. This is attested by their numerous contributions to Theosophical publications, as well as by Olcott's remark that the branch "has always been one of the best working nuclei of the Theosophical movement."[76] Berhampore lies southwest of Rajshahi in the Murshidabad district, north of Nadiya. Kaliprasanna thus lived in, or came from, the same region as Baradakanta and most likely coordinated his efforts with him. In the 1890s, he collaborated with Baradakanta on the Bengali Theosophical journal *Kalpa* and was also a frequent contributor to the *Path* and *Lucifer*, where he wrote, for instance, about karma and "magic among the Hindus."[77]

In his article for the *Theosophist*, Kaliprasanna declared, "The religious belief of almost all the Indo-Aryan sects is identical and similar, whether it be a Tantric, a Buddhist, a Vedantic, or a Vaishnava." He went on to explain that there was a general distinction between "Karma Kānda," the part of teaching dedicated to the method of worship, and "Gnyān Kānda," which dealt with the means of obtaining wisdom: "The doctrines laid in the 'Gnyān Kanda' are called secret doctrines, and are supposed to be known and understood by 'Yogees' and 'Paramahansas' only."[78] Kaliprasanna emphasized that the unity of all, veiled by Maya, lay at the core of that yogic, esoteric doctrine. He thus defined Tantra as lying at the root of all Aryan traditions, and as being separated into an esoteric and an exoteric part.

The next contribution to the discussion about Tantra, a letter, was published in the January 1883 issue of the *Theosophist*. It was less remarkable because of its length than because of its author, Rajnarayan Basu. As will be recalled, Rajnarayan had been a member of Debendranath Tagore's Tattavabodhinī Sabhā and was the president of the Ādi Brāhma Samāj. One of the most eminent intellectual voices in Bengal, he had translated the Upanishads into English and was a renowned nationalist, which earned him the title "grandfather of Indian nationalism."[79] One of his most widely acclaimed writings, "The Superiority of Hinduism" (*hindudharmmer śreṣṭhatā*, 1873), had been published in his own English translation in the same *Theosophist* issue that included Kaliprasanna's article.[80] Like many other Brahmos, Rajnarayan invoked the authority of the Tantras as a matter of course, for instance with a reference to the *Tantrasāra* in his "Superiority of Hinduism."[81] It is thus not surprising that Rajnarayan weighed in on the conversation about Tantra with a letter titled "The Tantras and Their Teachings,"[82] wherein he classified the scriptures into the three classes of Shakta, Vaishnava, and Buddhist: "Although most of these treat of the black art, we should learn from them the methods for controlling the forces of nature, which they teach without applying them to the accomplishment of malicious purposes if at all they successfully teach the same as they pretend. This would extend the dominion and resources of science to an extent not dreamt of in Europe."[83] According to Rajnarayan, the greatest principle underlying the Tantras was the realization that there is no evil but only "happiness in disguise; happiness arrising [*sic*] from the moral conciousness [*sic*] of triumph over evil." Clearly, Rajnarayan presented Tantra according to a Vedantic understanding of absolute unity. Like any science, it could be abused for malicious purposes and employed as black magic, but fundamentally it was far superior to Western forms of science. It is striking how consistently Tantra was framed with the notion of science in these articles, while its well-known associations with black magic warranted at least a disclaimer. This becomes tangible in a footnote by Blavatsky that was inserted right after the title "The Tantras," published in June 1883 by one "T.S." from Berhampore:

> For reasons of their own, the Aryas or the "reformers," as they and the Brahmos call themselves, regard *all* the *Tantras* as the most abominable works of sorcery that inculcate immorality. Some of the Tantric works and

> commentaries are certainly prohibited on account of their dealing with *necromancy* (modern Spiritualism). But the meaning in the real old *Tantras* remaining a dead letter to the uninitiated Hindus, very few can appreciate their worth. Some of the "White" *Tantras,* especially the one treated upon in the present article, contain extremely important information for the Occultists.[84]

While Blavatsky's dismissive stance toward the Ārya Samāj is as little surprising as her lashing out against Spiritualists, her differentiation between white and, implicitly, black Tantra demonstrates the significant impact that the new Bengali interventions had on the Theosophical perception of Tantra. To be sure, like Olcott, she still cautioned readers that Tantra would "also"[85] deal with necromancy and other reprehensible practices, but those "very few" who were able to understand the "real old" Tantras would uncover precious occult truths.

The article by T.S. underscores the value of Tantra as being first and foremost scientific. It was written in Berhampore, which links the author to Kaliprasanna and the Adhi Bhoutic branch. It is unclear who exactly T.S. was, but it is possible that he is Sachchidananda Swami, one of the most prolific writers on Tantra and a later reference for Woodroffe. This identity is indicated by the circumstance that his *Theosophist* article was later used for a series titled "Theory and Practice of Tantra" in the *Hindu Spiritual Magazine*, as well as in a series of monographs containing the same ideas, which will be discussed in the next chapter. "The word Tantra literally signifies science," explained T.S. right at the beginning of his *Theosophist* article. He differentiated between Shakta, Vaishnava, and Buddhist Tantras, although he noted that the term "Tantric" ordinarily referred to the Shakta variety. The article goes on to focus on the yogic aspect of Tantra, which rests on the worship of the "energy or Sakti, the highest deity."[86] Much of the ensuing discussion revolves around the polarity between Shiva and Parvati or Shakti, between Purusha and Prakriti, between male and female. The union of these principles would be achieved through "the absolute knowledge of *Yoga* which is at the centre, the highest point where both the positive and negative forces are equilibrated."[87] A footnote by Blavatsky clarified: "The above explanation of the allegory, and its secret meaning being found in the oldest works treating upon Aryan occultism, goes far to prove that the ancient Aryas know as much as we, if not more, of the physical sciences as taught to-day; western science having reached the present knowledge herself but very recently, comparatively speaking."[88]

As T.S. underlined a bit later, the "generation of everything" by the action of two principles "is a well known law of Occultism and admitted, in other terms, by modern science." It was through the female principle that man would be able to merge with the "One Absolute." Interestingly, T.S. goes on to provide a classification of yoga that is divided between "Brahma Yoga" and "Mantra Yoga." We learn that Brahma Yoga "is essentially the same as the *Raja Yoga* and is strongly recommended to all Tantrikas." Mantra Yoga, on the other hand, was subdivided into six branches, the first five of which constitute black magic, with the last branch providing "incantations" that are suited for those leading virtuous lives without inflicting any suffering upon animate beings and who never touch alcohol and abstain from intoxicating drugs.[89] A true Tantric, including even those following the *vāmācāra* or *virācāra* paths, would never actually consume intoxicating substances or commit any indecent acts. In "The Tantras in Buddhism," published in December 1883, T.S. stressed that all bad practices resulted from misunderstandings about Tantra, which he attributed to the "degeneration" of "*Sāktaism* (or *Tantricism*)," but also to that of Vaishnavism in Bengal.

These Bengali contributions are especially significant because of their vigorous approach to "black magic" and other negative practices associated with Tantra. Rather than denying their existence, it was argued that they resulted from misunderstandings (for instance, of esoteric doctrines), from the degeneration of once pure traditions, or simply from the bad characters of those who abuse or maliciously denounce Tantra. The supplement to the *Theosophist* issue of June 1883 saw the publication of an article that tackled an especially controversial topic: the ritual of *śāvasādhanā*, which required the practitioner to meditate on a corpse. It was based on a lecture held on April 28 at a meeting of the Dacca Theosophical Society by Kunjabihari Bhattacharya, who edited a homeopathic journal and would resurface as a revolutionary during the freedom struggle.[90] The article's description of *śāvasādhanā* contains an account of "the very mystic ceremony of *Bhutashuddhi*," which includes the performance of pranayama and the rising of the kundalini through "the six cycles (vital centres) of the body," notions that are frequently equated with Theosophical concepts. For instance, the kundalini is tentatively described as "a mystic Force in the seventh principle of man," the "thousand-leafed lotus" (the *sahasrāra*) is identified with "the Universal Ether," and karma with "Linga sarira or Astral body."[91]

Interestingly, a part of Kunjabihari's otherwise detailed description was censored by the editor because it contained some mantras, which, in the eyes of Blavatsky, were "not fit to be read by *uninitiated* Theosophists."[92]

That the true meaning of the Tantric works could be accurately comprehended only by the initiated is also underlined by Kunjabihari in the second part of his article: "These writings contain in them many of the greater mysteries of occult science, but like all other works on that subject such portions are garbed in a phraseology peculiar to the Occultists and which none but the initiated can comprehend." They might appear as "the emanations of a delirious brain" to the "superficial thinker," but "the student of Occult science" knows their significance. Echoing Baradakanta's contributions from 1880, Kunjabihari emphasized that these mysteries would enable the practitioner "to attain that mastery over the secret forces of Nature, to which all the crucibles, the scalpels, the microscopes, the spectroscopes and other instruments of boastful modern science can never afford a key."[93] It is no wonder that Theosophists were thrilled by these allusions to the key of the most powerful and esoteric of all Indian traditions. In a footnote, Blavatsky wrote:

> So little is known outside Bengal about Tantrik rites and ceremonies that space has been given this interesting paper, despite the disgusting and horrid ceremonial it describes. As there are both magic (pure psychic science) and sorcery (its impure counterpart) so there are what are known as the "White" and "Black" Tantras. The one is an expiation, very clear and exceedingly valuable of occultism in its noblest features, the other a devil's chap-book of wicked instructions to the would be wizard and sorcerer.[94]

This differentiation between black and white Tantra clearly paralleled that between black and white magic—and it paralleled the polemical distinctions between Hatha and Raja Yoga, as well as those between Spiritualism and occultism, that were unfolding in the same context. One result of this process was that Tantric elements became increasingly popular in Theosophical circles, although Blavatsky was at pains to insist that they be kept secret. This was mainly due to the demand of many Theosophists for practical experiences rather than lofty spiritual speculations. Increasing competition from other esoteric organizations, such as the Hermetic Order of the Golden Dawn, which had been founded in 1888, finally motivated Blavatsky to form an Esoteric Section or Eastern School in the same year.[95] The members of this

"Inner Group" were taught "practical occultism," including yoga with clearly Tantric elements.[96] Blavatsky drafted the lessons for this group, which were controversially published by Besant in the posthumous third volume of the *Secret Doctrine* in 1897. Blavatsky's interpretation of chakras, kundalini, and other concepts was fairly imaginative and often erroneous from a historical point of view and was influenced by her aggressive stance toward Tantra and Hatha Yoga, whose practice of pranayama, for instance, she believed would lead to "black magic and mediumship." Tantrikas, in this sense, are identified as black magicians who failed to grasp the esoteric meaning behind the science of breath: "By the Tāntrikas it is accepted literally, as relating to the regulation of the vital, lung breath, but by the ancient Rāja-Yogis as referring to the mental or 'will' breath, which alone leads to the highest clairvoyant powers, to the function of the Third Eye and the acquisition of the true Rāja-Yoga occult powers."[97] Blavatsky's attempts at harmonizing yogic concepts with her understanding of Theosophy were clearly driven by her claim to an exclusive access to esoteric knowledge, a claim that was also directed against Indians who disagreed with her. One of her central strategies was to ground her authority in what she termed the "Trans-Himalayan school, of the ancient Indian Raja-Yogis, with which the modern Yogis of India have little to do."[98] In her polemics, she thus increasingly referred to the hidden "Masters" or "Mahatmas" from whom she allegedly received esoteric instructions, rather than living Indian yogis or historical yogic traditions.

These claims to authority underline the ambiguity of the exchanges between Western Theosophists and Indians. On the one hand, there was undoubtedly an increasing influence of Indian authors in matters of yoga and Tantra; on the other, leading Theosophists such as Blavatsky and Olcott sometimes asserted their authority by detaching themselves from the knowledge of living or identifiable Indians—especially following the debacle with Dayananda. Nowhere is this clearer than in the case of the Mahatmas, the arcane masters who presumedly provided Blavatsky with instructions. She employed references to their teachings to reject criticism by Indians as "exoteric" misunderstandings; the initiation into the Mahatmas' esoteric knowledge proved a powerful weapon to ascertain authority. This is especially significant because the early interventions by the Mahatmas about yoga show little evidence of meditational and yogic practices that could be found on the Indian subcontinent. Rather, they described the use of magic mirrors and magnets, techniques that were typical for mesmerist and occultist practices but that were now "transferred to a fantastical Tibet."[99] Such tensions between

Theosophists like Blavatsky and her Indian interlocutors can be grasped in light of the example of the Basu brothers, whose work played an important role in the Theosophical discourse about yoga and Tantra.

The Basu Brothers

In 1887, Srishchandra Basu (1861–1918) published *The Esoteric Science and Philosophy of the Tantras*, a translation of the *Śiva Saṁhitā*, which we have already encountered as Olcott's major reference that had replaced the work of Sabhapati Swami. Srishchandra (whose last name is often spelled in the Sanskritized form, Vasu) was a Bengali civil servant and Sanskrit scholar from a Kayastha family. His father, Shyamacharan Basu, had been born in 1827 in the Bengali district of 23 Parganas and attended Alexander Duff's school in Calcutta.[100] Shyamacharan emerged as an influential educationist in the Education Department in Lahore, where Srishchandra grew up. Similar to his father, Srishchandra attended the Mission School of Lahore without converting to Christianity. In 1877, he entered the Lahore Government College. At this time, he became attracted to the Brāhma Samāj, the Ārya Samāj, and the Theosophical Society—simultaneously, it should be noted. He was an avid reader of the *Tattvabodhinī Patrikā*, which had originated as the organ of Debendranath Tagore's Tattavabodhinī Sabhā and was then the mouthpiece of the Calcutta Brāhma Samāj. Apart from his attraction to Brahmoism, Srishchandra was interested in Spiritualism and social reform. He partook in the student rebellion in Punjab in protest of the mistreatment of Indian students by European teachers, but he was not opposed to Western education in principle. His stance on this matter is illustrated by the fact that he, like his father, rejected efforts to reduce Western influence in the educational system, an endeavor that he considered regressive.[101]

Srishchandra joined the Theosophical Society at the end of 1880, after meeting Olcott and Blavatsky in Simla.[102] According to the Society's register, he joined on November 22 with the member number 690. It appears that he was authorized to accept new members in May 1881.[103] Having obtained his B.A. early in 1881, he also joined the Sādhāraṇ Brāhma Samāj and became acquainted with its leader, Shivanath Shastri. He developed into a prominent member of the Samadarśī Sabhā and hosted meetings of that faction at his house.[104] His relationship to Brahmoism seems to have cooled in 1883, when he stayed in Calcutta to arrange his marriage, but he maintained close contact with Brahmos throughout his life. His relationship to the Ārya Samāj was similarly shaped by both sympathy and distance. His biographer claims that he translated letters from Olcott and Blavatsky to Dayananda, and that his exchange with Dayananda inspired him to study the Vedas. He joined the Ārya Samāj only on the condition that he would not pledge the infallibility of the Vedas, a belief to which he could not bring himself and that would obviously have collided with his propagation of the Tantras.[105] While studying to become a *vakil*, a lawyer or solicitor, he started writing for the journal *Arya* in 1882, publishing a lecture he had given on the Ārya Samāj premises in 1881 titled "The Theory of Evolution from an Aryan Point of View."[106]

Since his college days, Srishchandra had supported the cause of a free India. His interactions with the Aryas, Brahmos, and Theosophists were firmly linked to these efforts. In 1883, he founded the Indian National Society and became an ardent writer of national songs and poems.[107] In June 1884, we find him voicing his defense of the Bengali nationalist Surendranath Bandyopadhyay in the *Regenerator of Aryavarta*, to which he was a frequent contributor.[108] Dedicated throughout his life to education, he founded, according to his biographer, the Indian Girls' Free High School in 1888.[109] We thus find in Srishchandra the typical combination of a progressive stance on education and science, the improvement of the education system in opposition to the exclusions related to sex and caste, the struggle for national independence, and political activism in reform-minded societies. An interest in Spiritualism and esotericism as offered by the Theosophical Society was evidently a natural ingredient in that mix.

It is against this background that Srishchandra's tireless efforts to edit and translate Sanskrit sources must be viewed. This specifically concerns his work on the Tantras and yoga, which he regarded as the central means for national and religious regeneration. In 1884, his translation of the *Śiva Saṁhitā* was first published in the *Arya* of Lahore and probably was the cause for the reference to that text in Olcott's 1885 introduction to *The Yoga Philosophy*. In 1887, the translation was published in book form as *The Esoteric Science and Philosophy of the Tantras* under the auspices of the Theosophical Society, and then again in 1893 with a dedication to Olcott "in recognition of his services for the revival of Aryan religion and ancient philosophy."[110] In 1895, he edited another seminal source text on yoga, the *Gheraṇḍa Saṁhitā*, and, as the reader might recall, he also edited the work of Sabhapati Swami. Together with his younger brother, Bamandas, Srishchandra established the renowned Panini Office to publish a wide range of texts, including the *Sacred Books of the Hindus* series, which was clearly a nod to Müller's *Sacred Books of the East*. Indeed, Srishchandra directly corresponded with Müller, who in turn quoted him in his *Six Systems of Indian Philosophy* (1899).[111]

After he had been posted as a *munsif* (a low judicial office) to Benares in 1896, Srishchandra became dedicated to the Indian Section of the Theosophical Society, whose headquarters had just been moved to the city. It appears, however, that his stance on the Society was anything but clear-cut. According to his biographer, he had a poor opinion of British Theosophists, whose "profession of universal brotherhood seemed to him lip-deep, for they did not rise superior to their prejudices against Indians, whom they considered an inferior race and a conquered people."[112] This opinion clearly did not extend to all British Theosophists, but it indicates an awareness of the ambiguities that have become apparent throughout this chapter. Similar sentiments come to surface in light of Srishchandra's engagement with Freemasonry, which began in 1896 and lasted only a few years. Again according to his biographer, he abandoned Freemasonry, "saying that it served no useful purpose in India. It benefited Christians mostly at the expense of the Hindus and Mussalmans."[113]

Srishchandra's idea of a revival of Hinduism clashed with *both* the hierarchies within the Theosophical Society and Brahmanical viewpoints. For instance, while he helped in the establishment of the Central Hindu College by Besant in 1898, he expressed his discomfort with its alleged embrace of "Brahmanical orthodoxy."[114] This grievance is highly significant, as it expresses the clash over different claims to "orthodoxy," at the center of which stood Tantra. It is clear that most Theosophists were still determined to adhere to the understanding of Brahmanical orthodoxy that, in the vein of diverse orientalist and Indian perspectives, was firmly opposed to the Tantras. Probably in reaction to this, Srishchandra published his own *Catechism of Hinduism* in 1899, which highlighted the role of the Tantras for turning Hinduism into a future universal religion of humanity.[115] This remarkable pamphlet was republished in 1919 as *Catechism of the Hindu Dharma* (note the replacement of *Hinduism* with *Hindu Dharma*) and demonstrates how inherently intertwined the defense of Tantra was, not only with the notion of science but also with Indian nationalism.

In his translation of the *Śiva Saṁhitā*, which, after all, bore the tile *The Esoteric Science and Philosophy of the Tantras*, this stance can be clearly observed. As Srishchandra explained in the introduction, the failure to recognize yoga as a science was due to "the ignorance of the real truths of Yoga," as well as "bigotry."[116] Some people would reject it because of "the disgusting spectacle of the ash-besmeared and lay beggar, the horrible self-inflictions of the Hatha Yogi," which could give the impression that yoga was nothing but humbuggery. "Scientists of our day," on the other hand, would not understand that yoga belongs to the "mental sciences" and cannot be judged according to the standards of the "physical sciences." Scientific experiments could be measured only in light of occult phenomena, but those could be produced only by yogis who strove for the attainment of *siddhi* (psychic powers). Most yogis would strive not for *siddhi* but for liberation (*mokṣa*). The *siddhas* who would be able to produce phenomena were extremely rare and hesitant to display their powers to strangers. They were difficult to approach because, like all "Aryas" and their allies, they carefully guarded their science and concealed their powers "from the gaze of the uninitiated profane."[117] Only those who are qualified (*adhikārī*) could hope to became a neophyte, and such people are not numerous: "We do not see Newtons, Franklins, Tyndalls and Drawins [*sic*] everywhere, and must we expect to see Yogis and Siddhas made out of ordinary men—men whose spirituality is altogether dormant or dead."[118]

It appears that Srishchandra regarded yoga as a distinctly elitist science that was open only to a few people with the right qualifications. The practice of that science was equated with occultism, magnetism, or occult philosophy;[119] it was also framed politically, as it would create abilities that turned a yogi into "the natural leader of humanity."[120] It is interesting to note that Srishchandra did not restrict the system of yoga to a Sanskritic Hindu sphere but regarded it as a system that developed methods depending on different contexts: "Thus the Tantriks have their own ways, the Sufis their own, and the Buddhists their particular system."[121] Not only did Srishchandra affirm Olcott's understanding of yoga as self-mesmerization,[122] but he also quoted from Arnold's *Light of Asia*[123] and, when explaining that the center of the nerve-force within the human body was located in the medulla oblongata, pointed out that "the effect of breathing on thought is very well explained by Swedenborg."[124] He also discussed methods that were "peculiar to the Persian" and described a method that was practiced by "a Mahomedan friend" in which the formula "Allah Hu" was used breathing in and out while throwing one's head back and forth—obviously a reference to *zikr*.[125] This shows that Srishchandra perceived yoga not only as scientific and suitable for creating a leadership of humanity but also as a system that manifested in different religious traditions, including Hinduism, Christianity, and Islam.

A look at the publications by Basu's younger brother, Bamandas (1867–1930), further elucidates this fascinating negotiation of the meaning of yoga and Tantra. In March 1888, Bamandas published "The Anatomy of the Tantras" in the *Theosophist*. He had entered the Medical College at Lahore in 1882 and taken up the parallel study of Ayurvedic medicine at the Oriental College, publishing a book about Indian medicinal plants. In July 1888, he left for England to finish his medical studies and returned in April 1891 to work in the Indian Medical Service, holding the rank of major.[126] The nationalist sentiments of Bamandas seem to have been more passionate than those of his older brother. His obituary in the *Modern Review*, the famous Calcutta-based periodical to which he frequently contributed, stated that he left the Service in 1907 because he had "too keen a sense of personal and national self-respect to relish being in harness . . . with military imperialists."[127]

After his retirement, Bamandas left for Allahabad and devoted himself to historical studies. He also actively promoted reformist ideas, such as female education and the abolishment of the caste system, while vehemently opposing Anglicization. In this light it is significant to note that he appeared as president of the anniversary event of Swami Shraddhananda's *gurukul*, an educational institution modeled after Arya ideals.[128] He published widely on subjects such as education and history, for instance the five-volume *Rise of the Christian Power in India*. As mentioned earlier, he also became the editor of the *Sacred Books of the Hindus* series. His study of Tantra is thus informed by a reformist, medical, and historical perspective that underlines the originality of his thought. He revered Swami Bhaskarananda of Benares—who had also initiated Bhudev Mukhopadhyay into Tantra—and had a photograph taken with him and Srishchandra.[129] In contrast to his brother, Bamandas took a significantly more critical stance toward Christianity and Islam, as his article in the *Theosophist* shows:

> Being considered as mystical works, the Tantras have not received that attention at the hands of Oriental scholars which their contents undoubtedly deserve. Though it is an undeniable fact that the magic and black arts form the chief topics in a Tantrik work, yet valuable information regarding the customs, manners, sciences, &c, of the Hindus during the Middle Ages, when groaning under the tyrannies of the Mohamedan rule, can be gathered from them when read between the lines.[130]

It appears that, according to Bamandas, an understanding of the Tantras would unearth wisdom that was lost due to a succession of conquest and oppression. For this reason, while praising the translation of his brother, Bamandas stressed that an "explanation of the Tantrik rituals and technical words" was necessary to grasp the meaning of the *Śiva Saṁhitā* and its "scientific truths." The yogis and Tantrics had gained knowledge of the nervous system through dissection, but the "language of the Tantras being too allegorical and too mystical to be understood by the uninitiated, it is very difficult to identify the *Nadis*, the *Chakras*, and the *Padmas* described in them." Bamandas claimed that they were identifiable by their description and mapped them on the nervous system, providing references to the *Śiva Saṁhitā* but also, in footnotes, to the *Ṣaṭcakranirūpaṇa* and the work of Ram Prasad.

The article deviates from Srishchandra's translation, which presents a six-chakra system plus the *sahasrāra*, whereas Bamandas placed a seventh chakra in the medulla oblongata, at the base of the brain, that is, below the sixth chakra instead of at the crown of the head. He associated the chakras with the nerve plexuses, which was a significant step in the development of modern yoga systems. This association was highly compatible with the mesmeric theories that emphasized the importance of the ganglia for interactions between a subtle and a material body through "fine" forces; this now became an integral point of reference for the explanation of yogic techniques. Notably, the association of the nervous system and the chakras is often traced to Vasant G. Rele's *Mysterious Kundalini* from 1927, which, however, appeared almost forty years after Bamandas's article and the introduction written by Srishchandra.[131]

Bamandas's article also contained a rebuttal of the earliest discussion of the chakras that had been made available to English readers in 1849, when the *Calcutta Review* published "Physical Errors of Hinduism." This prize essay had been written by Bipinbihari Shom, a Shudra who had attended the Free Church Institution in Calcutta. While he had not converted to Christianity, he was strongly anti-Brahmanical and directed his essay against the errors of the "Hindu Shastras," among which "the Tantras lie in the greatest obscurity," partly due to "the secret and impure natures of the rites which they teach," but also because of the widespread Puranic systems: "The Pandits of our country are for the most part either ignorant of this department of

Hinduism altogether, or they observe that secrecy which its doctrines require from them."[132] Shom summarized two Tantric theories that were illustrated by remarkable large illustrations: "The Tantric theory, on which the well known *yoga*, called Shat-chakra-bheda, is founded, supposes the existence of six main internal organs, called Chakras, or Padmas, all having general resemblance to that famous flower, the lotus. These are placed, one above the other, and connected by three imaginary chains, the emblems of the Ganges, the Jumna, and the Saraswati."[133] In addition to this six-chakra system, Shom described a ten-chakra system which he regarded as another "absurdity."[134]

The contrast to the Bengali intervention of the 1880s could hardly be more striking. It does not come as a surprise, then, that Bamandas referred to the author of this article as a "Hindu renegade" who, had he compared the chakras with the plexuses of modern anatomy, "would not have talked such nonsense."[135] Unlike the critics of Hindu medicine, and yoga or Tantra in particular, Bamandas stressed the scientific nature of this knowledge, a truth to which modern science could only aspire. He explained that the state of *samādhi*, far from being an absurd or superstitious notion, would be "the control of the sympathetic nervous system," the mastery over one's body after the spiritual nature of the practitioner had become dominant over the gross material aspects through *dhyāna* and *dhāraṇā*. Bamandas thus emphasized, "It behoves all students of Yoga and occultism then to gain a clear knowledge of these six *Chakras* from the contemplation of which he can aspire to attain to the stage of *Samādhi*."[136] Bamandas, then, not only directed polemics against Christian and Muslim influences but also presented Tantric yoga as a thoroughly scientific, esoteric practice that was of crucial importance for occultists.

The patterns that emerge in my analysis of these sources are strikingly consistent. Yoga was routinely framed by science and secrecy, aspects that were directly related to the supposed origins of Aryan civilization and its pristine wisdom that had to be revived. It was the ideas of Theosophists such as Blavatsky and Olcott that were most radically transformed in the process: rather than an export of Western esoteric ideas to India, we can observe how contributions by Indians, here especially Bengalis, actively shaped a prominent, complex discourse. The Bengali intervention left a deep impression on the discourse about yoga. For instance, the six-chakra system—which is first documented in the tenth- or eleventh-century *Kubjikāmata Tantra* but was one among many[137]—became established as the most common reference before Avalon cemented it as the de facto standard. The Bengali authors introduced concepts such as kundalini and the chakras, which became an integral part of understandings of yoga that remain influential up to the present day.

4
Reformism and Spiritualist Perspectives on Tantra

Since the 1880s, Theosophy was a key factor in Bengali debates about the role of Tantra in light of the relationship between religion and science. However, it was not the only movement discussed under the rubric of esotericism that played a role in this respect. This chapter will explore Spiritualism in Bengal and its ambiguous relationship with Theosophy. Both movements formed part of an ongoing discourse that voiced the ambition to merge "Western science" and "Eastern spirituality." There were other important factors that would be necessary for a comprehensive picture of that discourse, such as the extensive reception of Positivism in Bengal.[1] However, a comparison between Spiritualism and Theosophy is especially significant for our concerns, as Tantra featured prominently in both contexts.

It would be misleading to assume that Spiritualists and Theosophists formed two clearly distinguishable factions. Instead, they were determined by fluidities, overlaps, and tensions that can be discerned through a focus on central aspects in Spiritualist and Theosophical discourses: science, secrecy, colonialism, and the revival of Aryan dharma. These formed the conditions for the translingual practice of Bengalis who engaged with these discourses. Scholars have so far neglected Spiritualism in that regard, although Bengalis took up animated exchanges with North American and European Spiritualists, adherents of New Thought, and Transcendentalists in the years *before* the arrival of Theosophy in India. Even after the success of Theosophy, Spiritualism continued to thrive. Clearly, Indians not only engaged with Theosophy but also developed their ideas independent of it. Some kept the Society at a distance and were critical of the more conservative tendencies among Theosophists. These tendencies often aligned Theosophy with the "orthodox" camp, which will be further scrutinized in chapter 5; contrasting Theosophy with the Spiritualist milieu is an important prerequisite for understanding this complex situation.

Global Tantra. Julian Strube, Oxford University Press. © Oxford University Press 2022.
DOI: 10.1093/oso/9780197627112.003.0005

Pyarichand Mitra and Reformist Tantra

Spiritualism and an occupation with mesmerism had been popular in Bengal before the establishment of the Theosophical Society. Afterward there were Spiritualist and occultist individuals and groups in Bengal independent of the Theosophists, although they were often affiliated with them. Similar to the European and North American situation, overlaps and rivalries determined the relationship between such groups. The Theosophists were aware that they were not the first to introduce mesmerism into the educated circles at Calcutta. Olcott pointed out that a mesmeric hospital had been established by James Esdaile in Calcutta in 1846, under the patronage of Lord Dalhousie, the governor-general of India from 1848 to 1856, who is known for having introduced passenger trains, the electric telegraph, and uniform postage in India.[2] This was also acknowledged by Narendranath Sen as an important event.[3] Esdaile had been a civil assistant surgeon in Bengal and published a book, *Mesmerism in India,* in 1846, which was mainly concerned with defending mesmerism as a legitimate method of painless treatment. He maintained that the effects of mesmerism could be applied anywhere and that they had in fact been known and practiced in India since "remote antiquity."[4] Against the background of the orientalist scholarship that has been discussed in the first chapter, such an assessment is not surprising.

A range of sources attest to the popularity of mesmerism and Spiritualism among the Bengali intelligentsia. We learn from Bipinchandra Pal that Spiritualism "was much in vogue among some of our educated countrymen." According to him, the Brahmo leader Shivanath Shastri had been invited to a séance at the house of a friend in the 1860s and commenced to write automatically. After details of a family scandal he knew nothing about flowed out of his hands, he was so scared that he never practiced Spiritualism again.[5] As elsewhere across the globe, séances and other Spiritualist experiments or gatherings were very popular among the educated middle class and elite of Calcutta. The city produced some of the most renowned Spiritualists of India, including Pyarichand Mitra, the former member of Young Bengal and president of the Society for the Acquisition of General Knowledge. He was one of Bengal's most famous literati and had published, with *Ālāler gharer dulāl* (1855–1857/1858), a candidate for the "first Bengali novel," prior to Bankim's *Durgeśnandinī* (1865).[6]

In 1879, Pyarichand published *The Spiritual Stray Leaves,* a collection of short essays. The "critical notes" at the beginning of the book illustrate a lively correspondence with European and North American Spiritualists that predated the arrival of Theosophy. For instance, a letter from the leading American Spiritualist, Andrew Jackson Davis, lauded the first essay in the volume, "Psychology of the Aryas," as "exceedingly new and valuable, and I hope it will be widely circulated."[7] James Martin Peebles, another Spiritualist celebrity, regarded it as "excellent." Alfred E. Giles provided an extensive summary of and commentary on the pamphlet in the longest running and most important Spiritualist journal in the United States, *Banner of Light*, on March 31, 1877. He enthusiastically thanked the "native of Hindostan" for his significant insights that demonstrated the universal value of Spiritualism: "The essential identity of the religion or philosophy (for, go deep enough, religion and philosophy are one,) of the preeminent teachers of righteousness in all ages, and their re-statement in Christendom by Andrew Jackson Davis, when knowledge of them had become dim, we think appears also in the psychological teachings of the Aryas." This point had indeed been made by Pyarichand in his pamphlet, where the Vedas, Upanishads, the *Bhagavat Gītā*, and the Puranas are compared with European ideas ranging from Greek philosophy to Kant, Hegel, and Schelling: "The writings of some of the foreign metaphysicians are characterized by transcendentalism which remind us of the Arya train of thought."[8]

As Pyarichand explained, pondering the relationship between mind and matter was the basis of Aryan psychology, which ultimately led to the realization that mind could control matter. Such teachings could be found in ancient Egypt as well as in Persia: "The Sufees were Vedantists to the backbone," and "the doctrines of the New Platonists were tinged with Vedantism. Paul was thoroughly Vedantic in this teaching," and the same could be said about Hume and Fichte.[9] In his *Stray Thoughts on Spiritualism* from 1880, Pyarichand speculated that Hindus had come from the mouth of the Indus to Egypt and had spread their culture on the way: "The Chaldians, like the Egyptian priests and Aryas, were given to divination and occultism."[10] He was convinced that Aryan thought had promoted "spiritual culture," which, he stressed, was confirmed by Müller's observation that "the Aryas are the most spiritual of nations":[11] "It is thus evident that Inda [*sic*] was the cradle of spiritualism—the land where a deep conviction was entertained of the immortality of the the [*sic*] soul—of its returning to earth 'to sow righteousness and succour it' and of its endless progression in the spiritual world."[12]

We furthermore learn that mesmerism, electrobiology, and magnetism were not unknown to the ancient Aryans, who employed them during the

Vedic period.[13] In a chapter titled "Occultism and Spiritualism," Pyarichand points out that both of these sciences were "evolved by the will-force," but that occultism was only "partial" Spiritualism. He regarded Patanjali's *Yoga Sūtra* as "occultism or will-force developed to a high degree," but such methods would prepare the soul only for spiritual ascent. The acquisition of such power was in itself not sufficient for the attainment of "beatitude." Only the achievement of the "spiritual state" would lead to it, and this is what Spiritualism had to offer the individual.[14]

The practice of yoga was part of this process, but it was twofold: internal and external. Internal yoga consisted of "meditating quietly on the *invisible light* above and distinct from the brain in us," while external yoga was "the suppression of the breath and acquisition of supremacy over it." Both were complementary, as greater control over the body meant approaching "the soul region." This was the use of Spiritualism: "We have to raise ourselves on a non-molecular region."[15] Pyarichand emphasized that the "Arya philosophy" underlying this method was confirmed by "actual spiritual experience," and that for the previous sixteen years he had been "associated with spirits who are not away from me for a moment, and I am not only being spiritualised by them, but I am talking with them as I talk with those who are in flesh."[16]

Pyarichand clearly had his own ideas about the relationship between occultism and Spiritualism. This, however, did not motivate him to take an oppositional stance toward the Theosophists. Quite the contrary, he corresponded with both Olcott and Blavatsky in 1877 and was one of the driving forces behind the Theosophical relocation to India. On November 9, 1877, he wrote to Olcott—to whom he had sent his article "Psychology of Buddhist Aryans"—and let him know that he had submitted two papers to the *Spiritualist*, the oldest British journal of its kind. Interestingly, Pyarichand at the time had no hope for a branch of the Theosophical Society at Calcutta, as he complained that the only two "oriental scholars" in the city were Rajendralal Mitra, whom he regarded a materialist, and Reverend Banerjea, a Christian.[17] On December 12, 1877, Blavatsky lamented, "The Western world depends for its facts about the Orient upon missionaries, and civilians of various grades interested in supporting Christianity—the gigantic fraud of socalled 'civilized' nations." This resulted in "garbled facts," which is why she asserted, "Our work is to show the truth, and to do it, we count upon the help of our affiliated correspondents and the other native scholars whom they can enlist in the good cause."[18] Referring to Blavatsky's *Isis Unveiled* in a letter from February 6, 1878, Pyarichand reported that her work had not yet reached Calcutta but that he would make sure that it would be advertised in "native papers."[19] His enthusiasm for the Theosophical leaders' curiosity was expressed at the end of his *Stray Thoughts*, which once more underlines what united many Indians in their perception of Theosophy: "All honor also be to Brother Colonel Olcott and the venerable Madame Blavatsky for their most praiseworthy labors to prove that the West should receive light from the East, and not the East from the West."[20]

Pyarichand expressed his conviction that "[t]o understand the providence of God rightly, we must understand the soul. Theosophy is therefore the end—*yoga* and spiritualism are the means." He regarded this teaching as the essence of "Brāhma Dharma," and Brahmoism as a force next to Theosophy to diffuse it.[21] His reformist agenda, however, was more radical than that of other Bengali intellectuals, and it was closely tied to his praise of Spiritualism:

> It is not proper to teach Brahmoism alone from the Vedas, Upanishads, Puranas and Tantras. We must seek for it also in the Bible, the Koran, Zend-Avesta, and other sacred works. The true practice does not consist in merely changing the ritualism. How can we expect improvement unless we abolish caste, countenance the marriage of widows, intermarriages, prevent early marriages, promote female education and introduce females into society? Those who say these reforms will come in due time, speak vaguely, because until we take action in these matters, the evils will go on increasing. The investiture of a Brahman with sacred thread tends only to the perpetuation of bigotry and superstition.[22]

It is in this reformist, anti-Brahmanical sense that Pyarichand frequently referred to the Tantras. For instance, he invoked the *Mahānirvāṇa Tantra* as an authority for the improvement of women's rights.[23] Elsewhere he stressed that the "*Tantras* following the *Smritis* are equally, if not more, emphatic on the subject of woman."[24] Discussing the emergence of the worship of shakti during "the Mahommedan invasion," he wrote, "While the Tantrical practices were attended with abuse, they contributed to the elevation of the females by ennobling the *Sakti* principle in the estimation of men."[25]

The contrast to the positions of the Theosophical *Kalpa* authors is conspicuous, as the latter's stance toward the Brahmos illustrates. In the 1890s, the Brahmos had suffered from a steady decline in sociopolitical relevance, which was not least due to the success of the "revivalist" societies that will be the subject of the next chapter. The Bengali Theosophists' position on the Brahmos was somewhat ambiguous, as they shared some of the Brahmos' reformist convictions but insisted on the regeneration of the *sanātana dharma* rather than the creation of a new universal faith. In the *Kalpa* article that invoked the authority of the *Mahānirvāṇa Tantra*, the Brahmos are reprimanded for accusing traditional-minded Hindus of idolatry without understanding the ultimate insignificance of image-worship in the shastras.[26] One article even expected "the destruction of the Brāhma Samāj" by referring to an article in the Brahmo journal *Interpreter*, where it was lamented that more and more people would fall prey to sadhus, sannyasis, fakirs, and all kinds of religious charlatans. While the Brahmo author identified the lack of spiritual leadership and attention to matters spiritual within the Brāhma Samāj as the reason behind that, the *Kalpa* author had his own ideas: instead of getting agitated, the Brahmos would do well to read the documents published by the Theosophical Society, as they contained many a key to spiritual mysteries. This would lead to an understanding of the essence of Hindu dharma—and why would anyone wish to remain a Brahmo after that?[27]

While this implies shared goals and concerns between Bengali Theosophists, Brahmos, and an intellectual like Pyarichand, considerable differences emerge with respect to the question of caste. The Bengali Theosophists did not generally advocate for the abolition of caste distinctions. Quite the contrary, in his speech to the Bengal Theosophical Society, Rakhalchandra Sen attributed the degenerated present state of India not least to the dissolution of caste divisions. Similar to members of the Ārya Samāj, however, he did not perceive those divisions as rigid and insurmountable. Members of "lower" castes could elevate themselves to "higher" states through proper conduct of life. But while the ancient rishis had been able to raise Shudras from their Shudra-ness, the whole of India was now turning into a land of Shudras and *mlecchas* (savage foreigners). The only remedy was to learn the lessons of caste divisions from the Vedas and rejuvenate Vedic learning.[28] This is also underlined by a piece with the title "Hindu Dharma Is Entirely Liberal," wherein several examples are given of how people born into "low-caste" families were elevated to Brahmanhood.[29]

Another case in point is the status of women. In contrast to Pyarichand, who promoted the emancipation of women, the authors of *Kalpa* resolutely rejected "foreign" influences that worked toward that end. A reprint of an article by Nagendrabala Mustafi from the periodical *Bāmābodhinī Patrikā* questioned whether Hindu women of the past were really as unfree as present-day "enlightened," English-educated Hindu women thought. It even asked if the status of women in England had ever been superior to those in India and cited several examples that were intended to prove the opposite: not only were women held in high regard by Hindu kings, but they also benefited from an exceptional respect in Hindu scriptures and the life modeled after them. The respective standards, however, were rather conservative and consisted, first and foremost, in the ideal of chastity (*satītva*).[30] The author affirmed that the ideals for women should be sought in ancient India, not contemporary England.[31]

Another article polemicized against "civilized" Englishmen who were coming to India to provide Hindu men with "unsectarian" education, robbing them of the wisdom and customs of their forefathers. If Hindu dharma was still alive, it was thanks to Hindu *women* who had not yet been corrupted by secular education, due to the very fact that they had not received any. But their pristine attitude was under threat by "male-bashing free women" from the United States who had set up the Society for the Education and Liberation of the Women of India and plotted to convert Hindu women to Christianity. Hindu women should indeed be educated, but according to traditional ideals as embodied by Sita, Savitri, Mirabai, Gargi, Maitreyi, and others.[32] Another *Kalpa* author abhorred the consequences of the looming "new woman," who did not intend to stay under the control of men. Rather, she wanted to control her husband, with the most disgraceful outcomes: in Cincinnati, a husband had reportedly lodged a complaint in court against his wife, who forced him to do all kinds of household chores for one year and made him wear the clothes of servants. Other wives were even composing lists of dos and don'ts for their spouses.[33] Such were the outrageous outcomes of English education.

These issues of social reform highlight some differences between the position of Pyarichand and those of the contributors to *Kalpa*. With his Young Bengal background, Pyarichand was attracted to Spiritualism precisely because of its radical social reformist thrust, its advocacy of female emancipation, and the "democratic" practice of séances and other Spiritualist experiments, as opposed to the elitism of initiates that was propagated by the Theosophists. The Theosophical focus on *sanātana dharma* had a decisively conservative slant that strove for the revival of long-lost superior Aryan wisdom, although social reformist tendencies were by no means absent from Theosophy. This tension between what was considered tradition and reform also becomes tangible in the discussion of Tantra, which was presented as emancipatory by both the authors of *Kalpa* and Pyarichand, but with significantly different implications: while Pyarichand heralded the emancipation of women and disadvantaged castes, authors such as Baradakanta had in mind the emancipation of each individual practitioner, not so much in terms of social restructuring but in terms of attaining ultimate liberation through the realization of Brahman.

Yet, as Pyarichand's enthusiasm for Theosophy demonstrates, Spiritualism was not categorically separated from it. Rather, Spiritualist discourse in India took an idiosyncratic shape, while it engaged with both Spiritualist and Theosophical cohorts. A fixation on tradition (as in *sanātana dharma*) is largely absent from the ideas of Pyarichand. Like most Theosophists, however, he stressed the Aryan roots of true knowledge, which holistically comprised religion, science, and philosophy. While modern Western science had destructively dismantled that unity and indulged in gross materialism, "Hindu Spiritualism" supposedly employed scientific methods to elevate the individual spiritually. This was achieved through the practice of yoga, which Pyarichand divided into an "external" and "internal" practices: its occultist-practical aspect prepared the practitioner for the more advanced spiritual ascent. This division predated the Theosophical debates about yoga, which once more underscores that the Theosophists did not simply impose a Western understanding of yoga on local discourses.

Kshetrapal Chakravarti: "Tantra Is Science, Tantra Is Religion"

With these observations in mind, we can now turn to another important contribution to the debate about Tantra in the *Theosophist*. From October 1890 until January 1891, Kshetrapal Chakravarti (d. 1903) published an especially long series, "The Religious Aspects of the Early Tantras." Kshetrapal was the cofounder of the Baṅgīẏa Sāhitya Pariṣat·, the famous literary society that is still among the most eminent Bengali cultural institutions. Surprisingly little is known about this productive and quite influential writer. Even within the Pariṣat·, biographical information is scarce and limited to a short essay that admitted the incompleteness of its own account.[34] This might be due to the controversial circumstances under which Kshetrapal's links with the society were severed, highlighting the struggles for Bengali cultural identity that unfolded toward the end of the nineteenth century.

In 1873, Kshetrapal was among the first-year class of the Presidency College in Calcutta and had already made a name as an author for work published in several renowned reformist newspapers, including *Bāndhab*, *Sahacārī*, and the pioneering women's journal, *Baṅgamahilā*. After having a vision followed by an accident in his family in 1886, he immersed himself in the study of "Hindu dharma, philosophy, psychology, and yoga" (*hindudharmma, darśan, manobijñān o yog'śāstra*).[35] The result was the foundation of the Calcutta Psycho-Religious Society, which was later known as the Sri Chaitanya Yoga Sadhan Somaj. The young head of an old Calcutta family, maharaja Kumar Binaykrishna Dev Bahadur, became the patron of this society. In 1881, Kshetrapal published a newspaper article taking up the suggestion to create a Bengali literary society, which had originally been made in 1872 by the administrator and linguist John Beames, with the aim of "consolidating the language and giving it a certain uniformity, or in short, for creating a literary language."[36]

This project was finally realized on July 23, 1893, when Kshetrapal founded the Bengal Academy of Literature at the residence of Binaykrishna Dev in Calcutta's famous Shobhabazar neighborhood. Its cofounder was L. Liotard, a government official in the Indian Department of Revenue and Agriculture. Another leading figure in the society was Hirendranath Datt, an active Theosophist and later acquaintance of John Woodroffe.[37] The society published a periodical in English and Bengali, the *Bengal Academy of Literature*, which saw eleven numbers until June 1894. Kshetrapal contributed several pieces about Bengali dramas and the modern state of the Bengali language, which he regarded as disorderly and in urgent need of reform.[38]

The magazine's prominent use of English became the subject of controversial debates. The first to address this issue was the omnipresent Rajnarayan Basu, whose request to focus on the use of Bengali was acknowledged but ultimately dismissed by Kshetrapal and other members. After the matter had been discussed during the nineteenth meeting of the society, on December 24, 1893, the members "saw no reason to alter the existing practice."[39] This exchange between Rajnarayan and Kshetrapal was published in February 1894. It appears that the winds were changing, as it was declared in March that the journal's title would additionally be given as *Baṅgīya Sāhitya Pariṣad*, acknowledging the criticism of Rajnarayan and a more recent intervention from the magistrate and author Umeshchandra Batabyal.[40] More debates ensued in the following months, and the society was eventually reestablished as Baṅgīya Sāhitya Pariṣat·. Under its new president, Rameshchandra Datt, and vice presidents Rabindranath Tagore and Navinchandra Sen, the society developed into the highly influential cultural institution that we know today.

It appears that this refounded society cut its links with Kshetrapal, who had a rather antagonistic relationship with the literary world afterward. The fiery debates about the use of English or Bengali, but also Sanskrit, further demonstrate that the context in which Tantra was discussed by learned Bengalis toward the end of the nineteenth century was marked by struggles about Hindu identity and English education.[41] While neither Tantra nor yoga were brought up in the periodical of the Bengal Academy of Literature, its establishment followed Kshetrapal's efforts to propagate yoga as a means for national and religious regeneration, and it also coincides with a number of publications that he launched in the early 1890s. As in the cases of other Bengalis, the *Theosophist* was the first platform to disseminate his specific interpretation of Tantra. Apparently, the journal was now well established as a forum where such topics could be discussed freely.

In the issue of October 1890, Kshetrapal presented the early Tantrics as "students of nature" who, with impressive "intelligence and comprehensiveness," traced "the universe to one abstract force and expand the same to countless phases of life, intelligence and matter."[42] This focus on an impersonal force as object of worship was central to Kshetrapal's understanding of Tantra, which also was shaped by his Vaishnava background, already apparent in the name of his Sri Chaitanya Yoga Sadhan Somaj. Interestingly, he used the term "Vaishnavi Shakti" interchangeably with "Adya Sakti," which mirrored the practice of eulogizing Sita as shakti.[43] At the same time, Kshetrapal laid great emphasis on the impersonal character of shakti, an aspect that he elaborated in the second part of his article containing a criticism of both atheists and the worship of nature or a personal ("imaginary") God. Instead, "we find in the universe, a subtle, infinite, and almighty force in the atoms from which the earth and ultimately man *gradually evolved*."[44] Kshetrapal emphasized that the Tantrics had not rejected Vedic or Puranic teachings but examined and further elaborated them into a superior system. He paralleled this system with modern Spiritualism: "[I]n Tāntrik worship the woman is the most important factor, as she is made the subject or medium through whom the spirit is supposed to speak. The method of hypnotising individuals by passes, as is done in our days, was certainly not known to the Tāntriks of the ancient days, but they had their own method, which answered them admirably."[45] Through the use of wine and mantras (*bīja* and *japa*), the early Tantrics used to "magnetize" their "medium" during a "séance" and would set it "*en rapport* with the spirit invoked."[46]

Yet while "the power of woman" and her "fitness to mediumship" was thus first recognized in India by the Tantrics,[47] Kshetrapal pointed out central differences to modern Spiritualism: with regard to the "subjects" of Tantric worship, "the ancients of India invoke the souls of departed persons"; as for the "methods," they "as a rule looked more to their own psychic development than to physical manifestation"; and finally, their "objects" were "either temporal or spiritual, but in no case the mere satisfaction of curiosity or experiments to convince themselves or others of the existence of an after life." The attainment of siddhi was a central aim, but the "spiritual" achievement of "the union with the Deity" was the ultimate goal.[48] Kshetrapal sharply diverged from other discussions of Tantra through his explicit and positive depiction of transgressive ritual aspects. As he explained, man and woman were a "representation of Divine Love," and *sādhana* had consequently to be done in conjunction with both. The frankness with which the sexual element and ritual transgressions were discussed is remarkable:

> With the attainment of force they hope to rule, according to capacity, both the matter and the mind to the extent mentioned in the Tantras, irrespective of any distance of time and space. For public opinion they care not. Fear they have not. Uncleanliness and abomination, such as understood by the Hindus, are not to be found in their dictionaries. Fastings and penance they laugh at. Wine they require in moderate quantity to control the images of their mind, and woman to draw out their best nature at the time of Sadhana. At times their Sadhana flies off at a tangent and partakes the character of *Bir* (heroic) worship.[49]

This praise of the *vīra* (here Bengali *bīr*) mode of ritual practice sets Kshetrapal apart from those who wanted to downplay or philosophize the sexual element of Tantric worship, as well as the consumption of wine and other impure substances. He was careful to point out, however, that this should not be understood as licentiousness or arbitrariness, since the Tantrics distinguished between the few who "adhere strongly to religion" and the "vast mass" that was of a more changeable character: "It was in India and in India only that provisions of divers nature were advisedly made to suit different intellects and different dispositions."[50] Kshetrapal explained that this distinction led to different modes of worship, including forms for those whose inclinations were less ascetic:

> Thus when the Tantriks saw the people addicted to worldly pleasures, they sanctioned the pleasures, but at the same time inculcated a notion of worship in them. They gave them wine it is true, but they pointed out to them that it should only be used at the time of worship to concentrate their minds. They gave them woman, but they enjoined at the same time that she was the emblem of *Sukti* [shakti].[51]

Kshetrapal had presented a more extensive version of this paper at the general meeting of the Calcutta Psycho-Religious Society on May 30, 1890. In 1893, it was reprinted as a chapter in his collected *Lectures on Hindu Religion, Philosophy and Yoga*. This period marked his separation from the Baṅgīẏa Sāhitya Pariṣat·, which resulted in his ever-deeper immersion into the world of Spiritualism, New Thought, and Theosophy. It is no surprise that his commitment to yoga would lead him into the Theosophical debates revolving around its legitimacy. Yet when he published a leaflet in 1890 praising the benefits of Hatha Yoga, positive responses from the English press were not well received by some Theosophists. We find in the *Globe* of November 1, 1890, an angry letter by Walter Gorn Old (1864–1929), who had joined Blavatsky's Inner Group in London in August that year and held a number of high offices in the Society throughout the years, including that of the general secretary for England from 1890 to 1891.[52] In response to a positive note from October 30, which stated that Kshetrapal's leaflet suggested that there is more to the practice of yoga than "theosophical dilettantism," Old felt it necessary to clarify:

> [T]he Theosophical Society is in no way connected with the society to which you refer, either in its constitution or its objects; neither has Theosophy anything in common with the Hatha Yoga philosophy, which aims at the attainment of psychic and spiritual powers by certain physical restraints, such as swara (the breath) and asana (the posture). The effect of these methods upon the physical constitution is very deleterious, and the system has never been recognised as part of Theosophy, which is neither "theological dilettantism" nor Hatha Yoga, but the wisdom-religion of the ancient Sages, which underlies, as a basic truth, all the multiversant creeds and theologies of the past and present.[53]

This protest reflected the debates about Hatha and Raja Yoga. It is telling that Kshetrapal's Calcutta society was immediately perceived as a rival in that regard. Nevertheless, it is again impossible to draw a clear line between Theosophical positions and those of Kshetrapal, as his inclusion in the *Theosophist* conversation demonstrates. This is also reflected in his volume from 1893, where the content of the controversial leaflet is reprinted under the title "The Raj or Spiritual Yoga of the Hindus." It included a preface that stressed the preparatory function of Hatha Yoga, which had to be performed by the young yogi "before aspiring to Raj or the highest spiritual *yoga*."[54] Despite this new framing, the paper's main references still indicate the specific background of Kshetrapal's approach to yoga and Tantra: the *Śiva Saṁhitā* and the six chakras described in the *Mahānirvāṇa Tantra*.[55]

Kshetrapal also shared with other Bengali contributors to the *Theosophist* debate the conviction that Tantra was inherently scientific and, despite their many parallels, superior to modern science: "Unlike the scientists of the day who separate religion from science, these Tantriks sought nature to understand religion."[56] The ancient Tantrics had taught "the existence of a subtle force in man, known at present by the term 'animal-magnetism,'" and methods for using it.[57] As Kshetrapal put it, "*Tantra* is science, *Tantra* is religion."[58] However, he differed from other authors in his outright identification of Tantra with Spiritualism. According to him, the age of the Tantras had been

> the age of spiritualism—a word to be understood almost in the sense in which it is known at present in the West; for the elements comprising modern Spiritualism were not only understood and investigated, but were carried to a degree of success. We find in the *Tantras* directions for forming circles, for invoking high and low spirits, for automatic writings, and showing spirit-forms, &c., in mirror[s], and also directions for fascinating and hypnotising individuals. These all used to be done in a manner peculiar to India.[59]

Not only did Kshetrapal maintain that Spiritualism was not new to India, but he asserted that it had spread from India to "Egypt, Greece, Arabia, and China," which is why there was "not a subject now known in Europe and America in connection with Spiritualism which was not known before in India."[60] Moreover, Kshetrapal introduced a distinctly reformist thrust into his understanding of Tantra, which he outlined in a lecture, "On the Early Tantras of the Hindus," dedicated to Narendranath Sen "as a token of respect and gratitude."[61] Therein he stated that the age of the Tantras was "the age of reformation," which followed on the Brahmanical triumph over Buddhism in India. At that time, Tantrics allegedly took a stand against widespread corruption, after human selfishness had begotten "the corrupted rites, the false ideas, and the dogmatic tenets" that "led men to practise social abuses and crimes." Their task consisted "(1st) in collecting and arranging systematically the wisdoms of by-gone ages; (2nd) in purging whatever was considered unattainable and, false, whether in religion, science or politics; and (3rd) in imparting into these subjects fresh ideas and experience that appeared suitable to them."[62]

Similar to Pyarichand, Kshetrapal framed Tantra with a reformist program that aimed at rectifying social injustices. He also shared with him and Theosophical authors the conviction that Tantra was both religious and scientific and that it had spread from India to the rest of the world to form the basis of esoteric teachings. His activities underscore, however, that a Bengali intellectual did not have to go through Theosophical channels in order to discuss "occult phenomena" or the "occult sciences" in terms of Tantra. Like Pyarichand, Kshetrapal maintained close contacts to and exchanged extensive correspondence with Spiritualists and adherents of New Thought in the United States and Britain. These global connections underscore that the Theosophists did not have a monopoly in India.

Light of the East

The animated correspondence between Bengali, North American, and European intellectuals can also be observed in several English-language magazines that largely consisted of "exchanges" with publications such as the *Metaphysical Magazine* or *Progressive Thinker*. These periodicals were more inclined toward Spiritualism and New Thought, although they were generally not opposed to Theosophy. A notable example is *Light of the East*, which was published from September 1892 until April 1902 and bore the subtitle *A Hindu Magazine Devoted to Aryan Philosophy, Religions and Occultism*. Its editor, Sirishchandra Mukhopadhyay, later edited the *New Age* (Calcutta 1897–1901) and published editions of the *Mahābhārata* and *Bhagavad Gītā*. He also authored a Vaishnava work titled *The Imitation of Sreekrishna* (1894), in which he stressed that the practice of yoga was confirmed by modern science, particularly somnambulism and mesmerism.[63]

In the editorial of the first issue, we learn that Schopenhauer had predicted that the most remarkable event in the nineteenth century would be "the introduction of Aryan Religious Philosophy in the West." The triumph of science in the West had turned the attention of European thinkers to the "yet unexplored spiritual treasure of the East." The "sublime thinkers of Germany," dissatisfied with "the crude philosophy and material science of the West," were now looking to the Indian yogis for guidance. However, while those thinkers were influenced by "Hindoo Metaphysics," they had "failed to grasp its innermost essence, we mean, its practical side," as it could be discovered only through the sustained practice of yoga. Western physical science had been able to measure the "phenomenal aspects" of nature, but unlike the Indian rishis and yogis they were not capable of comprehending her "eternal truths," which Indians had achieved by virtue of their mastery of their "inner faculty, the faculty of hypersensual cognition." This method had been taught by "the great yogis" Jesus, Buddha, Shankara, Mohammed, and Chaitanya, all "glorious sons of Asia."[64] Consequently, the *Light of the East* declared its mission to be a mediator between the physics of the West and the "practical metaphysics" of the East, in order to set in motion an "inconceivable advancement of human knowledge."[65]

Obviously, the *Light of the East* expressed the same interests as their Theosophical counterparts, and the overall spirit appears to have been acknowledgment rather than adversity, as an approving reference to the journal in *Kalpa* confirms. Yet the affiliations of *Light of the East* were more strongly focused on authors such as Kshetrapal, who contributed pieces and clearly served as an important reference for the subjects of yoga and Tantra. His *Lectures* are positively reviewed, frequently promoted, and recommended for providing "a good deal of information regarding mystical subjects."[66] The journal proudly reproduced a note by Merwin-Marie Snell (1863–1921), the president of the scientific section of the World's Parliament of Religions, who lauded Kshetrapal's work especially for its "defence and exposition of the *Tantras*."[67] It also advertised for *The Yoga Shastras*, "as expounded in the Tantras" by an author who had taken on the name of the fourteenth-century Vedantist Madhvacharya. It explained the Tantras as "works on Mysticism for the development of psychic powers latent in man," for which yoga was the "stepping stone," a doctrine that was shared by Jesus Christ, Buddha, and Shankara, before Patanjali had systematized that "science."[68] In September 1895, the editors expressed their content with the great success of their journal, which was, according to them, "the only Hindu magazine treating of the various phases of Hindu Orthodoxy."[69]

Part of that "orthodoxy" was the Tantras, which are defended against criticism: "At the present time all the rites and ceremonies of Hinduism are guided by the injunctions of the Tantras and yet there is a deep-rooted belief in the mind of educated men that the greater part of the Tantras deal with black magic, mesmerism and kindred subject[s]." Such belief was due to a misunderstanding of the nature of the Tantras. They were intended for the Kali Yuga, when the vast majority of humankind was not able "to grasp the inner meaning of the sublime truths which lie hidden behind the esoteric garb of the Upanishads." The Tantras were of no use for those who could appreciate and admire the "high spirituality" of the Vedanta, but they were composed for those who still needed an element of "the pleasure of the senses" in religion.[70]

Such ideas had already been expressed in a series of articles called "Philosophy of the Tantras," penned by the manager of the *Light of the East*, Adharchandra Mitra. The series ran from December 1892 until March 1893, before it had to be canceled due to "circumstances of a private character" that compelled Adharchandra to cut off all connection with the journal, apparently on friendly terms.[71] In the published installments, Adharchandra was primarily concerned with establishing the fundamental unity of Vedanta and Tantra. He explained that, in the degenerate days of the Kali Yuga, the Hindu Shastras were violated by Western science and thought every moment of the day. The cornerstone of the Tantras was the prescription of "Karma Yoga," which Adharchandra contrasted with Hatha Yoga.[72] Unlike the opposition between Raja and Hatha Yoga that we have encountered within Theosophical debates, however, Hatha Yoga was rejected because it was thought to be too demanding for the short-lived men of the Kali Yuga. Karma Yoga revolved around proper conduct of life, with the aim of "spiritualizing" the practitioner. This was explained with reference to the *Mahānirvāṇa Tantra*, but also in a neighboring series of articles that explored the meaning of karma in the *Bhagavad Gītā*.[73]

Adharchandra put great emphasis on the necessity of keeping Tantric teachings secret. The religion appropriate for the Kali Yuga "must not preach openly the highest philosophy of the Vedantic doctrines." Instead, the disciple "must be initiated in the mystery by his *Guru* whose word will be the law to him," and he must observe "absolute *secrecy* in the mode of worship," which should be suited to the temperament of each individual, while making sure that this does not "clash against the social interests of the disciple." The religion must provide the "easiest and shortest path to *Mukti*" and promise the attainment of "*definite powers*" (*siddhi*). But it should also have bhakti as its "corner-stone" and make sure that every disciple adopts a "*personal* god" that suits his temperament.[74] Because of "false prophets," the Tantras had fallen into disrepute, as superficial inquirers had not been "initiated" into the "esoteric explanations" necessary to grasp their meaning.[75]

Adharchandra asserted that the philosophy of the Tantras was essentially that of the Upanishads, and that it was specifically designed for the realization of the Vedantic conception of an attributeless (*nirguṇa*) Brahman.[76] Like "all true religions" formed by "inspired men like the rishis," the Tantras taught the attainment of perpetual bliss and were aimed at rescuing the human mind from the clutches of materialism.[77] Through yogic practice, the consciousness of the gross or visible body (*sthūla śarīra*) could be withdrawn into the subtle body (*sūkṣma śarīra*) before it being absorbed into the universal mind, leading to liberation while living (*jīvanmukti*).[78] Yoga was thus a "process of spiritual purification" that required not only initiation but also hard practical work. This also pertained to the *pañcamakāra*, which disclosed "very highly spiritual interpretation, and at the same time are stern realities and have not the least shade of ambiguity."[79] The reason behind that was the "double aspect" of yoga, which, similar to Kshetrapal's description, was differentiated into "*bahir-yoga* or external worship" and "*antar-yoga* or internal worship."[80]

According to Adharchandra, Tantra encompassed both the realization of the (Vedantic) attributeless Brahman and highlighted the need of (Vaishnava) bhakti for spiritual progress. Its "practical" nature made it vastly superior to both speculative Western philosophy and Western scientific materialism. In that regard, it shared its core teachings with other "great religions," but it would be understood only after proper initiation, dedication to a guru, and the strict keeping of secrecy. We can see how this discussion of Tantra largely overlaps with the examples discussed so far. What is new is the emphasis on Vaishnavism, which we could similarly observe in Kshetrapal's writings. This relationship between Bengali Vaishnavism and Tantra is even more prominent in the thought of one of the most significant Vaishnava authors of the late nineteenth century.

Shishirkumar Ghosh and the *Hindu Spiritual Magazine*

Shishirkumar Ghosh (1840–1911) is an exceptionally influential example of the intersections between Theosophy, Spiritualism, and both Hindu reformism and revivalism. Born in Jessore, the district neighboring Nadiya, Shishir was an assiduous anticolonial author who began his journalistic career in the late 1850s, when he reported about the poor working conditions of indigo farmers. In 1868, Shishir and his brother Hemanta started the Bengali newspaper *Amṛta Bāzār Patrikā*, which became known for its anticolonial stance and was swiftly prosecuted for criminal defamation. Shishir was first drawn to the Brahmos. A self-fashioned agnostic, he championed social reform and, in 1875, founded the Indian League in Calcutta that strove for the stimulation of a sense of nationalism among the larger population and the encouragement of political education.[81] Around that time, Shishir developed an interest in Spiritualism and was provided with literature on "occult science" by Pyarichand.[82] Deeply impressed, he began to conduct séances—which he believed to be the first "on American principles" in India—and enthusiastically propagated them among his fellow Indians.[83] He quickly established contact with the Theosophists upon their arrival and joined the Society as the second member from Calcutta, on August 13, 1879.[84] It is telling that this period saw him turn away from his Brahmo leanings and become a vocal proponent of Vaishnavism. In the early 1880s, he began to propagate bhakti and retired from active politics. He also ceased the editorship of the *Patrikā*, which had already developed close links to conservative Hindu politics.

Varuni Bhatia has demonstrated that Shishir understood bhakti not only as individual devotion but as love for the homeland (*deś-bhakti*). He and his publishing house, the Amrita Bazar Patrika Press, played a formative role in the process of reframing and popularizing Chaitanya, the famous Bengali Vaishnava, among English-educated Hindus.[85] As Bhatia notes, this trajectory "from a firebrand journalist to an anticolonial organizer to a spiritualist, from a reformist Hindu to an orthodox Vaiṣṇava who adopts severely conservative stances on Hindu social and religious matters," is illustrative of broader contemporary trends. Shishir's interest in Spiritualism and Theosophy exemplifies "both the radical potential inherent in nineteenth-century antinomian movements and their protagonists, such as Euro-American spiritualists and transcendentalists, as well as its limits." Such limits were especially reached within the context of colonialism and its racial hierarchies and power dynamics.[86]

Significantly, Shishir's occupation with Brahmoism, Theosophy, and Spiritualism allowed him to engage with Vaishnava texts and "draw correspondences between *bhakti* as a specifically Vaiṣṇava affect of intimacy to one's chosen God and *bhakti* as a peculiarly Hindu manifestation of the universal phenomenon of religious experience."[87] These ideas were prominently expressed in Shishir's successful six-volume hagiography of Chaitanya, *Śrī amiẏa nimāi carita*, which he published from 1885 until 1910. Therein, he identified Bengal with the figure of Chaitanya itself, thus using the medieval thinker to assert national sentiments and Hindu identity.[88] In his prefaces, he presented anticolonial nationalism through bhakti as a collective of the weak and the emasculated against a masculine colonizing authority.[89] Vaishnava bhakti, then, was a means to asserting a specific Bengali cultural identity and consolidating anticolonial opposition. These ideas were propagated by Shishir in Bengali and in a wide range of English publications, including a two-volume version of his hagiography of Chaitanya, titled *Lord Gauranga* (1897–1898), another name for Chaitanya.[90]

Beginning in 1906, Shishir edited the *Hindu Spiritual Magazine*, which continued to be published at least until 1918.[91] It maintained close contacts with American Spiritualists, especially the circles around Peebles, and often referred to the *Progressive Thinker*, but also to the London Spiritualist journal *Light*. There were also manifest links to the South Indian group known as Latent Light Culture, which was based in Tinnevelly Bridge. Several members contributed articles dealing with the subject of occultism.[92] In the editorial of the first issue of his magazine, Shishir explained, "The object of the 'Hindu Spiritual Magazine' is to disseminate spiritual truths known in this ancient country but little known in the West, and those truths of the West which are similarly little known in the East. The Theosophists have done much to carry out this idea, but there is yet work for others."[93] He proudly reproduced a letter by Yatindramohan Tagore, in whose house Olcott had stayed when first arriving in Calcutta and where the Bengal Theosophical Society had been established. Stating that he could not think of a better "Hindu gentleman" to edit a magazine of this kind, Yatindramohan wrote that it "will certainly meet a want that has long been sadly felt, and will, I am sure, be hailed with joy by every one who feels a craving for occult knowledge and spiritual research." Shishir had so far been chiefly known as a "political character," but after publishing "so many religious works breathing deeply of devotional feelings and high spirituality," he should be even more widely known in connection with "spiritual culture."[94] This would be of great benefit, since the *Hindu Spiritual Magazine* (unlike Theosophical publications) would be mainly devoted to psychical research, "the greatest and most important subject that can engage the attention of man."[95] It might be surmised that this praise of psychical research was an outcome of the Mahatma letters scandal of the 1890s, which had discredited Theosophy in the eyes of many and certainly fueled occupations with other currents such as Spiritualism and New Thought.

In a series about "how Spiritualism came to India," Shishir provided an informative account of his personal history with Spiritualism. He explained that one of his seven brothers had committed suicide, which he attributed to "morbid religious feelings": "He had imbibed methodistical doctrines from the Brahmoism of those days which largely drew its instincts from Christian methodism. Our brother felt that he had committed [a] sin and would commit more as he grew up and that his best course would be to put an end to his life."[96] His faith in God was deeply shaken by this incident. But soon the family learned that "the Americans had discovered a way to open communication with the dead, and that they had published some books on the subject": "I had then no knowledge that India had also a large number of good books on similar subjects." After having received relevant tomes from Pyarichand, who worked as a librarian at the Calcutta Public Library, Shishir began to conduct séances and successfully established contact with his deceased brother. Shishir and his family quickly realized that this Spiritualist method had long been known in India; the raja of Krishnagar, Krishnachandra, had employed the service of an Indian medium in order to contact Lord Gauranga "more than a hundred years ago, long before the Fox family, the founders of modern spiritualism, came into existence."[97] In fact, the successful communication with the spirit world had long been proved in India by the deliberate separation of the "material body" and the "spiritual sense": "The Hindu, by the wonderful process called Yoga, for the first time disclosed to the outside world by Madame Blavatsky and her followers, the theosophists, succeeded in stepping out of the material body."[98]

Shishir's harsh criticism of Brahmoism stands in stark contrast to his advocacy of Spiritualism and his appreciation for Theosophy. While he renounced his former Brahmo leanings, his propagation of Bengali Vaishnavism appears to have gone hand in hand with Spiritualism. He welcomed Western efforts to counter materialism and engage Indian thought, but he also portrayed Western Spiritualist teachings and methods as inferior to the more ancient "Hindu" doctrines. In fact, the "rediscovery" of Indian Spiritualism appears to have been part of Shishir's anticolonial project. He pointed out that, despite "the *tornado* of the political life that we and our brothers had to lead," their belief in Spiritualism remained strong.[99] He described how countless Spiritualist circles were formed, featuring many well-known and respected persons.[100] Such activities were actively encouraged, for instance when the fifth issue of the *Hindu Spiritual Magazine*, from July 1906, provided instructions on "how to hold spiritual circles."[101] Clearly, the practice of Indian Spiritualism was regarded as an integral part of the propagation of Vaishnavism and its anticolonial thrust.

The *Hindu Spiritual Magazine* should consequently be viewed in an outspokenly political context. From such a perspective, it is especially remarkable that it featured several articles on Tantra and did not even shy away from an expanded discussion of the transgressive ritual of *śāvasādhanā*, which involved meditation on a corpse. This practice was praised for its "theurgic value" by its author, Ratneswar Chatterjee, a lawyer, and accompanied by an impressive painting in his possession.[102] Most striking, however, are two long article series about Tantra, which are probably the most extensive of their kind in any contemporary periodical.

The first was penned by Swami Dharmananda Mahabharati, who is most likely identical with the provincial secretary of West Bengal in Berhampore listed in the report of the thirteenth annual convention of the Indian Section of the Theosophical Society.[103] He published extensively in the journal *Kalpaka*, the mouthpiece of the Latent Light Culture, and also authored *The Yogi and His Message*, wherein he praised Jesus Christ as "the ideal yogi."[104] Beginning in September 1907, Dharmananda explained that the Tantras formed part of the Hindu Shastras. He recognized both conservative and reformist potential in those scriptures, as they were characterized "both by astute conservatism or bigotry on one hand, and that breadth and catholicity on the other," the latter being typical of Hindu thought.[105] Dharmananda regarded the Tantras as "an encyclopaedia of arts and sciences, both material and spiritual."[106] He provided a very instructive overview of popular Tantras in contemporary Bengal, in which he highlighted the *Mahānirvāṇa Tantra* was as "the most spiritual."[107]

According to Dharmananda, the Tantras were useful guides for different kinds of spirits, which made them valuable for Spiritualists.[108] But their most important and most scientific subject was the anatomy of the human body and its relation to the mind, as taught through the six chakras (*ṣaṭcakra*).

Similar to Bamandas Basu, Dharmananda praised this system as vastly superior to modern Western anatomy.[109] It employed "personal magnetism"[110] as well as electricity in a way that was "more easy and more scientific than that of the skilled medical authorities of the West."[111] As a "grand occult science of the Hindoos," Tantra was thoroughly practical rather than theoretical. And the ritual practice of *sādhana* stood at its center.[112] But the rigid requirements for its performance were not suited to everyone, and proper initiation was the only way to ascertain that suitability: "The practical side of Tantra, which is most essential and at the same time esoteric or hidden, must be learnt from the blessed mouth of the *gooroo* or spiritual guide."[113]

Interestingly, Dharmananda, similar to Shishir, regarded Vaishnava bhakti as superior to Tantra, although he emphasized that his own guru "made no distinction between a true Vaisnava and a true Tantrik."[114] He also stressed that "Tantrik Yogees" were often condemned for unjust reasons, out of ignorance—an argument that Dharmananda supported with a reference to the unbelief of Jews toward Jesus Christ.[115] The maintenance of its particular "spiritual truth" was a duty for each nation, as it was for every individual.[116] This once more highlights the relevance of Tantra for factional and national identities.

Beginning in September 1910, the *Hindu Spiritual Magazine* published an even longer article series on Tantra, which, with well over twenty installments, was the most extensive of its kind. It propagated an understanding that paralleled that of Dharmananda, but it also differed from it in some significant respects. It was written by Srimat Sachchidananda Swami, who appears to have had links to the Theosophical Society. Some of the series' content had been published in the *Theosophist* contribution by T.S. in 1883.[117] Sachchidananda was a prolific writer on Tantra and published a seven-volume work titled *Sanātan sādhan'tattva bā tantra-rahasya* (*The Eternal Principles of Sadhana, or The Secrets of Tantra*).[118] These volumes contain several illustrations that have most likely been drawn by the same artists as the article on *śāvasādhanā* in the *Hindu Spiritual Magazine*, which suggests a possible link between Sachchidananda and the author Ratneswar Chatterjee. In any case, Sachchidananda's work ran through several editions and was widely received, not least by Woodroffe, who invoked its authority in *Shakti and Shakta*.[119]

As the title suggests, *Sanātan sādhan'tattva bā tantra-rahasya* revolves around the notion of *sanātana dharma*, which is made explicit in the very first sentences of the book: "The Aryan dharma is the world's oldest true dharma [*satyadharmma*]. It is eternal and indestructible; for this reason, it is widely known as 'sanātandharmma.' "[120] Tantra, we learn, was revealed specifically to meet the needs of the Kali Yuga. Sachchidananda repeatedly emphasized that Shaktas, Vaishnavas, Shaivas, as well as the worshippers of Surya and Ganesha all followed legitimate paths, but that at the root of everything lay the realization of shakti as the only means to liberation.[121] Brahmans would engage in Tantric worship in secrecy and, in the modern age, kept their secrets as strictly as members of a Freemason's lodge—another instance of that widespread comparison.[122]

The core of Tantric teachings was formed by the dharma of the Kaulas (*kuladharmma*), who taught that the dharma of the Goddess or Mother was not only the most complete and best but also all-encompassing (*sarbbadharmma*). All dharmas of the world formed part of it, including Brahmans and Shudras; Shaktas and Vaishnavas; Aryas, non-Aryas, and Mlecchas; as well as Christians, Buddhists, and Jains: they were particular manifestations of what Sachchidananda called the Universal Worship (*sārbbajanīn dharmmānuṣṭhān*).[123] This idea was further developed in an English booklet with the title *Universal Worship and Equality*, in which Sachchidananda praised Chaitanya and Nanak as "reformers."[124] In his Bengali books, he declared that it was the Kaula dharma, as the essence of the Vedas, that lay at the root of all these particular religions.[125] Remarkably, Sachchidananda explained that the Theosophical Society (*tattva-sabhā*), as well as Masonic lodges, had understood that principle by admitting Hindus, Muslims, Brahmos, Christians, and others alike. This led him to propose that one could, in fact, talk about Aryan Kaula communities (*kaulacakra*) as "ancient Vedic lodges." The ideal of the Masonic "brother" and the principle of universal brotherhood consequently had their roots in Tantra.[126]

Sachchidananda regarded Tantra as the "fifth Veda" that mainly dealt with practical matters and focused on ritual practice, *sādhana*.[127] This was the focus of his series "Theory and Practice of Tantra" for the *Hindu Spiritual Magazine*, which was introduced by a definition that highlights Tantra as "the essence of the Vedas," as a psychological and physiological science, as well as decidedly "mystical."[128] According to Sachchidananda, the word "Tantra" had various shades of meaning, "all bearing the general sense of secret knowledge or esoteric lore."[129] In contrast to Dharmananda, he did not regard it as distinct from or even opposed to bhakti: "The spiritual character in Tantrik rites is the product of anxious work and *Bhakti* or devotion."[130] As a comprehensive compendium of knowledge, Tantra contains "speculative philosophy, religion, science, polity and occultism."[131] However, is was misunderstood due to the "moral and spiritual degeneration" of the Indian people.[132] False gurus would nowadays pose with sandal-paste-smeared foreheads and tridents, accompanied by unfortunate women. They indulged in the practice of *pañcamakāra* and were interested only in lust and money.[133] This outbreak of "Guruism" was the cause of great ruin and resulted in widespread misinterpretation of Tantric texts. Due to a lack of proper initiation into their esoteric meaning, they were erroneously taken literally.[134]

Sachchidananda professed that the phenomena of Tantra were entirely scientific and operated through "personal magnetism," which was "the main factor in the realisation of Divine Energy."[135] This method operated on the basis of scientific laws, for instance with regard to "mental magnetism stored up in [the practitioner's] brain battery."[136] Such energy could be harnessed and cultivated by means of the practice of pranayama and the flow of energy through the six chakras.[137] This would develop the nervous system and lead to an increase of the mind's power, which would become a veritable "battery of force."[138]

Western science would begin to extend its research in order to understand such processes, as the works of Herbert Spencer illustrated.[139] But it was a far cry from the wisdom of the Tantrics, who "dealt with physical sciences as are taught to-day," while Western science had "reached the present knowledge but very recently."[140] Consequently, the West would now look to the East for spiritual explanations, which, although it was in a feeble state: "To speak the truth, the East is now a copy of the West—a copy spoiled and disfigured by touches of selfishness and vanity." The development of the "mental organism" was thus a strenuous task in this purely materialistic age:

> [I]t appears to us that the condition of the Hindu is not hopeless yet. The mere fact that a spiritual Hindu still exists goes to prove it. A few years of well-directed efforts should suffice to revert to the culture of spirituality. But there is not time to waste, and we want workers, such as the late Mahatma Shishir Kumar Ghose was, and let them be really in earnest.[141]

Sachchidananda's discussion of Tantra reveals instructive differences from the series by Dharmananda. For instance, Sachchidananda did not separate ritual practice and bhakti, as both were inherently intertwined for him. His identification of Vaishnavism with "Tantrism" was significantly more unequivocal. However, both authors agreed on the high antiquity of Tantra, with

Sachchidananda even claiming that Tantra formed the basis of Universal Worship and drawing parallels to Theosophy and Freemasonry. Moreover, both authors regarded Tantra as a nonmaterialistic yet practical science that would lead to the spiritualization of the individual practitioner and even of the nation as a whole. Despite their invocation of ancient Aryan wisdom and *sanātana dharma*, both authors were explicitly reformist in outlook, with Dharmananda decrying conservatism and bigotry, and Sachchidananda praising the greatest teachers of humanity as "reformers." Once more, the lines between categories such as revivalism and reform are blurred, as these authors saw no contradiction between propagating *sanātana dharma* and denouncing the West as inferior to Eastern "scientific spirituality," while at the same time encouraging reform and positively engaging with Western thought.

The different viewpoints discussed in this chapter demonstrate how creatively and independently local actors engaged with Spiritualism, New Thought, and Theosophy against their own backgrounds.[142] Theosophical and Spiritualist journals functioned as nodal points for negotiations of the meaning of dharma and the relationship between Western education and Indian learning, not only on the level of personal networks and as a platform of communication but also through the criticism of the West voiced by actors such as Blavatsky. Her self-proclaimed disdain for the "so-called civilized nations" resulted from the conviction that the West had been corrupted by materialism, unbelief, and ignorance of esoteric truth. From such a perspective—which was shared by virtually all actors who moved within the circles of Theosophy and Spiritualism, Western or Indian—the revival of India would lead to the regeneration of the whole world. What "revival" was supposed to signify, however, was very much open for debate.

5
Revivalism and Theosophy

We have seen that actors from across the intellectual spectrum invoked the glory of ancient India and proclaimed its revival in terms that could be identified as both reformist and traditionalist. In most cases, this went hand in hand with an insistence on orthodoxy; however, how to define orthodoxy was hotly contested. In both Spiritualist and Theosophical circles, the revival of Aryan *sanātana dharma* was as much an integral part of discourse as in the blurry fields of revivalism and reformism. Yet the previous chapter demonstrated that certain Spiritualist perspectives on Tantra put a stronger emphasis, for instance, on female rights and the abolishment of caste hierarchies than was common among Bengali Theosophists and their Western partners. Not least for this reason, contemporaries usually situated Theosophy within the revivalist, orthodox camp.

This somewhat confusing situation necessitates an examination of how historical actors employed "revivalist" notions of *sanātana dharma*, what role Tantra played within these discourses, and how Theosophy can be situated in the unstable and heterogeneous landscape of so-called orthodox movements. First, this chapter will shed some light on the most prominent of all authorities in the discourses that have been observed so far, the *Mahānirvāṇa Tantra*. Its case allows for a diachronic perspective on the ambiguity of reform and revival stretching back to the eighteenth century; the *Mahānirvāṇa* is an outstanding example of how authority could be claimed through antiquity, tradition, and exclusive orthodoxy, while at the same time addressing issues of sex and caste that were eagerly taken up by nineteenth-century reformers.

Reform through the Authority of Antiquity: The *Mahānirvāṇa Tantra*

The *Mahānirvāṇa* was invoked as a major, if not the chief authority by virtually all actors who have been discussed so far. Rajnarayan Basu referred to it

Global Tantra. Julian Strube, Oxford University Press. © Oxford University Press 2022.
DOI: 10.1093/oso/9780197627112.003.0006

as "the best" of all Tantras,[1] while T.S. stressed that it was "the earliest, and is regarded by the *Tantrikas* as the most important of all."[2] In February 1889, the *Theosophist* even published a partial translation, which was possibly a follow-up to a discussion of the text in June 1886.[3] It is certainly the most frequently cited Tantra in Bengal, with Dharmananda stressing that it was "the most widely known" and "most largely published."[4] Its translation was the first publication by Avalon in 1913, which cemented its status as one of the most important Tantras in Bengal, if not the most important one.[5]

Although its proponents stressed the high antiquity of the *Mahānirvāṇa*, it was most likely composed in the second half of the eighteenth century and thus falls into the early colonial period.[6] Its philosophical and practical orientation is overtly Kaula, going as far as to declare that the *kula dharma* was the true and eternal dharma, the *satyadharma* and *sanātana dharma*.[7] This is based on the assumption—already expressed in the *Kulārṇava Tantra* and frequently highlighted by our Bengali authors—that Tantra is the mode of worship suitable for the Kali Yuga, whose inhabitants are not capable of adhering to the strict rites of the Vedas.[8] Consequently, Tantra is understood as the only path to liberation, not in opposition to the Vedas but as the revelation of their true core, as it was appropriate for the Kali Yuga.[9] This positioned the *Mahānirvāṇa* as a direct rival to Gaudiya Vaishnavism, which claimed that Chaitanya was the avatar of Vishnu in the Kali Yuga.[10]

The text is directed at Tantric initiates under the direction of a teacher (*kulācārya*). The more transgressive aspects of Tantra, most notably the "five Ms" (*pañcamakāra*), are discussed in a rather cursory manner. However, it would be somewhat misleading to perceive the *Mahānirvāṇa* as presenting a recently "sanitized" version of Tantra.[11] As mentioned earlier, the philosophical abstraction of Tantric rites and the substitution of impure elements such as alcohol, meat, and sexual intercourse was prevalent since the emergence of tenth-century Kashmir Shaivism, represented most prominently by Abhinavagupta.[12] It is thus inherently intertwined with the spread of Brahmanical culture in Bengal and its particular combination of Tantric and *smārta* lineages, rather than a modern attempt at sanitization. It is also important to note that the *Mahānirvāṇa*, like older Tantras, stressed the personal qualification (*adhikāra*) of the practitioner. Unlike the most advanced types of practitioners, *vīra* and *divya*, the lowest type of *paśu* was entirely unqualified for transgressive rites such as the consumption of alcohol, since he (the practitioner was assumed to be male) was neither capable of realizing the profound unity behind the illusionary distinction between pure and impure nor of controlling his desires and impulses.[13]

The *Mahānirvāṇa* maintains that there are only two rather than four stages of life (*āśrama*) in the Kali Yuga, namely that of the householder (*gṛhastha*) and the ascetic (*saṃnyāsin*). In contrast to Brahmanical norms, everyone can become an ascetic, not only Brahmans.[14] Notably, an ascetic is not bound to Brahmanical restrictions of food and caste, even outside of the Tantric ritual circle (*cakra*).[15] However, the *Mahānirvāṇa* prescribes substitutes for householders, for instance milk, sugar, and honey for alcohol. Instead of sexual union, the householder is supposed to meditate on the Goddess.[16] Even a *vīra* is allowed to have sexual intercourse only with his legal wife. If these prescriptions are followed, liberation (*mokṣa*) is possible within the material world (*jīvanmukti*), which is recognized as a manifestation of the Absolute and as ultimately identical with it. The practitioner is able to deify his body through the realization of the Absolute by means of the activation of the chakras and the awakening of the kundalini.[17]

While Goudriaan and Sanjukta Gupta noted that the scripture's ethical rules "breathe a conservative, upper middle class spirit,"[18] Urban has argued that it is marked by a significant "reformist agenda."[19] Such contradictory perceptions can be explained by the ambivalences within the text, which become plausible against the background of seventeenth-century Bengali Brahmanical culture. On the one hand, the text reproduces notions that are typical for Kaula practice. For instance, restrictions of caste and sex, and even religious differences are relaxed within the ritual setting of the *kulacakra*. It is possible for caste-less (*caṇḍālas*), Muslims and generally non-Hindus (*mlecchas*), and women to be initiated.[20] Outside of the *kulacakra*, however, caste norms (*varṇāśramadharma*) must not be violated.[21] On the other hand, more openly reformist tendencies manifest in the rejection of *sati*, the burning of widows.[22] Some of its legal prescriptions show influences of Muslim and even British law, which underscores that the Brahmanical analysis of dharma was anything but isolated from outside influences.[23] The *Mahānirvāṇa* should therefore be located within the social, political, and legal situation of early colonial Bengal.[24] Similar to the reception of Raghunandan at the end of the eighteenth century, it represents a harmonization of Tantra and *smārta* Brahmanical learning, denoting positions on "caste" (*varṇa*) and law that are typical for the Bengal School.[25]

The *Mahānirvāṇa Tantra* was very popular among the bhadralok and notably also within the Brāhma Samāj. The guru of Rammohan

Roy, Hariharananda Bharati, had written a commentary to the text, and Rammohan himself held it in high esteem.[26] Hence it is no surprise that the first edition of the text was published under the auspices of the Ādi Brāhma Samāj in 1876, based on three manuscripts, including one owned by Rammohan.[27] Urban has aptly explained the great appeal of the *Mahānirvāṇa* for reformers, with its claim to reveal ancient esoteric knowledge that is appropriate for the last phase of the Kali Yuga. It characterized Brahman as an impersonal Absolute; it contained a narrative of degeneration from the Golden Age; it displayed an ambivalent position toward the caste system; and it addressed legal issues such as marriage, inheritance, and the rights of non-Brahmans. The scripture thus offered a solution to the contradiction to the past golden age of India and the perceived flaws of modern Hinduism.[28]

Yet part of the *Mahānirvāṇa*'s success must also be the long-standing regional combination of *dharmaśāstra*, *smṛti*, and Tantra. In this light, the crucial point is not that the text was most likely an eighteenth-century production, although it claimed to be of old age.[29] It did formulate new doctrines, but within the established context of Tantric Brahmanical culture in Bengal, and by doing so it played into the extensive process of the renovation and reinterpretation of Shaiva-Shakta traditions since the end of the eighteenth century. Similar to the language of a "Shakta revival" during that period (which I discussed in chapter 1), it would be misleading to assume that this implied the restoration of an ancient purity. Rather, it was the expression of complex renegotiations that further unfolded throughout the nineteenth century.

Struggles about the Meaning of Revival and Reform

In the decades leading up to the end of the nineteenth century, a great number of self-consciously "traditionalist" or "orthodox" intellectuals began to take a stance against "reformers" such as the Brahmos or Aryas, whom they regarded as corrupted by English or generally Western influence. Ironically, those indicted reformers also claimed to eradicate such corruptions in order to restore the pure Hindu dharma of the lost golden age. Not least for this reason, it is futile to determine stable boundaries between reformism and orthodoxy. As the example of the Brāhma Samāj has shown, there could also be frictions and schism within one particular movement, for instance between those rejecting Christian elements, such as Rajnarayan's Ādi Brāhma Samāj, and those embracing them, such as Keshab's Nababidhān. The debates between these different actors revolved precisely around the question of what Hinduism, and by extension religion, meant in the first place.

This was anything but clear, as can be illustrated by an article by Umeshchandra Batabyal, the magistrate we have encountered in the debates within the Bangīya Sāhitya Pariṣat·. In 1893, he published an article asking, "What is the Bengali word for religion?" (*Rilijan śabder bāṃlā ki?*). Umeshchandra rejected the widespread practice of translating "religion" with "dharma" because the English notion of religion implied a differentiation between true and false religions. Dharma, in contrast, meant conduct and duty, but everyone's dharma was different. In Umeshchandra's opinion, the meaning of dharma was so far removed from religion that it would make little sense to translate it with that term.[30] Such uncertainties directly played into the debates about *sanātana dharma* precisely because many participants in those debates insisted that the ancient Aryans had, in fact, made no distinction between religion, science, and philosophy. Theosophists and Spiritualists, orthodox and revivalist actors, as well as reformers could thus invoke the restoration of a pristine unity in quite different yet interconnected ways. The Bengali Theosophical journal *Kalpa* is a case in point, as its title and programmatic editorial have shown. Evidently, historical actors used the term "revivalism" to reflect an attempt among educated Indians at revitalizing "traditional" and "orthodox" knowledge, often in explicit defiance of the colonial context.

The fundamental question was, of course, what was supposed to be revived or reformed. Nowhere were the answers to this question in unison. As the conflicts between the Brahmos and Aryas have shown, critical positions toward traditional customs and social structures could vary drastically. In a speech given to the Indian National Social Conference in 1897, the renowned reformer Mahadev Govind Ranade (1842–1901) formulated an especially clear reformist position.[31] Ranade had popularized the Prārthanā Samāj in Maharashtra, an organization that was founded after Keshab's visit to the state and that propagated a social reform program similar to that of the Brāhma Samāj. In his speech titled "Revival and Reform," Ranade highlighted the aspects that most reformers perceived as the most pressing matters: female education, widow remarriage, foreign travel, intercaste marriage, infant marriage, and the relationship between different religious groups.[32] He acknowledged that his orthodox opponents did address these issues, but he criticized their demand to revive, rather than reform, and return to "old ways, old authorities, old sanctions." As he pointed out, it was disputed what it was that should be revived, and that customs were not stable but had always been subject to change: "[I]n a living organism, as society is, no revival is possible."[33] It was not the external change of manners or habits that true reformers were pursuing, but an internal change that should rid society of oppression and submission, not only by foreign forces but precisely by the internal subordinations among castes, or man and woman.[34] It was those structures that generated dependence because of a blind fidelity to past authorities, and it was only after overcoming this that national independence would become possible.

A prominent response to this speech serves to illustrate that many contemporaries were not prepared to make such clear distinctions between the reformers and revivalists. It was penned by Lala Lajpat Rai (1865–1928), the famous Punjabi freedom fighter. He had joined the Ārya Samāj in the 1880s when he studied law in Lahore and became the first editor of the *Arya Gazette*. In contrast to Ranade, Rai pleaded for a focus on shared interests rather than differences. For instance—and quite remarkably for our concerns—he pointed out that Besant and the Theosophists were commonly regarded as revivalist, but that they were strictly opposed to infant marriages, a concern that was also shared by their rivals, the Aryas. The same could be said about the wish to abolish the countless subdivisions that had been introduced into the classical four-caste system. Similarly, Rai professed to know of no sensible revivalist who was seriously opposed to sea travel and female education or to the bettering of the status of disadvantaged castes. The only clear difference would revolve around widow remarriage, but this single question would not justify the bitter divisions between reformers and revivalists.[35]

Rai pointed out that the revivalists had emerged later than the Brahmo-led reformers, thanks to a wider diffusion of Sanskrit literature within the previous quarter of a century. Consequently, revivalists would simply call upon the shastras to introduce the very reforms that were demanded by the reformers; they just insisted on "national" rather than "rational" arguments, refusing the influence of Western education.[36] In the end, Rai turned around Ranade's question about what should be revived, asking if reform meant the adoption of European customs and laws. Revivalists would not want an "outlandish imitation of European customs and manners and an undiminished adoption of European vice"; they refused to admit that the institutions they wished to revive were dead, burned down, and gone. While their reformist opponents were fixated on European society, they were invoking the ancient shastras, traditions, and institutions to arrive at the same conclusion.[37] Social norms, especially those pertaining to family and caste, stand out as points of contention between those who regarded themselves as orthodox and those who proclaimed the need for reform.

Tantra as *Sanātana Dharma*

Tantra played a key role in the quarrels among those rival yet overlapping factions. In Bengal, the prominent role of the Tantras is mainly responsible for their often positive perception by reformers such as the Brahmos or the members of the Tattvabodhinī Sabhā. In contrast to the Aryas, Bengali reformers invoked the authority of the Tantras even when they were careful to warn of their "black-magical" side. Beginning with Rammohan's and his guru's occupation with the Tantras, Brahmo leaders such as Rajnarayan frequently referred to them. When Debendranath Tagore published his *Brāhma dharmma* around 1850, a book that was intended to be the official Brahmo scripture, he invoked not only the Upanishads, the Laws of Manu, and the *Mahābhārata*, but also the *Mahānirvāṇa*.[38] A discourse delivered to the Tattvabodhinī Sabhā in December 1839 was based on "all the Śāstras—the Smr̥tis, Purāṇas, and Tantras," citing even the *Kulārṇava Tantra*.[39] This tendency did not disappear with later Brahmos. Quite the contrary, even Keshab's New Dispensation contained Tantric elements, especially in its use of the image of "the Mother" and its attempt to prove the absolute unity of Vaishnava, Shakta, and Christian or Unitarian doctrines.[40]

This does not mean that the Brahmos were Tantrics, but it underlines how widespread and prominent the authoritative status of the Tantras was in Bengal. They were invoked by those who claimed to be progressive reformers, as well as by those who claimed to defend orthodoxy against foreign corruption. In the second half of the nineteenth century, the notion of *sanātana dharma* was increasingly employed to refer to an unchanging law that had governed India in its golden age and had to be revived in order to restore its former glory. The *Mahānirvāṇa*'s proclamation to reveal the *sanātana dharma* for the Kali Yuga, as well as its statements about caste, sex, and life conduct, made it especially attractive for nineteenth-century debates. What *sanātana dharma* should comprise was inevitably disputed. Brahmos like Shivanath Shastri reprimanded the pandits of Navadvip for taking conservative positions on social questions such as widow remarriage and the caste order.[41] At the same time, Brahmos resolutely rejected the Aryas' claim of the infallibility of the Vedas. Clearly, adherence to the Vedas was not the crucial point that separated orthodox and reformist positions, and neither can it be said, as Rai reminds us, that either camp was strictly opposed to social reform.

It was as late as the 1880s that a large number of conservative groups were founded that claimed to defend the *sanātana dharma* against the influences of both Western education and Indian reformers. These groups often took the form of *dharma sabhās* (dharma societies), the first of which had been established in Calcutta as early as 1831. The foundation of similar organizations received a stimulus by the Hindu Mela of 1867, but it was not until the 1880s that they were bourgeoning in all parts of India and became a substantial force within the political landscape. These groups were usually organized around leading figures and were rather mercurial. Sometimes "counterreformers" would gather around a popular publication such as the *Baṅgabāsī*, a journal with an associated press that had been started in 1881 to propagate a decidedly conservative agenda. By 1890, it sold twenty thousand copies every week and could boast fifty thousand subscribers.[42] The massive success of self-identifying orthodox movements soon eclipsed the Brahmos and underlines the force with which anticolonial sentiment and the wish for an affirmation of Hindu identity surfaced toward the end of the century.

The two leading figures in the organization of "Hindu orthodoxy" in late nineteenth-century Bengal were the English-educated Krishnaprasanna Sen (1849–1902) and Shashadhar Tarkachuramani (1851–1928), a pandit with a Sanskritic education. Their proclamation of the revival of Aryan Hindu civilization had an aggressive edge that was largely absent in other contemporary nationalist writers, such as Bankim and Bhudev.[43] Krishnaprasanna was born south of Navadvip and, as one might expect, brought up in an environment marked by Tantric worship. In the 1860s, he received an education in English and acquired knowledge of Christianity in the company of missionaries. He also made contact with Keshab and the Brahmos, but eventually seems to have been disappointed with them.[44] In the late 1870s, he took up missionary activity in the north of India to propagate his criticism of what he viewed as a Westernized, materialist culture.

In 1880, he established the Bhāratbarṣīẏa Ārya Dharma Pracāriṇī Sabhā (Indian Society for the Propagation of Aryan Dharma, BADPS), one of the few organizations that became a gravitational center in sociopolitical discourse over a longer period. One of its central aims was to "propagate Sanatan Hinduism as manifest in the sacred Vedas and thus to encourage the salvation of the common man," as well as to further "the study and propagation of the Aryan religion and culture." The association was "dedicated to the revival of Aryan religion as expounded in the *Vedas, Tantras* and *Puranas*."[45] This declaration put the BADPS at odds with the Aryas, who exclusively accepted the Vedas as an authority. Krishnaprasanna developed a spirited missionary activity, launching attacks on the Brahmos and Aryas, whom he accused of "denationalization."[46] His polemics against Christian missionaries were less intense, which suggests that he perceived the inner-Hindu threat to his understanding of *sanātana dharma* as more pressing.

In the year 1883, Shashadhar became formally associated with Krishnaprasanna and took up the position of minister of the BADPS. Hailing from Faridpur, Shashadhar had begun a modest career as a Sanskrit scholar and relocated to Calcutta in 1884, where he was first patronized by Bankim. Shashadhar's increasingly radical exposition of Hinduism, as well as his sharp criticism of Brahmoism and Christianity, attracted a large audience, but his eccentric ideas alienated moderate intellectuals. Rabindranath drew up several satirical pieces about the pandit's "Aryan excesses," which seemed to glorify an imagined Aryan past in an almost comical fashion.[47] Famously, Shashadhar attempted to prove the superiority of Hinduism by demonstrating its scientific character on the basis of magnetism and electricity, which ironically led other pandits to accuse the "Anglo-Vernacular" teachings of Shashadhar of doing justice neither to Hinduism nor to Western science.[48] This highlights very forcefully how misleading it would be to perceive even an "ultra-orthodox" figure like Shashadhar as a "traditional pandit" free from "foreign influences." Shashadhar affiliated himself more and more closely with the *Baṅgabāsī* group, was appointed a member of its Shastric Publications Board, and was entrusted with the production of affordable reprints of religious texts. In July and August 1883, he broke with the BADPS and founded a rival press and journal in Calcutta, which he called *Bed'byās*, in reference to the great mythical rishi Vedavyasa.

A large number of these competing societies, presses, and other groups were united in 1900 under the umbrella of the Bhārat Dharma Mahāmaṇḍal (BDM), which had convened in Delhi under the presidency of the maharaja of Darbhanga, Rameshwar Singh (1860–1929), who had also been a donor to the BADPS.[49] The BDM was formally established at Muttra in 1902 and moved its headquarters to Benares in 1905, with the maharaja occupying the position of general secretary. Within the following years, the BDM established six hundred branches, was affiliated with four hundred institutions, and employed nearly two hundred preachers. Despite its large size, it remained a markedly elitist organization that was funded by princes and religious leaders and whose active agents were pandits rather than common people.[50] The BDM's conservative agenda went as far as to uphold the prohibition of sea travel, which attracted a great deal of criticism and outright mockery. But it was not a uniform body representing a monolithic *sanātana dharma*, and its internal contradictions were readily pointed out by contemporaries. For instance, *sanātana dharma* was understood to represent a heavily caste-based, traditional form of Hinduism, yet it was declared in the first issue of *Mahāmaṇḍal Magazine* to be also "the universal Dharma for all mankind."[51] Moreover, the society was not categorically opposed to the notion of reform, as it announced its aim to "promote Hindu religious education in accordance with the Sanatan Dharma, to diffuse the knowledge of the Vedas, Smrtis, Purans and other Hindu Shastras and to introduce, in the light of such knowledge, useful *reforms* into Hindu Life and Society."[52]

Theosophy among the Revivalists

As has been illustrated by Rai's speech, many contemporaries counted the Theosophists among the revivalists as a matter of course. As remarkable as this might be at first glance, it is really no surprise, as the Theosophists expressly insisted on the revival of *sanātana dharma*, with the Bengal Theosophical Society referring to itself as the Bengali Theosophical Society for the Promotion of the Meaning of the Eternal Aryan Dharma. Bipinchandra Pal highlighted the role of Theosophy in his memoirs accordingly:

> [The Theosophical Society] was perhaps the most powerful of the forces that brought in this movement of Hindu religious revival and social reaction. This Society told our people that instead of having any reason to be ashamed of their past or of the legacies left to them by it, they have every reason to feel justly proud of it all, because their ancient seers and saints had been the spokesmen of the highest truths and their old books, so woefully misunderstood today, had been the repositories of the highest human illumination and wisdom. Our people had hitherto felt perpetually humiliated at the sense of their degradation. This new message, coming from

> the representatives of the most advanced peoples of the modern world, the inheritors of the most advanced culture and civilisation the world has as yet known, at once raised us in our own estimation and created a self-confidence in us that commenced to find easy expression in a new propaganda which, instead of apologising for our current and mediaeval ideas and institutions and seeking to reform and reconstruct these after modern European ideals, boldly stood up in defence of them.[53]

Amiya P. Sen has stated that "Theosophy did help to promote in the educated Hindu new measures of self-confidence but also lent themselves to grossly conservative uses."[54] These two aspects were not contradicting tendencies but part and parcel of the Theosophists' self-declared and perceived intention. The vague meaning of *sanātana dharma* and its ambivalent relationship with reform was one reason the camps of reform and revivalism were extremely volatile. Alliances were often built temporarily around a particular issue rather than a common ideology.[55] "Hindu revivalism" should be regarded as a fragmented and multifaceted, highly dynamic intellectual sphere, instead of a homogeneous current. For our concerns, it is most instructive to pay attention to the aspects that the orthodox and traditionalists shared, not only with the Brahmos and the Aryas but also with the Theosophists: the idea of a golden Aryan past that had to be saved from degeneracy; the claim to propagate a scientific form of religion that would not deny modernity but prove its superiority over modernity's materialistic, atheistic, and socially corruptive excesses; and the need to invigorate an Indian nation on the basis of that revival.

All participants in the debates about the meaning of Hinduism or *sanātana dharma* were motivated by the wish to separate "authentic" from "false" religion, but these negotiations were not straightforward, and most definitely not divided between Western and Indian actors. For instance, we find none other than Olcott among the founding members of the BDM.[56] Rameshwar Singh, its patron and general secretary, was an enthusiastic supporter of the Theosophists and cofounded, with Besant, the Banaras Hindu University in 1911. His elder brother and predecessor, Lakshmeshwar Singh (1858–1898), had joined the Theosophical Society as early as 1883 and was a generous supporter of the Theosophical Kashi Tattva Lodge in Benares—as we learn, for instance, from a report of the second anniversary meeting of the lodge, which was printed by none other than Shashadhar's Vedavyasa Press at Calcutta.[57] On April 29, the *Indian Mirror* proudly announced the maharaja's membership in the Theosophical Society: "Theosophy has its roots in the rich subsoil of Aryan Science, one would say it finds abundant nutriment there, for the vine is fast enwrapping the trunk of the tree of Anglo-Indian Empire."[58] Individuals across the intellectual spectrum were firmly convinced of this shared Aryan civilization, whose harmony of science and religion was to be restored as the remedy for an age of decay and degeneration. It is therefore quite likely that Shashadhar might have been inspired by Theosophy in his "scientific" interpretation of ancient Aryan wisdom.[59] The attitude among revivalists toward Theosophy was certainly varied and often ambiguous; Bhudev, for instance, referred to it as "adulterated Hinduism."[60] But it was precisely the internal tensions of Theosophy that made it highly attractive for both those who wanted to break down social norms in the spirit of universal brotherhood and those who wanted to uphold them on the basis of social hierarchies that are so typical of esoteric doctrines.

Baradakanta is an instructive example of these dynamics. In 1902, he published a book on the caste order (*varṇāśramadharma*), wherein he professed "the explanation of the esoteric significance of caste distinctions" (*jātibheder gūṛha tāt·paryya bibr̥ti* [*sic*]). To build his case, he engaged with Indian scriptures and the work of Shashadhar,[61] as well as with writings by Western orientalists, scientists, and Theosophists. The book was dedicated to Ray Jatindranath Chaudhuri, a prominent voice in the emergent National Congress movement who demanded increased governmental participation of Indians.[62] This dedication is significant, as Baradakanta's publication is marked by harsh criticism of Western influence on Indian society and what he considered the resulting corruption of the caste system. Baradakanta expressed his frustration with the lack of understanding of this system, which resulted in hypocrisies and abuses.

The only solution for this deplorable state of affairs was a strict return to the Aryan *sanātana dharma* as prescribed by the Vedas. Baradakanta protested vehemently against the claim, made by Western-educated Indians and Western scholars, that the caste system was a recent invention. Engaging with the work of Müller, he attempted to prove the contrary by citing a number of Vedic scriptures and the *Manusmr̥ti*.[63] In addition to these texts, it was Blavatsky's *Secret Doctrine* that helped him argue for the different qualities between "races" (*jāti*)[64] and types of people. According to him, the doctrine of caste (*varṇatva*) was a matter of the mind, not of the gross material body,[65] a point that he also saw confirmed by the writings of John Stuart Mill.[66]

We learn that the prescriptions of Vedic rules were important because caste depended not on hereditary transmissions but on the behavior of the individual and physical influences.[67] This shows that, for Baradakanta, caste was not a static system but dependent on personal development. Societal structures were essential to provide the necessary conditions for such development, and the West was certainly not to be viewed as a model in that regard. Even in materialistic communism, inequalities and discriminations were plenty, a case that Baradakanta made with reference to *The Study of Sociology* by Herbert Spencer (1873).[68] The Aryans were a spiritual people and in need of a particular way of living, which could only be guaranteed by a stable society built on the foundations of knowledge, preservation of society, earning, and caring. This would lead not to a selfish society based on economy but to a society based on dharma.[69] Aryan society was geared toward the uplifting of the spiritual part of man, providing rules according to individual qualification.[70] In such a system, no caste would be better or worse than the others, as all occupied their appropriate place. It was thus necessary to return to the *sanātana dharma*.

Baradakanta's argumentation is remarkable for its fluid combination of traditional scriptures and recent Western publications. His critique of Western food habits and advocacy of a vegetarian diet is another case in point, as he supports his points by references to Manu but also to Frederick William Pavy's *Treatise on Food and Dietetics* from 1874.[71] He also related the effects of kundalini shakti to the nerves in the spinal cord, citing *The Mechanism of Man* by Edward William Cox (1876) and *Animal Magnetism* by William Gregory (1877) to prove the effectiveness of Hindu dharma.[72] In this light, Baradakanta's plea for the restoration of the Aryan ways of life shows, first, how "revivalism" went hand in hand with an active and productive engagement with Western writings and concepts. Second, it demonstrates that his conceptualization of *sanātana dharma* was in itself decisively reformist. Not only did Baradakanta demand the radical reformation of the caste system, but his very life's work was marked by sustained efforts to further education and social reform. Theosophy provided an important framework for these efforts, both with regard to the legitimation of his ideas by contemporary science and the appeal for a return to an eternal secret (*gūṛha*) truth.

Thus Baradakanta once again serves as a highly instructive nodal point that connects the different threads of Theosophy, the manifold global discourses related to it, and the regional configuration of Bengal. This latter aspect has often been neglected in studies of Hindu revivalism, as Varuni Bhatia has argued in light of the "localized" dimension of Bengali Vaishnavism.[73] The same was certainly the case with Tantra. Not only was the "revival" of Vaishnavism inherently intertwined with the discourse about Tantra and Theosophy, as the case of Shishirkumar has shown, but it was also shaped by the same continuities and ruptures.

The scriptural corpus of the Bengali School served as the main textual authority within these nineteenth-century debates. The *Mahānirvāṇa* and the *Kulārṇava* Tantras, for instance, claimed the superiority of Tantra for the Kali Yuga and presented it as the *sanātana dharma*, in accordance with the Vedas, if not as their true core. Compendia such as the *Prāṇatōṣiṇī* and the *Tantrasāra* were widely used and accessible even for those who were not proficient in Sanskrit. All this underlines that Tantric rites were quite "mainstream" in Bengal and formed an integral part of both Brahmanical learning and popular practices. At the same time, however, Tantra had come under fire by Christian missionaries and some reformers, such as the Aryas. This tension manifested in the emphasis of secrecy and need of proper initiation by a qualified guru: the alleged corruption and degradation of Tantra, but also of Hindu society as a whole, could be explained by a loss of the true, hidden meaning of Tantra.

This tension was also one of the main characteristics of Theosophy, whose proponents referred to secrecy and initiation to affirm their authority over supposedly exoteric misunderstandings of an eternal, unchanging truth. This truth was contained in the *sanātana dharma*, which led to the proclamation of the restoration of true Aryan civilization. In practice, however, we can hardly observe the revival of an ancient tradition. Theosophists such as Baradakanta could invoke the ancient shastras, the writings of Shashadhar, and those of Blavatsky next to those by Spencer or Mill. The benefits of *sanātana dharma* were explained and legitimized on the grounds of modern Western science, social theory, and philosophy. Moreover, the return to the supposed eternal truths of Aryan wisdom required educational programs, the reevaluation of scriptures, reinterpretations of the caste systems, and a restructuring of society: revivalism always implied reform. These convoluted historical developments were structured by shifting hegemonic positions and constant renegotiations of meaning. The Bengali intervention in favor of Tantra is part of that story of claims of authority. Relevant to its understanding is the consideration of both diachronic developments and the new dynamics under colonialism, in which Theosophy played an extraordinary role.

6

Shivachandra Vidyarnava

One of the most vocal proponents of *sanātana dharma* was Shivachandra Bhattacharya Vidyarnava. His interpretation of Tantra, shaped by the Bengali School, was spread worldwide through the publications of Arthur Avalon. It will be recalled that he was the guru not only of John Woodroffe, Atalbihari Ghosh, and Pramathanath Mukhopadhyay but also of Baradakanta Majumdar. He moreover appears to have attracted the attention of Rameshwar Singh, the maharaja of Darbhanga, patron of the BADPS and supporter of the Theosophical Society, who is said to have become one of his disciples and patronized the publication of Shivachandra's writings.[1] In the 1890s, Shivachandra established his own "orthodox" society that opposed Western influence by invoking the Aryan *sanātana dharma* and aimed at forging an alliance between Shakta and Vaishnava currents.

Shivachandra (pictured on figure 6.1) had both direct and indirect links to practically all the contexts that have been discussed so far, yet there are differences that set him apart from our previous examples. In contrast to other proponents of Tantra, including swamis such as Dharmananda and Sachchidananda and even pandits such as Shashadhar, he did not openly engage with Western science, magnetism, or Theosophy. Quite the contrary, he refused to even learn English. In Shivachandra's *Tantratattva*, the famous work that was later translated as *Principles of Tantra*, we can observe how local rivalries and debates intermingled with the anticolonial stance of its author. On one hand, he engaged critically with Bengali Vaishnava traditions and Vedantic philosophy; on the other hand, he denounced English education and the reform movements allegedly corrupted by it, the Aryas and Brahmos. This engagement largely revolved around the notions of philosophy (Bengali *darśan*) and science (*bijñān*), which were dismissed in favor of Tantric ritual practice (*sādhan*). On these grounds, Shivachandra argued for the superiority of Tantra as a path to liberation based on practice and experience.

Global Tantra. Julian Strube, Oxford University Press. © Oxford University Press 2022.
DOI: 10.1093/oso/9780197627112.003.0007

Figure 6.1 Shivachandra Bhattacharya Vidyarnava.
Reproduced with permission by Rabindranath and Dipa Bhattacharya.

The Intellectual Atmosphere at Kumarkhali

Most of what we know about Shivachandra's life is derived from a biography written by one of his disciples, Vasantakumar Pal, a railway guard who was born in 1895 and entered service as a clerk in the Eastern Bengal Railway in 1919.[2] According to an interview that Kathleen Taylor has conducted with Samarendranath Bagchi, a retired judge of the High Court in Kolkata, Pal first encountered John Woodroffe and his wife, Ellen, on the Chittagong Mail. The couple was traveling to the birthplace of Shivachandra to pay their respects to "our most revered gurudev," and Pal was delighted to introduce himself as a fellow disciple.[3] This account appears to be somewhat dubious, since Pal had been employed by the railway only since 1919 and Shivachandra had passed away in 1914. While several scenarios could be imagined that would support the authenticity of Pal's account, these uncertainties underline the fact that much of the information about Shivachandra's life should be treated with caution.[4]

Be that as it may, Pal does provide a range of written and concrete oral sources that draw an informative image of Shivachandra's activities and the impact of his thought. Later writings about him largely rely on Pal, although they add a number of anecdotes in an often hagiographical fashion.[5] The most recent study by Kashinath Chakladar contains an instructive analysis of songs written by Shivachandra and information about his present-day descendants who take care of a small temple at Haora. I visited that temple several times in the fall of 2018 and, thanks to the kind hospitality of the family, can corroborate some of the accounts of their illustrious ancestor's life.

Shivachandra was born on May 16, 1860 (*jaiṣṭha* 2, 1267), in the village of Kumarkhali in the Nadiya district, which today is part of the Kushtiya district in Bangladesh.[6] This locality stood out as an intellectual and cultural hotspot well into the twentieth century. Kumarkhali is close to Shilaidaha Kuthibari, the famous residence established by Dvarkanath and Debendranath Tagore, which was regularly frequented by Rabindranath beginning in the 1890s.[7] Shivachandra's family had been living in Kumarkhali for a long time.[8] His lineage was full of renowned Tantrics and can be traced back for eleven generations.[9] Shivachandra's father, Chandrakumar, was especially celebrated for his learning, frequently consulted by pandits, and respected by Hindus and Muslims alike. The locality was marked by an intermingling of Tantric, Vaishnava, and Baul traditions, which were often shaped by Islam.

A common feature of the different accounts about Kumarkhali is the description of an intellectual atmosphere that transgressed religious and social divisions. The importance of this atmosphere for the interpretation of Tantra that was later propagated by Avalon can hardly be overestimated. In the second half of the nineteenth century, a personal network emerged at Kumarkhali and in neighboring parts of the Nadiya region that shaped many of the ideas that informed at least some of the participants of the Bengali intervention.

One the of nodal points of that network was Kangal Majumdar, who became famous under the name Kangal Harinath. The writer and composer of Baul songs was born in Kumarkhali and formed a group there that included a whole range of thinkers who were involved in contemporary debates about Tantra. These included Shivachandra, whose family had close ties to Kangal. Reportedly, Shivachandra's father had been the *dīkṣāguru* of Kangal and performed the so-called *hātekhaṛi* for Shivachandra, an important pre-*upāyana* ritual that is performed when the child is five years old.[10] Shivachandra remained closely associated with Kangal and was deeply influenced by his thought—he is said to have been his dearest disciple.[11] Throughout his life, Kangal was a strong advocate of the poor and disadvantaged castes. He had first attended a local English school, which he was forced to leave due to his poverty. In 1855, he set up a Bengali school in his village, followed by a girls' school the succeeding year.[12] In 1863, he started publishing his journal, *Grāmbārtā Prakāśikā* (*Village Publication*),[13] whose reputed contributors included Rabindranath. The journal was financially supported by Rabindranath's sister Svarnakumari Devi, who we met as a future member of the Theosophical Society in Calcutta. In his own contributions, Kangal promoted vernacular education and leveled criticism against social oppression, for instance against exploitation by British indigo farmers.

In 1880, Kangal established a Baul group at Kumarkhali that was known as Phikir Cāṁder Dal. Among his disciples were Akshaykumar Maitra, who would later make a name for himself as a historian and the cofounder of the Varendra Research Society; Mir Mosharraf Hossain (1847–1912), the first prominent Muslim author in Bengali whose work is still among the most widely read; and Dinendrakumar Ray (1869–1943), the novelist and future teacher of Aurobindo Ghosh.[14] Another disciple was Shivachandra's classmate Jaladhar Sen (1860–1939), Kangal's future biographer and a well-known writer whose numerous activities as editor included positions in the *Baṅgabāsī* and Narendranath Sen's *Indian Mirror*.[15] His autobiography, *Ātmajībanī o smṛti-tarpaṇ* (autobiography), includes one of the most instructive contemporary accounts of Shivachandra and his relationship with Woodroffe.[16]

The group surrounding Kangal also connected Shivachandra to the most famed of all Bauls, the celebrated Lalon Fakir (also known as Lalon Shah, among other names). Widely recognized as a beacon of Bengali culture, Lalon was known for his rejection of distinctions between caste and religion. His unique thought, which combined Tantric, Vaishnava, and Sufi elements, among others, is mainly known through the large number of his highly popular songs.[17] Kangal also ran one of the gymnasia (*ākhṛā*) that were established across the country to invigorate India's youth and foster anticolonial activity. It was there that Lalon and Shivachandra met for the first time and developed a close relationship.[18] It appears that Shivachandra was influenced by the Baul's understanding of harmony and openness, and Lalon, in turn, regularly visited Shivachandra to listen to his songs and perform some of his own.[19] In contrast to Shivachandra, Lalon's religious affiliation remains largely unclear—which is arguably the point of his conviction as a Baul—but the two men seemed to have shared a rejection of existing societal and religious biases. Shivachandra reportedly received the tile *phakir* himself,[20] although it is quite possible that his affiliation with Lalon might have been exaggerated by later authors.

What emerges from all historical accounts and his own writings, though, is Shivachandra's disagreement with traditionalist notions of caste hierarchies and his wish for the establishment of religious unity.[21] This demonstrates that his portrayal as a strictly "orthodox" and "traditionalist" pandit must be questioned. While his writings—which, significantly, he penned in Bengali rather than Sanskrit—do display an expertise in the shastras, his ideas were also significantly shaped by the Shakta poetry tradition of Bengal and the closely related Bauls. His rather unconventional stance is further underlined by the very fact that he would later take Woodroffe, a British Christian, as his disciple, and also in light of the activities of his earlier disciples, who paved the way for—and later formed part of—Arthur Avalon. One can hardly find a more impressive nodal point of global, regional, and local connections.

Vernacular Education and the Formation of a Tantric Pandit

From an early point on, Shivachandra's life was marked by the conflict between English and vernacular education. This is attested by Jaladhar, who was Shivachandra's classmate in the Bengali school at Kumarkhali that had been established by Kangal. The boys had entered the school at four years old, but Shivachandra was taken out after only two years. According to Jaladhar, Shivachandra's father, to whom he referred with the very intimate term *candrakākā*, was an "extremely spirited Brahman" who took issue with the material taught at the school.[22] One day, young Shivachandra was reading the *Caritābalī*, a translation of the exemplary lives of learned or heroic Europeans that had been composed by the great educationist and reformer

Ishvarchandra Vidyasagar on the basis of William Chambers's *Exemplary and Instructive Biography* (1836). The compilation contained the story of Valentine Duval (1695–1775), a French shepherd boy who, due to his diligence, became an eminent historian. When Chandrakumar saw his boy reading the story, he was outraged and decided that Shivachandra should from now on be home-schooled by his erudite grandfather Krishnashundar.

This reaction must be understood against the background of a far-reaching conflict over the material that was taught to children at school.[23] Ishvarchandra Vidyasagar had taken Chambers's stories about explorers, scientists, and other virtuous men to replace vernacular school primers such as the *Śiśubodh*, which contained the life stories of Hindu gods. This replacement drew wide criticism from those who regarded it as a blatant recasting of Indian culture after a European model.[24] As Gauri Viswanathan has shown, the use of English literature had been an important instrument for imparting European culture, and Christian morality specifically, since colonial policy would not allow for the Bible being taught in secular schools. "Secular" primers were an ideal way to communicate European and Christian values to young students without violating that policy.[25] That Chandrakumar took his son out of school was therefore an act of defiance against what he perceived as a replacement of traditional local culture with European culture.

Shivachandra was later sent to Navadvip, where he received instruction in a Vedic school (*catuṣpāṭhī*) and was educated in a Sanskrit school (*ṭol*). It is said that Shivachandra excelled at his studies and was put in contact with a number of distinguished professors, some of whom would later work at the Sanskrit College in Calcutta. Like his father, Shivachandra resolutely refused to learn English throughout his life.[26] After completing his Sanskrit studies, he moved to Calcutta to take the exam for the Vidyasagar title.[27] At that time, the government gave him the title of *kabirañjan* to honor his poetic achievements. Shivachandra allegedly never used this and numerous other titles that were bestowed upon him, due to what he regarded as an inflationary "disease of titles." He went as far as to reject the title of Vidyasagar in order to pay homage to his teacher in Calcutta, the eminent Jivananda Vidyasagar, whom he had allegedly impressed with his Sanskrit skills and his ability to spontaneously craft immaculate Sanskrit verses (*ślokas*). While many details of these accounts might have been colored by the hagiographical inclinations of Shivachandra's biographers, it emerges that he was a widely respected and talented Sanskrit scholar who made a point of taking a stand against the influence of English education.

Shivachandra's understanding of Tantra was shaped by local tradition at Nadiya and his education at Navadvip, which trained him in the Bengal School approach to *dharmaśāstra*, the Tantras, and New Logic (*navya nyāya*). However, it is likely that his ideas about Tantra were most significantly molded by his own family and the setting of Kumarkhali. His ancestors were reputed pandits, and he was probably initiated at home. The Bhattacharyas were said to have been in possession of rare old books and educational stories (*pūthi*) that were collected from different parts of India, Nepal, and Tibet.[28] In addition to the instructions by his elders, Shivachandra reportedly learned by reading these books, which is interesting insofar as he would later write such instructions himself, emphasizing the need of initiation by a guru to fully grasp their meaning. It might be for this reason that Shivachandra created unique worship rituals that observers noted were different from those of other practitioners (*sādhakas*) of his time.[29] As the invocation at the beginning of his main work, *Tantratattva*, suggests, he did not follow a single lineage but combined several schools and took initiation from different gurus.[30]

He refined his learning in Benares, where he purportedly started taking lessons under Ramram Swami and established himself as an accomplished pandit. Shivachandra passionately focused on the worship of the Goddess, specifically in her manifestations as Tara and Sarvamangala. He claimed to follow the Kaula path and was known for his extensive cremation ground rituals, including ritual practice on a corpse (*śāvasādhanā*).[31] His wife Manomohini functioned as his *śākti* during ritual practice. According to his grandson Rabindranath Bhattacharya, Manomohini also used to perform animal sacrifices and took part in rituals, a practice handed down to the present generation of the family.[32]

Shivachandra was famed for his highly elaborate pujas and would get furious if even the slightest detail was incorrectly performed. At his two weddings—he married a second time after his first wife passed away, leaving behind a daughter—he impressed the guests by his insistence on appearing with unkempt hair and walking to the wedding venue, contrary to established norms. During the ceremony, he laconically pointed out flawed pronunciations of *ślokas* and other mistakes by the priest, causing some discomfort among the number of eminent Sanskrit scholars present.[33] Again, the accuracy of such accounts is questionable, but Shivachandra's skills apparently left an impression among his contemporaries, and he formed close ties with a range of influential pandits in Benares and elsewhere, while traveling the country extensively.[34]

Public Activities and the Sarvamaṅgalā Sabhā

Shivachandra propagated his understanding of Tantra in public speeches, songs, and a substantial number of writings. Besides Bengali and Sanskrit, he spoke Hindi and engaged in debates with other learned men, especially in the north of India. He was widely known for his overwhelming oratory skills and his ability to captivate audiences, both learned and popular.[35] This is an aspect of his work that we can be sure about, since the power of his language is palpable in his publications, which include a range of books that were published in the 1890s.[36] It appears that *Tantratattva* was one of the first of these texts, as its preface was written in Benares in February or March 1890, although the first print edition appears to have been published several years later, in 1893, under the auspices of the Sarvamaṅgalā Sabhā. In 1891, Shivachandra published *Pīṭhmālā*, a rather technical handbook that lists sites where *japa* and other practices may be performed according to one's *iṣṭadevata*.[37] In a noteworthy passage, Shivachandra defended these instructions against "modern doubts" that suggested the names of some of those holy locations were later interpolations. As Shivachandra explained, contemporary names had been used in the Tantras to guide practitioners to liberation in the Kali Yuga, emphasizing that initiation was possible only in India, and more specifically in *āryāvarta*.[38]

A leading theme in these publications is relentless criticism of what Shivachandra regarded as a lack of knowledge among the pandits, the overall destitute state of traditional education, and the corruption of society by foreign influences. But here was hope: the transition from a period of darkness and decay to one of light and regeneration is the opening scene of *Rāslīlā* from 1896, which revolves around the fundamental unity between Shaktas and Vaishnavas. Shivachandra lamented that almost no one was left to offer initiation into the secret doctrine (*nigūṛh tattva*) of the shastras. Only waking up at the right hour could save society from doom. This meant overcoming the "malicious community" whose minds were distorted by the culture of "non-Āryyas." Shivachandra emphasized that, without the flowering of the knowledge of Brahman (*brahmabidyā*), truth would forever be beyond the grasp of common sense.[39] As will be recalled, the term *brahmabidyā* was usually used for translating Theosophy (for instance by Baradakanta at exactly the same time, but also by Max Müller), which underlines the importance of taking the local contexts of translingual practice into account;

Baradakanta's understanding of Theosophy did not accidentally parallel that of Shivachandra's *brahmabidyā*.

The same theme of decay and regeneration runs through the preface to *Gaṅgeś* (1898), a play that Shivachandra composed at the request of members of the Sarvamaṅgalā Sabhā to instruct the common people. Bemoaning that contemporary plays were based on fictional best-selling novels, he wished to present the life stories of the great men who should serve as ideals to human society—a goal that most likely reflected the experience of his school days. Shivachandra consequently wanted this work to be understood not as a play but as a true exposition of the life of the founder of New Logic, Gangesha Upadhyaya. In the preface, Shivachandra lamented that the knowledge of Gangesha's *siddhi-sādhanā* had been handed down for centuries but that *sādhakas* and professors would repeat the *ślokas* containing that wisdom without understanding them. Yet in secret (*nigūṛh bhābe*), the truth was germinating to blossom again and illuminate the minds of the ignorant.[40] Time and again, Shivachandra expressed his conviction that, as soon as the knowledge that had been handed down from guru to disciple in secret over the centuries became widely known, the regeneration of a world ravaged by modernity would be at hand. This is emphasized in the final scene of the play, in which a *bhairavī* deplores the current state of India, and Bengal in particular. The whole of India had turned into a cremation ground. Renewal would be possible only if people had learned again to devote themselves to the reality of the Mother unconditionally.[41]

Shivachandra regarded the corruption of Indian culture through ignorance and foreign domination as the main threat to this revival of *sanātana dharma*. It is therefore not surprising to find his contributions in journals such as the *Baṅgabāsī*, where he published an acclaimed series titled "Caṇḍītattva," and Shashadhar's *Bed'byās*. In the 1890s, he also edited his own monthly journal, *Śaibī*, whose copies seem to be lost.[42] Unlike other, ostensibly "orthodox" pandits, Shivachandra also appealed to a wider unlearned public with his devotional songs to the Goddess (*śyāmā saṅgīt*). A number of these songs, which followed the tradition of Ramprasad Sen and the contemporary Baul circle in Kumarkhali, were collected in a volume with the noteworthy title *Gītāñjali*.[43] This popular element in Shivachandra's activism is also evident through his contact with the famous *sādhaka* Vamakhepa (1837–1911), the "mad saint" of Tarapith.[44] One of the most important places of Tantric worship, Tarapith was also held in the highest esteem by Shivachandra.[45] Vamakhepa had been instrumental in popularizing the worship of the goddess Tara and was very much influenced by the poetry of Krishnachandra's court, especially by that of Kamalakanta Bhattacharya, who had also been a practitioner at Tarapith.[46] Evidently, Shivachandra was deeply involved not only in highly educated discussions with pandits but also in the popularizing devotional movement that fostered national sentiment.

In order to propagate his ideas, Shivachandra established the Sarvamaṅgalā Sabhā, named after his personal deity (*iṣṭadevī*), Sarvamangala. The society was based in Kumarkhali and Benares, but a number of branches were formed throughout India. Shivachandra became a vocal figure in the rapidly growing sphere of "orthodox" *sabhās*, among which his prime focus on Tantra stood out.[47] His closest collaborator was Danbari Gangopadhyay, an educated man from Kumarkhali who had close ties to Shivachandra's family and accompanied him everywhere. He became the society's secretary and seems to have worked largely in the background, since little information about him is available other than the fact that, somewhat ironically, he taught at the English School at Kumarkhali toward the end of his life.[48] What we do know is that the Sarvamaṅgalā Sabhā announced his establishment in reaction to a time of crisis and wished to cure "the diseased body of the society," in the words of Pal. This was to be accomplished by two aims. First, the *sabhā* professed to take on the fight against Western material science (*jaṛabijñān*) by promoting the "eternal Vedic dharma" (*sanātan vaidik dharma*) and forming a counterpoint to "the propaganda of Western materialist capitalists" (*pāścātyer dhanatāntrikdiger annadāsakuler apapracār*). Second, it should bridge the divisions between Shakta and Vaishnava factions and establish religious and social unity between them.[49]

The founding members of the Sarvamaṅgalā Sabhā consisted of a range of prominent and remarkably diverse figures, among them Shashadhar. We also find the renowned Vedanta pandit Kalibar Vedantabagish, who studied the yoga of Patanjali[50] and would later, by recommendation of Shashadhar, be the teacher of Swami Abhedananda of the Ramakrishna Vedanta Math.[51] Kalibar also provided information about "practical occultism" to a member of the Berhampore branch of the Theosophical Society.[52] Other members included Madangopal Gosvami and Krishnananda Swami, as well as the historian Bholanath Chakravarti.[53] It is perhaps most striking to find Bijaykrishna Gosvami (1841–1899) among these illustrious thinkers, a famous and highly influential Vaishnava reformer who had earlier been a follower of the Brāhma Samāj.[54] He was born to a Vaishnava family in Shantipur, Nadiya. After moving to Calcutta, he became a disciple of Debendranath in the late

1850s, completing a number of courses at the Calcutta Medical College with the support of his patron. In 1861, he joined the Brāhma Samāj and became one of Keshab's most ardent supporters. During the split between the Ādi Brāhma Samāj and Keshab's Bhāratbarṣīẏa Brāhma Samāj in 1866, he was one of the most vocal agents and exerted a growing influence on Keshab in the following years. He inspired Keshab to adopt the bhakti devotionalism of Chaitanya and shift his focus to native Bengali rather than foreign Christian elements.

With his unique blend of bhakti and Brahmo rationalism, Bijaykrishna established himself as the most widely known and influential proponent of Vaishnavism in Bengal. The course of his life parallels that of Shishirkumar Ghosh in several ways. His conviction had been that of a rational theist who heralded social reform, rejected the caste order, and proclaimed the "unity of God and the brotherhood of all men" in the spirit of Chaitanya.[55] Consequently, he grew critical of Keshab's new role as a prophet and avatar. This criticism was notably supported by rationalist arguments, since Bijaykrishna's goal had been, in the words of David Kopf, "to purify Vaishnavism from abuses through Brahmo rationalism."[56] He supported Shivanath Shastri's Sādhāraṇ Brāhma Samāj against Keshab on the issue of female rights, joined the Sādhāraṇ faction in 1878, and became its missionary. In 1866, however, charges were brought against him because of his alleged practice of idolatry (he was accused of worshiping an image of Radha-Krishna at Dacca) and because he had turned to popular Vaishnavism by joining the Kartābhajā community, which was regarded by Brahmos as backward and superstitious. After he had turned his back on the Brahmos in 1887, Bijaykrishna embraced his new role as a Vaishnava guru.

That Bijaykrishna became one of the founding members of the Sarvamaṅgalā Sabhā appears less surprising in light of this development; disillusioned with Brahmoism, he had gradually embraced regional Vaishnava traditions and rejected the influence of the Christian and Western philosophical ideas that were so prominent among Brahmos. At the same time, he supported social reform and took a demonstrably rationalistic stance. This made him compatible with the agenda of Shivachandra and his followers, which highlights the fact that "revivalists" were not necessarily united by a common ideology but by a shared set of issues and goals, in this case, the Sarvamaṅgalā Sabhā's aims to reject Western influences and promote unity among Hindus. At the same time, the background of its members illustrates the fluidity among Sanskritic learning, Shakta-Vaishnava devotional currents, reformist ideas in the vein of Brahmoism, and an openness to interact with the Theosophical Society. The "antireformist reformism" of an association such as the Sarvamaṅgalā Sabhā underlines that these discourses were not separated, and it illustrates how highly diverse individuals with various, even conflicting ideas attempted to work toward a common end.

Tantratattva: The Principles of Tantra

The ideas of Shivachandra were most prominently expressed in *Tantratattva*, a work that was published in two extensive volumes as an exposition of the true principles (*tattva*) of Tantra. About two decades after its original publication in Bengali, it was made available to a global readership by the English translation of Arthur Avalon. In parallel, at least one other Bengali edition was published by Shivachandra's son Mangalkumar in Kumarkhali in 1914. A renewed interest is attested by a 1972 print that was edited by Swami Prajnanananda of the Vedanta Math.[57] This and later editions were published by the popular Nababharat press that runs affordable and widely distributed prints.[58] The great impact of *Tantratattva* is not surprising. It addresses some of the most pressing issues of its day in an accessible and captivating yet highly erudite style that is marked by witty and poignant polemics. It is worth quoting a longer excerpt from the very beginning of the work, as it gives a flavor of Shivachandra's powerful language and addresses several central aspects of the book:

> By the grace of Sarvamangala, the drum of Sanātana Dharma seems to be again sending forth sweet and auspicious notes of triumph in Bhāratavarsha, the land of the Aryas. . . . Every scion of the Aryan race in India, be he intelligent or not, is today intoxicated with the sweet music of the charming mantra of the widespread agitation on the subject of the Sanātana Dharma, and is keeping time at every measure and dancing. In this great festival, in this ancient Durga festival of India, astrology, philosophy, Smriti, Purana, Veda, Vedanta, and many other musical instruments are playing in the extensive courtyard of the universe. But we are grieved to find that the great instrument of the Tantra Shastra, in which all other instruments are included, on which all other instruments depend, and which is the sole source of all yantras and mantras, is today silent. We know that the proper place for the playing of this instrument is not a courtyard,

> but the interior of the temple of Tantra Shastra, which is full of mantras; as also that the proper place for its discussion is not at a meeting or by society at large, but in the heart of the accomplished sādhaka. But what can we do? We are players on the outside.[59]

Obviously, the notion of *sanātana dharma* was central to Shivachandra's thought. The Aryan character of this dharma was stressed, as was the dependence of all other "instruments" on it. Tantra was therefore regarded not only as Aryan and Vedic but as the very essence of Aryan dharma. The ignorance of this instrument was condemned by Shivachandra as the prime cause of the poor state of Indian society. He was well aware of the paradox that the remedy for this universal degeneracy was shrouded in secrecy; the tension between secrecy and public instruction lies at the core of *Tantratattva*, which, obviously, had been written for the very purpose of instructing the public—in Bengali and then English, rather than Sanskrit. This underscores once more that Shivachandra, for all his professed rejection of English education—or rather, precisely because of it—was very much a participant in colonial discourse.

Time and again, Shivachandra denounced the corruption of a society that he perceived as deluded by "the outward pomp of philosophy and science [*darśanbijñānmaẏ*]," and that was "devoid of siddhi and sādhana." The Tantric guru stressed that every Aryan had a right to access that power through ritual practice, without the need for the mediation of a priest (*purohita*): "The object of this puja is not self-deception, but siddhi and sādhana for the self [*ātma*]."[60] Shivachandra regarded Tantra as the path to power that stood open to anyone who was qualified to enter it; by implication, it was the path that would lead the whole of India to liberation, as soon as it recognized the superiority of Tantra. The obstacles to that goal were to be found, according to Shivachandra, among the educated Indians. He lamented that Aryan society lay in ruins and its children lived at a distance from their Mother. The path of Tantra was "full of thorns" and lined with much dispute and many quarrels. This was due to three main causes, the first being the misdeeds of contemporaries: "Three classes of vipers [*tripuṣkara*] are riding together over the Tantra Shastra—namely, a number of short-sighted and illiterate traders, a few crafty discoverers of practices of magic, and some thoughtless and starving spiritual interpreters of the Shastra. Through them society is today going down to perdition."[61] Instead of listening to these deceitful voices, Shivachandra stressed the need for instruction by a guru and strict adherence to the Shastra: "From the Tantra alone must be learnt what the Tantra has said about the tattva of Tantra."[62] Second, Shivachandra lamented that people were convinced that the effects of worship (*upāsanā*) had to be believed before they were actually *experienced* in practice. This, in his opinion, was not only mistaken but also impossible, especially for the most secret of secrets (*gūṛhātigūṛhatam rahasya*) of Tantric worship. In fact, people had no knowledge about practices such as *ṣaṭcakra*, beyond widespread sensationalized accounts. In "the ever-new religious waves [*nityanaba dharmmataraṅga*] of the nineteenth century," many used terms such as *kulakuṇḍalinī* without comprehending them. Shivachandra was especially irked by a "class of yogis" who thought "there is really a lake of clear water within the body, and that lotuses blooming in them form the *ṣaṭcakra*!" Quoting a song by Ramprasad to illustrate the secret language used to describe Tantric concepts and yogic practices, Shivachandra mocked those who were not capable of understanding such encrypted expressions. Even worse were those who denounced Kali and Shiva, and Tantra as a whole; Shivachandra had no time for the words of those "non-Aryans."[63] But even among those who had been initiated—the third problem highlighted by Shivachandra—confusion and contradictions prevailed. Most were without direction, as guru lineages had declined and traditions faded.[64]

The main culprits behind these developments were identified as contemporary reformers who were influenced by Western education and had created a "pernicious system of non-Āryya education."[65] These were, most prominently, the members of the Brāhma and the Ārya Samāj. The latter were attacked for their criticism of image worship and idolatry, which they had adopted from Christian missionaries, Shivachandra implied. The language of idolatry, which had been given wide currency "by the community of unbelievers [*nāstik sampradāẏ*]," had misled "many senseless Hindus, both illiterate and literate," and generated a "class of born-blind educated fools." Half-"demons," these people were responsible for the ill fortune of India, as "all those spiritual principles propounded in the nineteenth century vomit only infidelity [*unbiṃśa śatābdīr ādhyātmik tattvasakal nāstikatāi udgīraṇ kare*]."[66]

Shivachandra's criticism of the Brahmos was much more extensive and at the same time considerably less polemical. This might have been the case because the Aryas were less influential in the Bengali context but also because

Brahmo positions were not as hostile to the Tantras as those of Dayananda's followers. It will be recalled that the *Mahānirvāṇa Tantra* enjoyed great popularity among Brahmos. The text itself contains formulations that are characteristic of Advaita Vedanta, such as the notion of *jīvanmukti* and the assertion that liberation is possible through an intellectual realization of the Absolute (*brahmā-jñāna*).[67] This becomes clear in light of the examples that are provided for the relation between the Absolute and the world.[68] These aspects indicate an intense exchange between Tantric and Advaita Vedanta schools in Bengal that warrants further scrutiny. In any case, it was not least for this reason that Shivachandra challenged his Brahmo opponents on the grounds of philosophical arguments instead of launching full-blown insults against them, as he would have with the Aryas.

The importance that Shivachandra attached to his Brahmo rivals becomes most tangible in his offensive against Rammohan, the modern individual whose ideas are most extensively challenged in *Tantratattva*. A whole chapter is dedicated to a refutation of Rammohan's understanding of a formless Brahman and what Shivachandra regarded as a flawed nondualism that misrepresented the relationship between Brahman, the material world, and the individual (*jīva*) inhabiting it. Shivachandra maintained that it was through *sādhana* rather than through intellectual reasoning that the true nature (*tattva*) of the world and the *jīva* could be understood, and eventually her or his oneness with Brahmamayi, the Mother of the Universe, which is a manifestation of the Absolute, Brahman.[69]

Shivachandra's education at Navadvip and Benares manifests in the vast corpus of Sanskrit texts that reflect the peculiarities of the Bengali School. These include Puranas that were of central importance for the Bengali School, notably the *Devī Bhāgavata* (also known as *Śrīmad Bhāgavata*) and the *Devī Māhātmya*, as well as a large number of Tantras from which Shivachandra drew quotes to support his argument. Among those, the *Mahānirvāṇa Tantra* unsurprisingly stands out as the foremost authority, next to the *Kulārṇava Tantra*. The *Śāradātilaka*, the *Gandharva Tantra*, the *Rudrayāmala Tantra*, or the *Yoginī Tantra* might also be singled out amid the most frequent references that underline Shivachandra's Kaula background. The pandit made a point of basing his arguments on (supposedly) old Tantras, as he emphasized that most nineteenth-century works were useless, if not dangerous, for a proper understanding of Tantra. He did hold two recent Bengali works in high esteem, however: "With the exception of the Prāṇatoṣiṇī and the Tantrasāra, all works which have been published on the subject of Tantra are but thorns on the path of truth."[70] His role as an exemplary Tantric pandit of the Bengal School is further highlighted by his frequent appraisals of Ramprasad Sen and other Shakta poets, as well as contemporary *sādhakas* such as Vamakhepa of Tarapith.

Its ostensibly "orthodox" stance notwithstanding, it would be too simplistic to regard *Tantratattva*, as Urban does, as a purely conservative, reactionary work.[71] As has become evident above, the self-proclaimed orthodox cohort was highly heterogeneous and driven by a reformist agenda that often overlapped with those of self-proclaimed reformers. Taylor was therefore right to underscore that Shivachandra should not merely be viewed as a reactionary, as he advocated the relaxation of caste-related and religious distinctions.[72] At the same time, it would be misleading to regard his efforts as socially "progressive," not only because said relaxations were understood to exclusively take place within a ritual context but also because they were far removed from contemporary sociopolitical ideas as they were articulated by Brahmos. Rather, they resulted from elements that had been particular to the Bengali School for centuries. Yet his aim of restoring *sanātana dharma* as the foundation of a future society was shared by many reformers, and several outright reformist individuals can be counted among his disciples and collaborators.

The prominence of the *Mahānirvāṇa Tantra* is crucial because it presented Tantra as the appropriate doctrine for the Kali Yuga and as the true *sanātana dharma*, invoking the authority of antiquity while displaying reformist tendencies. It also stressed the need for personal qualification (*adhikāra*) rather than predetermination by caste, religion, or sex: every householder could become a practicing ascetic, and distinctions of cast, religion, and sex were suspended within the ritual context. It also promised liberation while living (*jīvanmukti*) and emphasized the need for *sādhana*, through which the practitioner could realize the Absolute through Shakti, which manifested within the individual body as kundalini that could be raised by the means of yogic practice through the six chakras. These core characteristics of *Tantratattva* are in accordance with the contexts that have been discussed in previous chapters. At the same time, there are significant differences between *Tantratattva* and the approaches to Tantra that have been explored so far. Most important is the notion of science and its relationship to Tantric practice.

Science and *Sādhana* in *Tantratattva*

Like other authors, Shivachandra asserted the rationality of the Shastras, but his stance toward "science" is fundamentally dismissive. Rather, he emphasized the need for "knowledge" but stressed that knowledge was worthless without "practice" and "experience" demonstrating its efficiency. In order to understand his position toward science, it is necessary to discuss his opinion of rival contemporary movements and the ontology of shakti that he expounds as the foundation of worship and, eventually, liberation. Ritual practice (*sādhana*) was heralded by Shivachandra as the only viable path to liberation, and even to a basic understanding of the world.

The main intention of *Tantratattva* was to demonstrate that *sādhana* and the fruit of its successful performance, *siddhi*, were grossly misunderstood by the vast majority of people. Explaining that *sādhana* was of three kinds—physical, verbal, and mental—Shivachandra lamented that the country was crowded with people born of parents of different castes, foreigners (*mlecchas* and *yavanas*), and "people who adhere to other religious beliefs."[73] This was due to the Kali Yuga, with its bad practices. As a result, "India has to-day lost her old strength and the vigor of her austerities. Gone is that old faith, strength, and fortitude; gone is that courage."[74] What pained Shivachandra most was the emergence of a "guru profession," along with "political revolutions" and "a revolution in language"—a reference to British rule and education in English that is reminiscent of Sachchidananda's polemics against "Guruism."[75] True guruhood, in Shivachandra's eyes, could never be a profession, yet it now was centered on material wealth (*artha*) and causing great harm (*anartha*). Three classes of false gurus were responsible for this degradation: Vaishnava (*prabhu*, lord) and Brahmo (*bibhu*, omnipresent) gurus, who at least "originally" had based themselves on the Shastras; worse than those two classes was the third, consisting of "self-existent" (*svayambhu*) gurus without a proper lineage, who claimed to teach yoga. That "gang of men who are at heart atheists and Chandalas" could be found everywhere and had taken the place of the "true Yogis of yore."[76] Although they were devoid of any true worship and not concerned with caste rules (*barnāshram'dharmma*), such people and their male and female gurus professed to be followers of *āryya dharmma*. Shivachandra was most alarmed by "the fact that young men puffed up with their Western education [*pāścātyabidyābhimane sphītbakṣā*], but destitute of real worth, aimless and extremely lazy, show particular eagerness to learn this newly discovered yoga, which presents itself to them as a dharmma which may be followed without any labor, trouble, or cost to themselves."[77] The Vaishnava and Brahmo classes of professional gurus were steadily approaching the condition of those "unbelievers" (*nāstik*). In a highly sarcastic tone, Shivachandra reprimanded Vaishnavas for being "charmed by the glamour of love-maddening plays" and rejecting knowledge in favor of devotion (*bhakti*). Ignorant of the true meaning of worship, they were against mantra and any form of worship itself, inevitably causing the creation of a "non-Āryya society" and getting lost in self-indulgence.[78] Another class, the Brahmos, would think that "a man can never be a man's guru," that man's Supreme Guru would in fact be God (*īśvar*) and Nature (*prakṛti*).[79] Such a misconception could arise only when people failed to understand the necessity of receiving initiation, specifically "from a Tantric guru."[80] This was essential even for those who had amassed knowledge of the shastras and in old age decided to "set their minds to siddhi and sādhana." Great danger loomed for those who had learned without aid, as the *Kulārṇava Tantra* made it explicit that self-study was not possible. Initiation by a guru was always superior to "the load of lifeless blocks of wood which are various forms of worldly knowledge," and the prerequisite for entering the path to liberation.[81]

Possibly struggling with his own experiences, Shivachandra underlined that, no matter how many modern "degrees" a disciple had, he would still be a perfect ignoramus in the field of *sādhana*, and his vanity of worldly knowledge (*laukik bidyā*) was no match for the superior knowledge (*mahābidyā-tattvabidyā*) of the guru.[82] Shivachandra explained in great detail that the choice of a disciple (*śiṣya*) was a delicate matter and could be made only after careful and extensive examination. He was therefore alarmed by the Vaishnava and Brahmo gurus who had turned away from the shastra and had become "incarnations of abnormality" who "are in the habit of granting initiation at the rate of ten or twenty a day."[83]

As mentioned, his stance toward the Brahmos was complex. There are several reasons for this. First, Brahmo methods of propaganda and missionary work had served as a model for societies such as Shivachandra's. Generally, defenses of Hinduism were largely influenced by Brahmo teachings well into the 1870s and 1880s, making Brahmos a major and diverse cultural force in Bengal that no one could simply dismiss. Second, and more important, Brahmo positions toward the Tantras, unlike those of the followers of Dayananda's Ārya Samāj, were not categorically negative. Brahmos such as Rammohan and Rajnarayan held at least some Tantras, among them especially the *Mahānirvāṇa Tantra*, in high esteem—the same scripture that was served as one of Shivachandra's major authorities. Panchkari Bandyopadhyay, a prominent affiliate of Shivachandra, even attempted to prove that Rammohan had in fact been a Tantric.[84] Thus, from the perspective of Shivachandra, Brahmos had indeed originally based their creed on the shastras, but had become corrupted by foreign influences.

Shivachandra was not alone in challenging the "anti-idolatrous" Vedantic monotheism of the Brahmos. Ramakrishna especially had attracted a large following with his emphasis on the concept of *adhikari-bheda*, which prescribed different forms of worship depending on the individual practitioner's qualities and qualifications. This made it possible to harmonize image worship and the worship of multiple gods with the concept of a formless Brahman, since it could be argued that certain individuals were not (yet) capable of grasping the abstract, true nature of the godhead. It also countered the perception that Hinduism was just as good as any (monotheistic) religion, a tendency that Brahmos were often criticized for and that was especially pertinent in a period that saw the emergence of a "pan-Hindu" discourse.[85]

It does not come as a surprise, then, that a substantial and central part of *Tantratattva* revolves around Brahmo teachings. A whole chapter dealing with the different aspects or qualities of Brahman—the so-called *guṇas*—was in fact a response to the standpoint of Rammohan and his followers. In his discussion of "the play of guṇas" (*guṇalīlā*), Shivachandra highlighted the aspects of Brahman as Shiva, as Krishna, and as Shakti, providing a synthesis of Shakta and Vaishnava perspectives. Through Shakti, the Mother of the Universe, Brahman manifests in the dualistic material world. It is through her that Brahman establishes concordance between a seemingly conflicting mass of *guṇas*. Consequently, the *sādhaka* realizes the absolute Brahman through *sādhana*, by focusing on the Goddess (*devī*). This point is especially important because it pertains directly to the issue of image worship. Although the Mother is omnipresent, it is easiest for the individual (*jīva*) to worship one of her particular manifestations, or by means of a representation such as images or yantras. This, Shivachandra maintained, was misunderstood by those who had superficially studied the works of Vedanta and yoga, including the illustrious Rammohan. Rammohan had argued that an omnipresent being cannot be invoked through a material object: it would be futile to assume that the formless could be worshiped through form. Shivachandra argued that the "delusion" (*bhrānti*) of worshiping the Mother in a particular manifestation is not harmful but useful, as long as the *sādhaka* is aware of the ultimate oneness of all, which unfolds within the vast and seemingly contradictory play of the aspects of Brahman through shakti.[86]

In his criticism of worship practices, Rammohan had pointed out that there is no "here and there" for Brahman, who consequently cannot be invoked and told to "come" anywhere, for instance into an image. Shivachandra countered that it is precisely the delusion of "here and there" that the *sādhaka* acknowledges as *his* reality, and thus as the means to eventually realize Brahman: "This is what is called being too intelligent! Here Roy ought to have understood that what he was saying belonged to a different province [*adhikāra*] altogether. Its proper place is in the sphere of pure knowledge [*jñānakāṇḍa*]."[87] On these grounds, Shivachandra professed that Rammohan had profoundly misunderstood the nature of worship and its underlying ontology. It might be true that the Mother is invoked by saying "Come," but she is invoked not in her omnipresent totality but in her manifest form as Mother of the Universe.[88]

At the core of his argumentation, Shivachandra opposed to the nondualism of Rammohan his *qualified* Shakta nondualism that acknowledged the reality of the material world: all is ultimately one, but Brahman operates through shakti in the very real, material world. This encompasses the individual worshiper, who experiences shakti through *sādhana* as the *kulakuṇḍalinī*. In contrast to the abstract theorizing of the Vedantist, the Tantric devotee (*bhakta*) is a "world-conquering" (*bhubanabijaẏī*) individual who "boldly and proudly" acknowledges the great delusion of the material world, Mahāmāyā, as the Mother.[89] Instead of denying and fearing her, the Tantric practitioner embraces her:

> A sādhaka will here observe what a difference there is between sādhana and intellectual reasoning [*jñān-bicār*]—a difference as great as that between heaven and hell. Can the bubbles of intellectual [*jñān*] and scientific [*bijñān*] reasoning attract the notice of him who has sunk into the play of the waves of the charming sweetness of the charmer of the world? Ah, how sweet, how sweet, what an accomplishment in sādhana![90]

However, contemporary society was devoid of both *siddhi* and *sādhana*. For want of instruction by a competent guru, only a minuscule number of *sādhakas* could comprehend the aspects governing the material existence of individuals, while the mass of the population was either completely ignorant or misled by the doctrines of the nineteenth century. It was therefore no surprise that most contemporaries denied the workings of shakti, which can be employed by the initiated *sādhaka* through mantras and other means. The same cosmic powers form the basis for the worship of images:

> In fact, it is one of the terrible diseases of the nineteenth century to raise at every word the cry, "The laws of Nature [*prākrtik niẏama*] are violated." . . . In fact, the root of this objection is to be found, not in the nature of the Universe, but in the nature of the objector. He has, perhaps, with the narrow notions which are the product of his intellect and knowledge, understood Nature herself to be very narrow. . . . But, as a matter of fact, the law of Nature is one and inviolable, and consequently the appearance of the Devi, whose substance is consciousness in an earthen image, under the influence of Mantra, is natural and self-evident. Really this appearance is but manifestation.[91]

The goal of Tantric practice was to reach "the ultimate truth of Advaita," that is nondualism, the realization of the unity of everything. While Shivachandra's diverse disciples, such as Baradakanta, Woodroffe, and Pramathanath, asserted the rational and scientific character of Tantric *sādhana*,[92] their guru's position toward science was more indifferent: "This Shastra is neither philosophy nor science [*darśan bā bijñān nahe*]. It is the sādhana which leads to siddhi. It must be practiced as well as understood. By practice, even though without understanding, it will be made plain. But no amount of understanding without practice will effect this."[93] Shivachandra dismissed philosophy as mere abstraction and science as materialistic ignorance. Rather, he concentrated on the necessity of Tantric *practice*, which he regarded as superior to those who focused on the attainment of knowledge or devotion. In this model, modern science takes the lowest rank, overshadowed by insights that the Rishis had already gained millennia ago:

> The difference between the sight of those who nowadays display their knowledge of science [*bijñānbidyā*] by a discussion of the principles of matter [*bhūttattva*] and that of the Rishis is this: The former, in their short lives having seen but a small world, gasp out with tired voices: "Who knows what lies beyond this?" However, on seeing the world-play, one only feels that wonderful indeed must be the nature [*tattva*] of the real form of Her whose play it is, and that if one would have knowledge of that wonderful Shakti, there are no better means in human life than to study the principles

> of the universe. . . . The universe does not appear wonderful in the sight of him who has seen the primordial Shakti, the source of birth of this perfect play.[94]

For Shivachandra, the efficiency of *sādhana* as a method for realization was a proven fact, and the shastras teaching it were eternally true and infallible, as they were not merely the isolated experiences of individuals but revealed truth. The many who doubted that fact were, in his opinion, "made restless by the inconstant waves of glittering physical science [*cākcikyamaẏ bhūtbijñān*]."[95] The *sādhaka*, in contrast, operated in a threefold way toward the attainment of the nondualistic knowledge of Brahman: "(1) Hearing, thinking, and constant meditation, prescribed in the Vedanta philosophy; (2) practice of yoga; and (3) sādhana, consisting of a combination of the three things—karma [work, action], yoga, and jñān [knowledge], with bhakti as their root." This could be achieved only by following the Kaula path.[96]

The superiority of the Kaula path resulted from the impossibility of adhering to Vedic rules in the Kali Yuga. Attempts to become a true yogi on the Vedic paths were in vain, resulting in a being that was half-believer, half-unbeliever, half-man, half-lion, "a queer being" whose mind has become a vacuity by constant meditation upon a misty nothing.[97] Shivachandra also pointed out that nondualism—or monism, in the translation of Arthur Avalon—was not only attainable by the Vedantic philosophy taught by Shankara: "As a matter of fact, the principle of monism, which was taught by the Vedanta philosophy, has been brought into harmony with the principle of dualism in the Tantra Shastra."[98] The point was exactly to reach truth through the world of duality instead of its negation or rejection. Vedantists, Shivachandra maintained, were capable of "demolishing the opinion" of Nyaya philosophers, atheists, and others, but they could "only discuss," not attain, *siddhi*.[99]

It is at this point that Shivachandra cautiously touched upon the most controversial and notorious aspects of Tantric *sādhana*: the sexual unification of the male and female principles. He explained that knowledge of the interplay between Shiva and Shakti was the reason that, in the material world, men and women are the object of ritual practice. Even Shiva himself had to practice the "yoga of knowledge" (*jñānyog sādhana karite basiẏāchen*). Although he had created the world, he must worship the world before the "Shakti Tattva" could bloom in his heart.[100] What counted for

Shiva certainly counted for human beings: "It is by virtue of this direct knowledge of the Brahman in the form of Shiva and Shakti [*śibśaktimaẏ pratyakṣa brahmajñān*] that Tantric *sādhakas* ever conquer the world."[101] Shivachandra, however, made it clear that he was discussing "the secret principles of the yoga of knowledge" (*nigūṛh jñānyog-tattva*) that unconditionally required initiation by a guru.[102] The Tantra shastra had discovered a hidden path (*nigūṛh path*) that was not accessible to everyone.[103] This is why Shivachandra only hinted at the practice of *ṣaṭ-cakra-bhed*, or Kundalini Yoga, explaining that he "would not dare enter into the subject here in this short chapter" because it was too extensive and impossible to make the public understand the practice and that an explanation should properly be given by a guru. It was simply impossible to learn about it through writings, especially as no secrets should be revealed to all readers, who, as Shivachandra suspected, were not all "true sādhakas."[104]

Heralding the Dawn of a New Kaula Age

The two volumes of *Tantratattva* show Shivachandra's conviction that the true Aryan wisdom that had prevailed in India's golden age was lost to most contemporaries and corrupted by foreign education. Even most gurus were affected by that degeneration, leading the people away from truth. Only Tantric *sādhana* opened the path to liberation. Its method and underlying teachings were neither abstract philosophy nor vain, superficial physical science, but they led the practitioner to the realization of the true qualities of the universe. This knowledge, however, was accessible only to those who were qualified in the first place and then received initiation by a proper (Kaula) guru. The most profound teachings and practices were kept secret (*niguṛh*) and could not be learned—by any means—in an English school.

Shivachandra's eloquent polemics illustrate the dynamics and interconnectedness of Sanskritic learning, popular practices, and the always ambiguous propagation of *sanātana dharma*. He might have refused to learn English, but most of his disciples and collaborators did, and sometimes even received an English education and worked at institutions such as the High Court or English schools. The activities of these Bengali propagators of Tantra unveil a kaleidoscope of local Brahmanical Sanskritic culture, eclectic popular movements such as that of Kangal and the Bauls, and the colonial bhadralok who followed Shivachandra. These complex local and regional developments were shaped by local rivalries, for instance between Shakta and Vaishnava traditions, but such rivalries were renegotiated and redefined within the context of colonialism. As was the case with the negotiations of Vaishnavism as illustrated by Shishirkumar or Bijaykrishna, the negotiation of Tantra unfolded against a globally entangled background. Nowhere is this more tangible than in the fact that Shivachandra had decided to publish *Tantratattva* in Bengali and then have it translated into English.

In contrast to other Indian positions that have been discussed in previous chapters, Shivachandra did not engage in self-deprecation by admitting the inferiority of Indians in relation to their dominant, younger, Western brothers. He outright refused English education and cultural influences and did not adopt the narrative of racial hierarchies that has been exemplified by Theosophical and Brahmo accounts. What we can observe in his writings, most notably *Tantratattva*, is a narrative of degeneration and imminent regeneration of knowledge that would restore the eternal Aryan dharma to its former glory. This was to be achieved through Tantra. Although the truth was germinating in secret (*nigūṛh bhābe*), it certainly was not supposed to stay underground. Obviously, *Tantratattva* was supposed to reach a broad readership and bring about social transformation.

Interestingly, Shivachandra's scolding of philosophy and science extends beyond what he considered to be Western influences, to other Indian traditions of learning. To be sure, the lack of *siddhi* in Indian society was a result of foreign education, but Shivachandra made it very clear that only *Tantric sādhana* could bring about change. Dismissing Vedantic philosophy as mere speculation and modern science as worthless altogether, he insisted on the value of *sādhana* as being based on practice and experience. Granted correct initiation into its secrets by a qualified guru, a qualified (*adhikāra*) disciple would be able to acquire *siddhi* and conquer the world as a means of liberation. This was a result of the qualified nondualism expounded by Shivachandra or, as Andrew Sartori has called it, the "immanent monism" that was also proposed by contemporary Vaishnavas such as Bijaykrishna.[105] Its emphasis on the embrace of the material world and the acquisition of *siddhi* gave Tantra a decisively empowering thrust. This quality, as will be seen in the following chapter, directly played into the strongly nationalistic tendency that Shivachandra and his followers developed toward the end of the nineteenth century.

7

Tantra and Nationalism

The connection between Tantra and science has run like a red thread through the preceding chapters. This thread is inherently intertwined with the rise of national sentiment throughout the second half of the nineteenth century, as the *Theosophist* and related debates, the setting of Kumarkhali with Kangal's gymnasium, and Shivachandra's propagation of the regeneration of Aryan society have illustrated. It is well known that Tantra, or at least motifs taken from its reservoir, was popular among nationalists. Urban has argued that, for most Indians, and specifically for reformers and more conservative members of the nationalist movement, Tantra was a "terrible embarrassment" and a major reason for the supposed backwardness of India. It was only among the more radical, extremist wing of nationalists that Tantric notions and symbols have also been used positively.[1] This chapter adds complexity to this assessment, as we have seen that Tantra had been an integral part of *dharmaśāstra* in Bengal for centuries. Leading Brahmos from Rammohan to Rajnarayan have invoked the authority of several Tantras to substantiate their viewpoints, and references to the Tantras abound within explicitly conservative movements such as the BADPS.

This warrants closer scrutiny of the role of Tantra in the context of nationalism toward the end of the nineteenth century, and more concretely within the nationalist movement at the beginning of the twentieth known as Swadeshi. Against this broader background, the position of Shivachandra will be contrasted with those of two of his affiliates: Shashadhar Tarkacuramani and Pramathanath Mukhopadhyay, the friend and collaborator of Woodroffe. While all these authors were united in their ardent support for the nationalist cause, their stances toward Western science, although intimately related, are marked by instructive differences that will allow for a concluding analysis of the role of Tantra within the contexts of Hindu nationalism, public education, and the notion of esotericism.

Global Tantra. Julian Strube, Oxford University Press. © Oxford University Press 2022.
DOI: 10.1093/oso/9780197627112.003.0008

The Swadeshi Context

The activities of Shivachandra and his affiliates significantly contributed to the emergence of historical research on Bengali Tantra toward the end of the nineteenth century. The foundation of the Varendra Research Society was a milestone for a new approach to Bengal's past, which was characterized by the initiative of Bengali, rather than foreign, scholars. This directly played into national sentiment, which paralleled developments within the natural sciences. The chemist Prafullachandra Ray (1861–1944) was celebrated for putting Bengal on the map of scientific study. A regular supporter of the social welfare program of the Sādhāraṇ Brāhma Samāj and its girls' school in Calcutta, he not only contributed to contemporary scientific research, but he also opened the perspective on what was regarded as past Indian achievements in his *History of Hindu Chemistry from the Earliest Times to the Middle of the Sixteenth Century* (1902). The work depicted the evolution of "Hindu alchemy" in close relation to the development of Tantric rituals before a civilizational decline since the end of the sixteenth century, giving hope to a revitalization of the ancient knowledge that had once made India great.[2] For similar reasons, the studies of Jagadishchandra Bose (1858–1937) caused excitement among nationalists. His biophysical study of the electrical conduction of stimuli in plants earned him worldwide fame and was hailed by some as the greatest Swadeshi event of 1906.[3]

Indian historical research and science, in short, were integral to the nationalist movement. As Gyan Prakash has examined in some detail, nationalists, and especially those identifying as orthodox, had an often ambiguous relationship to science.[4] On one hand, modern European science served as the model for those who aspired to claim the scientific nature of their convictions. On the other hand, many self-styled orthodox nationalists rejected modern science in favor of an idealized and at times rather fantastical conception of a supposedly superior ancient "Hindu science." Such tensions can be prominently observed among the followers and collaborators of Shivachandra who claimed to oppose the influence of Western science, while at the same time stressing the scientific value of Tantra.

The formation of Shivachandra's Sarvamaṅgalā Sabhā and other "dharma societies" had been stimulated by the Hindu Mela, whose inauguration in 1867 is regarded as the first great expression of a growing sense of nationalism among educated Bengalis. The driving force behind the Mela was the English-educated intelligentsia of Calcutta, including several members of the

Tagore family and Brahmos such as Rajnarayan, who was among its most active contributors. Annual meetings were held until the 1890s, but the Mela's relevance was eclipsed since the 1870s due to a nationalist radicalization that intensified toward the end of the century. This development was significantly fueled by the repressive government of 1876–1880 under viceroy Lord Lytton, who was perceived as the embodiment of the racially charged disdain of a colonial administration that showed little concern for its Indian subjects.

These circumstances gave rise to the Swadeshi movement. Its most immediate cause was the Partition of Bengal in 1905, which had been drawn up by viceroy Lord Curzon.[5] Home to around 80 million people and encompassing Bihar and Orissa, the province of Bengal had been exceptionally large and difficult to govern. It was therefore decided to divide it between its western part and the newly created province of Eastern Bengal and Assam, with Dacca as its capital (see Figure 7.1). Although this was presented as a measure to improve administrative efficiency, the Partition appeared to be a blatant execution of colonial power to suppress the growing national sentiment among Bengali intellectuals. This was underlined by the overt antipathy of Lord Curzon toward the bhadralok, who rallied and petitioned against the plan without success. The Partition offended the cultural self-understanding of the Calcutta elite and exacerbated religious tensions, as it drove a wedge between

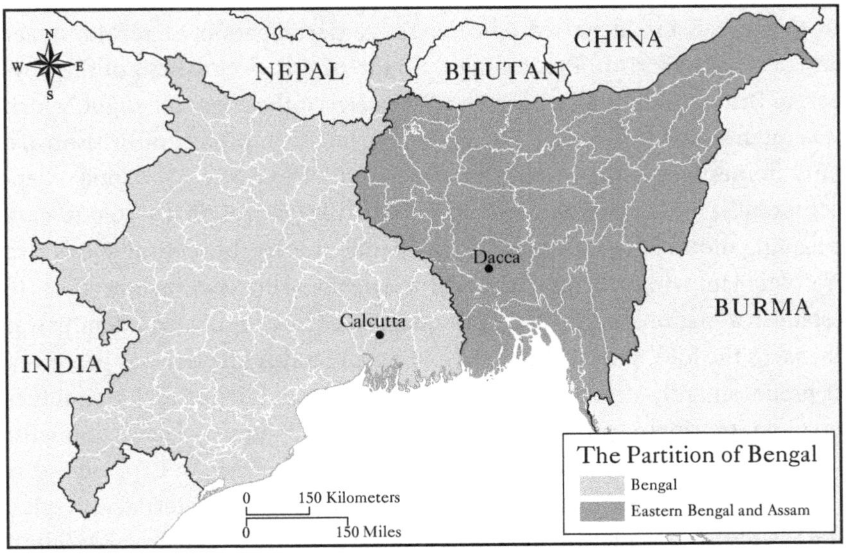

Figure 7.1 The Partition of Bengal.

a predominantly Hindu and a predominantly Muslim region. One result was the chiefly Hindu character of the Swadeshi movement, while Muslims were largely committed to protecting their newly acquired provincial power and formed the Muslim League in 1906.[6] More than a few contemporaries surmised that this was no accident on the part of the British but the successful execution of a "divide and rule" policy.

The repercussions of these developments can still be felt. Aside from inciting nationalism, they also profoundly affected Hindu-Muslim relationships and reshaped the administrative and sociopolitical landscape of the country. The end of the Partition of Bengal is usually dated to the year 1911, when the liberal Lord Hardinge, who was viceroy from 1910 to 1916, recommended the reunification of Bengal and, among other measures, relocated the capital of British India from Calcutta to Delhi in order to placate the Muslim minority. However, by no means did this put an end to the conflicts that the Partition helped to incite, as becomes most obvious in view of the fact that much of Eastern Bengal would later be encompassed by the states of East Pakistan and then Bangladesh. Neither did it quell political agitation, which is why it is difficult to pinpoint a definite end of the Swadeshi movement. The intervening years had produced a complicated landscape of rivaling factions, which embodied many of the tensions that continue to occupy Indian politics.

The spectrum of political demands within the Swadeshi movement ranged from the call for increased administrative participation to revolutionary anticolonial terrorism. Predominant Swadeshi tactics consisted of the boycott of British goods; large bonfires of Western clothes were set alight, which was often framed as a religious ceremony (*puja*). In protest of British rule, only domestic (*swadeshi*) textiles were worn. The movement soon swept across India and culminated in calls for self-rule (*swaraj*) that would remain a leading motto of the struggle for independence. The boycott of goods also translated into other forms of cultural and personal boycott, fueling efforts to establish a "national education." The question of Indian national identity was thrust to the fore, and it is important to note that this identity was perceived as predominantly Hindu.[7] The movement rapidly developed new techniques of militant action, a spirit that was reflected in the columns of new nationalist newspapers, most prominently *Bande Mātaram*, *Sandhyā*, and *Yugāntar*.

Not least because of its vast dimensions and countless internal struggles, the Swadeshi movement defies easy categorization. In his classic study, Sumit Sarkar has proposed a fourfold classification: moderates; the trend toward self-development without inviting an immediate political clash; political extremism using "extended boycott" or passive resistance; and terrorism.[8] In reality, boundaries between different factions were difficult to draw, especially since members tended to shift allegiances and changed or developed their political attitudes, often radically. Surendranath Bandyopadhyay (1848–1925) is usually regarded as the public voice of the movement. A teacher at the Calcutta College, he was the founder of the Indian National Association in 1876, which would later become the Indian National Congress. He was the editor of the weekly newspaper with the highest circulation, the *Bengalee*. In 1907, the Indian National Congress split into what can be classified as a moderate wing and an extremist, militant, revolutionary wing.

Next to Surendranath, the moderate spectrum included famous reformers such as Gopal Krishna Gokhale and Lala Lajpat Rai, whose opinion of revivalism was discussed in chapter 5. While these moderates advocated against violence and attempted to achieve their goals through political pressure and dialogue, younger militants such as Bal Gangadhar Tilak (1856–1920) called for revolutionary action. More passive forms of resistance were famously promoted by Bipinchandra Pal and, at least in public and to varying degrees, by Aurobindo Ghosh (1872–1950), who led the group surrounding *Bande Mātaram*.

Although the Swadeshi movement triggered a number of mass rallies, it remained largely elitist. Out of 186 persons convicted of revolutionary crimes or killed in committing them in the years between 1907 and 1917, no fewer than 165 were Brahmans, Kayasthas, and Vaidyas.[9] As Sarkar has pointed out, virtually no Swadeshi program was directed at peasants, rural areas, or any sphere beyond the concerns of advantaged castes. The lack of popular participation was thus the "Achilles' heel" of the movement.[10] This is underlined by the fact that most of the young extremists were barristers and had received an English education; their privileged status was determined by their caste but also by their education and training. Not least for this reason, the Swadeshi movement is permeated with conflicting attitudes toward British culture, and education in particular.

It is important to consider the Theosophical involvement in this regard. Annie Besant, called "Anna Bāsantī" in *Kalpa*, stands out as the most prominent politically active Theosophist. As is well known, she was elected president of the Indian National Congress in 1917. Another relevant, and earlier, example is Allan Octavian Hume, a relative of Woodroffe. Hume was a confidant of the liberal Lord Ripon, viceroy from 1880 to 1884, who faced stiff resistance from British lawmakers in his efforts to pass legislation that would bolster the rights of Indians.[11] He had joined the Theosophical Society in 1881 and is credited with organizing the Congress Party, whose first meeting he attended as the only British delegate. A range of Indian and non-Indian Theosophists took on leading positions during the Swadeshi period, for instance Narendranath Sen, the editor of the *Indian Mirror*, who was associated with both the Theosophical Society and Keshab's Nababidhān Brāhma Samāj. These connections highlight another important aspect of the Swadeshi movement, namely what Sarkar has called "the ideological conflict between modernism and traditionalism."[12] While this clash indeed stood at the core of the debates about Tantra, it has already become clear that the borders between such ideological standpoints were blurry.[13] This is evident considering the efforts of Shivachandra and his affiliates.

Awakening the Bloodthirsty Mother

It will be recalled that Shivachandra's writings, first and foremost *Tantratattva*, were published in the 1890s. Not surprisingly, Shivachandra, his associates, and his disciples became ardent promoters of the Swadeshi cause. The guru is known to have given several public speeches in support of the movement. One of these was held at the Kushtiya Swadeshi conference in 1905, which was presided over by the raja of Naldanga, the former patron of Baradakanta Majumdar. Its participants included Surendranath, Ambika Majumdar, the later president of the Indian National Congress, pandit Gishpati Kabyatirtha, as well as Jaladhar Sen and Akshaykumar Maitra.[14]

Shivachandra captivated the audience by speaking in a simple yet powerful Bengali, contrary to Surendranath, who was known for delivering his speeches in English, like most contemporary orators.[15] Giving a speech in Bengali was a political statement in itself, and it did not fail to resonate strongly with the popular audience, which was not rarely at a loss when listening to English. Shivachandra's popularizing agenda stood in stark contrast to those reformers who, like Surendranath, were mostly concerned with addressing English-educated Indians. For instance, all participants in the first Congress Party session, which had convened in December 1885 in Bombay, were English educated; more than half of them were lawyers, and the others journalists, businessmen, landowners, and professors. Shivachandra did not share such a background and could demonstrably not be bothered with addressing an English-speaking audience. He wore the attire of a *sādhaka* when he appeared on the stage, which made as much an impression as his use of Bengali. By appearing as a Tantric pandit, Shivachandra invoked widespread associations between Shaktism and nationalism. Adorned with a blood-red sandalwood tilak on his forehead, a necklace of *rudraksha* beads, and an ocher robe, Shivachandra raised his voice and, typically for his oratory style, engaged in a play of words that referred to the different forms of the Mother as an earthen image, the soil of the land, and the Mother of all and everything: "This is our Mother, but She is not simply soil—She is the true Mother. This Mother we must make into the real one and seize it; there is no other way. As we do not know this Mother and abandon her, we turn ourselves into dirt!"[16] The Bengali puns used in this passage invoked the identity of the Mother (*mā-ṭi*) with India's soil (*māṭi*) and its inhabitants, but also with the clay (*māṭi*) used for images of the Goddess, implying that the realization of ultimate unity in the Mother was the precondition for the awakening of the nation.[17] This idea was also expressed in several of Shivachandra's popular songs, which praised the Mother as the nurturer of the land and its children, voiced criticism of colonial oppression, and stressed the fact that one's duty to the Mother equaled one's duty to the homeland.[18] Surendranath, too, linked Swadeshi events with a puja of shakti, which was invoked by many nationalists as a force that had to be awakened in order to free India from its oppressors.[19] In her ferocious, terrifying, and gloriously combative manifestations as Kali and Durga, respectively, the Goddess was identified with Bengal or India and employed for the nationalist cause. The British journalist Valentine Chirol, known for his condescending observations of what he called the *Indian Unrest*, affirmed that tendency: "Nowhere is the cult of the 'terrible goddess,' worshipped under many forms, but chiefly under those of Kali and Durga, more closely associated with Indian unrest than in Bengal."[20] Indeed, this motif had peaked during the Swadeshi agitation, when, for instance, thousands of Bengalis gathered at the Kali temple in Calcutta on September 28, 1905, the new-moon day before the puja (*mahālaẏā*), and protested in favor of the movement.

The most famous and influential expression of the association of the Mother with the homeland is Bankim's song "Bande Mātaram," which was sung to a tune composed by Rabindranath and adopted as the unofficial Swadeshi hymn. It had been preceded by other songs that praised the Mother, most notably Dvijendranath Tagore's "Gloomy Is Your Moon-Face, O Mother India" (*malin mukhacandramā bhārat tomāri*) that had been sung at the inauguration of the first Hindu Mela. But it was Bankim's famous novel *Ānandamaṭh* that served as the main inspiration for Swadeshi nationalists. It was first published as a serial in *Baṅgadarśan* before it was printed in book form in December 1882, becoming "the single most important text for the radical nationalist movement in Bengal in the early twentieth century."[21] The song "Bande Mātaram" runs like a red thread through the novel, which soon developed into "the bible of armed revolutionaries."[22] It told the story of the historical rebellion of ascetics (*sannyāsīs*) in 1772, who had risen against the Muslim ruler in the north of Bengal. Driven by the famine of 1770 and excessive taxation by landlords, the *sannyāsīs* in the novel form a secret society whose headquarters are set up in a temple dedicated to the Mother.

Interestingly, Bankim depicted these ascetics simultaneously as Vaishnavas and followers of the Goddess. This becomes plausible when one realizes that the ascetics' fundamental creed is the *sanātana dharma*, handed down in secret in an age of oppression and darkness.[23] Bankim's prominent depiction of the role of dharma for India underlines the religious dimension of his oeuvre, which, as Hans Harder has pointed out, is often neglected in favor of his activities as a literate.[24] Lamenting his failure to free his Mother from the hands of unworthy foreigners, one of the protagonists is consoled by a healer, who explains the meaning of the "real" *sanātana dharma*. He expounds that the true "Hindu dharma" was based on knowledge (*jñān*), not action (*karma*), and differentiates between an outer (*bahirbbiṣaẏak*) and an inner (*antarbbiṣaẏak*) form of that knowledge. It is the inner knowledge that constitutes the crucial part of *sanātana dharma*, but it can be accessed only after outer knowledge has been acquired.[25] That outer knowledge, however, had been lost for a long time, since no one in the country was able to teach it. It was thus necessary to bring it in from another country, and since the English were very adept at outer knowledge, they should be made kings: "And when through this teaching our people are properly instructed about outer things, they will be able to understand the inner." After that, *sanātana dharma* will shine again, but as long as "the Hindu is not wise and virtuous and strong again," the British rule will persist.[26]

In order to understand this ambivalent stance toward British rule, it is illuminating to turn to another passage, where an initiate is led into the ascetics' temple. Therein, the Mother is depicted in three states that symbolize those of India: first, the Mother as she was in the past, glorious and perfect; then the Mother as Kali, the embodiment of oppressed India, fearsome and bloodthirsty; and third, the future, liberated Mother, radiant and gracious, after all children have embraced her.[27] It becomes clear that Kali was depicted at once as the symbol of degradation under foreign rule and the reservoir of power for its resurgence.[28] Thirsting for blood, she represented the power of revolutionary struggle that would restore a golden past and unite the children of India to lead them into a splendid future. This politicized form of Kali was enthusiastically adopted by revolutionaries, but also by prominent figures such as Vivekananda and Sister Nivedita, most famously in her book *Kali the Mother*. At the same time, the intention of Bankim's novel is anything but unequivocal, and it might very well be that this was quite intentional. The book can be interpreted as both a call for anticolonial insurgency and a defense of British rule, as the passage just quoted illustrates.[29] Much of Bankim's polemics are actually directed against Muslim rulers, while criticism of the British is more subtle and often communicated through puns and innuendo. Tellingly, in the serialized publication Bankim had the ascetics call for an attack on both the English and the Muslims, while the British were excluded in the first book version.[30]

When seen in this light, the passage about inner and outer knowledge seems to imply that the Indian people first had to acquire knowledge about the outer, material world from the English, who ruled not least through their scientific and military superiority. Only then could the inner knowledge, guarded by initiates such as the *sannyāsīs*, come to fruition. One could hence interpret the message as a call for the quiet preparation of independence under British rule, which would inevitably be overcome if the populace embraced the Mother and understood the true *sanātana dharma*.

In any case, numerous revolutionaries embraced the image of bloodthirsty Kali as a symbol of militant resistance. Aurobindo is among the most famous interpreters of the Mother along those lines. Before turning into one of the most influential religious leaders of India, he was devoted to radical politics during the Swadeshi period. He had been born into a privileged family—his maternal grandfather was the ubiquitous Rajnarayan—and sent to England for education, whence he returned in 1893 to work at the State Service in Baroda. He moved to Calcutta during the political upheavals in 1905 and joined the calls for self-rule (*swaraj*). Publicly proclaiming passive resistance, he secretly prepared for militant action with his brother Barindrakumar.[31] In 1902, he was among the founders of the Anuśīlan Samiti, the Society for Exercise, or Self-Cultivation. Already in the 1860s and 1870s, nationalists had founded gymnasia (*ākhṛā*) that promoted physical culture and religious teachings to educate the youth both physically and mentally. It might be recalled that Kangal established such a gymnasium at Kumarkhali. The strengthening of Indian bodies had been an important element in the Hindu Mela program and also within secret societies propagating violent acts of resistance.[32] Not surprisingly, the order of *sannyāsīs* in *Ānandamaṭh* had served as a model for such societies since the 1880s. Aurobindo and others turned "Bande Mātaram" into the rallying cry of the radicals and interpreted Bankim's story as an anticolonial call to revolution.[33]

Aurobindo, like other radicals, deemed his political convictions an integral part of his religious creed.[34] On January 19, 1908, he declared in a lecture to the Bombay National Union, "Nationalism is not a mere political program; Nationalism is a religion that has come from God."[35] He wrote elsewhere, "Nationalism is an *avatār* that cannot be slain. Nationalism is a divinely appointed shakti of the Eternal and must do its God-given work before it returns to the bosom of Universal Energy from which it came."[36] In 1905, Aurobindo published his most influential early political work, a pamphlet with the tile *Bhawani Mandir*. Therein he proclaimed the ideals of a secret religio-political order of young ascetics, which were ardently received among extremists.[37] Aurobindo declared that a nation *was* a shakti, the sum of all its inhabitants' shaktis.[38] The awakening of that power would lead India toward her own liberation but also toward the liberation of humanity:

> It is she who must send forth from herself the future religion of the entire world, the Eternal Religion which is to harmonise all religion, science and philosophies and make mankind one soul. In the sphere of morality, likewise, it is her mission to purge barbarism (Mlechchhahood) out of humanity and to Aryanise the world. In order to do this, she must first re-Aryanise herself.[39]

Like other participants in the discourse on *sanātana dharma* (here, "Eternal Religion"), Aurobindo tied the "true" Hindu religion to an Aryan past whose heritage was practically lost to India. A reawakening of that Aryan-ness would bring about India's independence and even elevate her to leader of the world. Shakti, in that sense, was the literal *power* of national renewal.[40] But it was also a force that would lead to the harmonization of religion, science, and philosophy. This demonstrates how closely interlinked these aspects were.

Toward the end of the nineteenth century, secret societies emerged as the hotbed for nationalists who propagated such ideas. In Aurobindo's case, the founding of secret societies could somewhat be regarded as a family tradition, illustrating the prominence of such tendencies among the Calcutta elite. Rajnarayan had founded a secret society himself, of which Rabindranath had been a member, and which was committed to revolutionary action.[41] Following the establishment of the Anuśīlan Samiti, Aurobindo's brother Barin headed the emergence of a more radical group that would become known under the name Yugāntar ("a new age, an epoch-making revolution"). Beginning in April 1906, a newspaper with that title was published and prosecuted for sedition six times before its eventual suppression in 1908. The notorious editorial of the paper illustrates why the authorities were alarmed by the appearance of the group:

> Will the Bengali worshippers of *Shakti* shrink from the shedding of blood? The number of Englishmen in this country is not above [150,000], and what is the number of English officials in each district? If you are firm in your resolution you can in a single day bring English rule to an end. Lay down your life, but first take a life. The worship of the goddess will not be consummated if you sacrifice your lives at the shrine of independence without shedding blood.[42]

The Yugāntar's overt call for violent action was no mere rhetoric. The group provided instructions for forming secret terrorist organizations, and Barin endeavored to collect weapons and craft bombs.[43] On April 30, 1908, members of the society made use of one of those bombs at Muzaffarpur. It was intended for Douglas Kingsford, who was being transferred from his position as chief presidency magistrate at Calcutta. Instead, the bomb tragically hit the carriage carrying his daughter. The incident caused great shock and provoked a swift crackdown. Police investigation led to the discovery of the Yugāntar headquarters at Barin's country house in a suburb of Calcutta. A number of arrests were made, including Barin and Aurobindo. In May 1908, the latter was taken into custody and sentenced to one year imprisonment. By 1910, following his sentence, Aurobindo turned away from revolutionary politics and became a spiritual teacher, creating his famous, still existing community at Pondicherry.

While Aurobindo's direct involvement in these acts of violence is contested, numerous Bengalis took the Mother's thirst for blood quite literally. Pandits such as Shivachandra certainly did not advocate such behavior, at least not in public, but their identification of the Mother with the motherland overlapped with, and probably informed, the ideas of more extremist revolutionaries. This was no coincidence, as it was especially in the Nadiya region that Shakta-inspired nationalism thrived and developed substantial networks. As the Report on the Anti-Partition and Swadeshi Movement in Bengal from September 1, 1906, remarked, the influence of the Brahmans of Shantipur and Navadvip had helped to make the Nadiya district "a happy hunting ground for political agitators."[44] The authorities took note that political Samitis were active at Krishnagar, Navadvip, Kushtiya, Ranaghat, and Kumarkhali. There were three Swadeshi dacoities in Nadiya in 1908 and 1909, which were thought to have been committed by the "Krishnagar gang" led by insurgents such as Jatindranath Mukhopadhyay.[45]

Known as Bagha Jatin due to his alleged barehanded fight with a Bengal tiger (*bāgh*), Jatindranath was born in the Kaya village in Nadiya. He passed his entrance examination for the Krishnagar Anglo-Vernacular School in 1898 and went to study at the Calcutta Central College.[46] Soon he became a follower of Vivekananda, who encouraged him to take up physical exercise, which made him a renowned strongman and fighter. According to police reports, however, it was chiefly his reputation for being a Brahmachari, a religious disciple, that earned him respect as an extremist leader.[47] Jatin was one of the founders of the Anuśīlan Samiti and is repeatedly highlighted in police reports, for instance in this one, about a secret meeting held in Calcutta in 1900: "The meeting resolved to start secret societies with the object of assassinating officials and supporters of Government. . . . One of the first to flourish was at Kushtea, in the Nadia district. This was organised by one Jotindra Nath Mukherjee."[48] The promotion of societies for political ends was "said to have spread to many of the districts of Bengal and to have flourished particularly at Kushtia, where Jatindra Nath Mukharji was leader."[49] In 1901, Jatin reportedly established a revolutionary society at Kaya.[50] After the disastrous Muzaffarpur bomb attack, he took over the leadership of the Yugāntar group.[51] He was responsible for the establishment of a network of different revolutionary branches, weapons caches, and hideouts.

Several sources claim that Jatin made contact with Shivachandra. As he was married to a woman from Kumarkhali, which is located in Kushtiya, this is not unlikely, although solid evidence is lacking. Purportedly, he was responsible for sending one of his friends, an atheist, to Shivachandra, who made such a strong impression on him that he became a devoted Shakta.[52] As in the case of other tales surrounding Shivachandra, the point here is not so much whether Bagha Jatin was really one of his disciples but that observers wanted to make this seemingly plausible connection: the Tantric guru was perceived as a proponent of the nationalist cause and a determined opponent of the influence of Western culture. Given his vocal support for the Swadeshi movement and the ideas that he spread in his writings and popular songs, this image is certainly warranted. It also fits with the activities of several of his associates, such as the revolutionary known as Tarapada Banerjee, who had been a member of the Yugāntar group before going to Tarapith and becoming one of Vamakhepa's principal disciples, taking on the name of Tarakhepa.[53] It appears that the same Tarakhepa was among the prominent guests at Shivachandra's funeral.[54] The Sarvamaṅgalā Sabhā's Swadeshi connections are further underlined by the fact that Bijaykrishna Gosvami was the guru of no fewer than four prominent figures of the movement, including Bipin.[55]

Shashadhar Tarkachuramani's Spiritual Science

Shivachandra's collaborator and fellow pandit Shashadhar is an instructive example of how these tendencies related to the subject of science. He was one of the most influential pandits who claimed the scientific superiority of Hindu dharma and shaped notions of Aryan-ness.[56] Both he and Shivachandra had written for *Baṅgabāsī* and *Bedᴵbyās*, were published by the same presses, and moved within the same personal networks.[57] It is therefore highly instructive to contrast his conceptualization of a "spiritual science" with Shivachandra's dismissal of science. This will underline common agendas, most notably a rejection of English education, but it will also demonstrate the heterogeneous positions within the "orthodox" camp on the meaning of dharma and science.

Historians of Bengal have tended to judge Shashadhar harshly. Tapan Raychaudhuri regarded him as part of a movement whose doctrine was "Hinduism *uber alles*" [*sic*] and that should be described by the epithet "aggressive chauvinism" rather than "revivalism." According to Raychaudhuri, Shashadhar "sought to justify every Hindu practice—ranging from child marriage and [sati] to popular beliefs in the occult implications of untimely sneezing or the clicking sound produced by house lizards." His attempts to elevate the knowledge of the ancient rishis over that of modern science were marshaled by "pseudo-scientific" arguments and constituted "pathetic attempts to bolster up Hindu self-esteem."[58] In light of political developments in India since the twentieth century, such judgments are understandable.

However, the theories of pandits like Shashadhar deserve to be examined more dispassionately within their historical context.[59] This is not least necessary because of their immense success. As Raychaudhuri pointed out, Shashadhar and his associates could fill town halls wherever they went, and the huge distribution of a paper like *Baṅgabāsī* underlines the attractiveness of their ideas. In fact, the "orthodox" movement, of which Shashadhar was an exceptionally radical representative, posed a most serious threat to the Brahmos, which were reduced to an object of ridicule on the pages of *Baṅgabāsī*.

A closer look at that context will serve to further elucidate the polemics against "reformers" and the influence of Western science as well as that the "scientific explanations" of Hinduism were very much in line with contemporary global debates about religion and, significantly, with those involving Theosophists in particular.[60] They were also widespread among Bengali intellectuals such as Bhudev Mukhopadhyay and Akshaychandra Sarkar.[61] These connections are confirmed by contemporary accounts. Bipin, for instance, remembered the "schools" led by Bankim and Shashadhar as the most influential representatives of "Hindu religious revival and Hindu social apologetics."[62] He wrote, "Religious ritualism, though sought to be defended by psuedo [*sic*] science, such as was found in the exegeses and apologetics of Pandit Shashadhar Tarkachudamani and the Theosophists, practically initiated a new movement of inner spiritual and religious culture which was distinct from all outer rituals and formularies."[63] That Bipin named the efforts of Shashadhar and the Theosophists in one breath underlines that Theosophy was an integral part of such debates, and that its connection with the "orthodox" milieu largely worked through the notions of science and revivalism. Indeed, we observed in the previous chapter how compatible his ideas were with those of the Theosophists, and it might be recalled that his Vedavyasa Press printed reports of Theosophical meetings. In 1884, he published his main work, a book with the programmatic title *Dharmmabyakhya* (*Explanation of Dharma*). It was printed by the Bangabasi Press and published by Bhudhar Chattopadhyay, who would soon launch *Bedbyās*. As the title implies, the book attempted to elucidate the meaning of dharma through a dialogue between a teacher (*ācārya*) and a disciple (*śiṣya*). Echoing the revivalist mood that also characterized the writings of Shivachandra, both Shashadhar and his publisher stressed that they were witnessing the "advancement of worldly knowledge about the gross material principles" (*sthūla-jaṛatattva-jñānbiṣaẏṇī-unnati*) after a period of disaster that had left India in ruins. While knowledge about things worldly and material was blossoming, knowledge about "fine" or "subtle" principles (*sūkṣṇatattva*) had degenerated and "the power of subtle philosophy" (*sūkṣṇadarśan śakti*) had waned. Due to "foreign education" (*bidēśīẏa śikṣā*), the ancient, lucid Aryan Shastras had been polluted and profaned; the dharma that they taught was neglected by an oppressed society that had lost its way.[64]

It was Shashadhar's aim to prove that dharma was based not on fiction and imagination but on teachings that were backed up by the discoveries of modern science, and vastly superior to them for the very reason that they did not foolishly draw a line between "gross" and "subtle" principles. Shashadhar based his explanation of the "practice of dharma" (*dharmmasādhana*) on the workings of shakti, which, he maintained, was not a material substance but the "repository" of material substance whose different manifestations pervaded, and essentially constituted, the universe.[65] The physical world, the individual *ātmāśakti*, and the diverse forms of shakti that affect the physical body (*śarīr*)—such tangible phenomena *are* shakti, the source and foundation of all things material (*śaktiī bhautik ālambana*).

This, the teacher tells his amazed disciple, explains the material forces of attraction (*ākarṣan*) between all bodies celestial and terrestrial, as well as those of magnets (*cumbak*).[66] Shakti also constitutes the functions of the nerves and the brain, and it manifests as the experience of consciousness (*caitanya*) and energy within the body. It is through shakti that the *jībātmā*, the individual *ātmā* or "soul," is formed, but also the human faculties of the intellect (*buddhi*), the mind (*man*), and the senses (*indriẏa*).[67] On these grounds, Shashadhar professed to "scientifically" justify the effectiveness of *sādhana*: since the individual is, like everything else, pervaded by shakti, the key to enlightenment is self-knowledge (*ātmajñān*), which ultimately leads to the realization of the all-pervading consciousness and Supreme Being (*paramātmā*).[68] The ancient Aryans had understood this and developed techniques such as meditation that employed electrical (*tāṛit·*) currents flowing through the body, thus uniting body and "soul" (*deha o ātmā*).[69] Similarly, the performance of *āsana* and the wearing of a tuft of hair (*śikhā* or *ṭiki*) could be explained by the workings of electromagnetic currents.[70] Religious practice is thus inherently intertwined with, and based on, principles such as magnetism and electricity that are only superficially explored by modern science, as the latter merely focuses on their material, gross aspects.

Such claims stood at the core of the agenda of *Bed'byās*, which was established in 1886 by Bhudhar Chattopadhyay. The paper ran through ten volumes until 1895 and, despite its considerable success, was struggling from a lack of funds and continuous ridicule by the badhralok intelligentsia. In 1892, *Bedlbyās* was declared the official mouthpiece of the Dharma Maṇḍalī, but the alliance broke apart only two years later due to internal struggles and a far-reaching controversy about the Age of Consent Bill from 1891, which was seen by many conservatives as an intrusion into traditional legislation.[71] The first editorial of *Bedlbyās* from April and May 1886 stated the intention of the paper as follows: "The glorious praise of the true Hindu Dharma is the goal of Bedlbyās. Today, many are curious to learn about the hidden secret of Dharma [*dharmmer nigūṛh rahasya*]. But sadly, the true explanation of Dharma is not published in any newspaper. Many have been led astray by reading delusions. This sight is hugely deplorable."[72] With the help of excellent pandits, the editor promised to provide a correct interpretation. He also stressed that it was the goal of the authors that "the outcome of politics would be just in the eyes of Hindus," making the political nature of the endeavor explicit. It is therefore telling that the first article was penned by Shashadhar and revolved around his conceptualization of a "spiritual science" (*adhyātmabijñān*). This term literally means "the science of *ātmā*," while *ātmā* can signify both the supreme divine Being and the individual. It can consequently pertain to both the metaphysical and physical realms, Shashadhar's point being that there is ultimately no separation between the two. The pandit elucidated this through an explanation of the principles of funeral rites (*śrāddhatattva*):

> The conclusion of the question concerning funeral rites derives from spiritual science. Through this science, one can understand bodily material things, the senses, the mind and the soul as well as their procedures, the conditions of death and rebirth, the principles of god and Brahman. This is why we have spiritual science. This is confirmed by Samkhya, Patanjali, Vedanta, Shruti, and all the other Shastras. All aspects of the principles of Shraddha rely entirely on this spiritual science. This spiritual science, in turn, is so dependent on other sciences that whoever is ignorant of the basic principles of these sciences would remain almost blind to the spiritual science, no matter how hard he labors.[73]

Hence, Shashadhar stressed that anyone who is unfamiliar with those sciences pertaining to the material aspects of being would not be able to comprehend the workings of the subtle, spiritual realm. He provided a list of sciences that are especially close to spiritual science: physical science (*bhautik-bijñān*), the science of electricity (*tāṛidbijñān*), astronomy (*jyotirbbijñān*), the science of psychology (*bhūt-bijñān*),[74] the science of shakti (*śakti-bijñān*), anatomy (*śarīrsthān bijñān*), and rhetoric (*bāgbijñān*).[75] In what follows, Shashadhar differentiated between those sciences that focus on gross (*sthūl*) substances and those that focus on subtle matter-substances (*sūkṣṇa bhūtpadārtha*).[76] One has to understand the gross aspects before proceeding to the subtle ones.

Shashadhar insisted that it would be mistaken to exclusively focus on either gross or subtle aspects. On one hand, he stressed that only ignorant people would believe that the true nature of matter can only be regarded in the scientific sense and that it is beyond the comprehension of the natural senses. On the other hand, an understanding of the physical substances was crucial to comprehend the workings of nature, such as the transmission of messages through electrical currents (that is, the telegraph). For this reason, it was necessary to master both the gross and the subtle sciences. Shashadhar explained that the "Aryan forefathers" had discovered this comprehensive knowledge, which formed the basis of their religious rites. If one wished to perform the funeral rites in accordance with the rishis, it was necessary to comprehend this.[77]

Similar to Shivachandra, however, Shashadhar considered the wisdom of the Aryan forefathers lost. Society had long fallen into a state of degeneracy and, due to the influence of foreign education, that downward spiral continued to accelerate. He elaborated this thought in an article for *Bedbyās*, which bears the telling title "Progress or Decline?" Again, the piece consists of a dialogue between a teacher and his disciple, which centers around the circumstance that, in the nineteenth century, many quarrels have arisen about the issues of progress or decline in India. The reason, we learn, was that there were different communities (*sampradāẏ*) with opposing opinions, four of which are singled out by the disciple:

1. Many gentlemen [*badhra santānagaṇ*] say, "Like the moon becomes larger every night during the period of the waxing moon, similarly India too is progressing on a daily basis. One feels remorseful and ashamed to publicly talk about the ugly and fallen state that India was in before the nineteenth century, reaching all the way back to the day of creation. It is a matter of great fortune for India that this eternal darkness has receded and ever since the introduction of western civilization and western education, the period of waxing moon has begun here."

2. Some other gentlemen [*badhralok*] say, "It is true that India is progressing now, but this progress is not greater than that of earlier times. Because India was developed in the past too. However, in the middle period, from a little before the Muslims, it witnessed colossal decline. In comparison to that, there is and has been a lot of progress nowadays."
3. Another group says, "There was neither any progress earlier nor is there any progress now. We do not even believe that real progress is possible. But if there is such a thing, it is still in the womb of the future."
4. Yet another group of gentlemen comes to the opposite conclusion. They say, "India is sinking every day into the depth of the ocean of regression nowadays. Only in the earliest times had India been at the zenith of progress."[78]

Confused by those opposed standpoints, for each of which there seemed to be good arguments, the disciple asks for guidance. As the teacher explains, progress or decline can be observed by anyone, but a sound judgment depends on what these words are supposed to mean. The meaning of words was anything but clear and depended on how different people employed them. For instance, the term "idolatry" had been introduced by the English, and English-educated Bengalis created an equivalent (*pauttalikatā*). But in condemning such a practice, they confused what they were talking about: from the viewpoint of the teacher, the worship of an image as an actual god or goddess would be illogical and against the shastra. But that is not what the worshiper does, as he worships not the clay idol itself but *ādyāśakti* and, through her, Brahman. A similar misunderstanding pertained to the English term "caste system," which, Shashadhar claimed, similarly to Baradakanta, was in fact quite different from the actual concept of *jātibhed*.[79]

In order to understand what the different groups meant when they talked about progress and decline, the disciple departs to question them and upon his return gives a summary of their responses. By "progress," the first group meant the establishment of schools, colleges, girls' and women's education, learning through English textbooks; an emphasis on the use of English that went as far as to postulate that one should even dream or think in that language; emulation of English clothes and habits, including the freedom of women, the showing of skin, relaxed rules for marriage and divorce, widow remarriage; and the abolishment of food and drink regulations. In the view of the second group, it was learning and education, that is to say the cultivation of natural science, chemistry, physical science, which declined under Muslim rule and were now progressing. The third group maintained that progress means the overall happiness of each and every individual. When all the people in India have no physical, mental, or familial unhappiness, discomfort, or shortages, only then will there be complete progress. But there is no evidence to suggest that this has ever been the case and, clearly, it is not the case even today. Hence, there has never been any real progress.[80] Listening to these responses, the teacher agrees that, from such viewpoints, progress and decline could be reasonably understood. It is the fourth group, however, that motivates him to explain his own perspective. According to the disciple, the fourth group says

> that only the expansion of the inner world or the growth of spiritual integrity or substance [*ādhyātmik sārabattā*] can be called progress. Good health, long life, strength, merit, courage, bravery, freedom, wealth, grace, fortune, and all such happiness, comfort, and tranquility that are possible in this world and hereafter, are all results of the expansion of the inner world of human beings. If human beings do not have any spiritual existence, then none of these things happen to them. . . . Hence, the increase of spiritual vigor [*ādhyātmik sārabattā*] is real progress, and if people do not possess any inner wealth, no matter how wealthy they might be from outside, all that would be considered decline.
>
> In ancient times, India possessed complete inner substance [*antaḥsārabattā*], [and] there was progress. Nowadays India is getting [more] bereft of any inner substance with each passing day. This is what can be called decline.[81]

The disciple wonders, however, what inner and spiritual substance or vigor are supposed to mean exactly. The teacher first responds by outlining the workings of Shakti and her different manifestations, referring to his *Dharmmabyakhya* for further details.[82] He then continues to expound the development of different qualities within the individual (the *guṇas* that are categorized as sattvic, tamasic, and rajasic). Because every individual and his or her consciousness are ultimately the sum of shakti, the practitioner was able to evolve through *sādhana* and conduct of life.[83] This, in short, is how real progress should be understood. The teacher makes it clear that English education offered no guidance on that path. Quite the contrary:

> The spread of schools, colleges, and primary schools, as well as the imitation of the English language and clothes is no progress, the earning of BAs, MAs, and so on, all those English books and the adoption of the English language are no progress, because if today's learning and the passing of exams mean the memorization of some words, or only knowing some truths and lies, then there is no connection whatsoever between them and the aforesaid types of improvement or degradation.[84]

The teacher acknowledges that both a Sanskrit school (*ṭol*) and an English college are places where students study and memorize things. But there was a vast difference between the English books taught at college and the Sanskrit shastras. The latter are not merely about learning things by heart but about the development of knowledge (*jñān*), the ability of philosophical discernment (*bibek*), and the renunciation of worldly matters (*bairāgya*), which eventually leads to liberation (*mukti*). The English language, and certainly college books, were devoid of such wisdom (more specifically, of *ātmatattva*, *brahmatattva*, *īśbartattva*, the principles of the *ātmā*, of Brahman, and of gods). Moreover, English books were so simple and shallow that there would be no hope at all of developing one's intellect (*dhīśakti*) through them.[85] In short, the teacher presents English education as restricted to the worldly material sphere, but also as inherently superficial and without any value for the development of the individual in the here and now, and consequently for his or her working toward liberation. In this, Shashadhar's position was in accordance with Shivachandra's understanding of education according to the "Aryan shastras," which he had outlined in an article for *Bed'byās* in July 1889.[86]

It can be concluded that Shashadhar shared with Shivachandra the conviction that the Aryan dharma had been lost in India, and that English education was nowadays mainly responsible for suppressing its revival. However, instead of dismissing the notion of science altogether, Shashadhar developed the concept of "spiritual science" that focused on the "subtle" aspects of being. Crucially, this spiritual science was *not* opposed to sciences focusing on the "gross" aspects of being, but interdependent. One outcome is a radical difference between the argumentation of Shivachandra and Shashadhar. The latter was at pains to explain, and legitimize, the practice of *sādhana* and the foundations of dharma on the grounds of physical concepts such as magnetism and electricity. Similar to Shivachandra, he stressed at the same time that the study of the Shastras did not merely lead to an understanding of the material world but also to an understanding of the universe, the development of the individual, to the realization of nondualism, and eventually to liberation.

Pramathanath Mukhopadhyay and National Education

The central role of science and education for the Tantric nationalism espoused by the members of the Sarvamaṅgalā Sabhā is vital for an understanding of the writings of an influential disciple of Shivachandra: Pramathanath Mukhopadhyay (1880–1973), whom Taylor mentioned as Woodroffe's second major collaborator after Atalbihari Ghosh.[87] Pramathanath was born in Chanduli in the district of Burdwan, about forty kilometers northwest of Navadvip. After obtaining an M.A. in philosophy, he was drawn to the "nationalist resurgence" and "dedicated himself to the service of the motherland," in the words of his later followers.[88] He became a professor at the National Council of Education, where he was a colleague of Aurobindo. Later he joined Ripon College, teaching philosophy, mathematics, and physics. Hence he stood at the heart of the controversial issue of education, which became an integral part of the Swadeshi movement.

The program of "national education" was significantly inspired by the activities of Satishchandra Mukhopadhyay (1865–1948), who had founded and edited the nationalist magazine *Dawn* (1897–1913).[89] In 1902, he founded the Dawn Society, which called for a radical reform of the university system. Several revolutionaries can be counted among its members, including Bagha Jatin. Its program was largely in line with Aurobindo's visions for educational and pedagogical reform. Satish also contributed to *Bande Mātaram* and maintained contact with Bijaykrishna. The Dawn Society was established in reaction to the Indian Universities Commission, which had been appointed in 1902 by Lord Curzon and was widely regarded as an attempt to control Indian universities in favor of the colonial administration. The Commission's recommendations were taken up in the Universities Act of 1904, which was seen by many as an attempt at turning universities into places where government clerks would be produced, while training in the arts, sciences, and technology was intentionally neglected. The resulting controversies directly played into the Swadeshi movement of 1905 and led, in 1906, to the foundation of the National Council of Education, which created the Bengal National College and Bengal National School. These institutions later merged to become the reputed Jadavpur University. Satish was a lecturer at the Bengal National College and successor to Aurobindo as its principal in 1907.

Pramathanath developed his philosophy within this highly political context. Like numerous authors we have encountered, he was convinced that the doctrines of the ancient rishis were confirmed by modern science and philosophy.[90] He dedicated most of his work to an understanding of mantras and yantras, as expounded by the Tantras.[91] As he wrote toward the end of his life, he held that "Tantra in its extended sense is the science (one may call it 'esoteric' when it ventures beyond the empirical) as well as the art of realization."[92] This realization was to be achieved through *sādhana*, which enabled the practitioner to turn shakti into an "operating energy" that could be accessed and employed with mantras—an exemplar of the attempt, in the words of Yelle, "to diagram various tropes of creation and produce a correspondence between language and reality so that the latter may be controlled by the former."[93] The most extensive discussion of this philosophy can be found in his six-volume magnum opus, *Japasūtram*.[94] Pramathanath later took on the name Swami Pratyagatmananda Saraswati and continued to write works about Tantra and science, revolving around *sādhana*.[95] This oeuvre deserves a study in its own right, as Pramathanath has been rightly deemed one of "the most intriguing and prolific" writers interpreting mantric utterances to a twentieth-century Indian audience.[96]

Whereas Shashadhar made vague allusions to Western science, which were usually restricted to evoking magnetism, electricity, or gravity, Pramathanath extensively and ingeniously engaged with Western philosophy and science, creating a unique and complex system of thought. Andrew Sartori has highlighted that he elaborated Shivachandra's qualified nondualism through the lens of German philosophical idealism, especially Hegel. Pramathanath claimed that modern idealism was approaching the truths discovered by the ancient Aryans, practically turning around the claim of scholars such as Müller that modern German idealism was the virile and mature stage of Aryan thought.[97] In his work *India: Her Cult and Education* from 1912, he described his vision that Hindu society was approaching "complete self-fulfillment" whose prerequisite was the strengthening of "the strategic points of his social constitution," so that "the necessity for adaptation" to outside influences would eventually be outgrown. The stages on that path were:

> *Self-awakening* in the bracing atmosphere of keen polarity and contact brought on by his present cycle; *Self-education* and *Self-concentration* by

> falling back upon the home sources and methods of life-culture, providing only an *irreducible minimum of inter-racial safeguard*; and *Self-fulfilment* and *Self-expansion* over a world which after its cycles of *Hellenisation*, *Romanization* and *Teutonization* now restlessly awaits a new cycle of *Indo-Aryanization*.[98]

Eventually, the role of "the Hindu" in this world-historical scheme was that of the "God-appointed High-priest" before "the altar of Humanity." Of course, in order to create the prerequisites for this development, Hindu society would first have to realize its self-fulfillment. Philosophy, as understood by Pramathanath, was the central force behind that realization, providing "a definite conception of what life in its individual and collective aspects ought to be, a distinct notion of the nature and conditions of life's self-fulfillment."[99] This would provide the framework for a "scheme of national education of India," animated by "patriotic devotion.[100] The key to this would be a comprehension of the particularities of the Indians (which Pramathanath basically equated with Hindus). On one hand, "human psychology is practically the same in its essential features all over the world and throughout history," and all was derived from the "primordial motherstuff of social life." On the other, races developed differently as they were subjected to the influences of "Nature." As Pramathanath explains with references to Darwin, Spencer, and Huxley, the "Indo-European families of the Aryan stock" have therefore evolved into different branches.[101] Nevertheless, they still shared the same foundations of the "philosophical method" required for the advancement of humanity: "India was undoubtedly the home of noble systems of philosophy, but so was also Greece and so has also been Germany." These systems were superior because they had been created by "a race that *lives* philosophy and not simply *produces* it."[102] It was thus vital for a "social mind" to "know its own constitution thoroughly and make the knowledge a source of power and an instrument for doing good," in order to move toward self-fulfillment.[103]

Pramathanath, then, strove for a comprehensive Indian history, which contained the keys to the self-knowledge required for India's self-realization. From his viewpoint, the first and foremost sources for this analysis were the *sadhus*, "the apostles and professors of realistic mysticism." Those were the privileged interpreters of Hindu civilization, "for whatever Hinduism may be, it is pre-eminently *a cult of experimental realization*, its basis being not dubious dialectics or mere theoretical assent playing fast and loose itself, but actual living experience, *not hypothesis but experiment*."[104] Other sources included the literature and tradition growing out of the Vedas; the lived lives of the millions of average people; the research of orientalist scholars; and finally, contemporary intellectual currents:

> Synthesis for the Hindu is not progressive construction but progressive restoration. This is impossible without a bracing atmosphere of polarisation, contrast. It is the contrast of Spinoza, Kant and Hegel that is clearing his vision of the old Vedanta and Sankara; he realizes what Vedanta is by seeing what it is not but what perhaps comes perilously near it. The contrast of Darwinism brings into relief his nebulous notions about Kapilism. The spiritualism and psychic research of modern Europe and America make instinct with life the dry bones of his belief in the occult and unseen. The polarity of the empirical positivism of the West brings into prominence his own transcendental positivism. Western science with her out-door method of induction has helped him to appreciate his own sublime science of Yoga with its mystic, in-door method of spiritual intuition.[105]

Tantric philosophy was the most noble and best approach to acknowledge and instrumentalize rather than reject such oppositions, as it embraced the real, material world as a means for spiritual growth and liberation. Generally, "the basis of Hindu society is *realistic idealism*," and its goal the establishment of a society "on a spiritual basis and moving to a spiritual end."[106] The specialty of Hindu society was the embrace of materialistic forces, which are gradually educated and elevated by spiritual forces, molding "the whole social order."[107]

> [Even] a metaphysical civilisation cannot do without a sound physical basis: a race-soul longing and striving after a supernatural state cannot afford to lose or neglect a thorough-going natural science and art. The Hindu has not reared his noble social edifice upon a mass of melting clouds: the scientific and natural basis of his society is not the loose gravel of old-world prejudice and antiquated dogma, but a solid body of profoundest truths that the high priests of Nature are fore-conceiving in their serenest divinations.[108]

The Hindu mastery of removing oneself from the need for adaptation to outside influences was the key to such an ideal development. This art was embodied by the ascetic exercises of the *sannyāsī*, which led to "the secret of safe and peaceful independence of the environment."[109] On these grounds, Pramathanath presented a philosophical system that, following Shivachandra, elevated experience and practice over abstraction and theorization. Tantric philosophy, like all true Aryan philosophy, was lived and applied in the actual world. In this light, the concrete outcomes of *sādhana* are explained by contemporary evolutionary and racial theories in the vein of Darwin, Spencer, and Huxley. Interestingly, this appreciation also included explicit references to Spiritualism and the "occult and unseen," as it proclaimed a synthesis of Western science and yoga.

While Shivachandra flatly ignored Western education and Shashadhar engaged with it only to demonstrate its inferiority, Pramathanath's thought constitutes a significantly different example. Like his fellows, he insisted on the superiority of the knowledge of the ancient rishis and attempted to prove that modern Western science and philosophy were only approaching what had been revealed millennia ago. At the same time, he profoundly engaged with Western science and philosophy, aiming to bring about a "synthesis" with Indian wisdom. Not unlike Aurobindo's wish for a future harmonization and Aryanization of the world, he envisioned "Indo-Aryanization" as the final cycle of a Hegelian world-historical scheme. Pramathanath went far beyond the superficial discourse about gross and subtle matter that can be found in Shashadhar's exposition and elaborated a remarkable interpretation of Shakta philosophy.

Perhaps most important, Pramathanath envisioned his future synthesis as a "progressive restoration" of Aryan civilization as the foundation for a future Hindu society that would lead India to independence and appoint it the leader of humanity. That was to be achieved through radical reform along the lines of "national education." This concept, however, was developed through an active engagement with European, particularly German philosophy and nationalism, which also makes Pramathanath a fascinating example of Indian nationalist concepts of "Germany" that, as Milinda Banerjee has shown, emerged through global exchanges.[110]

In stark contrast to Shivachandra's and Shashadhar's contempt for Western degrees (which was paralleled by Olcott's sarcasm about B.A.s as "Bad Aryans"), Pramathanath was among those nationalists who actually fought for the right of Indians to shape their universities beyond the requisites of colonial administration. His own engagement with Western philosophy, mathematics, and physics was far from superficial and substantially contributed to the elaboration of his philosophical system. Shaktism functioned as a far-reaching epistemology and ontology that informed concrete political and social demands. It was also the driving force between scientific and cultural projects, as the Varendra Research Society and the Sarvamaṅgalā Sabhā demonstrate. At the beginning of the twentieth century, such efforts culminated in the project that would indeed transform the perception of Tantra on a global level: Arthur Avalon.

8
Arthur Avalon and Tantrik Occultism

When John Woodroffe took part in the project of Arthur Avalon, he entered a stage that had already been set. Not only does this circumstance run contrary to the idea that Woodroffe was the mastermind behind Avalon; it also allows for connecting the threads that have been elucidated in the previous chapters, shining a light on a truly entangled global discourse that relates to broader questions about agency under colonialism, modernity, and the relationship between religion, science, nationalism, and esotericism. In this chapter, I will first discuss the relationship between Woodroffe and Shivachandra before turning to the personal network behind Avalon, taking into account Woodroffe's relationship to the circles around Shivachandra, the colonial elite of Calcutta, and the Theosophical Society. How Woodroffe and his affiliates related Tantra, Catholicism, and occultism will prove that Woodroffe's and Avalon's engagement with esotericism was anything but marginal. On the contrary, their ideas about national education, the relationship between East and West, and finally the very origin and future of religion can be understood only when taking this aspect into full account and recognizing it not as a Western import but as an integral part of a global discourse about Tantra in the nineteenth century.

Enter John Woodroffe

While we have already observed the tendency to exclusively focus on Woodroffe as the mastermind behind the project, some accounts depict him as a devout disciple of Shivachandra, exaggerating Woodroffe's dependency on the instructions of his guru. Echoing earlier sources, Kashinath Chakladar writes that Woodroffe had been "given the task" to propagate Tantra after his initiation. In this narrative, he was a master of both Sanskrit and Bengali who was responsible for the propagation and also for the translation of *Tantratattva* and other Tantric texts.[1] Writing in 1969, the famous art critic and historian Ardhendrakumar Gangopadhyay (O. C. Ganguly,

Global Tantra. Julian Strube, Oxford University Press. © Oxford University Press 2022.
DOI: 10.1093/oso/9780197627112.003.0009

1881–1974) even claimed that no judge since William Jones hat attained such a level of Sanskrit learning.[2] While these accounts highlight Shivachandra as the mastermind behind Woodroffe's efforts, they exaggerate the latter's capabilities for accomplishing the work of Avalon. In order to paint a more realistic picture, it is necessary to investigate the personal network that linked the two men.

All sources trace the first encounter between Woodroffe and Shivachandra to the Calcutta High Court, where Woodroffe had been raised to the Bench in 1904 and became chief justice in 1915. The court might appear a strange place for encountering Tantra, but it should be recalled that Tantra had formed an integral part of *dharmaśāstra* and the legal tradition in Bengal. Since the times of Raghunandan, pandits frequently referred to the Tantras in legal matters.[3] The *Mahānirvāṇa Tantra* is a highly influential case in point demonstrating that Tantra and law were inherently intertwined, especially as British colonial law actively engaged with *dharmaśāstra*.[4]

It appears that the High Court's Sanskrit interpreter Haridev Shastri introduced Woodroffe to his future guru.[5] Like several other sources, Jaladhar Sen mentioned in his memoirs that Haridev was Woodroffe's Sanskrit teacher.[6] Haridev was a reputed Sanskrit scholar and a professor at the Anglican Bishop's College in Calcutta. Moreover, he promoted the advancement of the social status of women based on the shastras. In 1910, he published *Bhārater śikṣita mahilā* (*The Educated Women of India*), which contained the lives of learned Hindu and Buddhist women and promoted the "manners, customs, modes of education and living of the Aryan ladies of India."[7] The work attracted a great deal of positive attention. On July 5, 1910, the *Amrita Bazar Patrika* praised Shastri for having done "a great service to Hinduism and to the improvement of the status of Hindu women" by publishing the book. As Haridev wrote in the preface to the second edition from 1914, Woodroffe found the book so precious that he promised to publish an English translation.[8] These plans had already been reported by the *Bengalee* on January 6, 1911. This marks the first public evidence of Woodroffe's collaboration with someone from the circle around Shivachandra, and it is remarkable that this collaboration revolved around the social question of Indian women.

While several sources suggest that it was through Haridev that Woodroffe got in touch with Shivachandra, the when and how remain largely unclear. Vasantakumar Pal reported that a case at the High Court required an expert opinion on "a special field of Hindu law [*hindu śāstra*]," and Haridev recommended his own guru, Shivachandra, who was then summoned to

Calcutta from Benares. It is said that Woodroffe was immediately impressed.[9] Taylor, who rightfully advises a healthy dose of skepticism about the hagiographical stories surrounding Woodroffe and Shivachandra, calculated that the meeting would have had to take place before 1906, which is roughly supported by an interview that she conducted in 1991 with Samarendranath Bagchi, the retired judge of the High Court, whose own guru had been a disciple of Shivachandra.[10]

We know with some certainty that Woodroffe posed as a disciple in a now famous photograph that was probably taken around 1912 at the sun temple of Konarak (see Figure 8.1). The thirteenth-century site was then located in a remote and beautiful area, "which I have known and enjoyed for many years," Woodroffe fondly recalled in his *Garland of Letters*.[11] The temple was of great archaeological and art historical interest and known for its erotic sculptures. Instead of posing as a curious scholar or impartial traveler, as most British did in such photographs, Woodroffe was wearing a white *dhoti* and an upper garment (*kṣaumvastra*): the dress of a *brahmacārī*, a disciple. Pal confirmed that Woodroffe regularly wore such attire.[12] Ardhendrakumar recalled in his memoirs the huge impression that this picture made on him when Woodroffe showed it to him. He reported that Woodroffe visited Konarak almost every weekend, taking the train to Puri and then traveling on by cart.[13] Abanindranath Tagore (1871–1951), the famous artist and founder of the Indian Society of Oriental Art, also mentioned the fascination that Konarak held for Woodroffe, which motivated him to visit the temple himself.[14]

This picture is hard evidence that Woodroffe's investment in Tantra went beyond mere scholarly curiosity. It will probably remain impossible to tell when and how exactly his interest in the subject was aroused, but Taylor thinks it "extremely unlikely" that he would have gone so far as to openly display an interest before the retirement of his father, James Tisdall, in 1904.[15] This would fit in with rumors about his practicing Tantric yoga with his friend, the art historian Ernest Binfield Havell (1861–1934), who left India in 1906. We know for sure that Woodroffe was one of several High Court judges who were among the founding members of the Indian Society of Oriental Art, along with Havell and his close friends Abanindranath and Gaganendranath Tagore (1867–1938), the celebrated painter. If Woodroffe started learning Sanskrit around that time, as is apparent by his collaboration with Haridev, reported in January 1911, and the picture at Konarak was taken around 1912, then this would indeed fit the timing of the first publications by Avalon in 1913.

Figure 8.1 John Woodroffe wearing a *dhoti*.
Reproduced from John Woodroffe, *The Serpent Power* (Madras: Ganesh & Co., 1973).

As one would expect, there are numerous stories of Woodroffe's initiation by Shivachandra.[16] Everything suggests that Woodroffe did indeed become a disciple of the Tantric guru and that he and his wife, Ellen, were initiated by him. According to Pal, Woodroffe visited Shivachandra's ashram in Benares with Haridev. The latter allegedly told Danbari Gangopadhyay, the secretary of the Sarvamaṅgalā Sabhā, details about these first meetings.[17] The account stresses the "mental magnetic attraction" that Woodroffe felt toward Shivachandra, which immediately illuminated his mind and induced a change of consciousness. Whether historically accurate or not, the episode's point is to assert that Woodroffe experienced the highest form of initiation. Bagchi maintained that Woodroffe's kundalini was immediately awakened as he was elevated from his low state, *paśubhāva*, to an illuminated one. Woodroffe, we learn, was unaware that he had just encountered his real guru (*sadguru*) and was tasked by Shivachandra to depart on a pilgrimage to find one. On this journey, Woodroffe had to master challenges that eventually led to the realization that he had already found his true guru in Shivachandra. The purpose of the tale is to show how a scientific-minded Western skeptic became convinced of the powers he had experienced without comprehending them. Eventually embracing Shivachandra, both Woodroffes received the first step of a gradual (*krama*) formal initiation at Benares.[18] Pal clarified that the final initiation (*mahāsamrāj abhiṣek*) was performed some days later by a Bengali *sādhikā* called Jayakali Devi.[19]

These stories are, at least in detail, most likely legendary. Taylor has concluded that we can accept that "Woodroffe was perceived as an initiated disciple by many people, both within and outside the circles around [Shivachandra]."[20] The events surrounding the latter's death at the end of March 1914 corroborate these connections. Shivachandra's funeral was a public event that allows for some contextualization and the identification of several disciples and supporters. Shivachandra had suffered an injury on his foot and died of an infection after enduring a great deal of pain.[21] As Pal reports, a memorial was arranged in Calcutta to commemorate the guru. Amritalal Basu (1853–1929), a celebrated playwright who is quoted by Haridev as one of those praising his book about the learned women of India,[22] presided over the meeting. Other participants included Hemendraprasad Ghosh (1876–1962), a leader of the extremist nationalist faction and a journalist who edited the pro-Congress *Basumatī*, as well as Atalbihari and Woodroffe, who was heartbroken and could hardly speak.[23]

It was purportedly Woodroffe who organized the appropriate funeral rite (*śrāddha*) for his guru, together with Haridev. Those who are said to have attended the funeral include Pramathanath Tarkacarya (probably Mukhopadhyay); Jatindranath Tantraratna (Panda), the leading disciple of Vamakhepa and temple priest at Tarapith; Tarakhepa (Manimohan Gosvami), another well-known disciple of Vamakhepa and anticolonial revolutionary of the Yugāntar group;[24] Swami Sadananda;[25] and the nationalist poet Saratchandra Chaudhuri.[26] Another meeting was later held for close disciples of Shivachandra, including Panchkari Bandyopadhyay, Madangopal Mukhopadhyay, Bhuluyababa (Kalidas Ghosh),[27] and Shivachandra's editor, the historian Bholanath Majumdar.[28]

No direct and reliable sources survive to validate the details of these events. The *Bengalee* of April 1, 1914, stated that Woodroffe had sent Haridev to Shivachandra's family with a generous gift of money, and the *Amrita Bazar Patrika* of April 2 reported a condolence meeting that had been organized at Kumarkhali by Jaladhar, however without providing any details other than that some of the speakers were moved. Jaladhar did not discuss the period after Shivachandra's death in his memoirs,[29] so it is impossible to tell whether the meeting at Kumarkhali was a separate event, whether the different meetings were confused, or whether they took place as reported at all. It seems reasonable to accept that Woodroffe showed support for the guru's family and expressed public grief.[30] The participants who are named in the reports were prominent public figures who would have protested a false association with the events in newspapers. This allows for the identification of a certain circle of disciples and supporters, who in several cases can be confirmed as collaborators of both Shivachandra and Woodroffe. Hence these accounts provide sufficient proof of the close relationship between Shivachandra and Woodroffe, as well as the fact that Woodroffe moved within, and closely cooperated with, the circles around the Tantric guru.[31]

Today, the intimacy between Shivachandra and Woodroffe is acknowledged in recurring media reports and numerous publications and by the descendants of Shivachandra. One of his grandsons, Rabindranath Bhattacharya, still takes care of a Sarvamangala temple at Haora, together with his wife, Dipa (Figure 8.2).[32] The temple houses a *mūrti* of Sarvamangala that had been kept by Shivachandra. It also honors the famous collaboration that is the subject of this chapter: on the wall behind the *mūrti* hang pictures of Shivachandra; his wife, Manomohini; Rabindranath's father, Kamalakumar; and the picture of Woodroffe at Konarak. The exceptional

Figure 8.2 Sarvamangala temple in present-day Haora.
Photograph by the author.

collaboration between the Tantric pandit and the British judge bears fruit up to the present day.

The Network behind Arthur Avalon

The idea that Woodroffe stood behind Avalon was actively promoted by the Indian participants on the project. Taylor surmised that Atalbihari's desire to propagate his own religious beliefs was his motive for upholding the deception that Woodroffe was "really" Avalon. According to Taylor, the real figure behind the pseudonym was not simply Atalbihari but rather "a symbiosis of the two."[33] Although she has meticulously proved that Atalbihari was indeed Woodroffe's main partner, it might be more appropriate to see Avalon not as a duo but as a team of several, and most likely altering, individuals. This is underlined by the fact that Woodroffe often referred to his "Indian friends" and informants,[34] but it is also evident in light of what has been discussed so far.

It should be noted that Atalbihari was not a pandit. Taylor could confirm that Atalbihari did, in fact, translate and edit several of the Avalon publications, but his granddaughter acknowledged that he had received the help of pandits from the Sanskrit College—and, it might be speculated, most likely from Shivachandra and his affiliates.[35] Atalbihari was a disciple of Shivachandra and has been linked by his descendants and by Pal to Haridev, who might therefore emerge as a likely candidate for having provided linguistic expertise.[36] Different sources also maintain that the Woodroffes had received initiation from the same *sādhikā* called Jayakali Devi who had also initiated Atalbihari and his second wife, Gauramma, who are referred to by their disciple names, Atalananda Saraswati and Srimati Gouramba Garu.[37] It has moreover been claimed that Atalbihari was the guru of Woodroffe, Havell, and their affiliate Norman Blount, an English jute broker. This, however, most likely refers to the *śikṣā guru* who teaches knowledge to his disciples rather than the *dīkṣā guru* who grants initiation. Several sources confirm that Atalbihari did read texts and teach lessons to several students, some of them foreigners like Woodroffe. He appears to have had international contacts, including in Germany and the United States, as is suggested by a note in Taylor's possession and by an article that Atalbihari penned for the Chicago-based *Occult Digest*.[38] What, according to Taylor, becomes evident from these accounts is that Atalbihari had a circle of European friends and students whom he instructed in Tantra. He indeed appears to have been "an extremely influential mediator of the Tantric tradition."[39]

The previous chapters have shown that societies played a key role in the activities of Avalon and their associates. An Āgamānusandhana Samiti (Agamas Research Society) was established to publish the *Tantrik Texts* series, in which Woodroffe invested a substantial amount of his own money. Its president was Rameshwar Singh, the maharaja of Darbhanga, whom we have encountered as a driving force behind the Bhārat Dharma Mahāmaṇḍal, as a supporter of the Theosophical Society, and allegedly as a disciple of Shivachandra. Dharmananda Mahabharati, in his series for the *Hindu Spiritual Magazine*, pointed out that the maharaja's library was "the most accomplished in Tantrik Sastras."[40] Rameshwar seems to have been the main financial sponsor of the Samiti after Woodroffe's departure, and was succeeded by his son Kameshwar Singh, who took over as president in 1931.[41] Atalbihari was named joint secretary of the society, alongside Woodroffe, but a fundraising pamphlet significantly downplayed Atalbihari's role. The text explains that the Samiti had begun "to take over and continue the work begun by Sir John Woodroffe to collect, preserve and publish and also correctly to interpret the Philosophy of the Agamik Scriptures." It is stressed that "Sir John Woodroffe has practically single-handed[ly] laboured at this task for several years, and has published and translated some original texts," while Atalbihari is described merely as "one of his collaborators" from the beginning of this work, which was now handed over to the Samiti as Woodroffe approached retirement.[42] This shows how much Atalbihari, and probably other coworkers as well, were willing to stay in the background in order to raise Avalon's profile. There can be little doubt that all those involved were very well aware of the fact that a British judge and Christian would be a more efficient spokesperson for the "rehabilitation" of Tantra than an Indian scholar, let alone a Tantric.

Another important example is the Varendra Research Society (Barendra Anusandhān Samiti), in which Atalbihari had been involved.[43] It was set up in 1910 by Saratkumar Ray, Ramprasad Chanda, and Akshaykumar Maitra, the historian from Kumarkhali and childhood friend of Shivachandra and Jaladhar, who had also been a member of the circle around Kangal Harinath. The society's aim was to promote the study of Bengali culture and history, especially in the Rajshahi region that had been the medieval kingdom of Varendra. Registered in 1914 as an association, the members started archaeological expeditions, conducted historical research, and collected antiquities and manuscripts. According to Pal, Woodroffe might even have become interested in Tantra after joining the society.[44] Samarendranath Bagchi, the High Court judge, claimed that Woodroffe had been inspired by Akshaykumar to study Sanskrit and Tibetan. Obviously, Akshaykumar had close links to Shivachandra and his disciples, including Haridev, who praised his work.[45] The centrality of Tantra to the Varendra Research Society and Varendra's scholarship was highlighted by Akshaykumar himself:

> [I]t is chiefly as a centre of Tantrika activity that Varendra deserves to be specially explored, to discover the images and manuscripts which alone are capable of explaining the various stages in the development of that mystic faith, which are now only dimly seen, or more frequently, vaguely imagined, to suit the theories which the students of Indian history are so eager to advance.[46]

The activities of Akshaykumar, Shivachandra, and Avalon evolved within the very same historical context and personal network. Of course, a large portion of the public was not prepared to embrace Tantra as a serious object of study, and even less so as the means for the regeneration of India. All propagators of Tantra faced a great deal of public resistance to their efforts, as is evident, for instance, in the memoirs of Jaladhar, who recounted his differences with Shivachandra over Tantra. Jaladhar emphasized that he had little knowledge of the subject and that his close friendship with Shivachandra remained unaffected by the disagreement. Yet he was struck with fear when he saw his friend dressed in a blood-red garment, a mark on his forehead, and adorned with umpteen necklaces. Knowing that he would engage in the practice of the transgressive "five Ms" (*pañcamakār*), Jaladhar was scared and reminded of the terrible description of a Tantric in Bankim's novel *Kapālakuṇḍalā*.[47] Although Shivachandra had given him his writings, he could not feel comfortable with his *tantra-mantra*:

> Shivachandra, Akshaykumar and I—these three people studied together at the feet of Kangal. Shivachandra attained siddhi through tantra-śāstra. Akshaykumar achieved profound expertise [*pāṇḍitya*] in tantra-śāstra, but he did not go through the practice of Tantra. And you can see what I have done. Kangal Harinath had once said, "All of you will grow up to be great." I tried to make sense of this statement in my own way, but that does not seem possible anymore. All three turned out to be different. One became

a clever person [*phikir*], one turned into a fakir [*phakir*], and the other became a wanderer [*musāphir*].[48]

Interestingly, Jaladhar recognized Tantra not as something that necessarily had to be practiced by a believer like Shivachandra but as a practice that could also be studied historically by someone like Akshaykumar. He recognized its intellectual and historical value, specifically for Bengali culture. Yet the demeanor of his old friend frightened him due to the widespread negative depictions of Tantrics. The significant point is that, around that time, Tantra had become the subject of scrutiny in exactly those Western-educated circles that Shivachandra denounced as responsible for the degeneration of Indian culture.

This even included the colonial elite, which can be illustrated by the aforementioned influential Indian Society of Oriental Art (ISOA). It first formally convened in 1907 but was a direct outcome of the contemporary art movement in Calcutta and the circle around Havell at the Government Art School that had formed in the preceding years. The society was representative of the highly educated bhadralok milieu and the New Bengal School, which promoted a decidedly "national" Indian art.[49] An exhibition with "national" artwork had already been organized on the occasion of the Mela in April 1867. Gaganendranath, one of the ISOA's founding members and a friend of Woodroffe and Havell, had been the first secretary of the Mela. At the same time, the ISOA was closely affiliated with the British colonial elite. During the first meetings, three attendees were High Court judges and four were members of the Tagore family. Its first president was Lord Kitchener, the chief of staff of the armed forces in India, followed by Woodroffe, who was succeeded by other British colonial administrators, including Lord Carmichael, the governor of Bengal. Of its 120 members in 1916, only 47 were Indian.

The ISOA organized successful exhibitions that also showed pieces from Tibet, China, and Japan. In 1911, it hosted a large exhibition at Allahabad as part of the United Provinces Exhibition organized by Ananda Coomaraswamy, who was allegedly introduced to Shivachandra by Woodroffe.[50] The ISOA also established links to William Rothenstein, who in 1910 had founded the Indian Society in London. He visited India in 1910–1911 with letters of introduction from Havell to Woodroffe and Abanindranath. This visit would result in a friendship with Rabindranath, who was consequently "discovered" by Western readers and received the Nobel Prize in 1913.[51]

In the same year that saw the first Avalon publications, Coomaraswamy and Sister Nivedita edited a volume of Hindu and Buddhist myths that was illustrated by Abanindranath and defended Indian beliefs and practices against colonial critique.[52] The ISOA is thus an outstanding example of a platform that merged arts and politics, but also colonizer and colonized. Tantra appeared to have played a prominent role within it. This can be illustrated by one of the Woodroffe's closest friends, James Cousins (1873–1956).[53] A bustling Theosophist, he was based at Madras and a close partner of Besant. He became an enthusiastic supporter of the Indian Society of Oriental Art. He accepted a personal invitation to its exhibition at Calcutta in January 1916 and arranged for its transfer to Madras, where it was held at the Young Men's Indian Association, a Theosophical organization that was modeled after and intended to challenge the Young Men's Christian Association.[54] Cousins and his wife, Margaret, stayed with the Woodroffes when he came for the 1917 Congress and praised the commodious, artistic, and philosophical atmosphere of their home.[55]

Cousins clearly came under the influence of Arthur Avalon's ideas, as can be illustrated by an article that he published in the *Modern Review* of February 1918 and that was later reprinted in Woodroffe's *Shakti and Shakta*. Cousins's understanding of Tantra is remarkable, as it demonstrates the influence of the contexts that formed the frame of reference for Theosophical engagements with the subject since the 1880s. Cousins wrote, "India is at present experiencing the interesting sensation of a national revival; and, like all other such happenings, a *national* revival is no more confined to nationality or nationalism than a religious revival is confined to religion."[56] This revival was not restricted to India but a worldwide phenomenon whose reverberations could be felt in the "political interpretation of nationality" as well as in the arts, science, and religion. Cousins praised the work of Avalon as "an integral and perhaps vitally important constituent of the revival" and claimed that his books "will rank among the precious things of the first quarter of the twentieth century in much the same way as 'The Secret Doctrine' of Madame Blavatsky and 'The Perfect Way' of Dr. Anna Kingsford ranked in the last quarter of the nineteenth."[57]

Cousins was aware of the controversies about Tantra within Theosophical circles. He explained that he had first encountered it "through a footnote in 'The Voice of the Silence,' in which Madame Blavatsky referred to several sects of 'sorcerers' as being 'all Tantrikas.'" Cousins rejected the assumption that Tantrikas were sorcerers, but he stressed that this was not necessarily implied in the footnote:

> In any case even if Madame Blavatsky adopted a hostile attitude to the Tantra, as she adopted a hostile attitude to spiritualism, we have the example of her great successor, Mrs. Besant, who has bridged the gulf between Theosophy and Spiritualism—or perhaps more accurately, between Theosophists and Spiritualists in their mutual search for the realization of the inner worlds of faculty and experience.[58]

While there were antinomian Tantric practices, such as those of the *vāmācāra* variety, these represented only a fraction of the Tantras and could not be applied to all Shaktas. And even these reprehensible practices were motivated not by sinister aims but by "the attainment of occult powers or spiritual illumination."[59] As a highly profound philosophy, it reconciled Vedantic monism and dualism. And even more significant, it transgressed the narrow confines of exoteric, superficial forms of religion:

> It is this recognition of psychic distinctions that marks the Tantra as a scripture that will appeal more and more to the future. Science has passed inwards from the physical to the psychical, and it will draw religion with it in due time, and leave those systems outside that have not a psychological basis to their faith and practice. In this respect the Agamas present a contrast to Christianity; not that the kernel of Christianity does not come from the same hidden Tree as all the other great Religions, but the overgrowths have, in the case of Christian faith and practice, obscured the implicit psychology of the system by sentimentality.[60]

It is this scientific character of Tantra—and its active, empowering embrace of the physical world and human nature through the employment of the divine Shakti—that stands in contrast with "simple religion, such as Christianity," which removes God from His creation as a single-sex entity. But it also contrasts with "simple" philosophy, which "reduces everything to abstraction." In Cousins's opinion, Tantra thus "unites the religious and philosophic functions of human natures by presenting a system which is in line with modern psychology."[61] These views on Tantra are an impressive illustration of the influence that the Avalon publications exerted in a milieu shaped by Theosophy, art, and discussions about the relationship between nationalism, religion, and science.

This mélange was fertile ground for the propagation of Tantra. At least three Europeans who were prominent in the art movement had been students of Atalbihari. Taylor obtained a photograph that shows Woodroffe, Atalbihari, and Hjalmar Ponten Moeller at Konarak wearing white *dhotis*, similar to the famous photograph of Woodroffe alone. Moeller was a Swedish businessman, diplomat, and prominent member of the ISOA, who had been initiated into Vaishnavism and also studied Tantric texts with Atalbihari. Taylor convincingly dated that picture to 1912. It was published in a Bengali magazine and caused a furor among the British in Calcutta.[62] In 1936, it was published by the newspapers *Bhāratbarṣa* and *Basumatī* in their obituaries of Woodroffe.[63] Another member of the ISOA was Blount, the Society's first joint secretary with Abanindranath. According to a rumor repeated by the artist Nandalal Bose, one of Abanindranath's former students, it was Blount who practiced Tantric *sādhanā* at Konarak with Woodroffe and Havell, with Atalbihari as their guru. Keeping in mind the photograph at Konarak, it is possible that Blount was confused with Moeller. In any case, both these men were friends of Atalbihari and visited him in his house at Chaibassa near Ranchi in Bihar, where it is said that Woodroffe practiced Tantra and studied Tantric texts with Atalbihari and other Europeans.[64]

The contrast between this milieu and that of Shivachandra may seem drastic at first glance, but those were precisely the Western and Western-educated circles where appreciation of Tantra flourished. This underlines how misleading it would be to perceive the renegotiation of Tantra simply as part of an "orthodox revivalist" movement against Western influences. In previous chapters, the prominent role of Theosophy for this context was evident, and the case of Cousins reminds us to now inspect the Woodroffes' relationship to the Society.

The Woodroffes and the Theosophical Society

Both John and Ellen Woodroffe had close links to the Theosophical Society. John wrote in Theosophical journals such as the *Theosophist*, the *Theosophical Review*, and the *Occult Review*, and he frequently quoted from publications such as the *Quest*. Most books published under the names of Avalon and Woodroffe were printed by the Theosophical publisher Ganesh & Co. in

Madras. As mentioned earlier, the maharaja of Darbhanga was a major supporter of the Āgamānusandhana Samiti, whose vice president was the maharaja of Cossim Bazar, Mahindrachandra Nandy, who was also a sponsor of the Banaras Hindu University that had been cofounded by Besant. Both Woodroffes, but especially Ellen, knew Besant, and it is reported that Ellen shared Besant's faith in Krishnamurti, the boy who was raised by Besant and Charles Webster Leadbeater to become the future "World Teacher," or "Maitreya."[65] The Woodroffes took Besant to Atalbihari's house in Calcutta, possibly in December 1917, when the Congress that elected Besant president was held in the city. The event coincided with the meeting of the Theosophical Society, alongside several other conventions, including that of the All India Cow Conferences Association, at which Woodroffe presided.

There is some evidence of the leading role that Ellen Woodroffe took in the couple's approach to Theosophy. The membership register of the Theosophical Society at Adyar suggests that she became a member on December 24, 1911—the same year Haridev Shastri publicly mentioned his collaboration with John.[66] As Taylor has pointed out, it would not have been surprising to find that Ellen, an exceptionally artistic and fashionable personality, was a member of the Society. Their son James even believed that "it was she who influenced her husband to take an interest in Indian religion."[67] John never formally joined the Society, but Florence Hume, the wife of James Tisdall Woodroffe, was a relative of Alan Octavian Hume, the influential Theosophist.[68] Therefore, his personal ties to the Society were rather intimate.

What we know for sure is that "Ellen Avalon" coedited one of the two publications from 1913, *Hymns to the Goddess*, parallel to *The Great Liberation*. This confirms that the Woodroffes' interest in Tantra was mutual at least in the beginning. It is highly significant that this collaboration was inaugurated in the *Theosophist* in October 1913, with a "Hymn to Durga." It was taken from a manuscript of the *Tārārahasyavṛttikā*, which was in the possession of the Varendra Research Society and was provided to Avalon by Akshaykumar.[69] In June 1914, another "Hymn to Prakṛti," taken from the *Prapañcasāra*, was printed in the journal.[70] An introduction highlighted the hymn's connections to the *Śāradātilaka* and the *Mahānirvāṇa Tantra*.[71]

It was apparently through Ellen that the couple also had connections to the French community, where Theosophy was quite popular. In 1917, Ellen established the French Literary Society in Calcutta, which once more underlines how active she was in the city's cultural scene.[72] John promoted the study of Tantra in French circles, especially when he lectured to the Association Française des Amis de l'Orient de Paris in 1921. This society had been established in the same year, during Rabindranath's second visit to Europe, by Paul Masson-Oursel (1882–1956) and Sylvain Lévi (1863–1935), two influential orientalists who would rely on the Avalon publications for their great appreciation of Tantra. Both men had close ties to Theosophy, which most likely led to another lecture that Woodroffe delivered to the Société Théosophique at Paris.[73]

Among the Theosophists who praised the pathbreaking work of Avalon was Friedrich Otto Schrader (1876–1961), the director of the Theosophical Society's library at Adyar from 1905 to 1916. In a combined review of *The Great Liberation*, the *Hymns to the Goddess*, and the inauguration of the *Tantrik Texts* series, Schrader applauded Avalon for exploring the Tantras, which had "hitherto played in Indology the part of a jungle which everybody is anxious to avoid."[74] After some critical remarks about issues of translation and transliteration, Schrader especially complimented the long introduction to *The Great Liberation*, which he regarded as a boon to knowledge about Tantra. In his review of the *Hymns*, he expressly commended Avalon for availing himself of "the assistance of the Tantrik gurus and pandits," since the study of Tantra "demands absolutely" the help of "authorised custodians of its traditions."[75] In his review of the first volume of *Principles of Tantra*, Schrader provided a summary of Shivachandra's arguments and praised Avalon's introduction as "a very remarkable work." He concluded that the "value of the book is undeniable, as nothing like it has been so far available to the western student."[76] This reception illustrates the fluidity between the academic orientalist and Theosophical milieu, in which Avalon was warmly received.

It bears noting that Woodroffe's articles in the *Theosophist* in 1913 were the first publications on Tantra in the journal since Kshetrapal Chakravarti's "Religious Aspects of the Early Tantras" from 1891, and it is most likely that this was no coincidence: Avalon was a direct follow-up to the Bengali intervention. In contrast to the Bengali intervention, however, this was a team effort consisting of Western and Indian members. Once more, they attempted to correct misconceptions among Theosophists rather than accepting the latter's teachings. A good illustration of this is Avalon's criticism of Charles Leadbeater (1854–1934), who had begun writing about chakras and the kundalini, most famously in his book *The Inner Life* from 1910.[77] In *The Serpent Power*, Avalon respectfully but firmly argued that Leadbeater's conceptualization of these Tantric elements was erroneous: "For though 'Theosophical' teaching is largely inspired by Indian ideas, the meaning which it attributes to the Indian terms which it employs is not always that given to these terms by Indians themselves."[78] Interestingly, this critique was extended to Indian Theosophists, and explicitly Srishchandra Basu, whose alleged deviation from Indian sources is tackled in a footnote to the same passage.[79]

This shows that it would be misleading to separate, as Taylor and McDaniel do, "Indian understandings" from those of "Western occultists."[80] Indians were very much part of Theosophy, and rivalries between different Indian authors were not less pronounced than those between Western Theosophists and non-Theosophical Indians. Avalon's own position toward the Society was critical yet appreciative, as becomes tangible in the introduction to the first volume of *Principles of Tantra*: "Since this work was first published the so-called 'progressive' movement has been followed by a reaction in the orthodox Hindu world, which is not without its own defects. The spread of Theosophical ideas first renewed an interest in the teachings of India's great past, and an awakening national spirit has done the rest."[81] While acknowledging Theosophy's contribution to the revival of Hindu orthodoxy, Avalon made it quite clear that Theosophy was flawed and unreliable. After all, the Avalon project was *not* presented as Theosophical. This appears to have been an outcome of the overall failure of the earlier Bengali intervention to rehabilitate the image of Tantra, and it might also have been a result of a general disappointment among Indian Theosophists after the scandals of the 1890s. Yet actors such as Baradakanta had not simply turned their back on Theosophy, and Woodroffe's personal ties to Theosophists, as well as his sustained activities in that milieu, underline the complexity of the situation. Once again, the picture is not one of clearly distinguishable factions and movements, but one of tangled connections and multidirectional exchanges.

The Science of Tantrik Spiritual Culture

The publications by Arthur Avalon demonstrate how deeply intertwined Theosophy, occultism, and other esoteric currents such as Spiritualism and New Thought were with the Bengali discourse about Tantra. Baradakanta is a good example of the creativity that marked Indian engagements with these areas. After initiating the Bengali intervention of the 1880s with his notion of "Tantrik Occultism," his introduction to the second volume of *Principles of Tantra,* at over a hundred pages long, is a potent illustration of how directly that earlier context relates to the activities of Shivachandra, providing the crucial framework for Avalon's work.[82]

For instance, Shivachandra's key arguments resurface in Avalon's introduction to the first volume. Immediately after Avalon's acknowledgment that the Theosophical Society "renewed an interest in the teachings of India's great past," we read that this interest was "due in part to the general religious revival in progress, and also to the increasing recognition of the necessity of sadhana (practice), as distinct from mere philosophizing, if any practical result is to be attained."[83] A true understanding of its performance, however, was absent from Indian society. Avalon lamented that "the English-educated Bengali community is without religion (Dharma) or action (Karma), and is devoid of the sense of nationality (Dharma), and caste."[84] This double translation of "dharma" with both "religion" and "nationality" underlines the political nature of the "renewal" of Tantra.

We have seen how Baradakanta linked Tantra, nationalism, Theosophy, and references to Western science in his journal *Kalpa* and his book *Barnāśram dharmma* from 1902. In his introduction to *Principles*, these aspects reappear in what Baradakanta presented as "the Science of Tantrik-Spiritual Culture."[85] As the case of Shishirkumar has illustrated, the promotion of "spiritual culture" has been a prominent aspect of Bengali nationalism, and in the case of Avalon and Baradakanta, its foundations were supposed to be Tantric. The core argument for this was Avalon's insistence that, according to the *Mahānirvāṇa*, Tantra "alone is fit for the century and the race at the present time."[86] In his own introduction, Baradakanta similarly stressed that the "Vaidik method" was unbearable for men of the Kali Yuga and, invoking the *Mahānirvāṇa*, emphasized that "esoteric Tantrism is as ancient as the Vedas." According to him, it was "only old wine in new jars which is presented by Shiva and Bhagavati to men of the Kali Yuga. An exoteric aspect, however, suitable for the generality of folk was added to the already extant esoteric path, which only a few are competent to pursue."[87] Tantric rules had been followed for thousands of years, but "it is to be deplored that, owing to English education, which has given a great impetus to intellectual culture, and has brought philosophy within the reach of all, the aspirations of many who are spiritually-minded far exceed their spiritual capacity."[88] It was hence necessary to lead Indian society back to its true dharma, and Baradakanta presented "Tantrik spiritual culture" as the path.

Baradakanta maintained that Tantra reconciled duality (*dvaita*) with nonduality (*advaita*). Shankara and Ramanuja had both been human expounders of Vedic law, representing the paths of *jñāna* and *bhakti*, respectively. Both their standpoints were, however, "pessimistic": "Such a system of spiritual culture is bound to fail, and to render religion an impossibility for the mass of the people."[89] The social consequences were disastrous: "Extreme Vedantik pessimism has rendered India what it is to-day—neither soaring to heaven nor blooming on earth."[90] According to the Tantras, the world was neither an illusion nor a nonreality. Rather, Tantric worship enabled the practitioner, "by higher processes of self-culture," to realize that the entire universe was to be regarded as the Mother, and all beings as part of Her. Liberation, from this standpoint, was attained by "eating the sweet fruit of the world" rather than rejecting it.[91] Hence liberation while living (*jīvanmukti*) was achieved by both *bhoga* and *yoga*, enjoyment and strict practice.[92] This was the essence of spiritual culture that would lead to the regeneration of India through the self-cultivation of the individual—a notion that paralleled contemporary occultist ideas.[93]

Echoing his earlier conceptualization of Tantrik Occultism, Baradakanta professed that the Tantric method worked because it was "an exact science, and does not shrink from the severest test which may be applied to it."[94] Tantra offered a key to "the inner temple of nature": the Tantric was "a theurgist and thaumaturgist, alchemist, herbalist, metallurgist, physician, astrologer, and astronomer. The Tantric's alchemy crossed the ocean and reaches Europe; his chemistry discovered ages ago many truths, some of which have dawned upon European scientists within but recent times." At the core stood the Tantric's "science of psycho-physical culture, which renders the physical body obedient to the will, and thus by certain postures not only enables him to ward off and cure diseases, but to control the mind."[95] This was the practice of yoga, which comprised the sexually connoted rising of the kundalini as the manifestation of the "vital Power of the universe" in the "centres of Power" within the human body.[96] The ancient Hindus had understood this, but that was no reason for Baradakanta to outright reject modern science that had reached India through English education:

> The Hindu of the old school takes it as an heirloom from his ancestors without ever trying to understand what it really is and how it can be utilized. He recites it parrot-like, and thinks he has done his duty. It is this indifference on the one hand, and apathy on the other, which has rendered the Hinduism of the present day almost a dead religion.[97]

Perhaps more clearly than anywhere else, Baradakanta here revealed his reasons for engaging so enthusiastically with Theosophy and Western science: he envisioned not simply a return to the past but a further illumination—and confirmation—of the ancient Tantric science by modern science. Baradakanta devoted a large part of his introduction to justifying yogic concepts through the lens of modern science and the esoteric movements that he considered part of it. For instance, he explained the awakening of the kundalini in terms of electricity, which could be manipulated and directed by "the Guru, the Mantrik Scientist." This claim was substantiated by references to the *Yoginī Tantra*, the *Rudra Yāmala*, the *Kulārṇava Tantra*, and Raghava Bhatta, but also to magnetism: "If there be reason to believe in transference of thought from a hypnotiser to his subject—and hypnotism has now been recognized as a science—there is no ground for disbelieving the transference of a power even subtler than a thought (which is a power as well) from a Guru to his disciples."[98]

These explanations obviously expand on Baradakanta's earlier writings, but the introduction to *Principles* also reveals a critical distancing from the Theosophical Society that might have grown in the intervening years. For instance, Baradakanta criticized interpretations of Indian concepts that are "borrowed from Theosophical literature."[99] Most curious is his rejection of the Theosophical distinction between Hatha and Raja Yoga. He was emphatic that pranayama was "indispensable" for the development of willpower: "Now, it must be distinctly understood that as Pranayama is Hatha Yoga, the elimination of the latter from Yoga-practice would be as beneficial to the practiser as the removal of his brain would be to a thinker."[100] Baradakanta acknowledged that Raja Yoga was "the most potent means to acquire" knowledge of Brahman,[101] but he underscored that "there is no royal road to Yoga, which is, in fact, nothing less than the complete reversal of the natural order of things in its aspirer."[102] In other words, Hatha Yoga was an integral part of yogic practice that should prepare the practitioner for the realization of Brahman. This broadside against the Theosophical yoga discourse most likely resulted from Baradakanta's disappointment over the eventual failure to establish a positive image of Tantra within the Society. Years later, the work of Arthur Avalon was a vehicle to communicate the same ideas to an even broader global readership independent of, yet still in dialogue with, Theosophy.

Science and Education, Eastern and Western

Baradakanta explicitly underlined the political nature of Tantrik spiritual culture: "The path of devotion—that is, the Kaula path—is therefore a blessing, not only individually, but socially."[103] This embrace of the Kaula perspective enabled Baradakanta to articulate a version of the "spiritual East" versus the "materialist West" scheme that was characteristic of the collaborators on the Avalon project. Rather than putting an emphasis on either spirituality or materialism, he highlighted both wealth and poverty in both extremes:

> Big religious bodies there are, but where is God? Whilst India has no faith in the world, and only a dreamy faith in heaven, the West seeks a heaven in this world. The best remedy for this disease is to be found in that religion which both fully recognizes the reality of the world, and regards it as the training-ground whereon man may grow into God.[104]

A Kaula, then, neither shrinks from the materiality of the world, nor does he (or indeed, she) deny the ultimate and absolute unity of everything. This is another key aspect of Baradakanta's embrace of both Tantra and Western science or occultism: the latter was of limited value, but it was crucial for comprehending the former. Rather than viewing materialism and spirituality as incommensurable, Baradakanta claimed that their best aspects were united in the Kaula path.

This merging of Western science and Shakta philosophy was, as we saw in the previous chapter, also typical of the thought of Pramathanath Mukhopadhyay and his propagation of "national education." Woodroffe eagerly adopted Pramathanath's key arguments and coauthored a whole series of books with him, titled *The World as Power* (1922–1929).[105] Woodroffe frequently described Pramathanath as a friend and cited his works especially for confirmation of the "practical," "experimental," and "realistic" character of Tantra, as well as for its accordance with Western philosophy, particularly Idealism and Monism.[106] Pramathanath clearly was one of Woodroffe's main partners, helping him, for instance, with the preparation of *The Garland of Letters* (1922).[107] Whole chapters from the pen of Pramathanath are reproduced in *Shakti and Shakta*, but also in the education-focused *Bharata Shakti* (1917). This underlines how the aspects of science and education were central to the discussion of the relationship between India and the West in the works of Avalon and the people behind that project.[108]

Indeed, Woodroffe made a point of engaging with living philosophical and religious thought in India. In the first volume of *World as Power*, he stated that "Indian Philosophy and Religion are too often treated in an archaeological way." He understood his work as being of direct and paramount relevance for present developments: "My own conviction is that an examinaton [*sic*] of Indian Vedantic Doctrine shows that it is, in important respects, in conformity with the most advanced scientific and Philosophie thought of the West, and that where this is not so it is Science which will go to Vedanta and not the reverse."[109] Like his Indian partners—and the numerous learned Bengalis we have encountered so far—Woodroffe was convinced that it was Western science that had most to learn from Indian traditions, and not the other way around.[110] His sincerity in engaging with contemporary Indian thought becomes evident not only in his extensive collaboration with Pramathanath but also through his many references to the work of Indian scientists, historians, and philosophers, most notably, Jagadishchandra Chattopadhyay's *Hindu Realism* (1912),[111] Brajendranath Seal's *Positive Sciences of the Ancient Hindus* (1915),[112] the experiments by Jagadish Bose, and the philosophical work of G. R. Malkani.[113] Woodroffe had close personal links to most of these authors, which underlines his deep involvement in the contemporary Indian intellectual landscape.

Stressing that the Shakta Tantras were a form of Advaita Vedanta, Woodroffe and Pramathanath believed that they were also in accordance with modern Monism. Rather than through "abstract speculation," Tantric *sādhana* led to the realization of ultimate nonduality through yogic *experience*.[114] In fact, the "currently accepted and orthodox scientific teaching" only confirmed ancient truths: "Alchemical and Mystical schools and lately systems of scientific monism which affirm unity in the form of a Fundamental Substance and its development into various modes of itself."[115] In order to verify these correlations, Woodroffe related the shastras to the work of scholars such as Haeckel, Huxley, William James, Oliver Lodge, Émile Boirac, and Gustave Le Bon.[116] Apart from Monism, Vitalism seemed to be especially "on the right track" in understanding the fact that "Life is a Power, a form of Consciousness which directs matter. But it is right to say that the cause of Life is immanent in matter as the Power which manifests as both Matter and Life."[117] It is not surprising, then, that Woodroffe welcomed movements that most enthusiastically embraced such ideas. Next to occultism, he regarded New Thought and Christian Science as especially promising trends in the West:

> What is called the "Philosophy of Life" and Doctrine of Power is now in vogue in the West. "New Thought" as it is called (so akin in some respects to Shakta doctrine) says "Within you is the Power." "Spiritual healing" is taught and practised by the followers of what is called "Christian Science" to whom man's mind is "mortal mind" and the world of matter is a kind of Maya. Great changes are taking place in Psychology. The debt of Theosophy to India is well known as also (though in another sense) of India to Theosophy which re-called to the Indian the value of his cultural inheritance. In Medical science, Psycho-therapy is establishing itself. An American critic reviewing one of the books which I have published on Tantra Shastra spoke of this Scripture as being "perhaps the most elaborate system of autosuggestion in the world." . . . All these western movements are further instances of the approximation, which is now taking place, of modern western and ancient Indian thought.[118]

The popularity of the philosophy and practice of "occult powers" and yoga in the West seemed only natural to Woodroffe against this background, as he saw the doctrines of modern Spiritualism confirmed by the shastras.[119] His approximation of occultist and Theosophical understandings of these practices is striking: "By occult phenomena we understand not something supernatural, something not related in a regular and constant form to the ensemble of the forces and laws of the universe which is throughout one, but as obeying one law governing all phenomena."[120] In the last title of the *World of Power* series, *Mahāmāyā,* from 1929, Woodroffe and Pramathanath stressed:

> In India, the Vedantic doctrine has afforded a wide and firm basis for the understanding of our common as well as "occult" experiences, and that doctrine is clear in its main outlines. On the practical side, too, the Indian genius has been remarkable for the courses of Sadhana or discipline it has evolved, suited to the varying temperament and competency of men, leading by steps to the highest stages of realization—"I am the Whole."[121]

In his essay, *Is India Civilized?*, Woodroffe wrote that, "in contrast to Spencer and the agnostic school, the Vedanta holds that the reality behind these phenomena is knowable, and is Consciousness itself." This was proven by "all high mystic experiences, whether in East or West." Yet, it was India that offered the most fruitful approaches to understanding them, as "established occult powers and phenomena now generally accepted, such as telepathy, thought-reading, hypnotism and the like, are only explainable on hypotheses which approach more nearly Eastern doctrine than any other theory which has in modern times prevailed in the West."[122] Woodroffe and his collaborators believed that "much of modern Western scientific teaching is consonant with and follows logically from the principles laid down in Indian Scriptures dealing with Power or Shakti." Rather than opposing Western and Indian science, these authors strove for mutual improvement based on the best aspects of both.[123]

The concept of national education was supposed to create the conditions for such an exchange. Pramathanath was a member of the National Council of Education, where Woodroffe lectured extensively in 1919.[124] It might be recalled that Woodroffe advocated for a "Religion of Power" that should regenerate Indian society through Shakta Tantra. The pertinent chapter in *Bharata Shakti* was penned by Pramathanath.[125] Awakening India's shakti was necessary because, according to Woodroffe, the preliminary to a union between East and West "is a free and truly Indian Self."[126] To realize this, an "Education upon National lines" was needed that would counter the dominance of the English language and by giving priority to vernacular education. This would "not necessarily mean neglect of English or other foreign language," but it would free India from the suffocating constraints of alien influences.[127]

Religion played a key role in this. As president of the Vivekananda Society, Woodroffe lauded Vivekananda's insistence on *svadharma*, quoting his statement "[O]ur strength, nay, our national life is in our religion."[128] Nalinimohan Chattopadhyay, a member of the Indian Rationalistic Society who was responsible for the publication of *Bharata Shakti*, similarly emphasized in the preface that the "basis of all culture and the maker of all nationality is Religion."[129] This, Woodroffe pointed out in his book *The Seed of Race* (1919), was inherently linked to "the Spirit of the Race, which *persists* throughout all the varying forms in which it clothes itself. This Spirit is a manifestation of the Essence of National Character, namely, the collective Sangskara."[130] While race obviously played a key role for Woodroffe's thought, he was wary of the category "Aryan" and, in contrast to most other authors we have encountered, generally rejected its use.[131] He explained:

> I am aware of the possibility that with the evolution of man many differences which now divide may disappear. I am as much opposed as any one else to Nationalism on its hind legs anywhere. My hope is the Confraternity

> of Men. I believe however in the possibility of the friendly co-existence of differing cultural characteristics, and that before India can fully express the more universal culture, which some believe the future may show, She must first realise, in its purity, or recover where it has been lost, Her Self.[132]

While this parallels the Theosophical notion of the brotherhood of humanity, it was not restricted to that context. We have seen in previous chapters how the consolidation of Indian national identity was widely regarded as the prerequisite for the realization of a future "universal culture" and "universal brotherhood," however different this state might have been envisioned. Common to such goals was the idea of a universalism that lay in the future but was rooted in the past.

Esoteric Universalism

One of the central aspects of Tantra frequently highlighted by the collaborators on the Avalon publications was its "all-comprehensiveness," which offered different paths to liberation according to the capacity and nature of each individual.[133] Tantra, we read in Baradakanta's introduction to the *Principles*, was "non-sectarian."[134] Not only did it proclaim the essential identity of Kali and Vishnu—and hence of Shaktism and Vaishnavism[135]—but the "most esoteric knowledge for the Supreme good of suffering humanity" that has been revealed by the great *sādhakas* enabled everyone to practice Tantric *sādhana* regardless of race, sex, or creed: "Hindus, Mahommedans, Christians, Parsees, Buddhists, nay, agnostics, if they choose, can enter this Yoga path without committing themselves to any particular form of religion. One's own religion, whatever it be, will, if practised through this esoteric path, lead the soul with scientific precision on to its destination."[136]

Woodroffe enthusiastically embraced this approach and related it extensively to Christianity. In the introduction to the first volume of the *Principles*, Avalon claimed that the teaching of Jesus Christ confirmed "our position, and proves the unity of truth in all revelations." The Christian "Word" was identical with "the Logos of the Greeks and Kabalists, and the Shabdabrahman of the Hindu."[137] However, in *Is India Civilized?*, Woodroffe cautioned that "institutional Christianity is not necessarily the same as the teaching of Jesus." Later historical developments, most notably secularism, had turned the Christianity of the Churches into something that was "rather the product of modern social and intellectual developments than of His essentially unworldly Yoga doctrines."[138] The implication is that Jesus was, in fact, a yogi. As Woodroffe wrote for the *Theosophical Review*, "degeneracy" from Christ's pristine teachings had been exacerbated by " 'Protestant' abolitions" of ritual and the impoverished mode of worship of the "reformer," which lacked "appeal and power."[139]

These attacks on "reform" and "Protestantism" were obviously linked to foreign criticism of "orthodox" Hinduism. Since Woodroffe perceived orthodox Hindus and Catholics as being on the same side in a vast struggle against modernity, it is no surprise that comparisons between Catholicism and Tantra abound in the Avalon and Woodroffe publications.[140] As early as the introduction to *The Great Liberation*, we read that "the Catholic Church possesses an elaborate ritual and a sadhana of its own which is in many points strikingly analogous to the Hindu system."[141] This was also repeatedly stressed by Pramathanath.[142] Against that background, Shivachandra's *Tantratattva* was perceived as a powerful means for forging an alliance against the corrupting powers of modernity: "In fact, in parts the book reads like an orthodox Catholic protest against 'modernism,' and is thus interesting as showing how many fundamental principles are common to all orthodox forms of belief, whether of West of East."[143]

It is striking that "occultism" was presented as an integral manifestation of that common tradition. For instance, we learn that the "methods of ancient Eastern science" were "psychic, or occult, or metaphysical and subjective," mirroring "the same psychic method" that formed the basis of the "sacraments of the Catholic Church and others of its ceremonies."[144] According to Woodroffe, the Tantras "are the expression of principles which are of universal application. The mere statement of religious truths avails not. What is necessary for all is a practical method of realization. This too the occultist needs."[145] Woodroffe's advocacy of occultism was vocal indeed, and based on the same values of science and universalism that he highlighted about Tantra:

> It has been well observed that there are two significant facts about occultism, namely its catholicity (it is to be found in all lands and ages) and its amazing power of recuperation after it has been supposed to have been disproved as mere "superstition." Even some quarter of a century ago . . . there were probably not a score of people in London (and those kept their preoccupation to themselves) who had any interest at all in the subject except from

> a purely antiquarian standpoint. Magic was dismissed by practically all educated men as something too evidently foolish and nonsensical to deserve attention or inquiry. In recent years the position has been reversed in the West, and complaint is again made of the revival of witchcraft and occultism to-day. The reason of this is that modern scientific investigation has established the objectivity of some leading phenomena of occultism.[146]

It does not come as a surprise, then, that Woodroffe leveled harsh polemics against "The Tantras and the Religion of the Shaktas" by Moriz Winternitz that was published in the *Ostasiatische Zeitschrift* in 1916.[147] As in his earlier work, Winternitz translated *sādhaka* as "magician" and dismissed those practices as superstitious magic and mysticism. Noting that the "learned Professor" had "evidently no liking for 'Occultism' and 'India-faddists,' " Woodroffe stated, "The mind which takes these views is like that of the Protestant who called the Catholic Mass 'Hocus Pocus.' It is superstitious trash to him but a holy reality to the believer. Such criticism involves the fallacy of judging others from one's own subjective standpoint."[148] This illustrates Woodroffe's conviction that Protestant bias was largely responsible for the degeneration of Christianity but also for the sorry state of present-day Hinduism. How closely these two were linked was stated quite unambiguously: "There is, in fact, no religion more Catholic than Hinduism."[149]

The central assumption behind that claim was the all-comprehensiveness, or literal catholicity, attributed to both Tantra and Catholicism. This went hand in hand with an affirmation of their "scientific" value and a common ancient root. One might surmise that this was the perspective of a Westerner, but these opinions were expressed earlier and simultaneously by authors such as Baradakanta and Pramathanath and also by Jnanendralal Majumdar, who, according to Shankarnath Ray, was among Woodroffe's main instructors.[150] A member of the Calcutta Mathematical Society and the Indian Research Society, Jnanendralal was the one who translated *Tantratattva* into English, as well as the *Īśopaniṣad* for the *Tantrik Texts* series.[151] In 1909, he published a work with the title *The Eagle and the Captive Sun*, wherein he compared "the different branches of Aryan mythology" and tried to prove the thesis of a "common home" of the ancient Aryans.[152] Greek, Norse, Iranian, and Indian myths were thus united in a primordial origin whose essentials had survived throughout the ages.

Similar ideas were also expressed by one of Shivachandra's affiliates, pandit Panchkari Bandyopadhyay (1863–1923), who was known for his studies on the historical importance of Tantra, especially for Bengal.[153] He even believed that the worship of shakti was the first established dharma, pioneered by the Naths, who had once been very influential in Bengal.[154] Against that background, Panchkari had joined Shivachandra's efforts to bridge sectarian differences, most importantly between Vaishnavas and Shaktas.[155] He even tried to convince the Brahmos of their own Tantric roots, claiming that Rammohan had relied on the Tantras and that the *Brāhma dharmma* (c. 1850) was based on Tantra.[156] Most responsible for the downfall of Tantra in Bengal was the influence of Europeans, which led to the oblivion of Bengali history and the emergence of pseudo-Vaishnavas and -Tantrics.[157] Panchkari thus praised the efforts of Avalon to revert this unfortunate development. He knew Woodroffe personally and mentioned attending one of his lectures.[158] In July 1913 (*śrābaṇ* 1320), Panchkari published an in-depth review of Avalon's work, which was translated at length in the introduction to the *Principles*.[159] Therein, Panchkari stressed that the Tantras contained nothing like idolatry or superstition:

> The special virtue of the Tantras lies in its mode of sādhana. . . . This is not mere philosophy—a mere attempt to ponder upon husks of words—but something which is to be done in a thoroughly practical manner. . . . We believe that the sādhana of the Moslems, and the Esoteric Reliion [*sic*, in Latin characters] or secret dharma-sādhana [*gupta dharmma-sādhanā*] of the Christians of the Roman Catholic and Greek Churches, is based on this groundwork of the Tantras.[160]

Panchkari believed that Tantra had been brought to India from Chaldea, and from there to Europe. Not only was its Shakta *sādhana* manifest in Buddhism, Confucianism, and Shintoism, but it was also prevalent in ancient Egypt, whence it was transmitted to Phoenicia and Greece. Eventually, it influenced primitive Christianity. Panchkari stressed that he had already expounded this theory a while back and was glad to see that Avalon had arrived at the same conclusion.[161] Similar to Krishnachandra's early claim about the intimate relationship between Egypt and India, this demonstrates how the "ancient wisdom narrative" that was supposed to explain the origins and diffusion of Tantra had not resulted from Woodroffe's perspective but was widespread among Bengali Tantrikas prior to the Avalon project. While the previous chapters have shown where such ideas came from and how they developed, it has now become evident that they resurfaced in, and indeed informed, the publications of Avalon and Woodroffe.

9

Conclusion

What a Global Religious History Could Offer

The chapters of this book have shown how modern understandings of Tantra have been shaped by global exchanges since at least the end of the eighteenth century. If global religious history could offer instructive insights into these entanglements, it has done so by relating fine-grained micro-analyses to broader historical developments, and by tracing and contextualizing the manifold connections among the global, regional, and local. Such connections emerged through publications, institutions, and the historical actors who established and animated them. Through translingual practices conditioned by these structures, a vastly diverse range of authors have presented us with their interpretations of religion, science, philosophy, dharma, esotericism, nationalism, race, modernity, reform, and orthodoxy. Tantra stood at their center. These interpretations can be fully grasped only when they are viewed within a metaphorical tangle of exchanges, the complexity of which culminated in the composite project of Arthur Avalon.

Behind the work of Avalon stood regional and local historical developments that I have most immediately traced back to the Bengali intervention of 1880, which in turn must be viewed in light of the diachronic background of Bengali Shakta traditions since the second half of the eighteenth century. Looking further back, to the sixteenth century, Tantra had been an integral part of Brahmanical learning in Bengal, but also of popular devotional poetry. Under the conditions of colonialism, it received political connotations that were bound up with anticolonial agitation, rivalries among Indian factions, and global debates about the meaning of religion. It was this specific environment that shaped the thought of a pandit such as Shivachandra, forming connections from the village of Kumarkhali, the district of Nadiya, and Bengal's cultural centers of learning, to Indian nationalism, orientalist scholarship, global reform and counterreform movements, and the global networks of Theosophy and related currents. The Theosophical Society established crucial lines of communications that were actively and

Global Tantra. Julian Strube, Oxford University Press. © Oxford University Press 2022.
DOI: 10.1093/oso/9780197627112.003.0010

deliberately used by Indian intellectuals as diverse as Baradakanta Majumdar and Rajnarayan Basu. It opened up a space that offered exceptional agency to the Bengali Tantrikas. However, Theosophy had no monopoly on these exchanges, as Indians such as Pyarichand Mitra, Shishirkumar Ghosh, and Kshetrapal Chakravarti enthusiastically and independently engaged with adherents of Spiritualism, New Thought, and Transcendentalism and Unitarianism across the globe.

We observed, time and again, how learned Bengalis and their Western interlocutors were mostly on the same page about issues such as the origin of "Aryan" religion and civilization, the alleged ailments of a materialist modernity, and colonial education and knowledge production. They readily identified yoga as an occult science, praised the esoteric wisdom guarded by Indian gurus, and propagated the scientific virtues of magic and occultism. This remarkable agreement becomes plausible in light of the vivid cultural and intellectual exchanges that have unfolded since the end of the eighteenth century, when orientalist scholarship engaged with the complex landscape of learning in Bengal.

An investigation of the background of the Bengali intervention thus required a contextualization that avoids a binary focus on center and periphery. In the context of Theosophy, and then especially in the circles around Woodroffe, the Calcutta bhadralok intelligentsia played a key role. Yet the debates about Tantra were shaped by developments that point far beyond the metropolis, to a village like Kumarkhali, cities such as Navadvip, Krishnagar, Berhampore, and Benares, and to the many branches that were established by the Theosophical Society, the Brahmos and Aryas, and the self-proclaimed orthodox *sabhās*. Brian Hatcher has expressed the need to consider the space beyond the metropolis by taking up the notion of "fluid landscapes," which were "marked by multiple, fluctuating regional borders and varying types of geological, political, and cultural frontiers against which change may be charted."[1] This perspective also helps sharpen the focus on the wider regional and global entanglements of Bengal's centers of learning. Navadvip and Krishnagar were not isolated spheres of "classical" learning but living and highly active intellectual environments that, as early as from the eighteenth century onward, were involved in shaping orientalist scholarship on India. While previous researchers have often focused on the metropolis of Calcutta, it has become clear how important it is to consider these dynamics.[2] That the activities unfolding in the village of Kumarkhali had a profound and lasting impact on the global discourse and practice of Tantra, both academic and nonacademic, forcefully highlights this.

Decentering the history of what I called "global Tantra" also means exploring the global connections emerging in those regional and local configurations. Global connections could have very different qualities, and they could evolve significantly within a short period of time. The decision of the Theosophical Society to relocate to India and learn from its inhabitants stands in stark contrast to orientalist scholars like Friedrich Max Müller who did not think it necessary to visit the region. Indeed, the Society is an instructive exemplar of the global mobility that increased in the second half of the nineteenth century, although this aspect would undoubtedly warrant complication by future research that should not only focus on the travels of Indian Theosophists in the West[3] but also explore the *limits* of mobility that most Indians faced as a matter of fact. This is an important aspect, as Sebastian Conrad has cautioned against an "obsession with mobility and movement" toward which global history sometimes gravitates.[4] In this sense, the concern of global religious history with connections and mobility should not obliterate the vast differences in agency faced by many individuals under the conditions of colonialism. A comparative study of the travel activities of Indian and Western Theosophists thus remains a desideratum, and I hope to have proposed several points where such studies could begin.

In a similar vein, it must be pointed out that intensifying global connections did not lead to homogeneity or harmony. Three aspects help to illustrate that the notions of entanglement and connection should not suggest that "everything is connected" and that an increase or intensification of global exchanges must not be viewed in simplistic and teleological terms of homogenization or diffusion of Western modernity. First, a focus on connections might distract from what Roland Wenzlhuemer has discussed as "non-connections."[5] Most of the readers of a publication like the *Theosophist* could not verify or falsify information themselves, due to spatial distance and/or lack of knowledge about the subjects that Theosophists explored so eagerly in India and in exchange with Indians. Yet these exchanges *did* exert influence extending far beyond the small circles of their initial participants; their ramifications can be observed across the spectrum of interpretations of "Tantra" all over the world.

Second, we have seen that Tantra was invoked for an assertion of Indian religious and national identity by individuals as diverse as Shivachandra, Baradakanta, Pramathanath, and Woodroffe. Increasing connections and mobility could stimulate nationalist tendencies and anticolonial struggles.[6] Many of the burning issues of present-day Indian politics, not least the Muslim-Hindu relations that were regrettably neglected in this study, directly result from the debates about *sanātana dharma* that have been examined here. They furthermore fed into Hindu sectarian conflicts, many of which were only taking shape or were significantly transformed toward the end of the century, as the case of the Sarvamaṅgalā Sabhā and similar societies has shown. The integrating language of entanglement and connections should not eclipse this conflictual potential.

Third, a focus on connecting structures might also result in neglect of local conditions that lie beyond the sphere of the written sources usually studied by historians. Especially in combination with technological advances in digitized historical research, it might lead, in the words of Lara Putnam, to "overemphasizing the importance of that which connects, and underestimating the weight of that which is connected: emplaced structures, internal societal dynamics."[7] This highlights another lacuna of this study, namely, South Asian actors who were neither colonial bhadralok nor Brahmanical pandits. A focus on subaltern contexts would be imperative for painting a more comprehensive picture, and it is to be hoped that future research will pay increased attention to them.

For these reasons, the genealogical perspective of global religious history is concerned with the fact that each exchange demands contextualization in its own right, considering ruptures, discontinuities, and dislocations. I hope I have succeeded in demonstrating the fractured and fluid nature not only of a movement like Theosophy but also of the many distinct, often rival voices of local and regional Indian interests. Tantra served as an instructive example for the many conflicts revolving around the meaning of Hinduism and dharma and its position within the colonial context.

Against that background, I have provided ample evidence that Theosophy and esotericism must not be viewed as a unilateral diffusion of Western knowledge. The very emergence of esotericism throughout the nineteenth century was inherently intertwined with the historical developments that also shaped the intellectual landscape of Bengal during the same period: learned debates about the origin, meaning, and future of religion; debates about (social) reform and its relationship with supposed orthodoxies; the issues of modernity and materialistic science; and colonial polities, most notably regarding education and nationalism. In India, Theosophists entered a complicated and vivid environment that included an active engagement of Indian intellectuals with fields such as Spiritualism, New Thought, Transcendentalism, and Unitarianism.

We have seen the central importance of societies for these exchanges, ranging from the Theosophical Society via the Brāhma and Ārya Samāj to the sphere of orthodox *sabhās*. The foundation of institutions such as the Varendra Research Society and the Agamas Research Society was instrumental in establishing modern research on the Tantras, and anticolonial or nationalist groups such as the Anuśīlan Samiti or the Yugāntar fueled the political thrust of Shaktism during the Swadeshi years, which would resurface even in the writings of Woodroffe. Future scholars could pursue research on this institutional aspect by concentrating on the many meetings and conventions that were organized by such groups, including the well-documented anniversary meetings of the Theosophical Society, which appear as hotspots for Indian nationalists, self-designated reformers and their revivalist adversaries, and a plethora of other voices. This would also benefit a more spatialized perspective on such interactions, as they became tangible in Olcott's lectures at the Calcutta Town Hall, a location that can be viewed, in the words of Hatcher, as "a kind of multicultural forum wherein the globally connected, yet locally articulated, worlds of Europeans and South Asians met, mingled, and meshed."[8] A systematic examination of such physical locations, including Adyar or Benares, promises to further flesh out the structural conditions that enabled global exchanges.

Many of the sources documenting these exchanges are provided by periodicals, which functioned as vital nodal points and forums on a global level, as in the case of the *Theosophist*, but also on various regional and vernacular levels, such as *Kalpa* and *Bedᵛbyās*, the *Indian Mirror*, *Amṛta Bāzār Patrikā*, and journals such as the *Hindu Spiritual Magazine* and *Light of the East*. These sources point toward an extensive nineteenth-century Indian discourse about religion and esotericism that awaits further exploration. Important steps in similar directions have recently been taken in the context of Vaishnava identities, which were significantly renegotiated through periodicals in the public sphere of colonial Bengal.[9] As Klaus Koschorke and Adrian Hermann have indicated, print media, and periodicals in particular, played a central role in "revivalist" movements across the globe, but a systematic survey and approach to periodicals within a "transregional public sphere" is still lacking.[10] While this present study has provided far-reaching insights into the role of periodicals, including the independence and creativity of Indian Theosophists that became evident in a journal like *Kalpa*, the bulk of source material awaits scrutiny and theoretical reflection.

An actor-focused perspective has helped to grasp the global connections that shaped understandings of Tantra while avoiding a simplistic binary between colonizer and colonized. One crucial insight resulting from this perspective is the fact that "Theosophy" was significantly shaped by actors such as the Aryas and Brahmos and the many individuals who traversed these and other milieus, such as Srishchandra Basu. An occupation with such actors is relevant to experts on esotericism because of the numerous eminent personalities involved in Theosophy, ranging from Rajnarayan Basu and the Tagores to Gandhi. The ideas debated in Theosophical contexts pertain to major issues like religious and national identities, race, gender, sexuality, orientalism, colonialism, and modern science and its relation to religion. This also implies that the Bengali intervention is by no means relevant only to specialists of Bengal: it is emblematic for broader historical developments, theoretical and methodological issues, and a concrete global discourse that continues to inform perceptions of Tantra and yoga.

Theoretical and methodological challenges arise not least because of the colonial framework and the racial hierarchies and ambiguities that can be discerned throughout this book. Global religious history attempts to avoid two misleading tendencies in scholarship on these issues: on one hand, assumptions about the harmlessness of "positive orientalism," the related idea that racial dynamics within Theosophy were apolitical, and the historiographical neglect of "non-Westerners" because of a diffusionist "export model" of "Western esotericism"; on the other hand, postcolonial claims of incommensurability, categorical denunciation of "cultural appropriation," an exclusive focus on oppressive structures, and resulting calls for segregated "indigenous historiographies." I have argued that both perspectives essentially reproduce the binaries, teleology, and Eurocentric-diffusionist assumptions that historical scholarship must complicate rather than reinforce.

Indeed, Theosophy functions like a burning glass for the many ambivalences and tensions that marked exchanges between Western Theosophists and their Indian partners and interlocutors. Gauri Viswanathan has pointed out how Annie Besant, despite her advocacy of self-rule, deemed the colonization of India necessary before universal brotherhood could be realized.[11] In the words of Peter van der Veer, Theosophy contained "a radical anticolonial and anticlerical universalism that opposed the Christian and racial notions of superiority which informed the prevalent British sense of being a 'nation with a mission.' This universalism, however, carried its own contradictions."[12] Theosophists such as Blavatsky reproduced racial stereotypes and colonial power structures, but they *did* side with the marginalized and oppressed.[13] All tensions and ambivalences notwithstanding, the situation was not one of outright exploitation, dominance, and cultural imperialism. It is precisely within the context of Theosophy that Indians could exert an extraordinary agency—depicting them merely as victims of colonial appropriation would historiographically deprive them of that agency.

The lens of translingual practice is a powerful tool for approaching these intricacies. It is not concerned with deciding whether a translation is "correct" or "accurate," but it attempts to reconstruct the conditions under which historical actors de facto established equivalences between languages. Bengalis such as Baradakanta were able to identify Tantra as occultism because of long-standing explanations of Indian ideas and practices with magnetism, electricity, and occult forces. Such perceptions might appear bizarre from a present-day perspective, but they were firmly established within scholarship throughout the nineteenth century and an integral part of orientalist studies since the late eighteenth century. I have shown that orientalist, Indological, and South Asian scholarship abounds with esoteric language consistently for well over two hundred years—again, preceding the emergence of currents such as Spiritualism and occultism, and significantly informing them. That present-day South Asian and Indological scholars approach Tantra in terms of esotericism, gnosis, Hermetic axioms, or occult powers is a direct outcome of this development. It was only reinforced by the vivid Theosophical-Tantrika exchange of the 1880s and 1890s that would form the foundations for the later Avalon project, which in turn cemented it.

The identification of Tantra with esotericism was not simply an orientalist projection. Indians actively engaged with and affected orientalist scholarship and esoteric discourse by identifying Indian concepts with terminology and practices that were labeled esoteric. In the process, they vehemently disagreed with orientalist viewpoints. This can be illustrated by Baradakanta's concepts of Tantrik Occultism and "Tantrik spiritual culture," as well as by the translation of Theosophy with terms such as *brahmabidyā*, which was also central to Shivachandra's proclamation of Tantra as *sanātana dharma*. That this was paralleled by Müller's own program of "theosophy" and his admonition that Olcott follow this "true Brahma-sophy" underlines the ambiguous role of orientalists within that context, which demands a study of its own. I have singled out several aspects that structured the historical conditions for such translations within a global context: debates about "true" religion; the relationship between science, religion, and philosophy; the notion of a shared Aryan civilization and the wish for the revival of its true essence; and esoteric universalism.

The idea that all great religious traditions were united by a common origin and/or a shared core of esoteric knowledge was commonplace not only among Indians but also among Theosophists and orientalists. In Indian discourse, such universalist notions were prominent at least since the late eighteenth century, as the examples of Krishnachandra and Rammohan illustrate; they were not simply adopted from Western orientalist scholarship but often, as in the case of Rammohan, *informed* that scholarship. While that circumstance requires further exploration, it goes without saying that, since the very inception of orientalist scholarship, the language of esotericism was used to differentiate between true and false religion, and it was related to India and "the East" accordingly by authors such as Jacques Matter and Henry Thomas Colebrooke. That later orientalists pursued the goal of restoring the pristine purity of a true religion of humanity has been exemplified by Müller. Tantra was central to these debates because it was perceived by many as being opposed to an alleged Vedic or Upanishadic "Brahmanical orthodoxy." Many Bengalis, from Shivachandra via Baradakanta, Srishchandra, Pyarichand, or Pramathanath, countered that Tantra was in full accordance with the Vedas and embodied not only the appropriate dharma for the Kali Yuga but the esoteric core of true religion.

It is telling that the Theosophists were perceived by contemporaries as part of the revivalist camp striving for the renewal of the true *sanātana dharma*, which underscores how misleading it would be to separate these discourses into Western and Eastern. Olcott was a founding member of the Bhārat Dharma Mahāmaṇḍal and toured Bengal lecturing about the "Bad Aryans" produced by Western education—criticism that fell on fertile ground among the intelligentsia of Calcutta and elsewhere. Local elites such as the maharaja of Darbhanga were involved in Theosophy and Tantra, but also in the Bhārat Dharma Mahāmaṇḍal and the Bhāratbarṣīẏa Ārya Dharma Pracāriṇī Sabhā. Shashadhar defended the shastras on the basis of Western science. Pramathanath profoundly engaged with Western philosophy and, together with Woodroffe, worked toward its "synthesis" with Shakta philosophy. Even Shivachandra, for all his polemics against Western influences, was surrounded by disciples and affiliates who engaged with Western knowledge, had received an English education, or were, like Woodroffe, Westerners. It was through his very criticism of Western influences and colonialism that he participated in a colonial discourse and would, through the work of Pramathanath, Baradakanta, Atalbihari, Woodroffe, and Avalon, exert a considerable, lasting global influence.

The notion of esotericism, then, stood at the center of these exchanges because it played prominent parts in virtually all the contexts that I have identified as crucial for the debates about Tantra. In accordance with Michael Bergunder's argument about the "twin birth" of religion and esotericism during the nineteenth century, I have demonstrated that it emerged within a global context and was significantly shaped by "non-Western" actors. Apart from the strictly historical perspective that determines my approach, it is worth briefly taking up my reflections, from chapter 1, on the notions of secrecy and initiation, as they run like a red thread through the sources that have been examined here. Orientalist scholars, such as Wilson in 1832, had emphasized that "left-hand" Tantrics had been enjoined in secrecy, and the notions of *rahasya*, *gupta*, and *gūṛha vidyā* (hidden or secret knowledge) abound in historical sources.[14] Indian actors compared Tantra to Western traditions precisely on these grounds, for instance when Baradakanta drew a parallel between Tantriks, Freemasons, and Rosicrucians. Such comparisons were prominent since at least the eighteenth century and commonplace throughout the nineteenth century, for instance in the *Journal of the Royal Asiatic Society* from 1852, where Edward Cockburn Ravenshaw compared the symbolism of the Shri Yantra with that of "esoteric" initiatory mystery cults in Egypt, Gnosticism, and Freemasonry.[15] Bengali authors such as Baradakanta and Rajnarayan—who referred to Shiva as "the Grand Master of the Tantric Masonhood"[16]—established such links, and the revolutionary societies discussed in chapter 7 were often inspired by Freemasonry or the Carbonari, combining their initiatory rituals with Tantric elements.[17] Differentiations between inner and outer teachings, or inner and outer yoga, were omnipresent and could be encountered in famous novels such as Bankim's *Ānandamaṭh*.

This was not simply the product of an orientalist gaze. We have seen that the genre of commentary aiming at unearthing the hidden meaning (*gūṛhārtha*) of a text had been widespread in India since the sixteenth century and formed an integral part of Brahmanical learning in Bengal. It fed directly into revivalist narratives of a period of decay that necessitates the explanation of hidden meanings to a misguided population, as in the proclamation of *Bedᵒbyās* to propagate the hidden secrets of dharma (*dharmmer nigūṛh rahasya*). Obviously, the emphasis on the need for initiation (*dīkṣā*) by a guru and the personal qualification (*adhikāra*) are historically central to Tantra and harmonize with occultist and even early mesmerist conceptualizations of the mastery of those occult forces that allegedly governed the arts of yoga and magic alike. As Rahul Peter Das and Carola Erika Lorea have discussed from both historical and ethnographical perspectives, secrecy and the use of coded language were and are vastly important to the Baul traditions of the Nadiya and neighboring regions and inherently intertwined with the devotional Shakta movement in which Shivachandra participated.[18] They are also essential to Vaishnava Sahajiya traditions, as has recently been discussed by Tony K. Stewart and Sukanya Sarbadhikary.[19] Secrecy, then, might very well be a useful structural aspect for comparing "esotericism" in different cultural contexts, as has been done by Hugh Urban.[20] However, as Lorea emphasizes, such comparisons bear the danger of misrepresentations and distortions if they are made without careful historical contextualization.[21] Hence global religious history maintains a genealogical focus on *how* historical actors have shaped the language of esotericism through translingual practice.[22] It thus makes a viable proposal for how to approach the thorny issue of religious comparativism.[23]

In sum, I hope to have provided insights into how historical developments shaped present perceptions of Tantra across the globe. More than shedding light on historical sources and their contexts per se, these insights also help us understand current scholarly perspectives on the subjects of Tantra, yoga, esotericism, and religion from a more theoretical angle. They allow for reflection on how we interpret sources and produce knowledge in the face of historical divisions between East and West, colonizer and colonized, notions of race and nation, orientalism, and religious conflicts. If this study paints a picture of blurred lines, fluid boundaries, and mutual exchanges, if it demonstrates complexity where historical polemics and current ideologies insist on binary dichotomies and incommensurability, then I have achieved a central goal that will hopefully inspire further discussions in a kindred spirit.

Notes

Introduction

1. For the commodification of Tantra especially, see Urban, "Tantra, American Style," and Urban, *Power*, esp. 165–196.
2. E.g., White, *Kiss*, xiii–xiv, 109, 258, where New Age forms of Tantra are dismissed as "invented nonsense" and a "pathetic hybrid." For other critical assessments, see Flood, *Tantric Body*, 187; Padoux, *Hindu Tantric World*, 175.
3. White, *Kiss*, 3; Flood, *Tantric Body*, 73.
4. A good basic introduction to the history of the Tantras, as well as categories such as Tantra and Tantrism, is Padoux, *Hindu Tantric World*. Interested readers may furthermore consult the cited works by White, Flood, and Urban. Essential specialized monographs include Gupta, Hoens, and Goudriaan, *Hindu Tantrism*; Goudriaan and Gupta, *Hindu Tantric*; Sanderson, "Śaivism" and "Śaiva Age"; Muller-Ortega, *Triadic Heart*; Brooks, *Secret*; Dyczkowski, *Journey*; Samuel, *Tantric Revisionings* and *Origins*; Biernacki, *Renowned Goddess*; Olesen, *Goddess Traditions*.
5. Sanderson, "Purity and Power."
6. For a discussion of these intricacies, see Jain, *Selling Yoga*, 95–129.
7. E.g., Urban, *Tantra*, 264–281; cf. Kripal, "Remembering Ourselves," 440.
8. For the sake of readability, the adjectives "Eastern" and "Western," as well as "the East" and "the West," will hereafter mostly be used without scare quotes.
9. Urban, *Zorba*, 3.
10. Ibid., 4–5, 10–15, 19, 181–184.
11. Srinivas, *Winged Faith*, 1–8, 23–35, 327–328.
12. Ibid., 7.
13. In what follows, the term "Theosophy" will be capitalized in order to refer to the ideas represented by the Theosophical Society. This is significant because the term "theosophy" is also used to refer to the teachings of *theosophers* (rather than Theosophists) such as Jacob Böhme and Louis-Claude de Saint-Martin. It should be noted, however, that this semantic differentiation is by no means consistent in either scholarship or historical sources.
14. Urban, *Tantra*, 208.
15. See Strube, "Hinduism," "Yoga and Meditation," and "Tantra." The emergence of New Age out of "Western esotericism" was first detailed by Hanegraaff, *New Age*, 365–513.
16. For an overview of these publications, see Taylor, *Sir John Woodroffe*, 129–136.
17. Urban, *Tantra*, 136.
18. White, *Kiss*, xi.
19. Kripal, "Remembering Ourselves," 446; cf. Kripal, *Kali's Child*, 28.

20. Urban, *Tantra*, esp. 165–202.
21. Urban, *Magia Sexualis*, 140–161; Djurdjevic, *India* and "Great Beast"; Newcombe, "Magic"; Granholm, "Serpent"; Bogdan, "Challenging."
22. Avalon, *Tantra of the Great Liberation* (1913), xv–xvi; cf. the publisher's note to Pratyagatmananda Saraswati and Woodroffe, *Sadhana*.
23. Cf. Woodroffe, *Shakti and Shakta* (1918), i.
24. See Woodroffe, *Bharata Shakti*, xx, and the discussion in Taylor, *Sir John Woodroffe*, 217–219.
25. Taylor, *Sir John Woodroffe*, 203–209.
26. See, for instance, Chakravarti, *Tantras*, v; Ray, *Religious Movements*, 68–73; Gupta, Hoens, and Goudriaan, *Hindu Tantrism*, 4; McDaniel, *Offering*, 76, 98; Padoux, *Hindu Tantric World*, 6; Sartori, "Beyond," 84–86.
27. De Michelis, *History*, 112–119.
28. Ibid., 29–30.
29. This is also emphasized by Taylor, *Sir John Woodroffe*, 236, cf. 233–234.
30. Cf. the plea in Strube and Krämer, "Introduction."
31. Taylor, *Sir John Woodroffe*, 148.
32. McDaniel, *Offering*, 278.
33. This has been extensively demonstrated by Chakrabarti, *Religious*.
34. Williams, *Hinduism*, 126–127; cf. Wilson, "Sketch," 224.
35. See chapter 6.
36. Cf. Bose, *Recasting*, 3.
37. The necessity for secrecy, *dīkṣā*, and the personal qualification (*adhikāra*) of the disciple are integral parts of the Tantric tradition and have been discussed from Abhinavagupta up to the present day. See Abhinavagupta, *Kula Ritual*, 73–79; also see the extensive treatment of the Kaula traditions in Muller-Ortega, *Triadic Heart* and Dyczkowski, *Canon*.
38. Cf. Strube, "Tantra as Experimental Science."
39. White, "Tantra."
40. Sartori, "Beyond," 84–89.
41. McDaniel, *Offering*, 74–75, 160–161, 176, 243, 259.
42. Ibid., 6–13.
43. E.g., ibid., 278.
44. Ibid., 9.
45. Weiss, *Emergence*, 1-2, 15-24, 98-101.
46. Hatcher, *Hinduism*, 59–60.
47. Cf. the overview in Hatcher, "Great Men."
48. Raychaudhuri, *Europe*, 9, cf. 336–338.
49. Sen, *Hindu Revivalism*, 10. In a recent piece, Sen reinforces this point within a Vaishnava context: Sen, "Theorising," 35, 37.
50. Hatcher, "Great Men," 137.
51. Cf. Hatcher, "Introduction," 9.
52. Wong and Sardella, "Vaiṣṇavism," 5–6.
53. Ibid., 5.

54. Hatcher, *Hinduism*, 3. For this reason, Hatcher proposes the notion of "religious polities" within a colonially defined "empire of reform" as a more useful analytical lens that avoids a normative discourse of religious reform. See 3–4, 8, 73–100.
55. Ibid., 32.
56. Ibid., 33–41; cf. Chatterjee, *Black Hole*, 75, from where this notion is borrowed.
57. Ghosh, "Innate Intuition," 3–7; also see Wong, "Against."
58. Prakash, *Another Reason*, 3–7.
59. Ibid., 6–7.
60. Dodson and Hatcher, "Introduction," 2–3 and, in addition to Hatcher's previous work on the subject, Hatcher, "Pandits."
61. See Bordeaux, "Mythic King" and Ehrlich, "New Lights."
62. Van der Veer, *Imperial Encounters*, 43.
63. Ballantyne, "Persistence," 138.
64. Singleton, *Yoga*, 84; Sen, *Hindu Revivalism*, 207.
65. Hatcher, *Hinduism*, 32. Hatcher's advocacy of a multiregional perspective is largely based on Asher and Talbot, *India*.
66. Bergunder, "Hinduism," 88–89. Cf. the detailed discussion in Bergunder, "Umkämpfte Historisierung."
67. See, for instance, the overall arguments in Kippenberg, *Discovering*; Nehring, *Orientalismus*; Krech, *Wissenschaft*; Hermann, *Unterscheidungen*; Masuzawa, *Invention*; Josephson, *Invention*; Krämer, *Shimaji Mokurai*; Cyranka, *Mahomet*; Tschacher, *Race*.
68. Kollmar-Paulenz, "Mongolische Geschichtsschreibung," 265–268; cf. Kollmar-Paulenz, "Lamas," 185–191.
69. Among notable exceptions is Conrad, "Cultural History," 619, 657–659.
70. For a constructive appeal to make deliberate use of that need, cf. Hermann, "Call."
71. Mazlish, *New Global History*, 1, 7–22. On the fuzzy relationship between global history and globalization, see Wenzlhuemer, *Globalgeschichte*, 25–29.
72. Mazlish, *New Global History*, 8, 9, 12.
73. Crossley, *What Is Global History*, 11–27.
74. Manning, *Navigating*, 3, 117.
75. Sachsenmaier, *Global*, 70–78.
76. Manning, *Navigating*, 169.
77. Wenzlhuemer, *Globalgeschichte*, 12–13.
78. Crossley, *What Is Global History*, 4, 102–121.
79. O'Brien, "Historiographical," 4.
80. Wenzlhuemer, *Globalgeschichte*, 10; cf. the cautionary stance in Sachsenmaier, "World History."
81. Fischer-Tiné, "Marrying," 50–51, 67–74. Also see the special issue "Global History and Microhistory" of *Past & Present* 242, no. 14, esp. Ghobrial, "Introduction," 10–17.
82. Wenzlhuemer, *Globalgeschichte*, 259–263.
83. Komlosy, *Globalgeschichte*, 14.
84. This point is frequently stressed by global historians, e.g., Manning, *Navigating*, 270–272 and Wenzlhuemer, *Globalgeschichte*, 79–84.

85. Conrad, *What Is Global History*, 12, 64–65; cf. Moyn and Sartori, "Approaches," 5–15.
86. Conrad and Randeria, "Einleitung," 40; cf. van der Veer, *Imperial Encounters*, 11.
87. Cf. Ballantyne, *Entanglements*, 17 and the overall argument in Ballantyne, *Webs*.
88. The creation of a comprehensible narrative also requires what has been called by Michel de Certeau a "scriptural inversion." Although genealogical research departs from the present, its narrative must depart from the past. See Certeau, *Writing*, 86–99.
89. Wenzlhuemer, *Globalgeschichte*, 14–23, 39–43.
90. Ibid., 23.
91. Ibid., 29. This spatial dimension is also why I find it useful to insert a regional level between the local and global. Although this distinction cannot be clear-cut, I find it analytically reasonable to differentiate between an investigation within a geographical area such as the Indian subcontinent and a much more confined space, such as the village of Kumarkhali.
92. Ibid., 145.
93. Ibid., 148–149, 184–185.
94. Baier, "Theosophical Orientalism," 315–318.
95. Hock, "Transkulturelle Perspektiven."
96. Hermann, *Unterscheidungen*, 32–35; cf. Hermann, "Buddhist Modernism," 55–56.
97. Raychaudhuri, *Europe*, 10, 33; Sen, *Hindu Revivalism*, 5.
98. E.g., Bhatia, *Unforgetting*, 58–59, 127 and "Psychic Chaitanya."
99. See, most recently, Bergunder, "Umkämpfte Historisierung," 56; Eßbach, *Religionssoziologie*, 156–166, 259–265, 309–316; Zander, *"Europäische,"* 44–45, 269–270, 339–340.
100. Mühlematter and Zander, *Occult Roots*.
101. Bayly, *Birth*, 365.
102. Osterhammel, *Transformation*, 813.
103. Conrad, "Cultural History," 582.
104. In fact, it also largely excludes nonwhite actors within "the West," as has been highlighted by Bakker, "Hidden Presence," 487; Gray, "Traumatic Mysticism," 206–216; Finely, Gray, and Page, "Africana Esoteric Studies"; and the contributions to Finley, Guillory, and Page, *Esotericism*. For the case of Theosophy, see Strube, "Theosophy and Race" and "Theosophy, Race, and the Study of Esotericism."
105. Hammer and Rothstein, *Handbook*.
106. Goodrick-Clarke, "Western," 303.
107. Rudbøg and Sand, *Imagining*. The only chapter that does revolve around a "non-Westerner" is a reprint of Michael Bergunder's 2014 article about Gandhi, "Experiments."
108. Baier, "Theosophical Orientalism," 309–310; cf. Baier, *Meditation*.
109. Chajes, *Recycled Lives*, 169.
110. Krämer and Strube, *Theosophy*.
111. See Hanegraaff, "Western Esotericism," 29–31.
112. Strube, "Towards"; cf. my earlier plea in Strube, "Transgressing Boundaries." The "orientalist baggage" of Western esotericism and its neglect of South Asian traditions

has also been addressed by Urban, "The Goddess," 2. For a broad discussion of the shortcomings of "Western esotericism," see Asprem and Strube, *New Approaches*, specifically Strube, "Towards."

113. Bergunder, "What Is Esotericism?," 29.
114. Pennington, *Was Hinduism Invented?*, 26; cf. Hermann, *Unterscheidungen*, 207–214.
115. Bergunder, "Religion," 110–112; Hatcher, "Colonial" and *Eclecticism*; for the case of Buddhism, see King, *Orientalism and Religion*, 151–152, cf. 217.
116. Bergunder, "Umkämpfte Historisierung," 103; cf. Strube, *Sozialismus*, 628–631.
117. Bergunder, "Religion," 117–123.
118. Ibid., 123.
119. Green, "Global Occult," 386.
120. Ibid., 385. The reconfiguration of space and time through technological developments such as the telegraph has been addressed in more detail by Wenzlhuemer, *Globalgeschichte*, 79–143.
121. For an extended discussion of sociological concepts of modernity and modernization with regard to global religious history, see Hermann, *Unterscheidungen*, 369–437.
122. Conrad, *Global History*, 76.
123. Conrad, "Greek," 21–23.
124. E.g., Moyn and Sartori, "Approaches," 15, 20; Manning, *Navigating*, 265–270.
125. Conrad, *Global History*, 69–70.
126. Subrahmanyam, *Europe's India*, 212. For the case studies, see 103–143. That such exchanges must be investigated with respect to "premodern" periods is only underlined by the fruitful engagement of global approaches with the history of science; see the contributions to Manning and Rood, *Global* and Manning and Owen, *Knowledge*.
127. Randeria, "Geteilte Geschichte," 87.
128. Fisher, *Hindu Pluralism*, 16.
129. As in Shmuel N. Eisenstadt's widely received notion of "multiple modernities." See Eisenstadt, *Multiple Modernities*.
130. Van der Veer, *Imperial Encounters*, 7, 160.
131. Drayton and Motadel, "Discussion," 7–13; cf. Manjapra, "Transnational Approaches."
132. Van der Veer, *Imperial Encounters*, 8–11.
133. Tweed, "Toward," 425; cf. Tweed, "American Occultism"; Banerjee, "Transversal Histories," 156 and *Mortal God*, 32–38. Also see the discussion in Banerjee, "All this is Indeed Brahman."
134. Foucault, "Nietzsche," 80–81, 89–91.
135. Asad, *Formations*, 16.
136. Bergunder, "What Is Religion?," 275–279; cf. Asprem and Strube, "Esotericism's Expanding Horizon."
137. Chakrabarty, *Provincializing*, 16, 255.
138. Eckert and Randeria, "Geteilte Globalisierung," 11.

139. Cf. the in-depth reflections in Okropiridze, "Interpretation Reconsidered" and Strube, *Sozialismus*, 29–37.
140. Bergunder, "What Is Esotericism?," 19–24 and "What Is Religion?," 259–273.
141. Laclau, "Why," 168.
142. Laclau, "Identity," 44–59.
143. Bergunder, "What Is Esotericism?," 25.
144. Ghobrial, "Introduction," 9.
145. Banerjee, "All This is Indeed Brahman," 83, 106.
146. Bergunder, "Comparison," 36–43; cf. Hermann, *Unterscheidungen*, esp. 195–254.
147. Cf. Bergunder, "Umkämpfte Historisierung" and Kleine, "Wozu außereuropäische Religionsgeschichte." For criticism of the assumption of cultural incommensurability, see Srinivas, *Winged Faith*, 27, 341 and Chakravarti, *Empire*, 16–17.
148. Cf. Bhabha, *Location*, 19, 37–38, 49–56.
149. Ibid., 6.
150. Asad, *Genealogies*, 18; Hall, "West," 276. Cf. Crossley, *What Is Global History*, 109–117.
151. Chakrabarty, *Provincializing*, 42–43.
152. Conrad and Randeria, "Einleitung," 51–52; van der Veer, *Imperial Encounters*, 3–13; Chidester, *Savage Systems*, xiii.
153. Fitzgerald, *Ideology*; McCutcheon, *Manufacturing Religion*.
154. Fitzgerald, "Introduction," 9.
155. Fitzgerald, *Ideology*, 134–135.
156. Conrad, *Global History*, 3–4; Conrad and Randeria, "Einleitung," 35–36; Yelle, *Language*, ix–x, 6–7. For a longue durée overview of diffusionist modes of writing history, see Crossley, *What Is Global History*, 28–46 and cf. 106–108.
157. Bergunder, "Religion," 87; this point is further developed in Bergunder, "Umkämpfte Historisierung"; cf. Hermann, *Unterscheidungen*, 200.
158. Yelle, *Language*, 4–5.
159. Conrad, *Global History*, 56–57; Moyn and Sartori, "Approaches," 18–20; for the case of Hinduism, see Frykenberg, "Constructions," 533–534 or King, *Orientalism*, 159.
160. Conrad, *Global History*, 74–75.
161. Fischer-Tiné and Gehrmann, "Introduction," 4–5.
162. Duara, "Asien"; Conrad and Randeria, "Einleitung," 33–34.
163. In addition to the work of Bergunder, important steps were taken by Granholm, "Locating" and Asprem, "Beyond"; cf. Roukema and Kilner-Johnson, "Editorial"; Asprem and Strube, "Esotericism's Expanding Horizon."
164. Strube, "Towards," 52–55.
165. Hanegraaff, "Globalization," 86, original emphasis.
166. For a detailed criticism of Hanegraaff's approach, see Strube, "Towards."
167. Strube, "Occultist," 575–577 and *Sozialismus*, 590–618; cf. Prothero, "From Spiritualism"; McVey, "Thebes"; Pasi, "Oriental Kabbalah"; Partridge, "Lost Horizon."
168. Godwin, *Theosophical*, 333–362.

169. In addition to Strube, "Towards," see Asprem and Strube, "Afterword" for the necessary consequences of the study of esotericism, namely, the abolishment of its ideologically charged Western demarcation.
170. Chakrabarty, *Provincializing*, 7–8, 12–15; cf. Asad, *Formations*, 13–14.
171. Chakrabarty, *Provincializing*, 28–29; cf. Randeria and Römhild, "Das postkoloniale Europa," 15–17; Sachsenmaier, *Global*, 39–45.
172. Forray, "William Q. Judge"; cf. Godwin, *Theosophical*, 363–379.
173. This will be discussed in chapter 3; it is briefly mentioned by Baier, "Theosophical Orientalism," 309–310.
174. Scott, "Miracle Publics"; about the Society for Psychical Research, see Oppenheim, *Other* and recently Noakes, *Physics and Psychics*.
175. Strube, "Theosophy and Race" and "Theosophy, Race, and the Study of Esotericism."
176. Partridge, "Lost Horizon," 329–330.
177. Ibid., 327.
178. For a criticism of that notion, see Strube, "Towards" and "Theosophy and Race."
179. Subrahmanyam, *Europe's India*, 213–215.
180. Lubelsky, "Mythological."
181. Bevir, "Opposition," "Theosophy," and "Theosophy and the Origins."
182. Viswanathan, "Ordinary Business" and *Outside*, 177–207.
183. Baier, "Theosophical Orientalism," 323–324.
184. Van der Veer, *Imperial Encounters*, 57.
185. Green, "Global Occult," 388–389.
186. Pasi, "Modernity."
187. Hanegraaff, "Globalization," 86.
188. Nandy, "History's Forgotten Doubles"; Lal, "Provincializing."
189. Fischer-Tiné, "Marrying," 55.
190. Strube, "Towards," 60.
191. This issue has been elucidated by Subrahmanyam, *Europe's India*, 283–285, in the context of premodern India.
192. Liu, *Translingual Practice*, xix, 2, 19.
193. Ibid., 5–6, 10; cf. Liu, "Legislating," 137.
194. Liu, "Legislating," 128 and "Question," 5. Several studies have proved the efficiency of adopting Liu's approach, for instance Hermann, *Unterscheidungen*, 219–232; Krämer, *Shimaji Mokurai*, 9–12 and "Euro-Asian."

Chapter 1

1. There exists no comprehensive and dedicated history of the Theosophical Society. See, however, the entries in Hammer and Rothstein, *Handbook*, and the recent discussions in Rudbøg and Sand, "Introduction," and Strube and Krämer, "Introduction."

2. Useful introductions and contributions to the debated meaning of esotericism include Hanegraaff, *Western Esotericism*; Bergunder, "What Is Esotericism?"; and Stuckrad, *Western Esoterisicm*. Also see the most recent discussions in Asprem and Strube, *New Approaches*.
3. Cf. the contributions to Rudbøg and Sand, *Imagining the East*, and Hanegraaff, "Western Esotericism and the Orient."
4. Bergunder, "Experiments."
5. Farquhar, *Modern Religious Movements*, 208–291.
6. Van der Veer, *Imperial Encounters*, 57.
7. See *The Theosophist* 1, no. 5 (1880): 108: "Our party should feel deeply grateful to the London 'Spiritualist' for the suggestion that Theosophy may be regarded as a 'subordinate branch of Spiritualism.' . . . This is extremely liberal; about as much so as for a Manchester man to concede that the British Empire is an auxiliary branch of the county of Lancashire."
8. Although there is now a wealth of valuable studies, a comprehensive, transnational history of Spiritualism remains to be written. One fundamental issue in the historiography of Spiritualism is the widespread assumption that Spiritualism started in the year 1848 after the famous "phenomena" observed by the Fox sisters in Hydesville, New York. While the succeeding media furor was largely responsible for creating a mass movement, Spiritualist groups had already existed and relied on ideas and currents that can be traced back at least to the beginning of the nineteenth century; see Cyranka, "Religious Revolutionaries"; Stuckrad, *Scientification*, 97; Godwin, *Theosophical*, 187–204. Among the numerous studies of Spiritualism and related contexts, such as Psychical Research, see, for overviews of national contexts, Oppenheim, *Other*; Braude, *Radical*; Owen, *Darkened*; Goldsmith, *Other*; Albanese, *Republic*, 177–329; Noakes, *Physics*; Linse, *Geisterseher*; Wolffram, *Stepchildren*; Edelman, *Voyantes*; or Sharp, *Secular*.
9. See Strube, "Socialist Religion," 373–374; Strube, "Baphomet," 64–69. I have extensively discussed this development in Strube, *Sozialismus*.
10. Baier, *Meditation*, 1:179–252; cf. Strube, "Yoga and Meditation" and "Hinduism."
11. See Strube, *Sozialismus*, esp. 524–534.
12. For a case study of this relationship between theories of natural forces and occultism, see Strube, *Vril*, 13–123.
13. Chajes, *Recycled Lives*, 134–135.
14. Asprem, *Problem*, 444–480; cf. Asprem, "Theosophical Attitudes."
15. Turner, *Between*, 68–103; Oppenheim, *Other*, 296–325.
16. Quoted in Bergunder, "Religion and Science," 121.
17. Stuckrad, *Scientification*, 94–112, here 94.
18. This has been broadly explored in the pioneering studies by Schwab, *Oriental Renaissance* and Halbfass, *India and Europe*. An in-depth study of Müller remains to be written.
19. Cf. the contributions to Mühlematter and Zander, *Occult Roots*.
20. Josephson-Storm, *Myth*, 115–116.
21. Urban, *Tantra*, 54–55.

22. Ibid., 51. Cf. the overview in Taylor, *Sir John Woodroffe*, 119–127.
23. Colebrooke, *Miscellaneous*, 3:157–158.
24. Mitra, *Indo-Aryans*, 2:404.
25. Williams, *Hinduism*, 116.
26. Ibid., 123.
27. Banerji, *Tantra in Bengal* (1978), 102.
28. Baier, *Meditation*, 1:324–329; Baier, "Theosophical Orientalism," 327–328.
29. Its author, Jnandev, claimed to be of the lineage of Matsyendra and Goraksha. For more background, see Novetzke, *Quotidian*, 221–229. The reference to the *Jñāneśvarī* is significant not only because of its connection to Nath traditions but also because of its formulations about social ethics, especially with regard to females and non-Brahmins, that were published in Marathi rather than Sanskrit (243–284). Unfortunately, the scope of this book does not allow for an investigation of the significant role of the Nath tradition for this debate. See White, *Alchemical Body* and *Sinister Yogis*; Samuel, *Origins*, 276–278; Bouillier, *Itinérance*; the respective contributions to White, *Yoga in Practice*; the selections in Mallinson and Singleton, *Roots*; and Mallinson, "Nāth Sampradāya."
30. Truth Seeker, "Yoga," 86–87. Indeed, the text contains a fascinating passage describing the rising of the kundalini. See Kiehnle, "Secret."
31. Truth Seeker, "Yoga," 87.
32. *The Theosophist* 1, no. 5 (1880): 113.
33. Urban, *Tantra*, 44–72.
34. Sarasvatī, "Arya Prakash," 66–67. Cf. the Bengali translation in Mukhopādhyāẏ, *Daẏānander svaracita jīban'bṛtta*, 27–28.
35. Bharadwaja, *Light*, 339.
36. Majumdar, "Tantric Philosophy," 173.
37. Ibid.
38. Ibid., 174.
39. Majumdar, "Glimpse," 244.
40. Ibid.
41. Majumdar, "Tantric Philosophy," 173.
42. Majumdar, "Occult Sciences," 53.
43. Ibid.
44. Cf. the overview in Strube, "Tantra," "Yoga and Meditation," and "Hinduism."
45. Cf. Sen, *Hindu Revivalism*, 258.
46. Chakrabarti, *Religious Process*, 111–113.
47. Sanderson, "Śaiva Age."
48. Bordeaux, "Mythic King," 99.
49. Urban, *Tantra*, 134–147; cf. White, "Introduction," 17.
50. Sanderson, "Purity and Power," 203; Sanderson, "Meaning," 79.
51. In 1887, William Joseph Wilkins wrote that it had been "estimated that of the Hindus in Bengal about three-fourths are devoted to the worship of Sakti" (*Modern Hinduism*, 91). This was affirmed in 1907 by John Campbell Oman, *Brahmans*, 24, on the basis

of the census of 1901. While these estimates should be taken with great caution, they underline the prominence of Shaktism in Bengal.

52. Among the vast literature that discusses the origins of Tantra, see Winternitz, *Geschichte*, 482; Banerji, *Tantra in Bengal* (1978), 32–33.
53. I am thankful to Michael Bergunder for sharing the draft of a chapter of his upcoming *Indische Religionsgeschichte* that revolves around this context.
54. McDermott, *Mother*, 20–22.
55. Bordeaux, "Mythic King," 197.
56. Ibid., 3.
57. Ibid., 21. Also see Dasgupta, "Maharaja." This is, interestingly, also highlighted in Bandyopādhyāẏ, *Bāṃlār Tantra*, 66.
58. Chakrabarti, *Religious Process*, 185–187. For a discussion of Tantra within the major Puranas, see Hazra, "Influence on the Tattvas," 680–681.
59. Chakrabarti, *Religious Process*, 193–194; cf. Brooks, *Secret*, 36.
60. Bordeaux, "Mythic King," 108.
61. Ganeri, *Lost*, 13, 17.
62. Bordeaux, "Mythic King," 59.
63. Ibid., 63; Sinha, *Pandits*, 15, 28. For a contextualization of Navya Nyāya, see Pollock, "New Intellectuals."
64. Ganeri, *Lost*, 39–59.
65. The local network of pandits, which Ganeri refers to as the "Navadvip establishment," is discussed in ibid., 81–88.
66. Bordeaux, "Mythic King," 11.
67. Ibid., 66–67.
68. Brown, Frykenberg, and Low, *Christians*, 51.
69. Bordeaux, "Mythic King," 68.
70. Ibid., 63; Sinha, *Pandits*, 25.
71. Hazra, "Influence on the Smṛti" and "Influence on the Smṛti 2."
72. See Hazra, "Influence on the Tattvas," 704. Tantric initiation was regarded as open to women and Shudras, given that they would not use the mantra "Om."
73. On the dating of the *Śāradātilaka*, see Sanderson, "Śaiva Age," 252.
74. See Bühnemann, "Śāradātilakatantra," 207.
75. Ibid., 206. The *Śāradātilaka*'s outstanding influence is attested by the numerous manuscript copies from all over the subcontinent, but also from the large number of texts that quote it as an authority, including several *smṛti* and many Tantric sources.
76. Hazra, "Influence on the Tattvas," 696.
77. For a comprehensive exploration of these practices, see Flood, *Tantric Body*. Also see the linguistic analysis of Tantric mantras in Yelle, *Explaining*, here esp. 39–44.
78. Hazra, "Influence on the Tattvas," 685–687, 694–697.
79. Ibid., 684, 697–698.
80. Ibid., 701.
81. Majumdar, "Glimpse," 244.
82. White, *Kiss*, 221.
83. Ibid., 257.

84. Hatcher, *Bourgeois*, 130, 179. These societies will be discussed in the next chapter.
85. About the prominence of the *Kulārṇava* in Bengal, also see McDaniel, *Offering*, 97–103.
86. Goudriaan and Gupta, *Hindu Tantric*, 147.
87. Banerji, *Tantra in Bengal* (1978), 111–114.
88. Bordeaux, "Mythic King," 107.
89. Pal, *Hindu Religion*, 67.
90. Bordeaux, "Mythic King," 176.
91. Bühnemann, "Śāradātilakatantra," 206, 208.
92. Sachchidananda, "Theory and Practice [1]," 39–40.
93. Majumdar, "Tantric Philosophy," 172.
94. The ambiguities related to this are expertly unraveled in Lorea, "I Am Afraid."
95. About Rāmprasād, see McDermott, *Mother* and McLean, *Devoted*. A selection of songs and poems can be found in McDermott, *Singing*.
96. McDermott, *Mother*; cf. Das Gupta, *Obscure*, 129.
97. For a comprehensive analysis, see Bhatia, *Unforgetting*. The broader context of Bengali Vaishnavism has recently been explored by Sardella and Wong, *Legacy*. Also see Ghosh, "Innate Intuition."
98. Ghosh, "Innate Intuition"; McDaniel, *Offering*, 4.
99. Chatterjee, "Goddess," 1480–1482; cf. Goudriaan and Gupta, *Hindu Tantric*, 180; McDermott, *Mother*, 31–33; McDaniel, *Offering*, 162.
100. Bordeaux, "Mythic King," 110–112.
101. Wong and Sardella, "Vaiṣṇavism," 4.
102. Ehrlich, "New Lights," 4–5.
103. *General Report*, 493–494.
104. Majumdar, *Shikshaka*, 1.
105. Ibid., 5. Also see the chapter on "rāj-kārya" (28–47).
106. Mukhurji, *Naldanga*, 111–121.
107. This also manifests in raja Pramathabhushan's family lore, which contains an account of Bhairavachandra Bhattacharya, a well-known worshiper of Kali who gathered many followers and performed miraculous deeds (ibid., 4–9).
108. *The Theosophist* 4, no. 5 (1883): 4.
109. *The Theosophist* 4, no. 8 (1883): 6.
110. Gombrich, *Theravāda Buddhism*; Prothero, *White Buddhist*; Bergunder, "Religion and Science," 125.
111. See Majum^{l}dār, *Bhūgol*; Majum^{l}dār, *Subhadrā*, which tells the story of the premarital life of Arjuna's wife; and the heavily edited Majum^{l}dār, *Śiśurañjan mahābhārat* that ends with the journey of the Pandavas to heaven. There are several other books by Baradakanta that deal with both social and educational subjects.
112. While Majum^{l}dār, *Yiśukhriṣṭa* does not provide an explicit exegesis, the book's terminology is an exemplar of an interpretation of Christianity from an Indian perspective. For instance, John the Baptist is depicted as the *guru* of Jesus, who in turn is referred to as an *avatār*, descended "to show mankind the way of dharma in the way of the guru" (mānab^{l}jātike dharmer path dekhāite gururūpe yini abatīrṇa) (16).

113. *Tattva* can designate a principle, truth, reality, or "true principle," according to Samkhya philosophy. *Dharma*, in turn, is often translated as "religion" but carries meanings that significantly differ from that European term: it can denote a law or rule of conduct, certain prescriptions or customary observances, degrees, established norms or practices, morality and ethics, and so on. *Vidyā*, finally, usually refers to knowledge, learning, or scholarship. The definitions of *vidyā* differ from school to school, but generally they describe a method of acquiring knowledge.
114. *Satya* is usually translated as "truth" or "reality," as it also signifies the uppermost of the seven worlds (*lokas*), the abode of Brahma.
115. These purposes can be found on the back cover of each issue.
116. "Kalper uday̐," *Kalpa* 1, no. 1 (1893): 1–4.
117. "Tattvaprabhā," *Kalpa* 2, nos. 2–3 (1894): 25–26.
118. *Kalpa* 3, nos. 5–6 (1895): 131.
119. "Hr̥day̐er dharmma," *Kalpa* 1, no. 1 (1893): 4–7.
120. Majumˡdār, "Dharmma-dveṣ," 17–19.
121. Majumˡdār, "Tattvabidyā o tattvasabhā," 34.
122. Ibid., 35.
123. Majumˡdār, "Tattvabidyā prabeṣikā," 59–60.
124. Ibid., 60–61.
125. "Bedāntadarśan," *Kalpa* 1, no. 1 (1893): 13.
126. *Kalpa* 1, no. 3 (1893): 49–54.
127. *Kalpa* 1, no. 3 (1893): 55–57.
128. *Kalpa* 2, nos. 2–3 (1894): 84.
129. "Śītalā debī," *Kalpa* 2, nos. 2–3 (1894): 51.
130. "Jāntab cumbak-śakti," *Kalpa* 2, nos. 2–3 (1894): 68–73.
131. *Kalpa* 3, nos. 5–6 (1895): 131.
132. "Jyotiṣ bijñān," *Kalpa* 2, no. 2 (1894): 38–42.
133. "Jñān māhātmyā," *Kalpa* 2, no. 2 (1894): 41–51.
134. "Ādyaśakti," *Kalpa* 3, nos. 5–6 (1895): 146–154.
135. "Pañcamakār," *Kalpa* 3, nos. 5–6 (1895): 187–190.
136. Taylor, *Sir John Woodroffe*, 137–152; cf. the contemporary observation of Farquhar, *Modern Religious Movements*, 305.
137. E.g., McDaniel, *Offering*, 69–70, or Sen Sharma, *Aspects*.
138. Avalon, *Principles*, vol. 1, preface, vii.
139. Ibid., xi.
140. Ibid., introduction, iv.
141. Yelle, *Language*, 33–70. Müller, who serves as Yelle's central example, will be discussed in chapter 2.
142. Woodroffe, *Bharata Shakti*, 40; cf. Woodroffe, *Seed*, 27.
143. Woodroffe, *Bharata Shakti*, 51, original emphasis; cf. Woodroffe, *Is India Civilized?*, 250.
144. Woodroffe, *Is India Civilized?*, 255.
145. This has been examined by Yelle, *Language*, 103–135, in light of Protestant polemics against mantras.

146. Woodroffe, *Is India Civilized?*, 38.
147. Taylor, *Sir John Woodroffe*, 187–189.
148. About national education in the Ārya context, see the in-depth study by Fischer-Tiné, *Gurukul*.
149. Avalon, *Principles*, vol. 1, preface, xix.
150. Woodroffe, *Shakti and Shakta*, 73.
151. Woodroffe, *Is India Civilized?*, 118; Woodroffe, *Shakti and Shakta*, 88–91, 106, 259. Cf. Strube, "Tantra as Experimental Science."
152. Woodroffe, *Shakti and Shakta*, 464.
153. Taylor, *Sir John Woodroffe*, 148.
154. Eliade, *Yoga*, 87–88.
155. Ibid., 116, 180, 352. It is also highlighted that, in Tantrism, it was the guru who transmitted that "esoteric doctrine" (206–207).
156. Das Gupta, *Obscure*, 242.
157. Banerji, *Tantra in Bengal* (1978), vi–vii, 1, 24.
158. Gupta, Hoens, and Goudriaan, *Hindu Tantrism*, 7–8.
159. Sanderson, "Śaivism," 667, 690–691; Sanderson, "Meaning," 57.
160. Padoux, *Vāc*, 58.
161. Padoux, *Hindu*, 11, 126.
162. White, *Kiss*, 16, 23, 79–81, 123; cf. White, "Tantra."
163. Burns, "Receptions," 35.
164. Brooks, *Secret*, 20.
165. Flood, *Tantric Body*, 163–164, 149–150, 163.
166. E.g., Fisher, *Hindu Pluralism*, 29, 49, 55, 59.
167. Ibid., 69.
168. Leyden, "On the Roshania," 376.
169. Colebrooke, "On the Philosophy," 450.
170. Hodgson, "Notices," 422.
171. Wilson, "Analysis," 384; Wilson, *Two Lectures*, iv.
172. For instance, Wilson, "Sketch," 221–228; cf. the remark in Wilson, "Summary," 58.
173. Sykes, "Notes," 252, 388, 448.
174. See Neugebauer-Wölk, "Historische Esoterikforschung," 41; Neugebauer-Wölk, "Der Esoteriker."
175. See Strube, "Socialism and Esotericism," 118–120 and, more extensively, *Sozialismus*, 97–147, 177–211. Also see the condensed overview in Strube, "Baphomet," 55–58. It should be noted that authors such as Matter had a background in High-Degree Freemasonry; further exploration of that background in light of the present subject would certainly be most fruitful.
176. Kippenberg, *Discovering*.
177. Such an approach has been proposed by Asprem, "Beyond." A similar comparison has been made by Urban, "Elitism." The relevance of secrecy for the study of esotericism has been extensively discussed by Stuckrad, *Locations*.
178. Ganeri, *Lost*, 6.

179. For a discussion of how such an approach can be fruitfully applied within the study of esotericism, see the comparativist perspective of global religious history in Bergunder, "Comparison."

Chapter 2

1. For an extensive treatment of Sinnett, see Harlass, *Orientalische Wende*.
2. Ransom, *Short History*, 545–546.
3. Ibid., 547.
4. This is the most quoted version today: "1. To form a nucleus of the Universal Brotherhood of Humanity, without distinction of race, creed, sex, caste or colour. 2. To encourage the study of comparative religion, philosophy and science. 3. To investigate unexplained laws of Nature and the powers latent in man" See ibid., 550–51.
5. "Lo! The 'Poor Missionary,'" *Theosophist* 1, no. 5 (1880): 112.
6. Ibid., 113.
7. "Our Duty to India," *Theosophist* 1, no. 5 (1880): 111.
8. "An Indian Patriot's Prayer," *Theosophist* 1, no. 5 (1880): 113.
9. Majumdar, "Glimpse," 244.
10. Ballantyne, *Orientalism*, 26–30.
11. See, e.g., the discussion in Arvidsson, *Aryan Idols*, here 7–8.
12. For an analysis of the notion of "Aryan" with regard to British India, see Trautmann, *Aryans*; cf. Schwab, *Oriental Renaissance*; King, *Orientalism and Religion*, 85. The classic study by Poliakov, *Le mythe aryen*, is still valuable as an overview. For an analysis in the context of Theosophy and its relation to German and Indian nationalism, see Myers, "Affinity."
13. See Gupta, *Notions*, 24–25, who notes that the "late colonial reorientation of 'Aryan' as a sociological and cultural concept had lineages not only in Orientalist legacies and the views of the British Sanskritists, but also in an indigenous connotative genealogy."
14. Banerjee, *Mortal God*, 291.
15. Cf., for the following, Ballantyne, *Orientalism*, 41–44.
16. Müller, *Chips*, 4.
17. Müller, *Introduction*, 66–67.
18. Müller, *India*, 23, original emphasis.
19. Müller, *Lectures*, 145.
20. Müller, *India*, 31–32.
21. Ibid., 116.
22. Ibid., 116–117.
23. Müller, *Chips*, 4.
24. Müller, *India*, 254.
25. Ibid., 117–118.
26. Müller, *Auld Lang Syne*, 4–5.
27. Partridge, "Lost Horizon," 312.

28. Josephson-Storm, *Myth*, 110–111.
29. Müller, *Life*, 233.
30. Ibid., 234.
31. This was the last part of a series of monographs titled *Natural Religion*, *Physical Religion*, and *Anthropological Religion*, respectively.
32. Müller, *Theosophy*, xvi.
33. Ibid., 474.
34. Ibid., 91–92.
35. Ibid., 92–95.
36. Ibid., 95.
37. Ibid., 105–106.
38. Olcott protested, "An entire misunderstanding. What I said was that, as young plants had to be manured, so I had noticed that new religions were commonly attended at the beginning by 'miracles'—i.e. psychic phenomena, which gave them quickly a grip on the public mind. And the observed wonders were multiplied indefinitely by partisan writers, who thought to thus fertilize them" (Müller, *Life*, 294).
39. Ibid., 294–295.
40. Ibid., 297.
41. Ibid., 298.
42. Ibid., 298–299.
43. Ibid., 299.
44. Van der Veer, *Imperial Encounters*, 49.
45. "Sonnets," *Theosophist* 1, no. 5 (1880): 112.
46. Deveney, *Astral Projection*, 60–61.
47. Viswanathan, "Colonialism," 36–37; cf. Ballantyne, *Orientalism*, 176–179.
48. Nanda, "Madame," 325–326.
49. Jones, "Arya Samaj," 39.
50. Jordens, *Dayaananda*, 78–81.
51. Ibid., 112–113.
52. Cf. the categorization in Jones, *Socio-Religious*, 3–4 and the criticism in Hatcher, *Hinduism*, 231–232, who argues that Jones "remained all too embedded in the key categories, tropes, and culturalist binaries" and relied "on an unstated teleology of the modern."
53. For a comparative study of Arya and Brahmo polemics against "idolatry," see Salmond, *Hindu Iconoclasts*. The ambivalence of the Arya engagement for women is highlighted by Kishwar, "Daughters." Rather than the emancipation of women, the goal of most Aryas was the establishment of a certain Hindu social norm.
54. O'Toole, "Secularising."
55. Zavos, *Emergence*, 49.
56. Ghai, *Shuddhi*.
57. Fischer-Tiné, *Gurukul*, "Inventing," and "From Brahmacharya."
58. Gupta, *Notions*, 23–30.
59. Kopf, *Brahmo Samaj*, 7–8; Zastoupil, *Rammohun Roy*, 39–56.

60. The exchanges between Unitarians and Brahmos are most extensively discussed by Lavan, *Unitarians* and Kopf, *Brahmo Samaj*; cf. the recent studies by Zastoupil, *Rammohun Roy* and Stevens, *Keshab*.
61. Zastoupil, *Rammohun Roy*, 25–26; Banerjee, "All This is Indeed Brahman," 83.
62. Bergunder, "Bhagavadgita"; also see Jackson, *Oriental Religions*, 69–73, 113; Versluis, *American Transcendentalism*, 99–104, 197, and, for the case of Emerson, Stievermann, *Sündenfall*, 785–788.
63. Killingley, *Rammohun Roy*, 60.
64. Jackson, *Oriental Religions*, 32.
65. Kopf, *Brahmo Samaj*, 4–5.
66. Hatcher, *Hinduism*, 225–226.
67. Lavan, *Unitarians*, 41–55.
68. For scholarship focusing on Emerson et alia, see, e.g., Hodder, "Best"; Robinson, "Emerson"; Altman, *Heathen*, 74–97.
69. For an overview of the reception by Transcendentalists and Unitarians, see Jackson, *Oriental Religions*; Versluis, *American Transcendentalism*; as well as the entries in Myerson, Petrulionis, and Walls, *Oxford*. For the U.S. context, also see Albanese, *Republic*, 162–171 and Conkin, *American Originals*.
70. Jackson, *Oriental Religions*; cf. the discussion in Versluis, *American Transcendentalism*, esp. chapters 8 and 9.
71. Stevens, *Keshab*, 179–181.
72. Hatcher, *Bourgeois Hinduism*, 28–29.
73. Chatterjee, "Our Modernity," 146–147.
74. Hatcher, "Remembering."
75. Kopf, *Brahmo Samaj*, 161–163.
76. Hatcher, *Bourgeois Hinduism*.
77. Dutt, *Essays*, 34.
78. Stevens, *Keshab*, 30.
79. Kopf, *Brahmo Samaj*, 179; Stevens, *Keshab*, 115–153.
80. Kopf, *Brahmo Samaj*, 17.
81. Jackson, *Oriental Religions*, 103–122; cf. Robinson, "Emerson"; Gura, *American*; and the respective chapters in Myerson, Petrulionis, and Walls, *Oxford*.
82. Jordens, *Dayaananda*, 75–94.
83. Kopf, *Brahmo Samaj*, 27.
84. Mullick, *First*.
85. Müller, *Life*, 59.
86. Ibid., 391, 397.
87. For more on the global connections of Keshab's thought, see Banerjee, *Mortal God*, 118–128.
88. For instance, see Jackson, *Oriental Religions*, 13–14 and Versluis, *American Transcendentalism*, 92–93; cf. the pioneering studies by Carpenter, *Emerson*, 67–102, and Christy, *Orient*, 15, 56–60.
89. Stevens, *Keshab*, 50.

90. With regard to the Theosophists, Brahmos, and Aryas, see Bevir, "Theosophy and the Origins," 105.
91. Olcott, *Old Diary*, 339–340.
92. *Indian Mirror*, March 9, 1879, 2.
93. *Indian Mirror*, May 11, 1879, 3.
94. *Indian Mirror*, March 30, 1879, 2.
95. In 1881, the *Indian Mirror* was careful to point out that the "Brahmos have never identified themselves with the Theosophists." *Indian Mirror*, February 20, 1881, 2.
96. Olcott, *Old Diary*, 340–341.
97. Mukhopadhyay, "Short History," 109–110.
98. *Full Report, Seventh Anniversary*, 12.
99. Olcott, "Theosophy," 116.
100. Ibid., 117.
101. Ibid., 118.
102. Ibid., 123.
103. Ibid., 127.
104. Ibid., 129, 143–144.
105. Ibid., 149, original emphasis.
106. *Full Report, First Anniversary*, 2.
107. Olcott, *Old Diary*, 341–342.
108. Their member numbers were 1,067 and 1,066, respectively. For a biographical sketch of Chattopadhyay, see Mukhopadhyay, "Mohini."
109. Gupta, *Notions*, 20.
110. Mukhopadhyay, "Short History," 113.
111. *Full Report, First Anniversary*, i; cf. Olcott, *Old Diary*, 342–343.
112. *Full Report, First Anniversary*, 2–3.
113. Ibid., 5.
114. Ibid., 6.
115. *Full Report, Seventh Anniversary*, 14, original emphasis. The copy used was probably falsely bound; it contains several identical pages on continuously numbered pages. The pagination might differ from other copies.
116. Ibid., 24.
117. Ibid., 30.
118. Ibid., 19.
119. Bhatia, *Unforgetting*, 13–15.

Chapter 3

1. *Full Report, Seventh Anniversary*, 10.
2. De Michelis, *History*, 9–12.
3. Alter, *Yoga*, 26.
4. De Michelis, *History*, 2–3.

5. Singleton, *Yoga*, 10.
6. De Michelis, *History*, 50, ch. 3.
7. Albanese, *Republic*, 206–220.
8. De Michelis, *History*, 110.
9. E.g., ibid., 140, 162–163.
10. Baier, *Meditation*, especially 1:178–428 and 2:429–542; also see Baier, "Mesmeric Yoga" and "Theosophical Orientalism."
11. This focus was consciously expressed by Singleton's notion of "transnational Anglophone yoga" (*Yoga*, 9–10).
12. Cf. the argument in Cantú, "Don't," where the perception of occultist engagement with yogic practices as "inauthentic" is criticized because it neglects the participation of South Asians in these exchanges.
13. De Michelis, *History*, 27–31. Cf. Faivre, *Access*, 10–15, where esotericism is defined based on a set of characteristics, or family resemblances.
14. F.T.S., "Yoga Vidya 1," 32.
15. See Strube, *Sozialismus*, 537–544; cf. Strube, "Baphomet," 69–73.
16. F.T.S., "Yoga Vidya 3," 84–85.
17. Baier, *Meditation*, 1:200–221; cf. Strube, "Yoga."
18. Baier, *Meditation*, 1:200–221.
19. The most extensive studies of that context are still Viatte, *Sources*, and Le Forestier, *Franc-maçonnerie*.
20. Hanegraaff, *Esotericism*, 260–277.
21. Strube, *Sozialismus*, 465. Lacordaire also wrote a preface to *Le monde occulte* (1851) by Henri Delaage, a socialist-occultist affiliate of Éliphas Lévi.
22. Baier, *Meditation*, 1: 221–243.
23. Matter, *Histoire*, 2:83; Matter, *Essai*, 4.
24. Matter, *Histoire*, 1:88–89.
25. Ibid., 98, 104, 196.
26. Strube, *Sozialismus*, 120; cf. Laurant, *Esotérisme*, 42; Le Forestier, *Franc-maçonnerie*, 419–420, 516–519, 594–595, 651–656, 803–810, 909–912; Keller, *Théosophe*.
27. Baier, *Meditation*, 1:183.
28. Williams, *Hinduism*, 126, 129.
29. Woodroffe, *Serpent Power*, 50; cf. Woodroffe, *The World as Power: Reality*, 115; Woodroffe, *The World as Power: Power as Life*, 29; Woodroffe and Mukhopādhyāya, *Mahāmāyā*, 183.
30. Majumdār, "Introduction," xxvi.
31. Gupta, Hoens, and Goudriaan, *Hindu Tantrism*, 8, 57.
32. Padoux, *Vac*, 24, 37–38; cf. White, "Introduction," 8, with reference to Madeleine Biardeau and Padoux; cf. White, "Tantra."
33. Notes from that meeting were published in *Theosophist* 2, no. 3 (1880): 46–48. Cf. Olcott, *Old Diary*, 213–225.
34. *Theosophist* 2, no. 3 (1880): 46.
35. Ibid., 47.
36. Olcott, *Old Diary*, 221.

37. Ibid., 224.
38. *Indian Mirror*, December 21, 1879, 2.
39. *Indian Mirror*, January 23, 1881, 2–3.
40. Ibid., 3.
41. *Theosophist* 2, no. 6 (1881): 132.
42. *Theosophist* 2, no. 3 (1880): 47.
43. Cf. Olcott, *Old Diary*, 222, where the Swami's assertion is stressed that "one *cannot* pass on to the practice of Rāja Yoga without first having subjugated the physical body by a course of Hatha Yoga, or physiological training."
44. Baier, *Meditation*, 1:332; cf. De Michelis, *History*, 178.
45. See Birch, "Meaning" and "Rājayoga"; cf. White, *Yoga Sutra*, 103–115.
46. Since the success of the *Haṭhapradīpikā*, the reconfiguration of Hatha Yoga by the Naths was highly influential and often became synonymous with yoga. See Mallinson, "Nāth Sampradāya" and "Śāktism and Haṭhayoga."
47. Singleton, *Yoga*, 52–53.
48. Paul, "Treatise," 312.
49. Ibid., 315.
50. Blavatsky, *Isis*, 2:590.
51. Owen, *Place*, 150.
52. Ibid., 46–47.
53. I thank Keith Cantú for sharing with me some preliminary results of his ongoing in-depth research on Sabhapati Swami.
54. See Cantú, "Sri Sabhapati Swami," where another account in Tamil explained that he sustained himself by his ancestral property and special goods.
55. An Admirer, "Madras Yogi."
56. Singleton, *Yoga*, 5.
57. Olcott, "Theosophy," 151–152.
58. Baier, *Meditation*, 1:328.
59. *Theosophist* 3, no. 11 (1882): 269.
60. Strube, *Sozialismus*, 528–529.
61. Jordens, *Dayaananda*, 213; van der Veer, *Imperial Encounters*, 55–56.
62. Singh, *Life*, 74–75.
63. Baier, *Meditation*, 1:297–299. About the concept of astral projection, see Deveney, *Astral Projection*, and Owen, *Place*, 150; cf. the sources in King, *Astral Projection*.
64. Cf. Singleton, *Yoga*, 168.
65. See Mitra, *Yoga Aphorisms*.
66. The year 1889 also saw an edition by William W. Judge, who made the language of the patchwork text more coherent and accessible.
67. Tatya, *Yoga Philosophy* (1882), ii–iii.
68. Ibid., v–vi.
69. Tatya, *Yoga Philosophy* (1885), vii–viii.
70. *Theosophist* 4, no. 3 (1882): 72.
71. Baier, *Meditation*, 1:360.
72. Mavalankar, "Philosophy," 176.

73. See Mookerjee, *Notes.*
74. *Path* 2, no. 4 (1887): 123.
75. Rajshahi was then referred to as Bauleah, the Rampore part of which served as the designation of this society. For the objectives of the branch, see *Theosophist* 4, no. 9 (1883): 7.
76. Olcott, *Old Diary*, 340.
77. Mukerji, "Magic."
78. Mukhopadhyay, "Tantric," 226.
79. Kopf, *Brahmo Samaj*, 315.
80. For a detailed examination of the fascinating exchange between Rajnarayan and Blavatsky, see Strube, "Rajnarayan Basu."
81. Bose, "Superiority," 14.
82. The letter had been forwarded by Shashibhushan Kumar.
83. Kumar, "Tantras."
84. *Theosophist* 4, no. 9 (1883): 226.
85. Tatya, *Yoga Philosophy* (1885), v.
86. T.S., "Tantras," 226.
87. Ibid., 227.
88. Ibid.
89. The branches listed are Maran, Uchatan, Stumbhan, Vasikaran, Sanmohan, and Santikarman.
90. Majumdar, *History*, 301. During the independence struggles, the former governor of Bombay, Lord Lamington, organized a meeting to "socialise" revolutionary tendencies. One of the speakers, Sir William Lee-Warner, referred to one of the revolutionaries, Kunjabihari, as "a dirty nigger," causing an uproar from the audience and inviting a punch from a man named Vasudeva Bhattacharya, who was later fined for the action.
91. It is worth nothing that the paper was forwarded by "Cally Coomar Dass," who might be identical with the Brahmo who, in 1857, published a widely noted universalist pamphlet "On the Supreme Being of Brahmo Theology."
92. Bhattacharya, "Description [1]," 10.
93. Bhattacharya, "Description [2]," 11–12.
94. Ibid., 12.
95. Baier, *Meditation*, 1:385–395.
96. For a discussion of the internal instructions distributed among members, see Leland, *Rainbow*, 117–127.
97. Blavatsky, *Collected Writings*, 615.
98. Ibid., 616.
99. Baier, *Meditation*, 1:338.
100. Bose, *Life*, 14–15. This is the only biography of Srishchandra and should be read with some caution due to its obviously hagiographical character.
101. Ibid., 90.
102. Ibid., 62–71, 166–170.
103. Ibid., 168.

104. Ibid., 98–99.
105. Ibid., 95–96.
106. This lecture was lauded by Blavatsky in the *Theosophist* of April 1882, where Srishchandra is simply mentioned as "one F.T.S.," that is, a Frater of the Theosophical Society. See *Theosophist* 3, no. 7 (1882): 181.
107. Bose, *Life*, 103–106. Here Srishchandra's biographer clearly exaggerates the role of his hero by suggesting that he inspired the foundation of the Indian National Congress.
108. Ibid., 92–94.
109. Ibid., 138–141. This episode warrants clarification, as Phanindranath mentions the "myth" that this school was actually founded by someone else, named Roshan Lal.
110. Singleton, *Yoga*, 44–49.
111. Ibid., 44–53. Cf. the correspondence with international scholars in Bose, *Life*, 156–160.
112. Bose, *Life*, 170.
113. Ibid., 200.
114. Ibid., 175–177.
115. Basu, *Catechism*, 5–6.
116. Basu, *Esoteric Science*, ii–iii.
117. Ibid., vi–vii.
118. Ibid., vii.
119. E.g., ibid., xiii–xiv.
120. Ibid., iv–v.
121. Ibid., xxii.
122. Ibid., liii–liv.
123. Ibid., xxv–xxvii.
124. Ibid., xliv–xlv.
125. Ibid., xlvi–xlvii.
126. Bose, *Life*, 136–138.
127. Chatterjee, "Baman Das Basu," 669.
128. Ibid., 673. About the gurukul, see Fischer-Tiné, *Gurukul*.
129. This can be found in the *Modern Review* article and also shows their common friend Mukunda Deb Mukherji. About Bhudev's initiation, see Sen, *Hindu Revivalism*, 173.
130. Basu, "Anatomy," 370.
131. Singleton, *Yoga*, 49–53.
132. Shom, "Physical," 437.
133. Ibid., 438. The names of the chakras are given as Mulādhāra Chakra, Linga Chakra, Nābi Chakra, Hrit Padma, Kantha Chakra, and Atma Chakra.
134. Ibid., 440. The chakras named are Adhāra Chakra, Adhistān Chakra, Manipura, Mānasha Chakra, Anāhata Chakra, Bishunda Chakra, Agyankhya Chakra, Balaban Chakra, Karpara Chakra, and on top Brahma-Randra.
135. Basu, "Anatomy," 371–372.
136. Ibid., 373.

137. Sanderson, "Śaivism," 687–688; Flood, *Tantric Body*, 158; Padoux, *Hindu*, 57; cf. Heilijgers-Seelen, "Doctrine."

Chapter 4

1. Forbes, *Positivism*; cf. Raychaudhuri, *Europe Reconsidered*, 22; Sen, *Hindu Revivalism*, 17, 213; Prakash, *Another Reason*, 58–59, 76–80, 227–228. For the case of Bankim, who was significantly influenced by Positivism but gradually moved away from it, see Sen, *Hindu Revivalism*, 112–113 and Harder, *Bankimchandra Chattopadhyay's Śrīmadbhagabadgītā*, 190–191.
2. Olcott, "Theosophy," 150; cf. Esdaile, *Natural*, vi–vii.
3. *Full Report, First Anniversary*, 5; cf. 15.
4. Esdaile, *Mesmerism*, 23, 60–61.
5. Pal, *Memories*, 402.
6. Harder, "Modern Babu," 371–374; Harder, "Migrant," 190.
7. Mittra, *Spiritual*, i.
8. Ibid., 3.
9. Ibid., 12–14.
10. Mittra, *Stray Thoughts*, 1.
11. Mittra, *Spiritual*, 5.
12. Ibid., 9; cf. Mittra, *Stray Thoughts*, 2.
13. Mittra, *Spiritual*, 16, 49.
14. Ibid., 50–51.
15. Mittra, *Stray Thoughts*, 6.
16. Mittra, *Spiritual*, 53.
17. Pyarichand Mitra to Olcott, November 9, 1877, archives of the Theosophical Society at Adyar.
18. Blavatsky to Pyarichand Mitra, December 12, 1877, archives of the Theosophical Society at Adyar.
19. Pyarichand Mitra to Blavatsky, February 6, 1878, archives of the Theosophical Society at Adyar. The file also includes a response by Blavatsky, who had received one of Mitra's books from 1877, a biography of David Hare (1775–1842), an influential educationalist in Bengal. Reading the book had "nearly reconciled me with European races, which I most cordially hate."
20. Mittra, *Stray Thoughts*, 23.
21. Ibid., 22–23. He lauded Debendranath Tagore for "toiling for years to diffuse *Brāhmadharma* as taught in the Vedas, Upanishads, and Darsanas."
22. Mittra, *Spiritual*, 64.
23. Ibid., 154.
24. Ibid., 163.
25. Ibid., 170.
26. "Jñān māhātmyā," *Kalpa* 2, no. 2 (1894): 41–51.

27. "Brāhmasamājer dhvaṃśa," *Kalpa* 2, nos. 2–3 (1894): 29–30.
28. *Kalpa* 1, no. 3 (1893): 55–57.
29. "Hindudharmma udāratā pūrṇa," *Kalpa* 3, nos. 7–10 (1895): 194–196.
30. "Hinduramaṇī," *Kalpa* 3, nos. 5–6 (1895): 133–140.
31. "Hinduramaṇī," *Kalpa* 3, nos. 7–10 (1895): 237.
32. "Hinduramaṇīr uddhār o śikṣā," *Kalpa* 3, nos. 5–6 (1895): 143–144.
33. "Bilātī nabaramaṇī (New woman)," *Kalpa* 3, nos. 5–6 (1895): 144–145.
34. See Bandyopādhyāẏ, "Kṣetrapāl Cakrabarttī Yog[l]śāstrī"; cf. the biographical information in the preface to Chakravarti, *Lectures*. The author of this preface, Pramatha Nath Mookerjee, is not to be confused with Woodroffe's later collaborator Pramathanath Mukhopadhyay, who was around twelve years old at the book's publication.
35. Bandyopādhyāẏ, "Kṣetrapāl Cakrabarttī Yog[l]śāstrī," 16.
36. Ibid., 16–17. Beames's suggestion had been published in *Bangadarśan* of āṣāṛh 1279, in an article titled "Bangīya Sāhitya Samāj."
37. Woodroffe and Hirendranath gave speeches at the tenth annual meeting of the Ram Mohan Roy Library; see Woodroffe, *Bharata Shakti*, 64.
38. *Bengal Academy of Literature* 1, no. 11 (1894): 3–4. Cf. Bandyopādhyāẏ, "Kṣetrapāl Cakrabarttī Yog[l]śāstrī," 20–21.
39. *Bengal Academy of Literature* 1, no. 7 (1894): 6.
40. *Bengal Academy of Literature* 1, no. 8 (1893): 1–2.
41. Ratte, *Uncolonised Heart*, 128–138.
42. Chakravarti, "Religious Aspects [1]," 23.
43. His references for this were the *Jñāna Saṅkalinī Tantra* and the *Śāradātilaka* (ibid., 24).
44. Chakravarti, "Religious Aspects [2]," 91.
45. Chakravarti, "Religious Aspects [1]," 26.
46. Ibid., 27.
47. Chakravarti, "Religious Aspects [3]," 209.
48. Chakravarti, "Religious Aspects [1]," 28.
49. Ibid., 25.
50. Chakravarti, "Religious Aspects [3]," 210.>
51. Ibid.
52. *International Theosophical Year Book*, 228.
53. *Globe*, November 1, 1890, 3.
54. Chakravarti, *Lectures*, 113.
55. Cf. ibid., 16, 121.
56. Ibid., 56.
57. Ibid., 57.
58. Ibid., 66.
59. Ibid., 14–15.
60. Ibid., 21. Also see 78–79, where some differentiations are made between "modern spiritualism of the West" and its Indian ancestor.
61. Ibid., 49.
62. Ibid., 51.
63. Mukhopadhyay, *Imitation*, xiv.

64. "The Signs of the Times," *Light of the East* 1, no. 1 (1892): 1–3.
65. Ibid., 8.
66. *Light of the East* 2, no. 9 (1894): 287.
67. *Light of the East* 3, no. 10 (1895): 321.
68. E.g., *Light of the East* 1, no. 12 (1893): 385.
69. *Light of the East* 4, no. 1 (1895): 1.
70. *Light of the East* 4, no. 1 (1895): 2.
71. *Light of the East* 1, no. 8 (1893): 229.
72. Mitra, "Philosophy 1," 119–120.
73. See ibid., 107, as well as Mitra, "Philosophy 3," 191–192 and Mitra, "Philosophy 4," 216–217.
74. Mitra, "Philosophy 1," 122, original emphasis.
75. Ibid., 123.
76. Mitra, "Philosophy 2," 148. Mitra cites the *Jñāna Sankalinī Tantra* to affirm that point (150). This scripture also served as an authority for Kshetrapal.
77. Ibid., 149–150.
78. Mitra, "Philosophy 3," 190.
79. Mitra, "Philosophy 4," 219.
80. Ibid., 218.
81. Bhatia, "Sisir's Tears," 6–7.
82. Ghose, "How Spiritualism [1]," 16–17. Shishir's engagement with Spiritualism has recently been discussed by Bhatia, "Psychic Chaitanya."
83. Ghose, "How Spiritualism 2," 86–87.
84. General Register, Theosophical Society, Adyar.
85. Bhatia, "Sisir's Tears," 2. For a concise overview of Bengali Vaishnavism within the context of nineteenth-century colonialism, see Bhatia, *Unforgetting*, 5–19.
86. Bhatia, "Sisir's Tears," 8.
87. Ibid.
88. Ibid., 4.
89. Ibid., 6, 15.
90. Cf. Bhatia, *Unforgetting*, 48–49.
91. After Shishir's "ascension" to the spirit world, his brother Motilal and his eldest son, Piyushkanti, took over the editorship. See *Hindu Spiritual Magazine* 5, no. 11 (1911): 400.
92. For more information about that elusive group, whose inner group was called the Holy Order of Krishna, see Bogdan, "Reception."
93. Ghose, "Introduction," 1.
94. Ibid., 2.
95. Ibid., 3.
96. Ghose, "How Spiritualism [1]," 15–16.
97. Ibid., 18.
98. Ghose, "How Spiritualism 2," 83.
99. Ghose, "How Spiritualism 3," 162.

100. Ibid., 163. The names that are listed are, in the original spelling, Dina Bandu Mitter, Shrish Chandra Vidyaratna, Sanjeeb Chandra Chatterjee, and Girish Chandra Ghose.
101. *Hindu Spiritual Magazine* 1, no. 5 (1906): 343–345.
102. See Chatterjee, "Sava-Sadhana," 347, and the frontispiece of the issue. Also see the article "Tantra-Shastra" by the lawyer Srish Chandra Biswas in *Hindu Spiritual Magazine* 6, no. 9 (1911): 202–208, and no. 10, 303–307.
103. See *The Indian Section of the Theosophical Society: Thirteenth Annual Convention Held at Adyar, Madras, December 28th and 29th, 1903*, appendix E, 4.
104. Mahavarati, *Yogi*, 5–29. That this work was authored by the same Dharmananda is affirmed by the recurrent references to Christianity in his Tantra series, for instance in Mahabharati, "Tantras [4]," 424–427, or Mahabharati, "Tantras [6]," 188. In the Tantra series, his name is given as both Mahabharati and Mahavarati.
105. Mahabharati, "Tantras [1]," 28.
106. Ibid., 29.
107. Mahabharati, "Tantras [2]," 108. This is affirmed by a reference to the scholarship of William Muir.
108. Mahabharati, "Tantras [5]," 95–96. This is followed by an extensive account of an "exorcism."
109. Mahabharati, "Tantras [2]," 110.
110. Mahabharati, "Tantras [3]," 343.
111. Mahabharati, "Tantras [4]," 418.
112. Mahabharati, "Tantras [3]," 340.
113. Ibid., 341. For more about the process of initiation, see Mahabharati, "Tantras [4]."
114. Mahabharati, "Tantras [1]," 32 and Mahabharati, "Tantras [4]," 424; cf. Ghose, *Lord Gauranga*, 172, 181, 202–203. Ghosh even assumed an outright conflict between Tantrics and Vaishnavas. Interestingly, this topic is discussed in different terms in the Bengali version, which would merit a closer comparative look. See, for instance, Ghoṣ, *Śrīamiẏa*, 28, where Tantric practice is depicted critically but more ambivalently.
115. Mahabharati, "Tantras [6]," 188.
116. Mahabharati, "Tantras [3]," 339.
117. Compare Sachchidananda, "Theory [9]" and T.S., "The Tantras."
118. The third edition of the first volume was published in 1927 by the Indian Art School. The present study uses the 1990 Nababharat edition.
119. Woodroffe, *Shakti and Shakta*, 145.
120. Saccidānanda Sarasvatī, *Sanātan sādhan'tattva*, 1.
121. Ibid., 5.
122. Ibid., 14–15.
123. Ibid., 28.
124. Sachchidananda, *Universal Worship*, 39. The booklet was published under the patronage of Jyoti Prasad Singh Deo, the zamindar of Panchkot in Western Bengal; see *Second Supplement*, 90.
125. Saccidānanda Sarasvatī, *Sanātan sādhan'tattva*, 30.

126. Ibid.
127. Ibid., 7.
128. Sachchidananda, "Theory [1]," 40.
129. Ibid.
130. Sachchidananda, "Theory [7]," 454.
131. Sachchidananda, "Theory [9]," 125.
132. Sachchidananda, "Theory [6]," 34.
133. Sachchidananda, "Theory [8]," 433.
134. Sachchidananda, "Theory [2]," 298–299; cf. Sachchidananda, "Theory [4]," 18–19.
135. Sachchidananda, "Theory [2]," 299–300; cf. Sachchidananda, "Theory [3]," 425.
136. Sachchidananda, "Theory [4]," 22–23.
137. Ibid., 24.
138. Sachchidananda, "Theory [5]," 99, 102–103.
139. Sachchidananda, "Theory [3]," 424.
140. Sachchidananda, "Theory [9]," 122, and Sachchidananda, "Theory [7]," 460.
141. Sachchidananda, "Theory [6]," 41–42.
142. Further research is needed to understand these intricacies and should consider contexts such as Freemasonry, Positivism, Unitarianism, and Transcendentalism.

Chapter 5

1. Kumar, "The Tantras."
2. T.S., "The Tantras," 227.
3. The partial translation is anonymous and differs from other English translations that were published elsewhere. The June 1886 article contained the discussion "'The Determination of Atma Gyanam' from the Maha-Nirvana-Tantra," penned by one "A.G." It is tantalizing to speculate that Atalbihari Ghosh, who would have been in his early twenties, might have been behind that translation, but there are no indications of that.
4. Mahabharati, "Tantras [2]," 108.
5. E.g., Ray, *Religious Movements*, 68; cf. Banerji, *Tantra* (1978), 102–111, with a list of editions.
6. Banerji, *Tantra* (1992), 112–119; Derrett, "Juridical Fabrication"; Urban, "Strategic Uses."
7. Avalon, *Tantra of the Great Liberation* (1913), 51–55, 357–358. Also see Halbfass, *Indien und Europa*, 217, 231.
8. Avalon, *Tantra of the Great Liberation* (1913), xlix–l; cf. Banerji, *Tantra* (1992), 50; Hazra, "Influence [3]," 681.
9. Urban, *Tantra*, 64–65.
10. Bhatia, "Images"; cf. Bhatia, *Unforgetting*, 9, 44, 116.
11. Urban, *Tantra*, 66.

12. This has been extensively discussed in Sanderson, "Purity," "Śaivism," "Meaning," and "Śaiva Age."
13. Flood, *Tantric Body*, 49–50; McDaniel, *Offering*, 92.
14. Avalon, *Tantra of the Great Liberation* (1913), 184.
15. Ibid., 191.
16. Ibid., 177–178.
17. Ibid., 136. The deification of the practitioner's body is discussed extensively in Flood, *Tantric Body*.
18. Goudriaan and Gupta, *Hindu Tantric*, 101.
19. Urban, *Tantra*, 70.
20. Avalon, *Tantra of the Great Liberation* (1913), 357. Cf. Urban, *Tantra*, 66; Derrett, "Juridical Fabrication," 146.
21. Avalon, *Tantra of the Great Liberation* (1913), 180. One notable exception is the introduction of a new form of marriage next to the socially established forms of Brahma marriage (*brāhma-udvāha*). This is the so-called Shiva marriage (*śaiva-udvāha*) that can be formed either for sexual union within the chakra or as a lifelong marriage that is publicly valid, although resulting children do not have full inheritance rights. See Derrett, "Juridical Fabrication," 149–151. For Tantric influences on social life and marriage in Bengal at the time of Raghunandan, see Hazra, "Influence [3]," 698–700.
22. Avalon, *Tantra of the Great Liberation* (1913), 245.
23. Derrett, "Juridical Fabrication," 149–164. About the British integration of *dharmaśāstra* into their legal system, see Yelle, *Language*, 137–160.
24. Urban, *Tantra*, 67.
25. Derrett, "Juridical Fabrication," 147–148.
26. See Urban, "Strategic Uses"; Urban, *Tantra*, 64; and Hatcher, *Hinduism*, 58, 183–184.
27. Goudriaan and Gupta, *Hindu Tantric*, 98.
28. Urban, *Tantra*, 69.
29. Goudriaan and Gupta, *Hindu Tantric*, 99.
30. Baṭabyāl, "Rilijan," 760–762. Umeshchandra proposed to instead use the term *pantha*, which signified different "paths." His deliberation is also highly interesting for the question of Muslim-Hindu relationships, which unfortunately cannot be discussed within the frame of this book.
31. Sturman, *Government*, 186–193.
32. With regard to the admission of converts from other faiths, Ranade emphasized that "in old times the non-Aryan races were brought within the fold of the Aryan system" ("Revival," 164).
33. Ibid., 169–171, 177–178.
34. Ibid., 172.
35. Rai, "Reform," 48–50.
36. Ibid., 50–51.
37. Ibid., 53–54.
38. Hatcher, *Bourgeois Hinduism*, 60–61. This text has also been influential for Dayananda, as shown by Jordens, *Dayananda*, 79–80.
39. Hatcher, *Bourgeois Hinduism*, 141–142.

40. Kopf, *Brahmo Samaj*, 251–252.
41. Bordeaux, "Mythic King," 79–80.
42. Sen, *Hindu Revivalism*, 207, 236; Raychaudhuri, *Europe Reconsidered*, 11.
43. Sen, *Hindu Revivalism*, 218; Harder, "Populärversionen."
44. Sen, *Hindu Revivalism*, 219–220.
45. Ibid., 222, 431–432.
46. Ibid., 224.
47. Ibid., 226.
48. Ibid., 233.
49. Farquhar, *Modern Religious Movements*, 316–323; Zavos, *Emergence*, 50–54.
50. Farquhar, *Modern Religious Movements*, 319–320.
51. *Mahāmaṇḍal Magazine* 1, no. 1: 8.
52. Farquhar, *Modern Religious Movements*, 317, my emphasis.
53. Pal, *Memories*, 425.
54. Sen, *Hindu Revivalism*, 17.
55. Ibid., 228.
56. Van der Veer, *Imperial Encounters*, 57.
57. *Report of the Second Anniversary*, 6.
58. Reprinted in *Theosophist* 4, no. 9 (1883): 3.
59. Sen, *Hindu Revivalism*, 219.
60. Raychaudhuri, *Europe Reconsidered*, 35.
61. The latter is quoted for a description of the characteristics of Kshatriyas (Majumˈdār, *Barnāśram dharmma*, 34).
62. Besant provided an account of Jatindranath's participation at the Eighth National Congress meeting at Allahabad in December 1892, as part of the Bengal delegation that included freedom fighters such as Surendranath Bandyopadhyay. In support of a resolution denouncing the lack of native government representation, Jatindranath criticized "all those appointments which can be safely given to the natives of the soil and which are filled by foreigners, as so many appointments robbed from the people to whom they belong by natural right." Besant, *How India*, 149.
63. Majumˈdār, *Barnāśram dharmma*, 2–8.
64. *Jāti* can be translated as "birth," "origin," "caste," "class," "kind," or "race." It is used in the text in practically all these meanings; in this passage, it is clearly related to Blavatsky's notion of "race."
65. Majumˈdār, *Barnāśram dharmma*, 17–18.
66. Ibid., 19–20.
67. Ibid., 27–28.
68. Ibid., 40.
69. Ibid., 42–44.
70. Ibid., 51.
71. Ibid., 71–75.
72. Ibid., 83–85.
73. Bhatia, *Unforgetting*, 15–16.

Chapter 6

1. Cākˡlādār, *Mahāsādhak*, 70, 87.
2. Some details about his employment emerge in the file of a court case about his retirement: AIR 1956 Cal 93, 59 CWN 1050, https://indiankanoon.org/doc/517629/, accessed March 7, 2021.
3. Taylor, *Sir John Woodroffe*, 98–99.
4. For instance, it could be that Pal had worked for the railway prior to his employment as a clerk, that the Woodroffes were traveling to Kumarkhali after Shivachandra's death, or that the dates provided to the court were not accurate. Since all witnesses have died, it will most likely remain impossible to verify Pal's account.
5. These include, most importantly, Cakrabartī, *Bāṃlār Sādhak*, 4:1–31; Rāy, *Bhārater Sādhak*; Datta, *Śibˡcandra*.
6. Pāl, *Tantrācārya*, 25, erroneously gives 1276 as the year, which contradicts other accounts, such as Rāy, *Bhārater Sādhak*, 113, and also logically conflicts with Shivachandra's age in light of his activities.
7. Rabindranath wrote some of his most highly praised work at this estate and translated his *Gītāñjali* into English, which earned him the Nobel Prize in 1913.
8. Pāl, *Tantrācārya*, 2–10; cf. Cākˡlādār, *Mahāsādhak*, 17–23.
9. See the appendix to Pal's biography, a copy of which was kindly given to me by Kathleen Taylor.
10. Sen, *Ātmajībanī*, 150; cf. Pāl, *Tantrācārya*, 25; Cākˡlādār, *Mahāsādhak*, 69. During the ritual, the priest would hold the child's hand and make it write the Bengali alphabet. Crook, *Transmission*, 106–107, 114; Bhattacharya, *Sentinels*, 123–124.
11. See Cākˡlādār, *Mahāsādhak*, 29–30, where a song by Shivachandra dedicated to Kangal is reproduced.
12. Shipra, Dastider, "Kangal Harinath," in Banglapedia, http://en.banglapedia.org/index.php?title=Harinath,_Kangal, accessed March 7, 2021.
13. Sen, *Ātmajībanī*, 75–78.
14. Pāl, *Tantrācārya*, 53; Cākˡlādār, *Mahāsādhak*, 29–30. Cf. Sen, *Ātmajībanī*, 64–65, 85–98. About Mir Mosharraf Hossain, see Bose, *Recasting*, 10–22.
15. Sen, *Hindu Revivalism*, 253; Sarkar, *Swadeshi*, 255–256.
16. Sen, *Ātmajībanī*, 149–156.
17. Lorea, "Playing," 426–427.
18. Pāl, *Tantrācārya*, 48. Allegedly, Lalon addressed Shivachandra with *dādāṭhākur*, an intimate and respectful expression.
19. Cākˡlādār, *Mahāsādhak*, 57–60, 67.
20. Ibid., 69.
21. Cf. the exemplary anecdote provided by Pāl, *Tantrācārya*, 206–207.
22. Sen, *Ātmajībanī*, 151–152.
23. This aspect is studied by Bhattacharya, *Sentinels*; Sengupta, *Pedagogy* and *Language*.
24. Bhattacharya, "Anglicized," 167–168; Sarkar, *Writing*, 254.
25. Viswanathan, *Masks*, 7–8, 45–67.
26. Cākˡlādār, *Mahāsādhak*, 37–42.

27. This title was bestowed because of excellency in Sanskrit linguistics and philosophy. It literally means "ocean of knowledge."
28. Pāl, *Tantrācārya*, 36–37; Cāk[l]lādār, *Mahāsādhak*, 44. After the death of Shivachandra's father, Chandrakumar, his jealous brother Satishchandra allegedly burned these writings, which had been guarded by the family for generations. According to Shivachandra's grandson Rabindranath and his wife, Dipa, the family also lost their possessions when relocating to West Bengal and due to a disastrous flood in the 1970s.
29. Pāl, *Tantrācārya*, 40.
30. Bidyārṇab, *Tantratattva*, 12. There he speaks of Kamadeva as his *tārkik* guru, of Kuladananda as his *paramguru*, and of Krishnananda as his *parāpara* guru.
31. His favorite *śmaśān* (cremation grounds) to perform *sādhana* was reportedly the Maṇikarṇikā Ghāṭ in Benares and the Vaidyanāth Dhām. See Cāk[l]lādār, *Mahāsādhak*, 54.
32. Interviews conducted by the author on October 10 and 21, 2018. Rabindranath's mother, Nirmala, used to take on such roles, and the important roles taken by the family's women can still be observed during Kali Puja.
33. Cāk[l]lādār, *Mahāsādhak*, 46.
34. Ibid., 80.
35. See, e.g., Pāl, *Tantrācārya*, 225 and Cāk[l]lādār, *Mahāsādhak*, 57.
36. These were *Rāslīlā*, *Mā*, *Pīṭhmālā*, *Stotramālā*, *Durgoṭsab*, *Karttā o man*, *Sbabhāb o abhāb*, and *Gaṅgeś*. See Pāl, *Tantrācārya*, 72; cf. Sengupta, *Sangsad Bāṅālī Caritābhidhān*, 512.
37. The authorities for these lists are the Tantras and Puranas. Special attention is paid to locations that, unlike normal *tīrthas*, are especially suited for worship, such as *siddhipīṭhās* (Bidyārṇab, *Pīṭhmālā*, 19–60) and *mahāpīṭhās*, which are defined as the places where gods and goddesses are immersed in their eternal *līlā*. The different occasions for worship are explained in some detail (66–87).
38. Ibid., 88–90.
39. Bidyārṇab, *Rāslīlā*, preface. Interestingly, Shivachandra again defends his exposition against nineteenth-century criticism, speculating that Vedavyasa might have anticipated it in the *Bhagavat Gītā* (20).
40. Bidyārṇab, *Gaṅgeś*, preface.
41. Ibid., 154–163.
42. The known dates of publication range from 1888 to 1905.
43. This title predates the world-famous collection by Rabindranath Tagore. For more information, see Cāk[l]lādār, *Mahāsādhak*, 81–86. For a comparison between Ramprasad's and Shivachandra's songs, see 135, 148.
44. Pāl, *Tantrācārya*, 53; Cāk[l]lādār, *Mahāsādhak*, 70. About Bamakhepa, see McDaniel, *Madness*, 127–133; cf. Cakrabartī, *Bāṃlār Sādhak*, 1:84–102; Kinsley, *Tantric*, 111; Ramos, *Pilgrimage*, 71–72.
45. Bidyārṇab, *Pīṭhmālā*, esp. 60–61.
46. Ramos, *Pilgrimage*, 82; McDermott, *Mother*, 349n.368,

47. For this reason, Farquhar was not quite correct when he wrote that there was "no modern organization" that had undertaken "to modernize or defend" what he referred to as the "Left-Hand Śāktas" (*Modern*, 304).
48. Pāl, *Tantrācārya*, 49–50; Cāk'lādār, *Mahāsādhak*, 47, 65.
49. Pāl, *Tantrācārya*, 146.
50. See Bedāntabāgīś, *Pātañjaldarśan o yog-pariśiṣṭa*.
51. Bagchi, *Swami Abhedananda*, 52. Abhedananda had close links to Theosophy and enthusiastically engaged with Spiritualism. He was also an acquaintance of Srishchandra Basu and stayed at his house; see Bose, *Life*, 164. A study of this fascinating personality is a desideratum. This is the more relevant as a direct line runs from Shivachandra to Abhedananda and then Swami Prajnanananda, the editor of later Bengali editions of *Tantratattva* who also knew Pramathanath Mukhopadhyay. Another influential swami who had similar links is Nigamananda. He, too, deserves further scrutiny. I am grateful for the hospitality at the Ramakrishna Vedanta Math at Kolkata, where I was allowed to study relevant material.
52. *Lucifer* 2, no. 12 (1888): 497–498.
53. Bholanath edited Shivachandra's book *Rāslīlā* under the auspices of the Sarvamaṅgalā Sabhā. In his own studies, he highlighted the bravery of ancient Bengalis, especially their opposition to Muslim rule. See Gupta, *Notions*, 340.
54. For biographical details, see Pal, *Saint*; Cakrabartī, *Bāṃlār Sādhak*, 2:118–151; Kopf, *Brahmo Samaj*, 219–227.
55. Kopf, *Brahmo Samaj*, 222.
56. Ibid., 226.
57. This edition includes an introduction by Prajnanananda and was based on a print from *āṣāṛh* 1317, that is June–July 1910. This suggests the existence of more than the two early editions from 1893 and 1914. See Bidyārṇab, *Tantratattva*.
58. The present work uses an edition from 1982. The Nababharat editions introduced chapter numbers, which in several instances subdivide the text in a different way than the Avalon translation. They also leave out several quotes and passages.
59. Bidyārṇab, *Tantratattva*, 3. The following translations are based on Arthur Avalon's *Principles of Tantra* and were modified especially regarding terminology. I chose not to translate several key terms that the reader is by now familiar with, and I decided to pay close attention to omissions and excessively free translations, both of which are characteristic of the Avalon translation. Cf. Avalon, *Principles*, 1:9–10.
60. Bidyārṇab, *Tantratattva*, 4; cf. Avalon, *Principles*, 1:11.
61. Bidyārṇab, *Tantratattva*, 5; cf. Avalon, *Principles*, 1:14.
62. Bidyārṇab, *Tantratattva*, 5; cf. Avalon, *Principles*, 1:14.
63. Bidyārṇab, *Tantratattva*, 6; cf. Avalon, *Principles*, 1:15–16.
64. Bidyārṇab, *Tantratattva*, 7–8; cf. Avalon, *Principles*, 1:17.
65. Bidyārṇab, *Tantratattva*, 575; cf. Avalon, *Principles*, 2:395.
66. Bidyārṇab, *Tantratattva*, 392–393; cf. Avalon, *Principles*, 2:140–141.
67. Avalon, *Tantra of the Great Liberation* (1913), 347.
68. Ibid., 350.

69. Bidyārṇab, *Tantratattva*, 160–161, 163; cf. Avalon, *Principles*, 2:224–225, 228. Also see Bidyārṇab, *Rāslīlā*, 26–71.
70. Bidyārṇab, *Tantratattva*, 5; cf. Avalon, *Principles*, 1:14.
71. Cf. Urban, *Tantra*, 139.
72. Taylor, *Sir John Woodroffe*, 100.
73. Bidyārṇab, *Tantratattva*, 46; cf. Avalon, *Principles*, 1:72.
74. Bidyārṇab, *Tantratattva*, 47; cf. Avalon, *Principles*, 1:74.
75. Avalon, *Principles*, 2:88.
76. Bidyārṇab, *Tantratattva*, 356–357; cf. Avalon, *Principles*, 2:88–89.
77. Bidyārṇab, *Tantratattva*, 357; cf. Avalon, *Principles*, 2:90.
78. Bidyārṇab, *Tantratattva*, 364–365; cf. Avalon, *Principles*, 2:104–106.
79. Bidyārṇab, *Tantratattva*, 367; cf. Avalon, *Principles*, 2:109.
80. Bidyārṇab, *Tantratattva*, 369; cf. Avalon, *Principles*, 2:112.
81. Avalon, *Principles*, 2:116, 118, 121.
82. Bidyārṇab, *Tantratattva*, 364; cf. Avalon, *Principles*, 2:104.
83. Avalon, *Principles*, 2:93–94.
84. Bandyopādhyāẏ, *Bāṃlār Tantra*, 42 and especially 123, 129.
85. Sen, *Hindu Revivalism*, 34, 47.
86. Bidyārṇab, *Tantratattva*, 413; cf. Avalon, *Principles*, 2:179. Here, Shivachandra quoted a song by the poet Digamvara Bhattacharyya to make his point.
87. Bidyārṇab, *Tantratattva*, 415; cf. Avalon, *Principles*, 2:181–182.
88. Bidyārṇab, *Tantratattva*, 417; cf. Avalon, *Principles*, 2:186–186.
89. Bidyārṇab, *Tantratattva*, 422–423; cf. Avalon, *Principles*, 2:194.
90. Bidyārṇab, *Tantratattva*, 428–429; cf. Avalon, *Principles*, 2:202.
91. Bidyārṇab, *Tantratattva*, 576; cf. Avalon, *Principles*, 2:396–397.
92. In addition to respective chapters of this book, see e.g., Pāl, *Tantrācārya*, 127; cf. Strube, "Tantra as Experimental Science."
93. Bidyārṇab, *Tantratattva*, 35; cf. Avalon, *Principles*, 1:24–25.
94. Bidyārṇab, *Tantratattva*, 25; cf. Avalon, *Principles*, 1:41.
95. Bidyārṇab, *Tantratattva*, 41; cf. Avalon, *Principles*, 1:63–64.
96. Bidyārṇab, *Tantratattva*, 407; cf. Avalon, *Principles*, 2:163–164.
97. Avalon, *Principles*, 1:75–77.
98. Ibid., 83. The notion of monism will be discussed in chapter 8.
99. Ibid., 86.
100. Bidyārṇab, *Tantratattva*, 56; cf. Avalon, *Principles*, 1:89–90.
101. Bidyārṇab, *Tantratattva*, 57; cf. Avalon, *Principles*, 1:91.
102. Bidyārṇab, *Tantratattva*, 56; cf. Avalon, *Principles*, 1:90.
103. Bidyārṇab, *Tantratattva*, 58; cf. Avalon, *Principles*, 1:92.
104. Bidyārṇab, *Tantratattva*, 552–553; cf. Avalon, *Principles*, 2:367–369.
105. Sartori, "Beyond," 85; cf. Sartori, "Categorial Logic."

Chapter 7

1. Urban, *Tantra*, 73–74.
2. Prakash, *Another Reason*, 102.
3. Sarkar, *Swadeshi*, 498.
4. Prakash, *Another Reason*.
5. Among the extensive writings on the subject, see the recent studies by Chatterji, *Bengal Divided*, and, although it focuses on the Partition's later ramifications, Sen, *Citizen Refugee*.
6. It is regrettable that the scope of this study largely excludes Muslim actors. For recent studies focusing on Islam during the Partition and its aftermath, see Ghosh, *Different Nationalisms*, and Bose, *Recasting*. Cf. Sarkar, *Swadeshi*, 405–464; Das, "Bengalischer Nationalismus," 187–188; Wolfers, "Born," 533.
7. About the dynamics between Hindu and Muslim anticolonial nationalist currents in the succeeding years, see Banerjee, *Mortal God*, 350–387. Cf. Sarkar, *Swadeshi*, 47–48, 79, 360; Raychaudhuri, *Europe*, 12; Sen, *Hindu Revivalism*, 368. Also see the in-depth exploration of Bengali language, culture, and Islam in Bose, *Recasting*.
8. Sarkar, *Swadeshi*, 33.
9. Ibid., 90.
10. Ibid., 78.
11. Among other measures, he expanded the powers of local government, lowered the salt tax, and liberalized the internal administration of British India. He allowed vernacular newspapers freedoms equal to English-language publications by repealing the Vernacular Press Act of 1878. In 1883, his so-called Ilbert Bill was passed only after he had been pressured to remove a provision to grant Indian judges the same rights as European judges in handling the cases of European defendants.
12. Sarkar, *Swadeshi*, 34.
13. About this "myth of rupture" between traditional and modern knowledge under colonialism, also see Yelle, *Language*, 12–18.
14. Pāl, *Tantrācārya*, 77–78; cf. Cākˡlādār, *Mahāsādhak*, 15.
15. Sarkar, *Swadeshi*, 276, 280.
16. Pāl, *Tantrācārya*, 76; cf. Cākˡlādār, *Mahāsādhak*, 15–16. The word *mā-ṭi* is a respectful/loving way to address a mother, while *māṭi* means earth, soil, clay, dirt, or dust.
17. Cf. Cākˡlādār, *Mahāsādhak*, 88.
18. Pāl, *Tantrācārya*, 107–115, 144–146, 200–201.
19. Ray, *Religious Movements*, 72.
20. Chirol, *Indian Unrest*, 18–19.
21. Urban, *Tantra*, 122.
22. Raychaudhuri, *Europe*, 132.
23. E.g., Caṭṭopādhyāẏ, *Ānandamaṭh*, 49.
24. See Harder, "Bankimchandra Chattopadhyay and Modern Hinduism," esp. 60–65.
25. Caṭṭopādhyāẏ, *Ānandamaṭh*, 131. Cf. Chatterji, *Ānandamaṭh*, 229, where *sanātana dharma* is translated as "Eternal Code."
26. Caṭṭopādhyāẏ, *Ānandamaṭh*, 131.

27. Ibid., 28–30; cf. Chatterji, *Ānandamaṭh*, 149–151.
28. Choudhuri, *Mother*, 39.
29. Historically, the relationship between warrior ascetic orders and the British was indeed ambiguous. While they were certainly opponents, the British were also adept at instrumentalizing such orders for their political aims. See Hatcher, *Hinduism*, 53–59.
30. Urban, *Tantra*, 124. For Bankim's ambivalent relationship toward Muslim and other "non-Hindu" religious communities, see Harder, "Bankimchandra Chattopadhyay (1838–94)"; cf. Harder, "Bankimchandra Chattopadhyay and Modern Hinduism," 65–69.
31. Heehs, "Aurobindo."
32. Sarkar, *Swadeshi*, 468.
33. Urban, *Tantra*, 94–95.
34. See Wolfers, "Born," where the interconnectedness of politics and spirituality in the thought of Aurobindo is emphasized. Cf. Wolfers, "Making."
35. Aurobindo, *Bande Mataram*, 652.
36. Iyengar, *Sri Aurobindo*, 377.
37. Urban, *Tantra*, 95.
38. Aurobindo, *Bande Mataram*, 65.
39. Ibid., 66.
40. Sarkar, *Swadeshi*, 272–273; Gordon, *Bengal*, 133; Urban, *Tantra*, 95–96.
41. Urban, *Tantra*, 91.
42. Chirol, *Indian Unrest*, 94.
43. Heehs, *Sri Aurobindo*, 53–54; also see Heehs, *Bomb*.
44. Quoted in Sarkar, *Swadeshi*, 375.
45. Ibid.
46. Mukherjee, *Two Great*, 163–164. Jatin's year of birth is often given as 1879.
47. Samanta, *Terrorism*, 2:393.
48. Ibid., 1:14.
49. Ibid., 2:509.
50. Sarkar, *Swadeshi*, 376.
51. Roy, *Memoirs*, 568–569; Sarkar, *Swadeshi*, 490.
52. Cāk'lādār, *Mahāsādhak*, 90; cf. Rāy, *Bhārater Sādhak*, 169–171.
53. Banerjee, *Logic*, 157; Ramos, *Pilgrimage*, 76–77.
54. Pal gives his civil name as Manimohan Gosvami, while contemporary reports identify Tarakhepa as Tarapada Banerjee. See Samanta, *Terrorism*, 1:60.
55. Sarkar, *Swadeshi*, 28. The others were Asvinikumar Datta, Satischandra Mukhopadhyay, and Monoranjan Guha Thakurta.
56. Harder, "Populärversionen," 83–84.
57. *Bedbyās* itself was printed by the Bangabasi Steam Machine Press (*baṅgabāsī ṣṭīm meśin pres*) in Calcutta.
58. Raychaudhuri, *Europe*, 9–10.
59. Cf. Sen, *Hindu Revivalism*, 15.
60. Ibid., 219.
61. Ibid., 163.

62. Pal, *Memories*, 425–426.
63. Ibid., 428. Ironically, such "orthodox" ambitions had been prepared and inspired by the Brahmos: "Hinduism in my boyhood was almost exclusively a personal religion with a social aspect that was organised in the festivities of the external *pujas*. The only form of what might deserve to be called congregational worship was found in the Vaishnava *keertanas* and in the Vaishnava *Mahotshavas*. The higher and the more educated classes had no participation in these. It was the Brahmo Samaj which first introduced congregational worship in modern India. With this Hindu revival and reaction, *Hari Sabhas* commenced to grow up everywhere which inaugurated a kind of congregational worship. At meetings of these *Sabhas*, scripture texts were read and expounded by some Pandit and hymns or *bhajans* were sung. All this was clearly a reproduction of the Brahmo mode of worship."
64. Tarkacuṛāmaṇi, *Dharmmabyākhyā*, 1–3.
65. Ibid., 72: "śaktir ādhāra bhaudītik padārtha nahe, bhautik padārther ādhārī śakti."
66. Ibid., 72–74.
67. Ibid., 80, 157–160, 219–221.
68. Ibid., 86–88.
69. Ibid., 138.
70. Cf. Ibid., 320.
71. Sen, *Hindu Revivalism*, 229–230. The Bill had raised the age of consent for sexual intercourse from ten to twelve years.
72. "Uddēśya," *Bedbyās* 1, no. 1 (1886): 1.
73. Tarkacuṛāmaṇi, "Śrāddhatattva," 1.
74. The meaning of *bhūt* is ambiguous and could also signify "spirit." In the parlance of other pandits, including Shivachandra, *bhūt* clearly refers to a physical, material science. In Shashadhar's writings, the differentiation is not so clear-cut, which might very well have been intentional: ultimately, spirit and matter were not separate.
75. Tarkacuṛāmaṇi, "Śrāddhatattva," 2.
76. The ambiguity of *bhūt* as both matter and spirit is even more prominent here.
77. Tarkacuṛāmaṇi, "Śrāddhatattva," 3.
78. Tarkacuṛāmaṇi, "Unnati ki abanati?," 33–34.
79. Ibid., 34–35. It might be recalled that Baradakanta did, in fact, cite Shashadhar in his *Barnāśram dharmma*.
80. Ibid., 36–38.
81. Ibid., 38–39.
82. Tarkacuṛāmaṇi, "Unnati o abanatir artha [1]," 116–120.
83. Tarkacuṛāmaṇi, "Unnati o abanatir artha 2," 187–188.
84. Ibid., 189.
85. Ibid., 190.
86. Bidyārṇab, "Śikṣā," 88.
87. Taylor, *Sir John Woodroffe*, 134.
88. Pratyagatmananda Saraswati, *Complete Works*, 7.
89. For an overview, see Mukherjee and Mukherjee, *Origins*.
90. Pratyagatmananda Saraswati, *Complete Works*, 7–8.

91. For a concise summary of his approach, see Pratyagatmananda Saraswati and Woodroffe, *Sadhana*, 1–26.
92. Ibid., 23.
93. Yelle, *Explaining*, 20–54, here 55.
94. For a summary in English, see Pratyagatmananda Saraswati, *Japasutram*.
95. Cf. the later booklet, Pratyagatmananda Saraswati, *Science and Sādhanā*.
96. Alper, *Understanding*, 442.
97. Sartori, "Beyond," 87–88; cf. chapter 2 of the present study.
98. Pratyagatmananda Saraswati, *Complete Works*, 82, original emphasis.
99. Ibid., 1.
100. Ibid., 4–6.
101. Ibid., 10–18.
102. Ibid., 18, original emphasis.
103. Ibid., 30.
104. Ibid., 41.
105. Ibid., 44.
106. Ibid., 65.
107. Ibid., 69.
108. Ibid., 72.
109. Ibid., 73–74.
110. Banerjee, "German Foundations."

Chapter 8

1. Cāk'lādār, *Mahāsādhak*, 72, 75.
2. Gaṅgopādhyāẏ, *Bhārater*, 90.
3. Hazra, "Influence of Tantra on the Tattvas," 703.
4. See Yelle, *Language*, 137–160. Also see the discussion in Hatcher, *Hinduism*, 84–88, where he writes that the British "prioritized original purity and stasis over historical change and the governing agency of communities," thus putting their engagement with *dharmaśāstra* to political use.
5. Taylor, *Sir John Woodroffe*, 37, 102.
6. Sen, *Ātmajībanī*, 154.
7. Śāstrī, *Bhārater*, preface, 13.
8. Ibid., preface, 1–2.
9. Pāl, *Tantrācārya*, 54. Cf. Gaṅgopādhyāẏ, *Bhārater*, 89–90, who probably relied on Pal, as argued by Taylor, *Sir John Woodroffe*, 94.
10. Taylor, *Sir John Woodroffe*, 101.
11. Woodroffe, *Garland*, ix.
12. Pāl, *Tantrācārya*, 82.
13. Gaṅgopādhyāẏ, *Bhārater*, 91; cf. Taylor, *Sir John Woodroffe*, 93.
14. Ṭhākur and Canda, *Joṛāsāṁkor dhāre*, 172, 174–175.

15. Taylor, *Sir John Woodroffe*, 14. Taylor suspected that he might have been drawn to it secretly much earlier. In 1894, John's mother had died, and a cryptic remark in a lecture from 1917 might imply that he was consoled by Shivachandra's friend Vamakhepa, who pointed out the immortality of the Mother of the Universe. The lecture was delivered to the Société Artistique et Littéraire Française de Calcutta and was included in Woodroffe, *Shakti and Shakta*, 696. The anecdote was about "a man who I know and who had lost his mother." However, the *ante quem* of this anecdote, should it refer to Woodroffe himself, would be Vamakhepa's death in 1911 and thus not of much help for a "much earlier" dating.
16. For a summary of those by Pal, Ray, and Bagchi, see Taylor, *Sir John Woodroffe*, 102–104.
17. Pāl, *Tantrācārya*, 57–58.
18. Ibid., 58–64, 67.
19. Ibid., 178. The initiation was performed by "sprinkling" (*siñcan*).
20. Taylor, *Sir John Woodroffe*, 105.
21. Pāl, *Tantrācārya*, 94–97; cf. Sen, *Ātmajībanī*, 155.
22. See the preface to Śāstrī, *Bhārater*.
23. Pāl, *Tantrācārya*, 102–103.
24. Tarakhepa is also named Tarapada Banerjee. It is unclear whether these are two different people, if authors confused them, or if the use of different names was intended to obstruct the work of intelligence officers investigating revolutionary activities.
25. Not to be confused with Vivekananda's follower, who died in 1911.
26. Pāl, *Tantrācārya*, 104–105.
27. Cakrabartī, *Bāṃlār Sādhak*, 4:89–110.
28. Pāl, *Tantrācārya*, 118–119. The text also mentions a letter that was sent to Woodroffe from the district and session judge Phanindramohan Chattopadhyay.
29. Sen, *Ātmajībanī*, 156.
30. This is also the conclusion of Taylor, *Sir John Woodroffe*, 106.
31. For some other accounts, see Pāl, *Tantrācārya*, 174–176, and Taylor, *Sir John Woodroffe*, 107–109, 112–113.
32. Interviews conducted on October 10 and 21, 2018. According to Rabindranath, Shivachandra had five children when he passed away. Rabindranath has five brothers, but the surviving family is scattered. It appears that the direct lineage of Shivachandra will come to an end, as Rabindranath represents the last generation of priests. However, according to several interviews conducted in Haora and Shibpur, the Sarvamaṅgalā Sabhā still has active members.
33. Taylor, *Sir John Woodroffe*, 236.
34. See, for instance, Avalon, *Tantra of the Great Liberation* (1927), xi.
35. Taylor, *Sir John Woodroffe*, 205.
36. Cf. ibid., 37, 94, 98.
37. Ibid., 96–97. Atalbihari used the name Atalananda on the publications in *Tantrik Texts* from nos. 16 to 20.
38. Taylor, *Sir John Woodroffe*, 209. The article with the title "The Teachings of the Tantra" was published in *Occult Digest* of April 1930.

39. Taylor, *Sir John Woodroffe*, 97.
40. Mahabharati, "Tantras [2]," 108.
41. Taylor, *Sir John Woodroffe*, 211–212.
42. Ibid., 204.
43. See, for instance, Ghosh, "Śiva and Śakti."
44. Pāl, *Tantrācārya*, 69.
45. Śāstrī, *Bhārater*, preface, 7.
46. Maitra, "Stones," 590.
47. The story prominently features a Tantric Kapalika. Building on the imagery of earlier Sanskrit works, Bankim depicted this figure in a gruesome way that invoked cremation ground rituals and sexual perversion. See Urban, *Tantra*, 121–122.
48. Sen, *Ātmajībanī*, 153–154. The implication of his statement is that Akshaykumar attained cleverness by becoming a lawyer, while the Tantric Shivachandra devoted himself to asceticism (*sannyāsa*).
49. This nationalist dimension of art has been explored by Mitter, *Art*.
50. Taylor, *Sir John Woodroffe*, 104–105.
51. Ibid., 69–70.
52. Chakrabarti, *Religious Process*, 4–5.
53. For more information on Cousins, see Hashimoto, "Irish."
54. Taylor, *Sir John Woodroffe*, 70.
55. Ibid., 45, 73.
56. Cousins, "Agamas," 147.
57. Ibid., 148.
58. Ibid.
59. Ibid., 150.
60. Ibid., 151.
61. Ibid., 153.
62. Taylor, *Sir John Woodroffe*, 94–95.
63. Pāl, *Tantrācārya*, 83.
64. Taylor, *Sir John Woodroffe*, 95–96.
65. Ibid., 44.
66. Under number 46,571, it lists one "N. Woodroff" at Calcutta. It is very likely that this is a spelling mistake, as several such cases can be found in the otherwise meticulous register.
67. Taylor, *Sir John Woodroffe*, 18–19.
68. Ibid., 12.
69. *Theosophist* 35, no. 1 (1913): 59.
70. *Theosophist* 35, no. 9 (1914): 363–370. The *Prapañcasāra* was published as the third volume of *Tantrik Texts*.
71. *Theosophist* 35, no. 9 (1914): 364, 367.
72. Taylor, *Sir John Woodroffe*, 20.
73. Both are reprinted in Woodroffe, *Shakti and Shakta*, 688–724.
74. *Theosophist* 35, no. 1 (1913): 138–144, here 138.
75. Ibid., 143. Schrader was here quoting from the preface to the *Hymns*.

76. *Theosophist* 35, no. 11 (August 1914): 741–750, here 749–750.
77. For an extensive discussion of this controversy, see Leland, *Rainbow*, 192–210.
78. Woodroffe, *Serpent Power*, 6–19, here 15.
79. Avalon there reprimanded Srishchandra for identifying the *liṅga śarīra* with the Theosophical concepts of the "etherial duplicate" and the "Astral body." This is remarkable insofar as other parts of the Avalon/Woodroffe textual corpus are not hesitant in drawing similar parallels—most likely because such differing statements might have come from different authors behind Avalon.
80. Taylor, *Sir John Woodroffe*, 149; McDaniel, *Offering*, 278.
81. Avalon, *Principles*, 1:x.
82. The introduction was signed by Baradakanta in Benares on March 23, 1914.
83. Avalon, *Principles*, 1:x–xi.
84. Ibid., xxix.
85. This notion was not coined by Woodroffe, as is suggested by Sartori, "Beyond," 86.
86. Avalon, *Principles*, 1:xxix.
87. Majumdār, "Introduction," v–vii, here vii.
88. Ibid., x–xi.
89. Ibid., xi–xii.
90. Ibid., cxlviii.
91. Ibid., xiv.
92. Ibid., cxlix.
93. One of the most impressive and influential examples is Éliphas Lévi, the "founder" of occultism, who envisioned the "self-creation" of the individual as the first step toward the regeneration of society. See Strube, "Socialist Religion," 378.
94. Majumdār, "Introduction," xl.
95. Ibid., xvi.
96. E.g., ibid., xxi, xxxi–xxxii, cii. Sexuality is discussed by Baradakanta quite frankly, an aspect that warrants closer attention.
97. Ibid., xxxix.
98. Ibid., liii.
99. Ibid., xix. In this passage, he rejected the "Veil of Prakriti," explaining the place of prakriti in Shakta philosophy.
100. Ibid., civ; cf. lxxiii.
101. Ibid., cx.
102. Ibid., cv.
103. Ibid., cxlviii.
104. Ibid., cxlviii–cxlix. Here, Baradakanta again invoked the *Kulārṇava Tantra*.
105. Not all volumes are officially coauthored, but Pramathanath's contribution is highlighted in the first volume; see Woodroffe, *The World as Power: Reality*, 15–16.
106. References abound in *Bharata Shakti*. Woodroffe frequently cited him as a "friend," for instance in *Shakti and Shakta*, 28, 75, 665 and *Serpent Power*, 302.
107. Woodroffe, *Garland*, 40.
108. Cf. Strube, "Tantra as Experimental Science."
109. Woodroffe, *The World as Power: Reality*, 6–7.

110. This was especially argued for the case of Advaita, which is reminiscent of many contemporary arguments, for instance Akshaychandra Sarkar's conviction that Western science confirmed Advaitism; see Sen, *Hindu Revivalism*, 163.
111. Jagadishchandra was mostly known as an expert on Kashmir Shaivism and published, in 1911, the first volume of the Kashmir Series of Texts and Studies. He was friends with Woodroffe and also collaborated with Theos and Pierre Bernard (about the former, see Hackett, *Theos Bernard*, where Jagadishchandra is not mentioned). In 1898, he delivered lectures in Belgium that were published as *La philosophie ésotérique de l'Inde* under the pseudonym Brahmacharin Bodhabhikshu. A German translation was published as *Die Geheim-Philosophie der Indier* (2nd edition, 1906). This connection warrants further exploration.
112. Brajendranath, a member of the Sādhāraṇ Brāhma Samāj, had suggested Woodroffe as the chair of the Ram Mohan Roy Library, where the latter gave a lecture on March 20, 1915, and was introduced by Brajendranath. See Taylor, *Sir John Woodroffe*, 79. It is remarkable that Brajendranath, like Bamandas Basu, had criticized Bipinbihari Shom's article "Physical Errors of Hinduism" from 1849 (Taylor, *Sir John Woodroffe*, 172). For more on Seal, see Prakash, *Another Reason*, 100–101.
113. About Malkani, an outstanding Vedantist philosopher of colonial India who engaged with the thought of Hegel, see Deshpande, "G. R. Malkani."
114. Woodroffe, *The World as Power: Reality*, 89, 107.
115. Woodroffe and Mukhopādhyāya, *The World as Power: Power as Matter*, 15.
116. For an analysis of that engagement, see Taylor, *Sir John Woodroffe*, 194–202.
117. Woodroffe, *The World as Power: Power as Life*, 21–22; cf. x–xi.
118. Ibid., xxi–xxii; cf. Woodroffe, *Shakti and Shakta*, 127.
119. Woodroffe, *The World as Power: Power as Mind*, xv–xvi, 30.
120. Ibid., 108–109. He here referred to the work of Madame de Staël and Boirac.
121. Woodroffe and Mukhopādhyāya, *Mahāmāyā*, 188.
122. Woodroffe, *Is India Civilized?*, 113–115.
123. Woodroffe and Mukhopadhyaya, *The World as Power: Causality and Continuity*, vi–vii. See also the following objection to criticism that "an attempt has been made to read something into such Scriptures which is not there."
124. Woodroffe, *Garland*, preface.
125. Woodroffe, *Bharata Shakti*, 54–61.
126. Ibid., xvi.
127. Ibid., xvii, 40–41; Woodroffe, *Seed*, 27–28, 33. Also see Woodroffe, *Bharata Shakti*, 75–79, about university education. Havell's criticism of foreign influences is approvingly cited.
128. Woodroffe, *Bharata Shakti*, 49–51.
129. Ibid., viii. About Nalinimohan and the Indian Rationalistic Society, see Taylor, *Sir John Woodroffe*, 83–85.
130. Woodroffe, *Seed*, 10–11.
131. Ibid., 15. For a more detailed treatment of his racial ideas, see Taylor, *Sir John Woodroffe*, 85–87.
132. Woodroffe, *Seed*, 39.

133. Avalon, *Principles*, 2:xi.
134. Ibid., xv, xix–xx.
135. Ibid., lxxx–lxxxi.
136. Ibid., c.
137. Avalon, *Principles*, 1:xxxvii. On the following page, this is related to the theory of a common "root-language of the human race."
138. Woodroffe, *Is India Civilized?*, 58–59.
139. See the reprint of this article in Woodroffe, *Shakti and Shakta*, here 407.
140. Cf. Strube, "Tantra und Katholizismus."
141. Avalon, *Tantra of the Great Liberation* (1927) xii; cf. similar statements in Avalon, *Principles*, 1:lxxi; Woodroffe, *Shakti and Shakta*, 164–165, 195–196, 208.
142. E.g., in Woodroffe, *Shakti and Shakta*, 61–62; Pratyagatmananda Saraswati, *Complete Works*, 51; Woodroffe, *Bharata Shakti*, 59.
143. Avalon, *Principles*, 1:xvi.
144. Avalon, *Tantra of the Great Liberation* (1927), civ.
145. Woodroffe, *Shakti and Shakta*, 62.
146. Ibid., 88.
147. See Winternitz, "Tantras."
148. Woodroffe, *Shakti and Shakta*, 106.
149. Ibid., 408.
150. Rāy, *Bhārater Sādhak*, 174.
151. Avalon, *Principles*, 1:xvii.
152. Majumdar, *Eagle*, iii–iv.
153. Bandyopādhyāẏ, *Bāṃlār Tantra*, 119–134.
154. Ibid., 82.
155. See ibid., 18, where Bijaykrishna Gosvami is especially lauded. Also see 103, where one of Shivachandra's songs is referenced to discuss the worship of Devi.
156. Ibid., 123. As mentioned earlier, the book did invoke the authority of the *Kulārṇava* and the *Mahānirvāṇa*.
157. Ibid., 128–130. Interestingly, Rammohan and Ishvarchandra Vidyasagar are highlighted as two "pure Bengalis," in contrast to Keshabchandra and Rabindranath, who were influenced by European culture. Panchkari also attributes the degeneration of Tantra to the Kanyakubja Brahmins who had recently moved to Bengal, as well as to negative tendencies among Tantrics themselves (123).
158. Ibid., 1.
159. Avalon, *Principles*, 2:xxii–xxix.
160. Bandyopādhyāẏ, "Mahāyogī sāhitya," 365: "tantrer biśiṣṭā uhār sādhanā-paddhatite. . . . ihā kebal philasaphi nahe, bacaner tūṣa cūrṇa karibār ceṣṭā nahe, 'hāte hetere' kariẏā karmmiẏā dekhibār biṣaẏ. . . . mane haẏ, musalmānder sādhanā, romān-kāthalik o grīkcarccer khrīṣṭāndiger Esoteric Reliion [*sic*] bā gupta dharmma-sādhanā ei tantrer bedīr upar pratiṣṭita." Cf. Avalon, *Principles*, 2:xxiv.
161. Bandyopādhyāẏ, "Mahāyogī sāhitya," 365; cf. Avalon, *Principles*, 2:xxiv–xxv.

Chapter 9

1. Hatcher, *Hinduism*, 50.
2. Ibid., 67.
3. An important step for research on the travels of Indian Theosophists is Mukhopadhyay, "Mohini."
4. Conrad, *What Is Global History*, 16, 225–226. Also see Ghobrial, "Introduction," 6–8.
5. Wenzlhuemer, *Globalgeschichte*, 76–78.
6. Fischer-Tiné, "Marrying," 51.
7. Putnam, "The Transnational," 377–378.
8. Hatcher, *Hinduism*, 38.
9. Dey, "Piety"; Bhatia, "Psychic Chaitanya."
10. Koschorke and Hermann, "Beyond," 228–230, 234–241.
11. Viswanathan, *Outside*, 200.
12. Van der Veer, *Imperial*, 64.
13. Josephson-Storm, *Myth*, 117.
14. Wilson, "Sketch," 225.
15. Ravenshaw, "Note," 76–77.
16. Kumar, "Tantras."
17. See Sarkar, *Swadeshi*, 313–314, 468, 483; Urban, *Tantra*, 123; cf. Bolle, *Persistence*, 79–102; Choudhuri, *Mother*, 56.
18. Das, "Problematic," 415–416; Lorea, "I Am Afraid."
19. Stewart, "Power" and Sarbadhikary, "Sahajiya Texts."
20. See Urban, "Elitism," who concludes that secrecy does not denote countercultural or subversive behavior but should be viewed as a highly elitist, hierarchically structured endeavor. For the ambivalence of secrecy in Tantra, which was often more important than actually keeping a secret, also see White, *Kiss*, 157. Cf. Urban's discussion of the political ramifications of secrecy in the context of colonialism in *Tantra*, 75–87, 131–133. The aspect of "advertised secrecy" is a fundamental issue in the study of esotericism and has been addressed in the light of neoliberal consumerism and commodification in Crockford, "What."
21. From an ethnographical perspective, Lorea has pointed out that the gaze of academics has created a "myth of secrecy" that stands in contrast to a much more "flexible reality of accessible, though esoteric, religious groups that continuously negotiate their balance between secrecy and disclosure" ("I Am Afraid," 3, 8, 16).
22. In what way this historical perspective could be complemented with approaches from sociology, anthropology, and related disciplines will hopefully emerge in future scholarly dialogue. A promising route has been proposed in Asprem, "Beyond," 20–30, where a comparative lens is suggested that does not necessarily require evident historical connections.
23. Cf. Bergunder, "Comparison."

Bibliography

Primary Sources

Abhinavagupta. *The Kula Ritual as Elaborated in Chapter 29 of the Tantrāloka*. Translated by John R. Dupuche. Delhi: Motilal Banarsidass, 2006.

An Admirer. "The Madras Yogi Sabhapaty Sawmi." *Theosophist* 1, no. 6 (1880): 145–147.

Aurobindo, Sri. *Bande Mataram: Early Political Writings*. Pondicherry: Sri Aurobindo Ashram, 1973.

Avalon, Arthur. *Principles of Tantra: The Tantratattva of Ṣhrīyukta Ṣhiva Chandra Vidyārnava Bhattāchāryya Mahodaya*. Vol. 1. London: Luzac, 1914.

Avalon, Arthur. *Principles of Tantra: The Tantratattva of Ṣhrīyukta Ṣhiva Chandra Vidyārnava Bhattāchāryya Mahodaya*. Vol. 2. London: Luzac, 1916.

Avalon, Arthur. *Tantra of the Great Liberation (Mahānirvāna Tantra)*. Madras: Ganesh, 1913.

Avalon, Arthur. *Tantra of the Great Liberation (Mahānirvāna Tantra)*. 2nd ed. London: Luzac, 1927.

Bandyopādhyāẏ, Brajendranāth. "Kṣetrapāl Cakrabarttī Yog'śāstrī" (1371). In *Sāhitya-Sādhak-Caritmālā*, edited by Brajendranāth Bandyopādhyāẏ, vol. 87, 15–26. Kalikātā: Baṅgīẏa Sāhitya Pariṣaṯ, 1964.

Bandyopādhyāẏ, Pāṁckaṛi. *Bāṃlār Tantra*. Edited by Bimalendu Cakrabartī. Calcutta: Beṅgal Pābliśārs, 1942.

Bandyopādhyāẏ, Pāṁckaṛi. "Mahāyogī sāhitya." *Sāhitya* 24, no. 4 (1913): 363–368.

Basu, Baman Das. "The Anatomy of the Tantras." *Theosophist* 9, no. 102 (1888): 370–373.

Basu, Srischandra. *A Catechism of Hinduism*. Benares: Freeman, 1899.

Basu, Srischandra. *The Esoteric Science and the Philosophy of the Tantras: Shiva Sanhita*. 2nd ed. Calcutta: Heeralal Dhole, 1893.

Baṭabyāl, Umeścandra. "Rilijan śabder bāṃlā ki?" *Sahitya* 4 (1893): 760–765.

Bedāntabāgīś, Kālībar Bhaṭṭācāryya. *Pātañjaldarśan o yog-pariśiṣṭa*. 4th ed. Calcutta: Haripad Bhaṭṭācāryya, 1907.

Besant, Annie. *How India Wrought for Freedom: The Story of the National Congress Told from Official Records*. Adyar: Theosophical Publishing House, 1915.

Bharadwaja, Chiranjiva. *Light of Truth, or An English Translation of the Satyarth Prakash the Well-Known Work of Swami Dayananda Saraswati*. Allahabad: K. C. Bhalla, 1939.

Bhattacharya, Kunjabihari. "A Description of the Tantrik Mystical Rites and Ceremonies Known as 'Savasadhana [1].'" *Theosophist* 4, no. 9, Supplement (1883): 10–11.

Bhattacharya, Kunjabihari. "A Description of the Tantrik Mystical Rites and Ceremonies Known as 'Savasadhana [2].'" *Theosophist* 4, no. 10, Supplement (1883): 11–12.

Bidyārṇab, Śib'candra Bhaṭṭācāryya. *Gaṅgeś*. Calcutta: Dānbāri Gaṅgopādhyāẏ, 1898.

Bidyārṇab, Śib'candra Bhaṭṭācāryya. *Pīṭhmālā*. Kumārkhālī: Sarbbamaṇgalā Sabhā, 1891.

Bidyārṇab, Śib'candra Bhaṭṭācāryya. *Rāslīlā*. Kumārkhālī: Bholānāth Cakrabartti, 1896.

Bidyārṇab, Śib'candra Bhaṭṭācāryya. "Śikṣā." *Bed'byās* 4, no. 4 (1889): 86–88.

Bidyārṇab, Śib'candra Bhaṭṭācāryya. *Tantratattva.* 2nd ed. Calcutta: Nababhārat Pābliśārs, 1982.
Bidyārṇab, Śib'candra Bhaṭṭācāryya. *Tantratattva.* Edited by Svāmī Prajñānānanda. Calcutta: Nababhārat Pābliśārs, 1973.
Blavatsky, Helena Petrovna. *Collected Writings.* 2nd ed. Vol. 12. Wheaton, IL: Theosophical Publishing House, 1987.
Blavatsky, Helena Petrovna. *Isis Unveiled: A Master-Key to the Mysteries of Ancient and Modern Science and Theology.* 2 vols. Vol. 2. New York: J. W. Bouton, Bernard Quaritch, 1877.
Bose, Phanindranath. *Life of Sris Chandra Basu.* R. Chatterjee, 1932.
Bose, Raj Narain. "Superiority of Hinduism to Other Existing Religions: As Viewed from the Stand-Point of Theism." *Theosophist* 4, no. 1 (1882): 13–16.
Cāk'lādār, Kāśīnāth. *Mahāsādhak tantrācārya Śib'candra Bidyārṇab.* Kolkata: Pustaka Bipaṇi, 2006.
Cakrabartī, Gaṅgeś'candra. *Bāṃlār Sādhak.* Vol. 1. Calcutta: Sadgrantha Prakāśan, 1972.
Cakrabartī, Gaṅgeś'candra. *Bāṃlār Sādhak.* Vol. 2. Calcutta: Sadgrantha Prakāśan, 1927.
Cakrabartī, Gaṅgeś'candra. *Bāṃlār Sādhak.* Vol. 4. Calcutta: Biśvabaṇī Prakāśanī, 1948.
Caṭṭopādhyāẏ, Baṅkim'candra. *Ānandamaṭh.* Calcutta: Baṅgīya Sāhitya Pariṣat, 1937.
Caṭṭopādhyāẏ, Baṅkim'candra. *Baṅkim Racanābalī.* Edited by Yogeścandra Bāgal. Vol. 2. Calcutta: Sāhitya Saṃsad, 1954.
Chakravarti, Kshetrapal. *Lectures on Hindu Religion, Philosophy and Yoga.* Calcutta: New Britannia Press, 1893.
Chakravarti, Kshetrapal. "The Religious Aspects of the Early Tantras [1]." *Theosophist* 12, no. 1 (1890): 23–29.
Chakravarti, Kshetrapal. "The Religious Aspects of the Early Tantras [2]." *Theosophist* 12, no. 2 (1890): 91–93.
Chakravarti, Kshetrapal. "The Religious Aspects of the Early Tantras [3]." *Theosophist* 12, no. 4 (1891): 208–210.
Chatterjee, Ramananda. "Baman Das Basu." *Modern Review* 48 (1930): 667–675.
Chatterjee, Ratneswar. "Sava-Sadhana." *Hindu Spiritual Magazine* 7, no. 11 (1913): 334–347.
Chatterji, Bankimcandra. *Ānandamaṭh, or The Sacred Brotherhood.* Translated by Julius J. Lipner. Oxford: Oxford University Press, 2005.
Chirol, Valentine. *Indian Unrest.* London: Macmillan, 1910.
Colebrooke, Henry Thomas. *Miscellaneous Essays.* Vol. 3. London: Trübner, 1873.
Colebrooke, Henry Thomas. "On the Philosophy of the Hindus, Part III." *Transactions of the Royal Asiatic Society of Great Britain and Ireland* 1 (1827): 439–460.
Cousins, James H. "The Agamas and the Future." *Modern Review* 23, no. 2 (1918): 147–153.
Dutt, Shoshee Chunder. *Essays on Miscellaneous Subjects.* Calcutta: Military Orphan Press, 1854.
Esdaile, James. *Mesmerism in India, and Its Practical Application in Surgery and Medicine.* London: Longman, Brown, Green, and Longmans, 1846.
Esdaile, James. *Natural and Mesmeric Clairvoyance, with the Practical Application of Mesmerism in Surgery and Medicine.* London: Hippolyte Bailliere, 1852.
Farquhar, John Nicol. *Modern Religious Movements in India.* 1915; London: Macmillan, 1929.
F.T.S. "Yoga Vidya 1." *Theosophist* 1, no. 1 (1879): 31–32.
F.T.S. "Yoga Vidya 3." *Theosophist* 1, no. 4 (1880): 84–86.

A Full Report of the Proceedings of the First Anniversary Meeting of the Bengal Theosophical Society, Held at the Town Hall, Calcutta, on May 21, 1883. Calcutta: Sen Press, 1883.

Full Report of the Proceedings of the Seventh Annivesary Meeting of the Theosophical Society, Held at the Framji Cowasji Institute, Bombay, on the 27th November, 1882. Calcutta: New Sanskrit Press, 1883.

Gaṅgopādhyāẏ, Arddhendrakumār. *Bhārater Śilpa o Āmār Kathā.* Calcutta: Amiẏarañjan Mukhopādhyāẏ, 1969.

General Report on Public Instruction in the Lower Provinces of the Bengal Presidency for 1868–1869. Calcutta: Baptist Mission Press, 1869.

Ghoṣ, Śiśir'kumār. *Śrīamiẏa nimāi carit.* Calcutta: Kāminī Prakāśālaẏ, 2000.

Ghose, Shishir Kumar. "How Spiritualism Came to India [1]." *Hindu Spiritual Magazine* 1, no. 1 (1906): 15–22.

Ghose, Shishir Kumar. "How Spiritualism Came to India, Pt. 2." *Hindu Spiritual Magazine* 1, no. 2 (1906): 81–87.

Ghose, Shishir Kumar. "How Spiritualism Came to India, Pt. 3." *Hindu Spiritual Magazine* 1, no. 3 (1906): 161–165.

Ghose, Shishir Kumar. "Introduction." *Hindu Spiritual Magazine* 1, no. 1 (1906): 1–3.

Ghose, Shishir Kumar. *Lord Gauranga, or Salvation for All.* Calcutta: Golap Lal Ghose, 1897.

Ghosh, Atalbihari. "Śiva and Śakti." In *Varendra Research Society's Monographs*, vol. 6, 12–16. Rajshahi: Varendra Research Society, 1935.

Hodgson, Brian Houghton. "Notices of the Languages, Literature, and Religion of the Bauddhas of Nepal and Bhot." *Asiatic Researches* 16 (1828): 409–449.

The International Theosophical Year Book. Adyar: Theosophical Publishing House, 1937.

Kumar, Shashibhushan. "The Tantras and Their Teachings." *Theosophist* 4, no. 4 (1883): 95.

Leyden, John. "On the Roshania Sect and Its Founder Bayezid Ansari." In *Asiatic Researches*, vol. 11, 363–405. London: J. Cuthel, 1812.

Mahabharati, Dharmananda. "Tantras and the Tantrikas [1]." *Hindu Spiritual Magazine* 2, no. 7 (1907): 28–32.

Mahabharati, Dharmananda. "Tantras and the Tantrikas [2]." *Hindu Spiritual Magazine* 2, no. 8 (1907): 103–112.

Mahabharati, Dharmananda. "Tantras and the Tantrikas [3]." *Hindu Spiritual Magazine* 2, no. 11 (1907): 339–345.

Mahabharati, Dharmananda. "Tantras and the Tantrikas [4]." *Hindu Spiritual Magazine* 2, no. 12 (1907): 417–427.

Mahabharati, Dharmananda. "Tantras and the Tantrikas [5]." *Hindu Spiritual Magazine* 4, no. 2 (1909): 95–108.

Mahabharati, Dharmananda. "Tantras and the Tantrikas [6]." *Hindu Spiritual Magazine* 4, no. 3 (1909): 188–197.

Mahabharati, Dharmananda. "Tantras and the Tantrikas [7]." *Hindu Spiritual Magazine* 4, no. 5 (1909): 348–356.

Mahavarati, Dharmananda. *The Yogi and His Message.* Calcutta: Goswami J. J. Bharati, 1904.

Maitra, A. K. "The Stones of Varendra." *Modern Review* 7, no. 6 (1910): 588–590.

Majumdar, Barada Kanta. "A Glimpse of Tantrik Occultism 1." *Theosophist* 1, no. 10 (1880): 244–245.

Majumdar, Barada Kanta. "The Occult Sciences." *Theosophist* 2, no. 3 (1880): 53–54.

Majumdar, Barada Kanta. *The Shikshaka or Monitor Being a Series of Moral and Civil Discourses for the Instruction of Young Proprietors of Land.* 1876.

Majumdar, Barada Kanta. "Tantric Philosophy." *Theosophist* 1, no. 7 (1880): 173–174.

Majumdār, Baradā Kānta. "Introduction: Vaidik and Tāntrik Systems of Spiritual Culture Compared." In *Principles of Tantra*, edited by Arthur Avalon, i–cxlix. London: Luzac, 1916.

Majumdar, Jnanendralal. *The Eagle and the Captive Sun.* Calcutta: Bhattacharya & Sons, Kegan, Paul, Trench, Trübner, 1909.

Majumˈdār, Baradākānta. *Barnāśram dharmma: Jātibheder gūṛha tāt·paryya bibr̥ti.* 1902; Calcutta: Sadeś, 2005.

Majumˈdār, Baradākānta. *Bhūgol.* Calcutta: Sanyal and Sons, 1898.

Majumˈdār, Baradākānta. "Dharmma-dveṣ o Sāmpradāẏikatā." *Kalpa* 1, no. 2 (1893): 17–19.

Majumˈdār, Baradākānta. *Śiśurañjan mahābhārat.* Śiśurañjan granthābalī. Calcutta: Asutosh Library, 1914.

Majumˈdār, Baradākānta. *Subhadrā.* Calcutta: Asutosh Dhar, 1913.

Majumˈdār, Baradākānta. "Tattvabidyā o tattvasabhā." *Kalpa* 1, no. 3 (1893): 33–36.

Majumˈdār, Baradākānta. "Tattvabidyā prabeṣikā." *Kalpa* 1, no. 4 (1893): 59–61.

Majumˈdār, Baradākānta. *Yiśukhriṣṭa.* 5th ed. Calcutta: Asutosh Library, 1946.

Matter, Jacques. *Essai historique sur l'Ecole d'Alexandrie.* Paris: F. G. Levrault, 1820.

Matter, Jacques. *Histoire critique du gnosticisme et de son influence sur les sectes religieuses et philosophiques des six premiers siècles de l'ère chrétienne.* 2 vols. Paris: F.-G. Levrault, 1828.

Mavalankar, Damodar K. "The Philosophy and Science of Vedantic Raja Yoga." *Theosophist* 5, no. 6 (1884): 176.

Mitra, Adhar Chandra. "Philosophy of the Tantras, Pt. 1." *Light of the East* 1, no. 4 (1892): 119–123.

Mitra, Adhar Chandra. "Philosophy of the Tantras, Pt. 2." *Light of the East* 1, no. 5 (1892): 148–151.

Mitra, Adhar Chandra. "Philosophy of the Tantras, Pt. 3." *Light of the East* 1, no. 6 (1892): 190–192.

Mitra, Adhar Chandra. "Philosophy of the Tantras, Pt. 4." *Light of the East* 1, no. 7 (1892): 216–219.

Mitra, Rajendralal. *The Yoga Aphorisms of Patanjali.* Calcutta: Asiatic Society of Bengal, 1883.

Mitra, Rajendralala. *Indo-Aryans: Contributions towards the Elucidation of Their Ancient and Mediaeval History.* Vol. 2. Calcutta: W. Newman, Edward Stanford, 1881.

Mittra, Peary Chand. *The Spiritual Stray Leaves.* Calcutta: Thacker Spink, 1879.

Mittra, Peary Chand. *Stray Thoughts on Spiritualism.* Calcutta: I. C. Bose, 1880.

Mookerjee, Kali Prosanna. *Notes on Engineering.* Patna: Kali Prosanna Mookerjee, 1873.

Mukerji, Kali Prasanna. "Magic among the Hindus." *Lucifer* 8, no. 46 (1891): 334–335.

Mukhopādhyāẏ, Debendranāth. *Daẏānander svaracita jībanˈbr̥tta.* Kolkata: Shishirkumar Ghosh, 1908.

Mukhopadhyay, Kaliprasanna. "The Tantric and Puranic Ideas of the Deity." *Theosophist* 3, no. 9 (1882): 226–227.

Mukhopadhyay, Sirish Chandra. *The Imitation of Sreekrishna: Quotations from the Hindu Religious Literature for Each Day in the Year.* Calcutta: J. N. Mullick, 1894.

Mukhurji, Amvikacharan. *Naldanga and the Naldanga Raj Family.* Calcutta: Hare Press, 1911.

Müller, Friedrich Max. *Auld Lang Syne, Second Series: My Indian Friends.* London: Longmans, Green, 1899.

Müller, Friedrich Max. *Chips from a German Workshop.* Vol. 1. London: Longmans, Green, 1868.

Müller, Friedrich Max. *India, What Can It Teach Us?* London: Longmans, Green, 1883.

Müller, Friedrich Max. *Introduction to the Science of Religion: Four Lectures Delivered at the Royal Institution, with Two Essays on False Analogies, and the Philosophy of Mythology.* London: Longmans, Green, 1873.

Müller, Friedrich Max. *Lectures on the Origin and Growth of Religion as Illustrated by the Religions of India.* London: Longmans, Green, 1878.

Müller, Friedrich Max. *The Life and Letters of the Right Honourable Friedrich Max Müller.* Edited by Georgina Adelaide Müller. Vol. 2. London: Green, 1902.

Müller, Friedrich Max. *Theosophy, or Psychological Religion.* London: Longmans, Green, 1893.

Olcott, Henry Steel. *Old Diary Leaves: The Only Authentic History of the Theosophical Society, Second Series, 1878–83.* London: Theosophical Publishing Society, Theosophist Office, 1900.

Olcott, Henry Steel. "Theosophy, the Scientific Basis of Religion." In *Theosophy: Religion and Occult Science*, edited by Henry Steel Olcott, 116–165. London: George Redway, 1885.

Oman, John Campbell. *The Brahmans, Theists and Muslims of India: Studies of Goddess Worship in Bengal, Caste, Brahmaism and Social Reform, with Descriptive Sketches of Curious Festivals, Ceremonies and Faquirs.* London: Fisher Unwin, 1907.

Pāl, Basantakumār. *Tantrācārya Śib'candra Bidyārṇab.* Kuc'bihār: Tribṛtta Prakāśanī, 1972.

Pal, Bipin Chandra. *Memories of My Life and Times.* Calcutta: Modern Book Agency, 1932.

Pal, Bipin Chandra. *Saint Bijayakrishna Goswami.* Calcutta: Bipinchandra Pal Institute, 1964.

Paul, Navinchandra. "A Treatise on the Yoga Philosophy 1." *Theosophist* 1, no. 12 (1880): 312–315.

Pratyagatmananda Saraswati, Swami. *The Complete Works of Swami Pratyagatmananda Saraswati.* Vol. 1. Chanduli: Saranam Asram, 1980.

Pratyagatmananda Saraswati, Swami. *Japasutram: The Science of Creative Sound.* Madras: Ganesh, 1971.

Pratyagatmananda Saraswati, Swami. *Science and Sādhanā.* Calcutta: Sm. Sudha Basu, 1962.

Pratyagatmananda Saraswati, Swami, and John Woodroffe. *Sadhana for Self-Realization (Mantras, Yantras and Tantras).* Madras: Ganesh, 1963.

Rai, Lala Lajpat. "Reform or Revival?" In *Lala Lajpat Rai: Writings and Speeches*, edited by Vijaya Chandra Joshi, vol. 1, 45–54. Delhi: University Publishers, 1966.

Ranade, Mahadeva Govind. "Revival and Reform." In *Religious and Social Reform: A Collection of Essays and Speeches by Mahadeva Govind Ranade*, edited by M. B. Kolasker, 156–178. Bombay: Gopal Narayen, G. Claridge, 1902.

Ravenshaw, Edward Cockburn. "Note on the Sri Jantra and Khat Kon Chakra (Six-Angled Wheel), or Double Equilateral Triangle." *Journal of the Royal Asiatic Society of Great Britain and Ireland* 13 (1852): 71–80.

Rāy, Śankar'nāth. *Bhārater Sādhak.* Vol. 11. Kolkata: Karuṇā Prakāśanī, 1958.

Report of the Second Anniversary of the Kasi Tattva Sabha Theosophical Society. Calcutta: Vedavyasa Press, 1887.

Saccidānanda Sarasvatī, Śrīmat· Svāmī. *Sanātan sādhan'tattva bā tantra-rahasya: Sādhan-pradīp.* Vol. 1. Calcutta: Nababhārat Pābliśārs, 1990.

Sachchidananda, Srimat Swami. "Theory and Practice of Tantra [1]." *Hindu Spiritual Magazine* 5, no. 7 (1910): 39–43.

Sachchidananda, Srimat Swami. "Theory and Practice of Tantra [2]." *Hindu Spiritual Magazine* 5, no. 10 (1910): 296–301.

Sachchidananda, Srimat Swami. "Theory and Practice of Tantra [3]." *Hindu Spiritual Magazine* 5, no. 12 (1911): 422–428.

Sachchidananda, Srimat Swami. "Theory and Practice of Tantra [4]." *Hindu Spiritual Magazine* 6, no. 1 (1911): 18–25.

Sachchidananda, Srimat Swami. "Theory and Practice of Tantra [5]." *Hindu Spiritual Magazine* 6, no. 2 (1911): 97–103.

Sachchidananda, Srimat Swami. "Theory and Practice of Tantra [6]." *Hindu Spiritual Magazine* 7, no. 1 (1912): 34–42.

Sachchidananda, Srimat Swami. "Theory and Practice of Tantra [7]." *Hindu Spiritual Magazine* 7, no. 6 (1912): 453–461.

Sachchidananda, Srimat Swami. "Theory and Practice of Tantra [8]." *Hindu Spiritual Magazine* 7, no. 12 (1913): 427–436.

Sachchidananda, Srimat Swami. "Theory and Practice of Tantra [9]." *Hindu Spiritual Magazine* 8, no. 2 (1913): 118–128.

Sachchidananda, Srimat Swami. *Universal Worship and Equality.* Calcutta: Bolaye Chand Mullick, 1911.

Sarasvatī, Dayānanda. "Arya Prakash: The Autobiography of Dayanund Saraswati, Swami 2." *Theosophist* 1, no. 3 (1879): 66–68.

Śāstrī, Harideb. *Bhārater śikṣita mahilā* (1910). 2nd ed. Calcutta: Kalej Pres Em Si Cakrabarttī, 1914.

Second Supplement to Who's Who in India, Brought up to 1914, Popular Edition. Lucknow: Newul Kishore Press, 1914.

Sen, Jaladhar. *Ātmajībanī o Smr̥ti-Tarpaṇ.* Kolkata: Jijñāsā Ejensij, 1960.

Shom, Bipin Behari. "Physical Errors of Hinduism." *Calcutta Review* 11 (1849): 397–444.

Sykes, William Henry. "Notes on the Religious, Moral, and Political State of India before the Mahomedan Invasion." *Journal of the Royal Asiatic Society of Great Britain and Ireland* 6 (1841): 248–450.

T.S. "The Tantras." *Theosophist* 4, no. 9 (1883): 226–228.

Tarkacuṛāmaṇi, Śaśadhar. *Dharmmabyākhyā.* Calcutta: Baṅgabāsī Ṣṭīm Meśin Pres, 1884.

Tarkacuṛāmaṇi, Śaśadhar. "Śrāddhatattva." *Bed'byās* 1, no. 1 (1886): 1–5.

Tarkacuṛāmaṇi, Śaśadhar. "Unnati ki abanati?" *Bed'byās* 1, no. 2 (1886): 33–39.

Tarkacuṛāmaṇi, Śaśadhar. "Unnati o abanatir artha [1]." *Bed'byās* 1, no. 5 (1886): 113–120.

Tarkacuṛāmaṇi, Śaśadhar. "Unnati o abanatir artha 2." *Bed'byās* 1, no. 8 (1886): 184–190.

Tatya, Tukaram, ed. *The Yoga Philosophy: Being the Text of Patanjali, with Bhoja Raja's Commentary, a Reprint of the English Translation of the above, by the Late Dr. Ballatyne and Govind Shastri Deva, to Which Are Added Extracts from Various Authors, with an Introduction by Colonel Henry S. Olcott, President of the Theosophical Society.* Bombay: Bombay Branch, Theosophical Society, 1882.

Tatya, Tukaram, ed. *The Yoga Philosophy: Being the Text of Patanjali, with Bhoja Raja's Commentary, with Their Translations in English by Dr. Ballantyne and Govin Shastri*

Deva, an Introduction by Col. Olcott and an Appendix. 2nd ed. Bombay: Subodha-Prakash Press, 1885.
Ṭhākur, Abanīndranāth, and Śrīrānī Canda. *Joṛāsāṁkor dhāre*. Calcutta: Biśvabhāratī Granthālaẏ, 1985.
The Indian Section of the Theosophical Society: Thirteenth Annual Convention Held at Adyar, Madras, December 28th and 29th, 1903, n.p., n.d.
Truth Seeker. "Yoga Philosophy." *Theosophist* 1, no. 4 (1880): 86–87.
Wilkins, William Joseph. *Modern Hinduism: An Account of the Religion and Life of the Hindus in Northern India*. London: T. Fisher Unwin, 1887.
Williams, Monier. *Hinduism*. London: Society for Promiting Christian Knowledge, Pott, Young, 1878.
Wilson, Horace Hayman. "Analysis of the Kah-Gyur." *Journal of the Asiatic Society of Bengal* 1 (1832): 375–392.
Wilson, Horace Hayman. "Sketch of the Religious Sects of the Hindus." *Asiatic Researches* 17 (1832): 169–313.
Wilson, Horace Hayman. "A Summary Account of the Civil and Religious Institutions of the Sikhs." *Journal of the Royal Asiatic Society of Great Britain and Ireland*. (1847): 43–59.
Wilson, Horace Hayman. *Two Lectures on the Religious Practices and Opinions of the Hindus*. Oxford: John Henry Parker, 1840.
Winternitz, Moriz. "Die Tantras und die Religion der Śāktas." *Ostasiastische Zeitschrift* 3 (1916): 153–163.
Winternitz, Moriz. *Geschichte der indischen Litteratur*. 2nd ed. Vol. 1. Leipzig: C. F. Amelangs Verlag, 1909.
Woodroffe, John. *Bharata Shakti: Collection of Addresses on Indian Culture*. 3rd ed. 1917; Madras: Ganesh, 1921.
Woodroffe, John. *The Garland of Letters (Varnamālā): Studies in the Mantra-Shāstra*. Madras: Ganesh, Luzac, 1922.
Woodroffe, John. *Is India Civilized? Essays on Indian Culture*. Madras: Ganesh, 1918.
Woodroffe, John. *The Seed of Race*. Madras: Ganesh, 1919.
Woodroffe, John. *The Serpent Power: Being the Shat-Chakra-Nirupana and Paduka-Panchaka*. 2nd ed. Madras: Ganseh, 1924.
Woodroffe, John. *Shakti and Shakta: Essays and Addresses on the Shakta Tantrashastra*. 3rd ed. Madras: Ganesh, Luzac, 1929.
Woodroffe, John. *The World as Power: Power as Life*. Madras: Ganesh, 1922.
Woodroffe, John. *The World as Power: Power as Mind*. Madras: Ganesh, 1922.
Woodroffe, John. *The World as Power: Reality*. Madras: Ganesh, 1922.
Woodroffe, John, and Pramatha Nātha Mukhopādhyāya. *Mahāmāyā: The World as Power: Power as Consciousness*. Madras: Ganesh, 1929.
Woodroffe, John, and Pramathanatha Mukhopadhyaya. *The World as Power: Causality and Continuity*. Madras: Ganesh, 1923.
Woodroffe, John, and Pramathanātha Mukhopādhyāya. *The World as Power: Power as Matter*. Madras: Ganesh, 1923.

Secondary Sources

Albanese, Catherine L. *A Republic of Mind and Spirit: A Cultural History of American Metaphysical Religion*. New Haven, CT: Yale University Press, 2007.

Alper, Harvey P. *Understanding Mantras*. Albany: State University of New York Press, 1989.

Alter, Joseph S. *Yoga in Modern India: The Body between Science and Philosophy*. Princeton, NJ: Princeton University Press, 2004.

Altman, Michael J. *Heathen, Hindoo, Hindu: American Representations of India, 1721–1893*. New York: Oxford University Press, 2017.

Arvidsson, Stefan. *Aryan Idols: Indo-European Mythology as Ideology and Science*. Chicago: University of Chicago Press, 2006.

Asad, Talal. *Formations of the Secular: Christianity, Islam, Modernity*. Stanford, CA: Stanford University Press, 2003.

Asad, Talal. *Genealogies of Religion: Discipline and Reasons of Power in Christianity and Islam*. Baltimore, MD: Johns Hopkins University Press, 1993.

Asher, Catherine B., and Cynthia Talbot. *India before Europe*. New York: Cambridge University Press, 2006.

Asprem, Egil. "Beyond the West: Towards a New Comparativism in the Study of Esotericism." *Correspondences* 2, no. 1 (2014): 3–33.

Asprem, Egil. *The Problem of Disenchantment: Scientific Naturalism and Esoteric Discourse, 1900–1939*. Numen Book Series 147. Leiden: Brill, 2014.

Asprem, Egil. "Theosophical Attitudes towards Science: Past and Present." In *Handbook of the Theosophical Current*, edited by Olav Hammer and Mikael Rothstein, 405–427. Leiden: Brill, 2013.

Asprem, Egil, and Julian Strube. "Afterword: Outlines of a New Roadmap." In *New Approaches to the Study of Esotericism*, edited by Egil Asprem and Julian Strube, 241–251. Leiden: Brill, 2021.

Asprem, Egil, and Julian Strube. "Esotericism's Expanding Horizon: Why This Book Came to Be." In *New Approaches to the Study of Esotericism*, edited by Egil Asprem and Julian Strube, 1–19. Leiden: Brill, 2021.

Asprem, Egil, and Julian Strube, eds. *New Approaches to the Study of Esotericism*. Leiden: Brill, 2021.

Bagchi, Moni. *Swami Abhedananda: A Spiritual Biography*. 3rd ed. Calcutta: Ramakrishna Vedanta Math, 2018.

Baier, Karl. *Meditation und Moderne: Zur Genese eines Kernbereichs moderner Spiritualität in der Wechselwirkung zwischen Westeuropa, Nordamerika und Asien*. 2 vols. Würzburg: Königshausen & Neumann, 2009.

Baier, Karl. "Mesmeric Yoga and the Development of Meditation within the Theosophical Society." *Theosophical History* 16, nos. 3–4 (2012): 151–161.

Baier, Karl. "Theosophical Orientalism and the Structures of Intercultural Transfer: Annotations on the Appropriation of the Cakras in Early Theosophy." In *Theosophical Appropriations: Esotericism, Kabbalah, and the Transformation of Traditions*, edited by Julie Chajes and Boaz Huss, 309–354. Beer Sheva: Ben-Gurion University of the Negev Press, 2016.

Bakker, Justine M. "Hidden Presence: Race and/in the History, Construct, and Study of Western Esotericism." *Religion* 50, no. 4 (2020): 479–503.

Ballantyne, Tony. *Entanglements of Empire: Missionaries, Māori, and the Question of the Body*. Durham, NC: Duke University Press, 2014.

Ballantyne, Tony. *Orientalism and Race: Aryanism in the British Empire*. Houndmills: Palgrave Macmillan, 2002.

Ballantyne, Tony. "The Persistence of the Gods: Religion in the Modern World." In *World Histories from Below: Disruption and Dissent, 1750 to the Present*, edited by Antoinette Burton and Tony Ballantyne, 137–168. London: Bloomsbury Academic, 2016.

Ballantyne, Tony. *Webs of Empire: Locating New Zealand's Colonial Past.* Wellington: Bridget Williams Books, 2012.

Banerjee, Milinda. "'All This is Indeed Brahman': Rammohun Roy and a 'Global' History of the Rights-Bearing Self." *Asian Review of World Histories* 3, no. 1 (2015): 81–112.

Banerjee, Milinda. "German Foundations of Indian Nationalism: Hohenzollerns, Habsburgs, and Hegel in Indian Political Thought, ca. 1870–1910." (forthcoming).

Banerjee, Milinda. *The Mortal God: Imagining the Sovereign in Colonial India.* Cambridge: Cambridge University Press, 2018.

Banerjee, Milinda. "Transversal Histories and Transcultural Afterlives: Indianized Renditions of Jean Bodin in Global Intellectual History." In *Engaging Transculturality: Concepts, Key Terms, Case Studies*, edited by Laila Abu-Er-Rub, Christiane Brosius, Sebastian Meurer, Diamantis Panagiotopoulos, and Susan Richter, 155–169. Abingdon: Routledge, 2019.

Banerjee, Sumanta. *Logic in a Popular Form: Essays on Popular Religion in Bengal.* London: Seagull, 2010.

Banerji, Sures Chandra. *Tantra in Bengal: A Study in Its Origin, Development, and Influence.* Calcutta: Naya Prokash, 1978.

Banerji, Sures Chandra. *Tantra in Bengal: A Study in Its Origin, Development, and Influence.* 2nd ed. New Delhi: Manohar, 1992.

Bayly, Christopher A. *The Birth of the Modern World, 1780–1914: Global Connections and Comparisons.* Malden, MA: Blackwell, 2004.

Bergunder, Michael. "Comparison in the Maelstrom of Historicity: A Postcolonial Perspective on Comparative Religion." In *Interreligious Comparisons in Religious Studies and Theology*, edited by Perry Schmidt-Leukel and Andreas Nehring, 34–52. London: Bloomsbury Academic, 2016.

Bergunder, Michael. "Die Bhagavadgita im 19. Jahrhundert." In *Westliche Formen des Hinduismus in Deutschland*, edited by Michael Bergunder, 187–216. Halle: Franckesche Stiftungen, 2006.

Bergunder, Michael. "Experiments with Theosophical Truth: Gandhi, Esotericism, and Global Religious History." *Journal of the American Academy of Religion* 82 (2014): 398–426.

Bergunder, Michael. "Hinduism, Theosophy, and the Bhagavad Gita within a Global Religious History of the Nineteenth Century." In *Theosophy across Boundaries: Transcultural and Interdisciplinary Perspectives on a Modern Esoteric Movement*, edited by Hans Martin Krämer and Julian Strube, 65–107. Albany: State University of New York Press, 2020.

Bergunder, Michael. *Indische Religionsgeschichte vom 16. bis zum frühen 20. Jahrhundert.* forthcoming.

Bergunder, Michael. "'Religion' and 'Science' within a Global Religious History." *Aries* 16, no. 1 (2016): 86–141.

Bergunder, Michael. "Umkämpfte Historisierung: Die Zwillingsgeburt von 'Religion' und 'Esoterik' in der zweiten Hälfte des 19. Jahrhunderts und das Programm einer globalen Religionsgeschichte." In *Wissen um Religion: Erkenntnis—Interesse: Epistemologie und Episteme in Religionswissenschaft und Interkultureller Theologie*, edited by Klaus Hock, 47–131. Leipzig: Evangelische Verlagsanstalt, 2020.

Bergunder, Michael. "What Is Esotericism? Cultural Studies Approaches and the Problems of Definition in Religious Studies." *Method and Theory in the Study of Religion* 22, no. 1 (2010): 9–36.

Bergunder, Michael. "What Is Religion? The Unexplained Subject Matter of Religious Studies." *Method and Theory in the Study of Religion* 26 (2014): 246–286.

Bevir, Mark. "In Opposition to the Raj." *History of Political Thought* 19 (1998): 61–77.

Bevir, Mark. "Theosophy and the Origins of the Indian National Congress." *International Journal for Hindu Studies* 7, nos. 1–3 (2003): 99–115.

Bevir, Mark. "Theosophy as a Political Movement." In *Gurus and Their Followers*, edited by Antony Copley, 159–179. Delhi: Oxford University Press, 2000.

Bhabha, Homi K. *The Location of Culture*. 1994; London: Routledge, 2004.

Bhatia, Varuni. "Images of Nabadwip: Place, Evidence and Inspiration." In *Time, History and the Religious Imaginary in South Asia*, edited by Anne Murphy, 167–185. Abingdon: Routledge, 2011.

Bhatia, Varuni. "The Psychic Chaitanya: Global Occult and Vaishnavism in *Fin de Siècle* Bengal." *Journal of Hindu Studies* 13 (2020): 10–29.

Bhatia, Varuni. "Sisir's Tears: *Bhakti* and Belonging in Colonial Bengal." *International Journal of Hindu Studies* 21 (2017): 1–24.

Bhatia, Varuni. *Unforgetting Chaitanya: Vaishnavism and Cultures of Devotion in Colonial Bengal*. New York: Oxford University Press, 2017.

Bhattacharya, Nandini. "Anglicized—Sanskritized—Vernacularized: Translational Politics of Primer Writing in Colonial Bengal." In *Language Policy and Education in India: Documents, Contexts and Debates*, edited by M. Sridhar and Sunita Mishra, 166–183. Oxon: Routledge, 2017.

Bhattacharya, Tithi. *The Sentinels of Culture: Class, Education, and the Colonial Intellectual in Bengal (1848–85)*. New Delhi: Oxford University Press, 2005.

Biernacki, Loriliai. *Renowned Goddess of Desire: Women, Sex, and Speech in Tantra*. Oxford: Oxford University Press, 2007.

Birch, Jason. "The Meaning of Haṭha in Early Haṭhayoga." *Journal of the American Oriental Society* 131, no. 4 (2011): 527–554.

Birch, Jason. "Rājayoga: The Reincarnations of the King of All Yogas." *International Journal of Hindu Studies* 17, no. 3 (2013): 399–442.

Bogdan, Henrik. "Challenging the Morals of Western Society: The Use of Ritualized Sex in Contemporary Occultism." *Pomegranate* 8, no. 2 (2006): 211–246.

Bogdan, Henrik. "Reception of Occultism in India: The Case of the Holy Order of Krishna." In *Occultism in a Global Perspective*, edited by Henrik Bogdan and Gordan Djurdjevic, 177–201. Abingdon: Routledge, 2014.

Bolle, Kees W. *The Persistence of Religion: An Essay on Tantrism and Sri Aurobindo's Philosophy*. Leiden: E. J. Brill, 1971.

Bordeaux, Joel. "The Mythic King: Raja Krishnacandra and Early Modern Bengal." Ph.D. thesis, Columbia University, 2015.

Bose, Neilesh. *Recasting the Region: Language, Culture, and Islam in Colonial Bengal*. Delhi: Oxford University Press, 2014.

Bouillier, Véronique. *Itinérance et vie monastique: Les ascètes Nāth Yogīs en Inde contemporaine*. Paris: Maison des Sciences de l'Homme, 2008.

Braude, Ann. *Radical Spirits: Spiritualism and Women's Rights in Nineteenth-Century America*. Boston: Beacon Press, 1989.

Brooks, Douglas. *The Secret of the Three Cities: An Introduction to Hindu Śākta Tantrism.* Chicago: University of Chicago Press, 1990.

Brown, Judith M., Robert Eric Frykenberg, and Alaine M. Low. *Christians, Cultural Interactions, and India's Religious Traditions.* Grand Rapids, MI: W. B. Eerdmans, RoutledgeCurzon, 2002.

Bühnemann, Gudrun. "The Śāradātilakatantra on Yoga: A New Edition and Translation of Chapter 25." *Bulletin of SOAS* 74, no. 2 (2011): 205–235.

Burns, Dylan. "Receptions of Revelations: A Future for the Study of Esotericism and Antiquity." In *New Approaches to the Study of Esotericism*, edited by Egil Asprem and Julian Strube, 20–44. Leiden: Brill, 2021.

Cantú, Keith. "'Don't Take Any Wooden Nickels': Western Esotericism, Yoga, and the Discourse of Authenticity." In *New Approaches to the Study of Esotericism*, edited by Egil Asprem and Julian Strube, 109–126. Leiden: Brill, 2021.

Cantú, Keith. "Sri Sabhapati Swami." In *Brill's Encyclopedia of Hinduism*, edited by Knut A. Jacobsen. Leiden: Brill, forthcoming.

Carpenter, Frederic Ives. *Emerson and Asia.* Cambridge, MA: Harvard University Press, 1930.

Certeau, Michel de. *The Writing of History.* New York: Columbia University Press, 1988.

Chajes, Julie. *Recycled Lives: A History of Rebirth in Blavatsky's Theosophy.* New York: Oxford University Press, 2019.

Chakrabarti, Kunal. *Religious Process: The Purāṇas and the Making of a Regional Tradition.* New Delhi: Oxford University Press, 2001.

Chakrabarty, Dipesh. *Provincializing Europe: Postcolonial Thought and Historical Difference.* Princeton, NJ: Princeton University Press, 2000.

Chakravarti, Ananya. *The Empire of Apostles: Religion, Accommodation, and the Imagination of Empire in Early Modern Brazil and India.* New Delhi: Oxford University Press, 2018.

Chakravarti, Chintaharan. *Tantras: Studies on Their Religion and Literature.* Calcutta: Punthi Pustak, 1963.

Chatterjee, Kumkum. "Goddess Encounters: Mughals, Monsters and the Goddess in Bengal." *Modern Asian Studies* 47, no. 5 (2013): 1435–1487.

Chatterjee, Partha. *The Black Hole of Empire: History of a Global Practice of Power.* Princeton, NJ: Princeton University Press, 2012.

Chatterjee, Partha. "Our Modernity." In *Empire and Nation: Selected Essays*, edited by Partha Chatterjee, 136–152. New York: Columbia University Press, 2010.

Chatterji, Joya. *Bengal Divided: Hindu Communalism and Partition, 1932–1947.* Cambridge: Cambridge University Press, 2002.

Chidester, David. *Savage Systems: Colonialism and Comparative Religion in Southern Africa.* Charlottesville: University Press of Virginia, 1996.

Choudhuri, Keshab. *The Mother and Passionate Politics.* Calcutta: Vidyodaya Library, 1979.

Christy, Arthur Edward. *The Orient in American Transcendentalism: A Study of Emerson, Thoreau, and Alcott.* New York: Columbia University Press, 1932.

Conkin, Paul K. *American Originals: Homemade Varieties of Christianity.* Chapel Hill: University of North Carolina Press, 1997.

Conrad, Sebastian. "A Cultural History of Global Transformation." In *A History of the World*, vol. 4: *An Emerging Modern World, 1750–1870*, edited by Sebastian Conrad and Jürgen Osterhammel, 411–659. Cambridge, MA: Harvard University Press, 2018.

Conrad, Sebastian. "Greek in Their Own Way: Writing India and Japan into the World History of Architecture at the Turn of the Twentieth Century." *American Historical Review* 125, no. 1 (2020): 19–53.

Conrad, Sebastian. *What Is Global History?* Princeton, NJ: Princeton University Press, 2016.

Conrad, Sebastian, and Shalini Randeria. "Einleitung: Geteilte Geschichten—Europa in einer postkolonialen Welt." In *Jenseits des Eurozentrismus: Postkoloniale Perspektiven in den Geschichts- und Kulturwissenschaften*, edited by Sebastian Conrad, Shalini Randeria, and Regina Römhild, 32–70. Frankfurt am Main: Campus Verlag, 2013.

Crockford, Susannah. "What Do Jade Eggs Tell Us about the Category 'Esotericism'? Spirituality, Neoliberalism, Secrecy, and Commodities." In *New Approaches to the Study of Esotericism*, edited by Egil Asprem and Julian Strube, 201–216. Leiden: Brill, 2021.

Crook, Nigel. *The Transmission of Knowledge in South Asia: Essays on Education, Religion, History, and Politics*. Delhi: Oxford University Press, 1996.

Crossley, Pamela Kyle. *What Is Global History?* Cambridge, UK: Polity, 2008.

Cyranka, Daniel. *Mahomet: Repräsentationen des Propheten in deutschsprachiger Literatur des 18. Jahrhunderts*. Göttingen: Vandenhoeck & Ruprecht, 2018.

Cyranka, Daniel. "Religious Revolutionaries and Spiritualism in Germany around 1848." *Aries* 16, no. 1 (2016): 13–48.

Das, Rahul Peter. "Bengalischer Nationalismus und die Konstruktion einer austroasiatischen Vergangenheit." In *"Arier" und "Draviden": Konstruktionen der Vergangenheit als Grundlage für Selbst- und Fremdwahmehmungen Südasiens*, edited by Michael Bergunder and Rahul Peter Das, 181–205. Halle: Verlag der Franckeschen Stiftungen, 2002.

Das, Rahul Peter. "Problematic Aspects of the Sexual Rituals of the Bauls of Bengal." *Journal of the American Oriental Society* 112, no. 3 (1992): 388–432.

Dasgupta, Ratan. "Maharaja Krishnachandra: Religion, Caste and Polity in Eighteenth Century Bengal." *Indian Historical Review* 38, no. 2 (2011): 225–242.

Das Gupta, Shashibhusan. *Obscure Religious Cults*. 3rd ed. Calcutta: K. L. Mukhopadhyay, 1969.

Datta, Hārādhan. *Śib'candra Bidyārṇab*. Calcutta: Adhyaẏan, 1967.

De Michelis, Elizabeth. *A History of Modern Yoga: Patañjali and Western Esotericism*. London: Continuum, 2004.

Derrett, John D. M. "A Juridical Fabrication of Early British India: The Mahānirvāṇa-Tantra." *Zeitschrift für Rechtswissenschaft* 69, no. 2 (1968): 138–181.

Derrett, John D. M. "A Juridical Fabrication of Early British India: The Mahānirvāṇa-Tantra." In *Essays in Classical and Modern Hindu Law*, edited by John D. M. Derrett, vol. 2, 138–181. Leiden: E. J. Brill, 1977.

Deshpande, Sharad. "G. R. Malkani: Reinventing Classical Advaita Vedānta." In *Philosophy in Colonial India*, edited by Sharad Deshpande, 119–135. New Delhi: Springer, 2015.

Deveney, John Patrick. *Astral Projection or Liberation of the Double and the Work of the Early Theosophical Society*. Fullerton, CA: Theosophical History, 1997.

Dey, Santanu. "Piety in Print: The Vaishnava Periodicals of Colonial Bengal." *Journal of Hindu Studies* 13, no. 1 (2020): 30–53. https://doi.org/https://doi.org/10.1093/jhs/hiaa003.

Djurdjevic, Gordan. "The Great Beast as a Tantric Hero: The Role of Yoga and Tantra in Aleister Crowley's Magick." In *Aleister Crowley and Western Esotericism*, edited by Henrik Bogdan and Martin P. Starr, 107–140. Oxford: Oxford University Press, 2012.

Djurdjevic, Gordan. *India and the Occult: The Influence of South Asian Spirituality on Modern Western Occultism*. New York: Palgrave Macmillan, 2014.

Dodson, Michael S., and Brian A. Hatcher. "Introduction." In *Trans-Colonial Modernities in South Asia*, edited by Michael S. Dodson and Brian A. Hatcher, 1–12. Abingdon: Routledge, 2012.

Drayton, Richard, and David Motadel. "Discussion: The Futures of Global History." *Journal of Global History* 13, no. 1 (2018): 1–21.

Duara, Prasenjit. "Asien neu denken: Zum Verständnis einer zusammenwachsenden Region." In *Jenseits des Eurozentrismus: Postkoloniale Perspektiven in den Geschichts- und Kulturwissenschaften*, edited by Sebastian Conrad, Shalini Randeria, and Regina Römhild, 526–553. Frankfurt am Main: Campus Verlag, 2013.

Dyczkowski, Mark S. G. *The Canon of the Śaivāgama and the Kubjikā Tantras of the Western Kaula Tradition*. Albany: State University of New York Press, 1988.

Dyczkowski, Mark S. G. *A Journey in the World of Tantras*. Varanasi: Indica Books, 2004.

Eckert, Andreas, and Shalini Randeria. "Geteilte Globalisierung." In *Vom Imperialismus zum Empire: Nichtwestliche Perspektiven auf Globalisierung*, edited by Andreas Eckert and Shalini Randeria, 9–33. Frankfurt am Main: Suhrkamp, 2009.

Edelman, Nicole. *Voyantes, guérisseuses et visionnaires en France*. Paris: Michel, 1995.

Ehrlich, Joshua. "New Lights on Raja Krishnachandra and Early Hindu-European Intellectual Exchange." *Journal of the Royal Asiatic Society* 31, no. 1 (2021): 159–171.

Eisenstadt, Shmuel N. *Multiple Modernities*. New Brunswick, NJ: Transaction, 2002.

Eliade, Mircea. *Yoga: Immortality and Freedom*. New York: Pantheon Books, 1958.

Eßbach, Wolfgang. *Religionssoziologie*. Vol. 1: *Glaubenskrieg und Revolution als Wiege neuer Religionen*. Paderborn: Wilhelm Fink, 2014.

Faivre, Antoine. *Access to Western Esotericism*. Albany: State University of New York Press, 1994.

Finley, Stephen C., Biko Mandela Gray, and Hugh R. Page, Jr. "Africana Esoteric Studies and Western Intellectual Hegemony: A Continuing Conversation with Western Esotericism." *History of Religions* 60, no. 3 (2021): 163–187.

Finley, Stephen C., Margarita Simon Guillory, and Hugh R. Page Jr., eds. *Esotericism in African American Religious Experience: "There Is a Mystery."* Leiden: Brill, 2014.

Fischer-Tiné, Harald. *Der Gurukul Kangri oder die Erziehung der Arya-Nation: Kolonialismus, Hindureform und "nationale" Bildung in Britisch-Indien (1897–1922)*. Würzburg: Ergon-Verlag, 2003.

Fischer-Tiné, Harald. "From Brahmacharya to 'Conscious Race Culture': Victorian Discourses of 'Science' and Hindu Traditions in Early Indian Nationalism." In *Beyond Representation: Colonial and Postcolonial Constructions of Indian Identity*, edited by Crispin Bates, 230–259. Oxford: Oxford University Press, 2006.

Fischer-Tiné, Harald. "Inventing a National Past: The Case of Ramdev's Bharatvarsh ka Itihas (1910–14)." In *Hinduism in Public and Private Reform, Hindutva, Gender, and Sampraday*, edited by Antony Copley, 110–139. New Delhi: Oxford University Press, 2003.

Fischer-Tiné, Harald. "Marrying Global History with South Asian History: Potential and Limits of Global Microhistory in a Regional Inflection." *Comparativ* 28, no. 5 (2018): 49–74.

Fischer-Tiné, Harald, and Susanne Gehrmann. "Introduction: Empires, Boundaries, and the Production of Difference." In *Empires and Boundaries: Rethinking Race, Class, and*

Gender in Colonial Settings, edited by Harald Fischer-Tiné and Susanne Gehrmann, 1–22. Abingdon: Routledge, 2008.

Fisher, Elaine M. *Hindu Pluralism: Religion and the Public Sphere in Early Modern South India.* Oakland: University of California Press, 2017.

Fitzgerald, Timothy. *The Ideology of Religious Studies.* Oxford: Oxford University Press, 2000.

Fitzgerald, Timothy. "Introduction." In *Religion and the Secular: Historical and Colonial Formations*, edited by Timothy Fitzgerald, 1–12. London: Equinox, 2007.

Flood, Gavin D. *The Tantric Body: The Secret Tradition of Hindu Religion.* London: I. B. Tauris, 2006.

Forbes, Geraldine Hancock. *Positivism in Bengal: A Case Study in the Transmission and Assimilation of an Ideology.* Calcutta: Minerva Associates, 1975.

Forray, Brett. "William Q. Judge's and Annie Besant's Views of Brahmin Theosophists." *Theosophical History* 10, no. 1 (2004): 5–34.

Foucault, Michel. "Nietzsche, Genealogy, History." In *The Foucault Reader*, edited by Paul Rabinow, 76–100. New York: Pantheon Books, 1984.

Frykenberg, Robert Eric. "Constructions of Hinduism at the Nexus of History and Religion." *Journal of Interdisciplinary History* 23, no. 3 (1993): 523–550.

Ganeri, Jonardon. *The Lost Age of Reason: Philosophy in Early Modern India, 1450–1700.* Oxford: Oxford University Press, 2011.

Ghai, R. K. *Shuddhi Movement in India: A Study of Its Socio-Political Dimensions.* New Delhi: Commonwealth, 1990.

Ghobrial, John-Paul A. "Introduction: Seeing the World Like a Microhistorian." *Past & Present* 242, no. 14 (2019): 1–22.

Ghosh, Abhishek. "Innate Intuition: An Intellectual History of Sahajajñāna and Sahaja Samādhi in Brahmoism and Modern Vaiṣṇavism." *Religions* 10, no. 6 (2019): 1–26.

Ghosh, Semanti. *Different Nationalisms: Bengal, 1905–1947.* Oxford: Oxford University Press, 2016.

Godwin, Joscelyn. *The Theosophical Enlightenment.* Albany: State University of New York Press, 1994.

Goldsmith, Barbara. *Other Powers. The Age of Suffrage, Spiritualism, and the Scandalous Victoria Woodhull.* New York: Knopf, 1998.

Gombrich, Richard F. *Theravāda Buddhism: A Social History from Ancient Benares to Modern Colombo.* London: Routledge & Kegan Paul, 1988.

Goodrick-Clarke, Nicholas. "Western Esoteric Traditions and Theosophy." In *Handbook of the Theosophical Current*, edited by Olav Hammer, 261–307. Leiden: Brill, 2013.

Gordon, Leonard A. *Bengal: The Nationalist Movement, 1876–1940.* New York: Columbia University Press, 1974.

Goudriaan, Teun, and Sanjukta Gupta. *Hindu Tantric and Śākta Literature.* Wiesbaden: Harrassowitz, 1981.

Granholm, Kennet. "Locating the West: Problematizing the 'Western' in Western Esotericism and Occultism." In *Occultism in a Global Perspective*, edited by Henrik Bogdan and Gordan Djurdjevic, 17–36. London: Acumen, 2013.

Granholm, Kennet. "The Serpent Rises in the West: Positive Orientalism and Reinterpretation of Tantra in the Western Left-Hand Path." In *Transformations and Transfer of Tantra in Asia and Beyond*, edited by István Keul, 495–519. Religion and Society. Berlin: De Gruyter, 2012.

Gray, Biko. "The Traumatic Mysticism of Othered Others: Blackness, Islam, and Esotericism in the Five Percenters." *Correspondences* 7, no. 1 (2019): 201–237.

Green, Nile. "The Global Occult: An Introduction." *History of Religions* 54, no. 4 (2015): 383–393.

Gupta, Sanjukta, Dirk Jan Hoens, and Teun Goudriaan. *Hindu Tantrism.* Leiden: Brill, 1979.

Gupta, Swarupa. *Notions of Nationhood in Bengal: Perspectives on Samaj, c. 1867–1905.* Leiden: Brill, 2009.

Gura, Philip F. *American Transcendentalism: A History.* New York: Hill and Wang, 2007.

Hackett, Paul G. *Theos Bernard, the White Lama: Tibet, Yoga, and American Religious Life.* New York: Columbia University Press, 2012.

Halbfass, Wilhelm. *India and Europe: An Essay in Understanding.* Albany: State University of New York Press, 1988.

Halbfass, Wilhelm. *Indien und Europa: Perspektiven ihrer geistigen Begegnung.* Basel: Schwabe, 1981.

Hall, Stuart. "The West and the Rest: Discourse and Power." In *Formations of Modernity*, edited by Stuart Hall and Bram Gieben, 275–320. Cambridge, UK: Polity Press, Blackwell, 1992.

Hammer, Olav, and Mikael Rothstein, eds. *Handbook of the Theosophical Current.* Leiden: Brill, 2013.

Hanegraaff, Wouter. *Esotericism and the Academy: Rejected Knowledge in Western Culture.* Cambridge: Cambridge University Press, 2012.

Hanegraaff, Wouter. "The Globalization of Esotericism." *Correspondences* 3, no. 1 (2015): 55–91.

Hanegraaff, Wouter. *New Age Religion and Western Culture: Esotericism in the Mirror of Secular Thought.* Leiden: State University of New York Press, 1996.

Hanegraaff, Wouter. *Western Esotericism: A Guide for the Perplexed.* London: Bloomsbury Academic, 2013.

Hanegraaff, Wouter. "Western Esotericism and the Orient in the First Theosophical Society." In *Theosophy across Boundaries: Transcultural and Interdisciplinary Perspectives on a Modern Esoteric Movement*, edited by Hans Martin Krämer and Julian Strube, 29–64. Albany: State University of New York Press, 2020.

Harder, Hans. "Bankimchandra Chattopadhyay (1838–94)—Begründer kommunalistischer Ideologien?" In *Religion—Macht—Gewalt: Religiöser "Fundamentalismus" und Hindu-Moslem-Konflikte in Südasien*, edited by Christian Weiß, Tom Weichert, Evelin Hust, and Harald Fischer-Tiné, 57–70. Frankfurt am Main: IKO-Verlag für Interkulturelle Kommunikation, 1996.

Harder, Hans. "Bankimchandra Chattopadhyay and Modern Hinduism." In *The Oxford History of Hinduism: Modern Hinduism*, edited by Torkel Brekke, 54–71. Oxford: Oxford University Press, 2019.

Harder, Hans, ed. *Bankimchandra Chattopadhyay's Śrīmadbhagabadgītā: Translation and Analysis.* New Delhi: Manohar, 2001.

Harder, Hans. "Migrant Literary Genres: Transcultural Moments and Scales of Transculturality." In *Engaging Transculturality: Concepts, Key Terms, Case Studies*, edited by Laila Abu-Er-Rub, Christiane Brosius, Sebastian Meurer, Diamantis Panagiotopoulos, and Susan Richter, 185–195. Abingdon: Routledge, 2019.

Harder, Hans. "The Modern Babu and the Metropolis: Reassessing Early Bengali Narrative Prose (1821–1862)." In *India's Literary History: Essays on the Nineteenth Century*, edited by Stuart Blackburn and Vasudha Dalmia, 358–401. Delhi: Permanent Black, 2004.

Harder, Hans. "Populärversionen des 'Arierturms' in Indien um die Wende zum 20. Jahrhundert." In *"Arier" und "Draviden": Konstruktionen der Vergangenheit als Grundlage für Selbst- und Fremdwahrnehmungen Südasiens*, edited by Michael Bergunder and Rahul Peter Das, 79–92. Halle: Verlag der Franckeschen Stiftungen, 2002.

Harlass, Ulrich. *Die orientalische Wende der Theosophischen Gesellschaft*. Berlin: De Gruyter, 2021.

Hashimoto, Yorimitsu. "An Irish Theosophist's Pan-Asianism or Fant-asia? James Cousins and Gurcharan Singh." In *Theosophy across Boundaries: Transcultural and Interdisciplinary Perspectives on a Modern Esoteric Movement*, edited by Hans Martin Krämer and Julian Strube, 345–371. Albany: State University of New York Press, 2020.

Hatcher, Brian A. *Bourgeois Hinduism, or the Faith of the Modern Vedantists: Rare Discourses from Early Colonial Bengal*. New York: Oxford University Press, 2008.

Hatcher, Brian A. "Colonial Hinduism." In *A Continuum Companion to Hindu Studies*, edited by Jessica Frazier, 171–184. New York: Continuum, 2011.

Hatcher, Brian A. *Eclecticism and Modern Hindu Discourse*. New York: Oxford University Press, 1999.

Hatcher, Brian A. "Great Men Waking: Paradigms in the History of the Historiography of the Bengal Renaissance." In *Bengal: Rethinking History: Essays in Historiography*, edited by Sekhar Bandyopadhyay, 135–163. New Delhi: Manohar, 2001.

Hatcher, Brian A. *Hinduism before Reform*. Cambridge, MA: Harvard University Press, 2020.

Hatcher, Brian A. "Introduction." In *Hinduism in the Modern World*, edited by Brian A. Hatcher, 1–12. Abingdon: Routledge, 2015.

Hatcher, Brian A. "Pandits at Work: The Modern Shastric Imaginary in Early Colonial Bengal." In *Trans-Colonial Modernities in South Asia*, edited by Michael S. Dodson and Brian A. Hatcher, 45–67. Abingdon: Routledge, 2012.

Hatcher, Brian A. "Remembering Rammohan: An Essay on the (Re-)emergence of Modern Hinduism." *History of Religions* 46, no. 1 (2006): 50–80.

Hazra, Rajendra Chandra. "Influence of Tantra on the Smṛti-Nibandhas [1]." *Annals of the Bhandarkar Oriental Research Institute* 15, nos. 3–4 (1933): 220–235.

Hazra, Rajendra Chandra. "Influence of Tantra on the Smṛti-Nibandhas Part 2." *Annals of the Bhandarkar Oriental Research Institute* 16, nos. 3–4 (1934): 202–211.

Hazra, Rajendra Chandra. "Influence of Tantra on the Tattvas of Raghunandana." *Indian Historical Quarterly* 9 (1933): 678–704.

Heehs, Peter. "Aurobindo Ghose and Revolutionary Terrorism." *South Asia* 15, no. 2 (1992): 47–69.

Heehs, Peter. *The Bomb in Bengal: The Rise of Revolutionary Terrorism in India, 1900–1910*. New Delhi: Oxford University Press, 1993.

Heehs, Peter. *Sri Aurobindo, a Brief Biography*. Delhi: Oxford University Press, 1989.

Heilijgers-Seelen, Dory. "The Doctrine of the Ṣaṭcakra According to the Kubjikāmata." In *The Sanskrit Tradition and Tantrism*, edited by Teun Goudriaan, 56–65. Leiden: Brill, 1990.

Hermann, Adrian. "Buddhist Modernism in 19th Century Siam and the Discourse of Scientific Buddhism: Towards a Global History of 'Religion.'" *Journal of the South and Southeast Asian Association for the Study of Culture and Religion* 5 (2011): 33–56.

Hermann, Adrian. "A Call for a Permissible Plurality within Theory-Building in a Time of Excess." *Method & Theory in the Study of Religion* 30, no. 4 (2018): 487–497.

Hermann, Adrian. *Unterscheidungen der Religion: Analysen zum globalen Religionsdiskurs und dem Problem der Differenzierung von "Religion" in buddhistischen Kontexten des 19. und frühen 20. Jahrhunderts.* Göttingen: Vandenhoeck & Ruprecht, 2015.

Hock, Klaus. "Transkulturelle Perspektiven auf polyzentrische Strukturen." In *Veränderte Landkarten auf dem Weg zu einer polyzentrischen Geschichte des Weltchristentums: Festschrift für Klaus Koschorke zum 65. Geburtstag*, edited by Ciprian D. Burlacioiu and Adrian Hermann, 295–314. Wiesbaden: Harrassowitz, 2013.

Hodder, Alan D. "'The Best of Brahmins': India Reading Emerson Reading India." In *Ralph Waldo Emerson: Bicentenary Appraisals*, edited by Barry Tharaud, 177–201. Trier: Wissenschaftlicher Verlag, 2006.

Iyengar, K. R. *Sri Aurobindo: A Biography and a History.* 3rd ed. Vol. 1. Pondicherry: Sri Aurobindo International Centre of Education, 1972.

Jackson, Carl T. *The Oriental Religions and American Thought: Nineteenth-Century Explorations.* Westport, CT: Greenwood Press, 1981.

Jain, Andrea R. *Selling Yoga: From Counterculture to Pop Culture.* New York: Oxford University Press, 2015.

Jones, Kenneth W. "The Arya Samaj in British India 1875–1947." In *Religion in Modern India*, edited by Robert D. Baird, 27–54. New Delhi: Manohar, 1994.

Jones, Kenneth W. *Socio-Religious Reform Movements in British India.* Cambridge: Cambridge University Press, 1989.

Jordens, J. T. F. *Dayananda Sarasvati: His Life and Ideas.* 1978; Delhi: Oxford University Press, 1997.

Josephson, Jason Ānanda. *The Invention of Religion in Japan.* Chicago: University of Chicago Press, 2012.

Josephson-Storm, Jason Ānanda. *The Myth of Disenchantment: Magic, Modernity, and the Birth of the Human Sciences.* Chicago: University of Chicago Press, 2017.

Keller, Jules. *Le théosophe alsacien Frédéric-Rodolphe Saltzmann et les milieux spirituels de son temps: Contribution à l'étude de l'illuminisme et du mysticisme à la fin du XVIIIe et au début du XIXe siècle.* Bern: Peter Lang, 1985.

Kiehnle, Catharina. "The Secret of the Nāths: The Ascent of Kuṇḍalinī According to Jñāneśvarī 6.151–328." *Bulletin des Études Indiennes*, nos. 22–23 (2005): 447–494.

Killingley, Dermot. *Rammohun Roy in Hindu and Christian Tradition: The Teape Lectures 1990.* Newcastle upon Tyne: Grevatt & Grevatt, 1993.

King, Francis, ed. *Astral Projection, Ritual Magic and Alchemy.* London: Neville Spearman, 1971.

King, Richard. *Orientalism and Religion: Postcolonial Theory, India and "the Mystic East."* London: Routledge, 1999.

Kinsley, David R. *Tantric Visions of the Divine Feminine: The Ten Mahāvidyās.* Berkeley: University of California Press, 1997.

Kippenberg, Hans G. *Discovering Religious History in the Modern Age.* Princeton, NJ: Princeton University Press, 2002.

Kishwar, Madhu. "The Daughters of Aryavarta: Women in the Arya Samaj Movement in Punjab." *Indian Economic and Social History Review* 23, no. 2 (1986): 151–186.

Kleine, Christoph. "Wozu außereuropäische Religionsgeschichte? Überlegungen zu ihrem Nutzen für die religionswissenschaftliche Theorie- und Identitätsbildung." *Zeitschrift für Religionswissenschaft* 18 (2010): 3–38.

Kollmar-Paulenz, Karénina. "Lamas und Schamanen: Mongolische Wissensordnungen vom frühen 17. bis zum 21. Jahrhundert: Ein Beitrag zur Debatte um aussereuropäische Religionsbegriffe." In *Religion in Asien? Studien zur Anwendbarkeit des Religionsbegriffs*, edited by Peter Schalk, 151–200. Uppsala: Uppsala Universitet, 2013.

Kollmar-Paulenz, Karénina. "Mongolische Geschichtsschreibung im Kontext der Globalgeschichte." In *Geschichten und Geschichte: Historiographie und Hagiographie in der asiatischen Religionsgeschichte*, edited by Peter Schalk, 247–279. Uppsala: Uppsala Universitet, 2010.

Komlosy, Andrea. *Globalgeschichte: Methoden und Theorien*. Wien: Böhlau Verlag, 2011.

Kopf, David. *The Brahmo Samaj and the Shaping of the Modern Indian Mind*. Princeton, NJ: Princeton University Press, 1979.

Koschorke, Klaus, and Adrian Hermann. "'Beyond Their Own Dwellings': Die Entstehung einer transregionalen und transkontinentalen indigen-christlichen Öffentlichkeit." In *"To Give Publicity to Our Thoughts": Journale asiatischer und afrikanischer Christen um 1900 und die Entstehung einer transregionalen indigen-christlichen Öffentlichkeit*, edited by Klaus Koschorke, Adrian Hermann, Frieder Ludwig, and Ciprian Burlacioiu, 227–260. Wiesbaden: Harrassowitz Verlag, 2018.

Krämer, Hans Martin. "Euro-Asian Political Activist and Spiritual Seeker: Paul Richard and Theosophy." In *Theosophy across Boundaries: Transcultural and Interdisciplinary Perspectives on a Modern Esoteric Movement*, edited by Hans Martin Krämer and Julian Strube, 317–344. Albany: State University of New York Press, 2020.

Krämer, Hans Martin. *Shimaji Mokurai and the Reconception of Religion and the Secular in Modern Japan*. Honolulu: University of Hawaii Press, 2017.

Krämer, Hans Martin, and Julian Strube, eds. *Theosophy across Boundaries: Transcultural and Interdisciplinary Perspectives on a Modern Esoteric Movement*. Albany: State University of New York Press, 2020.

Krech, Volkhard. *Wissenschaft und Religion: Studien zur Geschichte der Religionsforschung in Deutschland 1871 bis 1933*. Tübingen: Mohr Siebeck, 2002.

Kripal, Jeffrey J. *Kali's Child: The Mystical and the Erotic in the Life and Teachings of Ramakrishna*. Chicago: University of Chicago Press, 1995.

Kripal, Jeffrey J. "Remembering Ourselves: On Some Countercultural Echoes of Contemporary Tantric Studies." *Religions of South Asia* 1, no. 1 (2007): 11–28.

Laclau, Ernesto. "Identity and Hegemony: The Role of Universality in the Constitution of Political Logics." In *Contingency, Hegemony, Universality: Contemporary Dialogues on the Left*, edited by Judith Butler, Ernesto Laclau, and Slavoj Žižek, 44–89. London: Verso, 2000.

Laclau, Ernesto. "Why Do Empty Signifiers Matter to Politics?" In *The Lesser Evil and the Greater Good: The Theory and Politics of Social Diversity*, edited by Jeffrey Weeks, 167–178. London: Rivers Oram Press, 1994.

Lal, Vinay. "Provincializing the West: World History from the Perspective of Indian History." In *Writing World History 1800–2000*, edited by Benedikt Stuchtey and Eckhardt Fuchs, 271–289. Oxford: Oxford University Press, 2003.

Laurant, Jean-Pierre. *L'ésotérisme chrétien en France au XIXe siècle*. Lausanne: L'Age d'Homme, 1992.

Lavan, Spencer. *Unitarians and India: A Study in Encounter and Response.* Boston: Beacon Press, 1977.

Le Forestier, René. *La franc-maçonnerie templière et occultiste aux XVIIIe et XIXe siècles.* Paris: Aubier-Montaigne, Editions Nauwelaerts, 1970.

Leland, Kurt. *Rainbow Body: A History of the Western Chakra System from Blavatsky to Brennan.* Lake Worth, FL: Ibis Press, 2016.

Linse, Ulrich. *Geisterseher und Wunderwirker: Heilssuche im Industriezeitalter.* Frankfurt am Main: Fischer, 1996.

Liu, Lydia He. "Legislating the Universal: The Circulation of International Law in the Nineteenth Century." In *Tokens of Exchange: The Problem of Translation in Global Circulations*, edited by Lydia He Liu, 127–164. Durham, NC: Duke University Press, 1999.

Liu, Lydia He. "The Question of Meaning-Value in the Political Economy of the Sign." In *Tokens of Exchange: The Problem of Translation in Global Circulations*, edited by Lydia He Liu, 13–41. Durham, NC: Duke University Press, 1999.

Liu, Lydia He. *Translingual Practice: Literature, National Culture, and Translated Modernity.* Stanford, CA: Stanford University Press, 1995.

Lorea, Carola Erika. "'I Am Afraid of Telling You This, Lest You'd Be Scared Shitless!' The Myth of Secrecy and the Study of the Esoteric Traditions of Bengal." *Religions* 9, no. 6 (2018): 1–24. https://doi.org/https://doi.org/10.3390/rel9060172.

Lorea, Carola Erika. "'Playing the Football of Love on the Field of the Body': The Contemporary Repertoire of Baul Songs." *Religion and the Arts* 17, no. 4 (2013): 416–451. https://doi.org/https://doi.org/10.1163/15685292-12341286.

Lubelsky, Isaac. "Mythological and Real Race Issues in Theosophy." In *Handbook of the Theosophical Current*, edited by Olav Hammer and Mikael Rothstein, 335–355. Leiden: Brill, 2013.

Majumdar, Ramesh Chandra. *History of the Freedom Movement in India.* Vol. 2. Calcutta: Firma K. L. M., 1963.

Mallinson, James. "Nāth Sampradāya." In *Brill's Encyclopedia of Hinduism Online*, edited by Knut A. Jacobsen, Helene Basu, Angelika Malinar, and Vasudha Narayanan, 2018. http://dx.doi.org/10.1163/2212-5019_beh_COM_9000000067.

Mallinson, James. "Śāktism and Haṭhayoga." In *Goddess Traditions in Tantric Hinduism: History, Practice and Doctrine*, edited by Bjarne Wernicke Olesen, 109–140. Abingdon: Routledge, 2016.

Mallinson, James, and Mark Singleton, eds. *Roots of Yoga.* Milton Keynes: Penguin Random House, 2017.

Manjapra, Kris. "Transnational Approaches to Global History: A View from the Study of German-Indian Entanglement." *German History* 32 (2014): 274–293.

Manning, Patrick. *Navigating World History: Historians Create a Global Past.* New York: Palgrave Macmillan, 2003.

Manning, Patrick, and Abigail Owen, eds. *Knowledge in Translation: Global Patterns of Scientific Exchange, 1000–1800 CE.* Pittsburgh, PA: University of Pittsburgh Press, 2018.

Manning, Patrick, and Daniel Rood, eds. *Global Scientific Practice in an Age of Revolutions, 1750–1850.* Pittsburgh, PA: University of Pittsburgh Press, 2016.

Masuzawa, Tomoko. *The Invention of World Religions, or How European Universalism Was Preserved in the Language of Pluralism.* Chicago: University of Chicago Press, 2005.

Mazlish, Bruce. *The Idea of Humanity in a Global Era.* New York: Palgrave Macmillan, 2009.

Mazlish, Bruce. *The New Global History.* New York: Routledge, 2006.

McCutcheon, Russell T. *Manufacturing Religion: The Discourse on Sui Generis Religion and the Politics of Nostalgia.* Oxford: Oxford University Press, 2003.
McDaniel, June. *The Madness of the Saints: Ecstatic Religion in Bengal.* Chicago: University of Chicago Press, 1989.
McDaniel, June. *Offering Flowers, Feeding Skulls: Popular Goddess Worship in Bengal.* Oxford: Oxford University Press, 2004.
McDermott, Rachel Fell. *Mother of My Heart, Daughter of My Dreams: Kālī and Umā in the Devotional Poetry of Bengal.* New York: Oxford University Press, 2001.
McDermott, Rachel Fell. *Singing to the Goddess: Poems to Kālī and Umā from Bengal.* Oxford: Oxford University Press, 2001.
McLean, Malcolm. *Devoted to the Goddess: The Life and Work of Ramprasad.* Albany: State University of New York Press, 1998.
McVey, Geoffrey. "Thebes, Luxor, and Loudsville, Georgia. The Hermetic Brotherhood of Luxor and the Landscapes of 19th-Century Occultisms." In *The Occult in Nineteenth-Century America*, edited by Cathy Gutierrez, 153–181. Aurora, CO: Davies Group, 2005.
Mitter, Partha. *Art and Nationalism in Colonial India, 1850–1922.* Cambridge: Cambridge University Press, 1995.
Moyn, Samuel, and Andrew Sartori. "Approaches to Global Intellectual History." In *Global Intellectual History*, edited by Samuel Moyn and Andrew Sartori, 3–30. New York: Columbia University Press, 2013.
Mühlematter, Yves, and Helmut Zander, eds. *Occult Roots of Religious Studies: On the Influence of Non-Hegemonic Currents on Academia around 1900.* Berlin: De Gruyter, 2021.
Mukherjee, Haridas, and Uma Mukherjee. *The Origins of the National Education Movement.* Calcutta: Jadavpur University, 1957.
Mukherjee, Uma. *Two Great Indian Revolutionaries: Rash Behari Bose and Jyotindra Nath Mukherjee.* Calcutta: Firma K. L. Mukhopadhyay, 1966.
Mukhopadhyay, Mriganka. "Mohini: A Case Study of a Transnational Spiritual Space in the History of the Theosophical Society." *Numen* 67, nos. 2–3 (2020): 165–190.
Mukhopadhyay, Mriganka. "A Short History of the Theosophical Movement in Colonial Bengal." *Parlokatatta* 4 (2016): 103–132.
Muller-Ortega, Paul Eduardo. *The Triadic Heart of Śiva: Kaula Tantricism of Abhinavagupta in the Non-dual Śaivism of Kashmir.* Albany: State University of New York Press, 1989.
Mullick, Sunrit. *The First Hindu Mission to America: The Pioneering Visits of Protap Chunder Mozoomdar.* New Delhi: Northern Book Centre, 2010.
Myers, Perry. "Affinity and Estrangement: Transnational Theosophy in Germany and India during the Colonial Era (1878–1933)." In *Theosophy across Boundaries: Transcultural and Interdisciplinary Perspectives on a Modern Esoteric Movement*, edited by Hans Martin Krämer and Julian Strube, 217–252. Albany: State University of New York Press, 2020.
Myerson, Joel, Sandra Harbert Petrulionis, and Laura Dassow Walls. *The Oxford Handbook of Transcendentalism.* New York: Oxford University Press, 2010.
Nanda, Meera. "Madame Blavatsky's Children." In *Handbook of Religion and the Authority of Science*, edited by James R. Lewis and Olav Hammer, 279–344. Leiden: Brill, 2010.
Nandy, Ashis. "History's Forgotten Doubles." *History and Theory* 34, no. 2 (1996): 44–66.

Nehring, Andreas. *Orientalismus und Mission: Studien zur Repräsentation der südindischen Kultur und Religion durch deutsche Missionare 1840–1945*. Wiesbaden: Harrassowitz, 2003.

Neugebauer-Wölk, Monika. "Der Esoteriker und die Esoterik: Wie das Esoterische im 18. Jahrhundert zum Begriff wird und seinen Weg in die Moderne findet." *Aries* 10, no. 2 (2010): 217–231.

Neugebauer-Wölk, Monika. "Historische Esoterikforschung." In *Aufklärung und Esoterik: Wege in die Moderne*, edited by Monika Neugebauer-Wölk, Renko Geffarth, and Markus Neumann, 37–72. Berlin: De Gruyter, 2014.

Newcombe, Suzanne. "Magic and Yoga: The Role of Subcultures in Transcultural Exchange." In *Yoga Traveling: Bodily Practice in Transcultural Perspective*, edited by Beatrix Hauser, 57–79. Cham, Switzerland: Springer, 2013.

Noakes, Richard. *Physics and Psychics*. Cambridge: Cambridge University Press, 2019.

Novetzke, Christian. *The Quotidian Revolution: Vernacularization, Religion, and the Premodern Public Sphere in India*. New York: Columbia University Press, 2016.

O'Brien, Patrick. "Historiographical Traditions and Modern Imperatives for the Restoration of Global History." *Journal of Global History* 1, no. 1 (2006): 3–39.

Okropiridze, Dimitry. "Interpretation Reconsidered: The Definitional Progression in the Study of Esotericism as a Case in Point for the Varifocal Theory of Interpretation." In *New Approaches to the Study of Esotericism*, edited by Egil Asprem and Julian Strube, 217–240. Leiden: Brill, 2021.

Olesen, Bjarne Wernicke. *Goddess Traditions in Tantric Hinduism: History, Practice and Doctrine*. Abingdon: Routledge, 2016.

Oppenheim, Janet. *The Other World: Spiritualism and Psychical Research in England 1850–1914*. Cambridge: Cambridge University Press, 1985.

Osterhammel, Jürgen. *The Transformation of the World: A Global History of the Nineteenth Century*. Princeton, NJ: Princeton University Press, 2014.

O'Toole, Therese. "Secularising the Sacred Cow: The Relationship between Religious Reform and Hindu Nationalism." In *Hinduism in Public and Private: Reform, Hindutva, Gender and Sampraday*, edited by Antony Copley, 84–109. Oxford: Oxford University Press, 2003.

Owen, Alex. *The Darkened Room: Women, Power and Spiritualism in Late Victorian England*. Philadelphia: University of Pennsylvania Press, 1990.

Owen, Alex. *The Place of Enchantment: British Occultism and the Culture of the Modern*. Chicago: University of Chicago Press, 2004.

Padoux, André. *The Hindu Tantric World: An Overview*. Chicago: University of Chicago Press, 2017.

Padoux, André. *Vāc: The Concept of the Word in Selected Hindu Tantras*. Albany: State University of New York Press, 1990.

Pal, Pratapaditya. *Hindu Religion and Iconology According to the Tantrasāra*. Los Angeles: Vichitra Press, 1981.

Partridge, Christopher. "Lost Horizon: H. P. Blavatsky and Theosophical Orientalism." In *Handbook of the Theosophical Current*, edited by Olav Hammer and Mikael Rothstein, 309–333. Leiden: Brill, 2013.

Pasi, Marco. "The Modernity of Occultism: Reflections on Some Crucial Aspects." In *Hermes in the Academy: Ten Years' Study of Western Esotericism at the University of Amsterdam*, edited by Wouter J. Hanegraaff and Joyce Pijnenburg, 59–74. Amsterdam: Amsterdam University Press, 2009.

Pasi, Marco. "Oriental Kabbalah and the Parting of East and West in the Early Theosophical Society." In *Kabbalah and Modernity: Interpretations, Transformations, Adaptations*, edited by Boaz Huss, Marco Pasi, and Kocku von Stuckrad, 151–166. Leiden: Brill, 2010.

Pennington, Brian K. *Was Hinduism Invented? Britons, Indians, and the Colonial Construction of Religion*. Oxford: Oxford University Press, 2005.

Poliakov, Léon. *Le mythe aryen: Essai sur les sources du racisme et des nationalismes*. Paris: Calmann-Lévy, 1971.

Pollock, Sheldon. "New Intellectuals in Seventeenth-Century India." *Indian Economic & Social History Review* 38, no. 1 (2001): 3–31.

Prakash, Gyan. *Another Reason: Science and the Imagination of Modern India*. Princeton, NJ: Princeton University Press, 1999.

Prothero, Stephen R. "From Spiritualism to Theosophy: 'Uplifting' a Democratic Tradition." *Religion and American Culture: A Journal of Interpretation* 3, no. 2 (1993): 197–216.

Prothero, Stephen R. *The White Buddhist: The Asian Odyssey of Henry Steel Olcott*. Bloomington: Indiana University Press, 1996.

Putnam, Lara. "The Transnational and the Text-Searchable: Digitized Sources and the Shadows They Cast." *American Historical Review* 121, no. 2 (2016): 377–402.

Ramos, Imma. *Pilgrimage and Politics in Colonial Bengal: The Myth of the Goddess Sati*. Abingdon: Routledge, 2017.

Randeria, Shalini. "Geteilte Geschichte und verwobene Moderne." In *Zukunftsentwürfe: Ideen für eine Kultur der Veränderung*, edited by Jörn Rüsen, Hanna Leitgeb, and Norbert Jegelka, 87–96. Frankfurt am Main: Campus, 1999.

Randeria, Shalini, and Regina Römhild. "Das postkoloniale Europa: Verflochtene Genealogien der Gegenwart." In *Jenseits des Eurozentrismus: Postkoloniale Perspektiven in den Geschichts- und Kulturwissenschaften*, edited by Sebastian Conrad, Shalini Randeria, and Regina Römhild, 9–31. Frankfurt am Main: Campus Verlag, 2013.

Ransom, Josephine. *A Short History of the Theosophical Society*. Adyar: Theosophical Publishing House, 1938.

Ratte, Lou. *The Uncolonised Heart*. London: Sangam Books, 1995.

Ray, Benoy Gopal. *Religious Movements in Modern Bengal*. Santiniketan: Visva-Bharati, 1965.

Raychaudhuri, Tapan. *Europe Reconsidered: Perceptions of the West in Nineteenth Century Bengal*. Delhi: Oxford University Press, 1988.

Robinson, David M. "Emerson, the Indian Brahmo Samaj, and the American Reception of Gandhi." In *A Power to Translate the World: New Essays on Emerson and International Culture*, edited by David LaRocca and Ricardo Miguel-Alfonso, 43–60. Lebanon, NH: Dartmouth College Press, 2015.

Roukema, Aren, and Allan Kilner-Johnson. "Editorial: Time to Drop the 'Western.'" *Correspondences* 6, no. 2 (2018): 109–115.

Roy, Manabendra Nath. *M. N. Roy's Memoirs*. Bombay: Allied, 1964.

Rudbøg, Tim, and Erik Reenberg Sand. *Imagining the East: The Early Theosophical Society*. Edited by Tim Rudbøg and Erik Reenberg Sand. New York: Oxford University Press, 2020.

Rudbøg, Tim, and Erik Reenberg Sand. "Introduction." In *Imagining the East: The Early Theosophical Society*, edited by Tim Rudbøg and Erik Reenberg Sand, 1–12. New York: Oxford University Press, 2020.

Sachsenmaier, Dominic. *Global Perspectives on Global History: Theories and Approaches in a Connected World.* Cambridge: Cambridge University Press, 2011.

Sachsenmaier, Dominic. "World History as Ecumenical History?" *Journal of World History* 18, no. 4 (2007): 465–489.

Salmond, Noel A. *Hindu Iconoclasts: Rammohun Roy, Dayananda Sarasvati and Nineteenth Century Polemics against Idolatry.* Kolkata: Sampark, 2004.

Samanta, Amiya K., ed. *Terrorism in Bengal: A Collection of Documents on Terrorist Activities from 1905 to 1939.* Vols. 1 and 2. Calcutta: Government of West Bengal, 1995.

Samuel, Geoffrey. *The Origins of Yoga and Tantra: Indic Religions to the Thirteenth Century.* Cambridge: Cambridge University Press, 2008.

Samuel, Geoffrey. *Tantric Revisionings: New Understandings of Tibetan Buddhism and Indian Religion.* Aldershot: Ashgate, 2005.

Sanderson, Alexis. "Meaning in Tantric Ritual." In *Essais sur le Rituel III: Colloque du Centenaire de la Section des Sciences religieuses de l'École Pratique des Hautes Études*, edited by Anne-Marie Blondeau and Kristofer Schipper, 15–95. Louvain-Paris: Peeters, 1995.

Sanderson, Alexis. "Purity and Power among the Brahmans of Kashmir." In *The Category of the Person: Anthropology, Philosophy, History*, edited by Michael Carrithers, Steven Collins, and Steven Lukes, 190–216. Cambridge: Cambridge University Press, 1985.

Sanderson, Alexis. "The Śaiva Age: The Rise and Dominance of Śaivism during the Early Medieval Period." In *Genesis and Development of Tantrism*, edited by Shingo Einoo, 41–350. Tokyo: University of Tokyo, Institute of Oriental Culture, 2009.

Sanderson, Alexis. "Śaivism and the Tantric Traditions." In *The World's Religions*, edited by Stewart Sutherland, Leslie Houlden, Peter Clarke, and Friedhelm Hardy, 660–704. London: Routledge and Kegan Paul, 1988.

Sarbadhikary, Sukanya. "Sahajiya Texts of Nadia: Beyond Reform and Revival." In *The Legacy of Vaiṣṇavism in Colonial Bengal*, edited by Ferdinando Sardella and Lucian Wong, 167–184. Abingdon: Routledge, 2020.

Sardella, Ferdinando, and Lucian Wong, eds. *The Legacy of Vaiṣṇavism in Colonial Bengal.* Abingdon: Routledge, 2020.

Sarkar, Sumit. *The Swadeshi Movement in Bengal, 1903–1908.* New Delhi: People's Publishing House, 1973.

Sarkar, Sumit. *Writing Social History.* Delhi: Oxford University Press, 1997.

Sartori, Andrew. "Beyond Culture-Contact and Colonial Dicourse: 'Germanism' in Colinial Bengal." *Modern Intellectual History* 4, no. 1 (2007): 77–93.

Sartori, Andrew. "The Categorial Logic of a Colonial Nationalism: Swadeshi Bengal,1904–1908." *Comparative Studies of South Asia, Africa and the Middle East* 23, nos. 1–2 (2003): 271–285.

Schwab, Raymond. *The Oriental Renaissance: Europe's Rediscovery of India and the East, 1680–1880.* New York: Columbia University Press, 1984.

Scott, J. Barton. "Miracle Publics: Theosophy, Christianity, and the Coulomb Affair." *History of Religions* 49, no. 2 (2009): 172–196.

Sen, Amiya P. *Hindu Revivalism in Bengal, 1872–1905: Some Essays in Interpretation.* Oxford: Oxford University Press, 1993.

Sen, Amiya P. "Theorising Bengal Vaiṣṇavism: Bipin Chandra Pal and New Perspectives on Religious Life and Culture." In *The Legacy of Vaiṣṇavism in Colonial Bengal*, edited by Ferdinando Sardella and Lucian Wong, 33–56. Abingdon: Routledge, 2020.

Sen, Uditi. *Citizen Refugee: Forging the Indian Nation after Partition.* Cambridge: Cambridge University Press, 2018.

Sengupta, Papia. *Language as Identity in Colonial India: Policies and Politics.* New York: Springer, 2017.

Sengupta, Papia. *Pedagogy for Religion: Missionary Education and the Fashioning of Hindus and Muslims in Bengal.* Berkeley: University of California Press, 2011.

Sengupta, Subodhcandra, ed. *Sangsad Bāṅālī Caritābhidhān.* Calcutta: Sahitya Sangsad, 1976.

Sen Sharma, Debabrata. *Aspects of Tantra Yoga.* Varanasi: Indica Books, 2007.

Sharp, Lynn L. *Secular Spirituality: Reincarnation and Spiritism in Nineteenth Century France.* Lanham, MD: Lexington Books, 2006.

Singh, Chhajju. *The Life and Teachings of Swami Dayanand Saraswati.* New Delhi: Jan Gyan Prakashan, 1971.

Singleton, Mark. *Yoga Body: The Origins of Modern Posture Practice.* Oxford: Oxford University Press, 2010.

Sinha, Samita. *Pandits in a Changing Environment: Centres of Sanskrit Learning in Nineteenth Century Bengal.* Calcutta: Sarat Book House, 1993.

Srinivas, Tulasi. *Winged Faith: Rethinking Globalization and Religious Pluralism through the Sathya Sai Movement.* New York: Columbia University Press, 2010.

Stevens, John A. *Keshab: Bengal's Forgotten Prophet.* New York: Oxford University Press, 2018.

Stewart, Tony K. "The Power of the Secret: The Tantalising Discourse of Vaiṣṇava Sahajiyā Scholarship." In *The Legacy of Vaiṣṇavism in Colonial Bengal*, edited by Ferdinando Sardella and Lucian Wong, 125–166. Abingdon: Routledge, 2020.

Stievermann, Jan. *Der Sündenfall der Nachahmung: Zum Problem der Mittelbarkeit im Werk Ralph Waldo Emersons.* Paderborn: Schöningh, 2007.

Strube, Julian. "The 'Baphomet' of Eliphas Lévi: Its Meaning and Historical Context." *Correspondences* 4 (2017): 37–79.

Strube, Julian. "Hinduism, Western Esotericism, and New Age Religion in Europe." In *Handbook of Hinduism in Europe*, edited by Knut A. Jacobsen and Ferdinando Sardella, 152–173. Leiden: Brill, 2020.

Strube, Julian. "Occultist Identity Formations between Theosophy and Socialism in Fin-de-Siècle France." *Numen* 64, nos. 5–6 (2017): 568–595.

Strube, Julian. "Rajnarayan Basu and His 'Science of Religion': The Emergence of Religious Studies through Exchanges between Bengali and Christian Reformers, Orientalists, and Theosophists." *Method and Theory in the Study of Religion* 33, no. 4 (2021): 289–320.

Strube, Julian. "Socialism and Esotericism in July Monarchy France." *History of Religions* 57, no. 2 (2017): 197–221.

Strube, Julian. "Socialist Religion and the Emergence of Occultism: A Genealogical Approach to Socialism and Secularization in 19th-Century France." *Religion* 46, no. 3 (2016): 359–388.

Strube, Julian. *Sozialismus, Katholizismus und Okkultismus im Frankreich des 19. Jahrhunderts: Die Genealogie der Schriften von Eliphas Lévi.* Religionsgeschichtliche Versuche und Vorarbeiten. Berlin: De Gruyter, 2016.

Strube, Julian. "Tantra." In *Dictionary of Contemporary Esotericism*, edited by Egil Asprem. Leiden: Brill, forthcoming.

Strube, Julian. "Tantra as Experimental Science in the Works of John Woodroffe." In *Occult Roots of Religious Studies: On the Influence of Non-Hegemonic Currents on Academia around 1900*, edited by Yves Mühlematter and Helmut Zander, 132–160. Berlin: De Gruyter, 2021.

Strube, Julian. "Tantra und Katholizismus im Kontext einer globalen Religionsgeschichte." In *Weltreligion im Umbruch: Transnationale Perspektiven auf das Christentum in der Globalisierung des 19. Jahrhunderts*, edited by Olaf Blaschke and Francisco Javiér Ramón Solans, 338–362. Frankfurt: Campus, 2019.

Strube, Julian. "Theosophy and Race." In *Theosophy and the Study of Religion*, edited by Charles Stang and Jason Ānanda Josephson, forthcoming.

Strube, Julian. "Theosophy, Race, and the Study of Esotericism." *Journal of the American Academy of Religion* (forthcoming).

Strube, Julian. "Towards the Study of Esotericism without the 'Western': Esotericism from the Perspective of a Global Religious History." In *New Approaches to the Study of Esotericism*, edited by Egil Asprem and Julian Strube, 45–66. Leiden: Brill, 2021.

Strube, Julian. "Transgressing Boundaries: Social Reform, Theology, and the Demarcations between Science and Religion." *Aries* 16, no. 1 (2016): 1–11.

Strube, Julian. *Vril: Eine okkulte Naturkraft in Theosophie und esoterischem Neonazismus.* Paderborn: Wilhelm Fink, 2013.

Strube, Julian. "Yoga and Meditation in Esoteric Traditions." In *Routledge Handbook of Yoga and Meditation Studies*, edited by Suzanne Newcombe and Karen O'Brien-Kop, 130–145. Abingdon: Routledge, 2020.

Strube, Julian, and Hans Martin Krämer. "Introduction." In *Theosophy across Boundaries: Transcultural and Interdisciplinary Perspectives on a Modern Esoteric Movement*, edited by Hans Martin Krämer and Julian Strube, 1–26. Albany: State University of New York Press, 2020.

Stuckrad, Kocku von. *Locations of Knowledge in Medieval and Early Modern Europe: Esoteric Discourse and Western Identities.* Leiden: Brill, 2010.

Stuckrad, Kocku von. *The Scientification of Religion: An Historical Study of Discursive Change, 1800–2000.* Berlin: DeGruyter, 2014.

Stuckrad, Kocku von. *Western Esoterisicm: A Brief History of Secret Knowledge.* London: Equinox, 2005.

Sturman, Rachel Lara. *The Government of Social Life in Colonial India: Liberalism, Religious Law, and Women's Rights.* New York: Cambridge University Press, 2012.

Subrahmanyam, Sanjay. *Europe's India: Words, People, Empires, 1500–1800.* Cambridge, MA: Harvard University Press, 2017.

Taylor, Kathleen. *Sir John Woodroffe, Tantra and Bengal: An Indian Soul in a European Body?* Richmond, UK: Curzon, 2001.

Trautmann, Thomas R. *Aryans and British India.* Berkeley: University of California Press, 1997.

Tschacher, Torsten. *Race, Religion, and the "Indian Muslim" Predicament in Singapore.* New York: Routledge, 2018.

Turner, Frank M. *Between Science and Religion: The Reaction to Scientific Naturalism in Late Victorian England.* London: Yale University Press, 1974.

Tweed, Thomas A. "American Occultism and Japanese Buddhism: Albert J. Edmunds, D. T. Suzuki, and Translocative History." *Japanese Journal of Religious Studies* 32, no. 2 (2005): 249–281.

Tweed, Thomas A. "Toward a Translocative History of Occult Buddhism: Flows and Confluences." *History of Religions* 54, no. 4 (2015): 423–433.
Urban, Hugh B. "Elitism and Esotericism: Strategies of Secrecy and Power in South Indian Tantra and French Freemasonry." *Numen* 44, no. 1 (1997): 1–38.
Urban, Hugh B. "The Goddess and the Great Rite: Hindu Tantra and the Complex Origins of Modern Wicca." In *Magic and Witchery in the Modern West*, edited by Shai Feraro and Ethan Dole White, 21–42. Cham, Switzerland: Palgrave Macmillan, 2019.
Urban, Hugh B. *Magia Sexualis: Sex, Magic, and Liberation in Modern Western Esotericism*. Berkeley: University of California Press, 2006.
Urban, Hugh B. *The Power of Tantra: Religion, Sexuality, and the Politics of South Asian Studies*. London: I. B. Tauris, 2010.
Urban, Hugh B. "The Strategic Uses of an Esoteric Text: The Mahanirvana Tantra." *South Asia* 18, no. 1 (1995): 55–81.
Urban, Hugh B. "Tantra, American Style: From the Path of Power to the Yoga of Sex." In *Transformations and Transfer of Tantra in Asia and Beyond*, edited by István Keul, 457–494. Berlin: De Gruyter, 2012.
Urban, Hugh B. *Tantra: Sex, Secrecy Politics, and Power in the Study of Religions*. Berkeley: University of California Press, 2003.
Urban, Hugh B. *Zorba the Buddha: Sex, Spirituality, and Capitalism in the Global Osho Movement*. Oakland: University of California Press, 2015.
van der Veer, Peter. *Imperial Encounters: Religion and Modernity in India and Britain*. Princeton, NJ: Princeton University Press, 2001.
Versluis, Arthur. *American Transcendentalism and Asian Religions*. Oxford: Oxford University Press, 1993.
Viatte, Auguste. *Les sources occultes du romantisme: Illuminisme, Théosophie 1770–1820*. 2 vols. Paris: Champion, 1928.
Viswanathan, Gauri. "Colonialism and the Construction of Hinduism." In *The Blackwell Companion to Hinduism*, edited by Gavin Flood, 23–44. Malden, MA: Blackwell, 2005.
Viswanathan, Gauri. *Masks of Conquest: Literary Study and British Rule in India*. New York: Columbia University Press, 1989.
Viswanathan, Gauri. "The Ordinary Business of Occultism." *Critical Inquiry* 27, no. 1 (2000): 1–20.
Viswanathan, Gauri. *Outside the Fold: Conversion, Modernity, and Belief*. Princeton, NJ: Princeton University Press, 1998.
Weiss, Richard. *The Emergence of Modern Hinduism: Religion on the Margins of Colonialism*. Oakland: University of California Press, 2019.
Wenzlhuemer, Roland. *Globalgeschichte schreiben: Eine Einführung in 6 Episoden*. Konstanz: UVK Verlagsgesellschaft, 2017.
White, David Gordon. *The Alchemical Body: Siddha Traditions in Medieval India*. Chicago: University of Chicago Press, 1996.
White, David Gordon. "Introduction." In *Tantra in Practice*, edited by David Gordon White, 3–38. Princeton, NJ: Princeton University Press, 2000.
White, David Gordon. *Kiss of the Yogini: "Tantric Sex" in Its South Asian Contexts*. Chicago: University of Chicago Press, 2003.
White, David Gordon. *Sinister Yogis*. Chicago: University of Chicago Press, 2009.
White, David Gordon. "Tantra." In *Brill's Encyclopedia of Hinduism Online*, edited by Knut A. Jacobsen, Helene Basu, Angelika Malinar, and Vasudha Narayanan, 2018. http://dx.doi.org/10.1163/2212-5019_beh_COM_9000000067.

White, David Gordon, ed. *Yoga in Practice*. Princeton, NJ: Princeton University Press, 2012.

White, David Gordon. *The Yoga Sutra of Patanjali: A Biography*. Princeton, NJ: Princeton University Press, 2014.

Wolfers, Alex. "Born Like Krishna in the Prison-House." *South Asia* 39, no. 3 (2016): 525–545.

Wolfers, Alex. "The Making of an Avatar: Reading Sri Aurobindo Ghose (1872–1950)." *Religions of South Asia* 11, nos. 2–3 (2017): 274–341.

Wolffram, Heather. *The Stepchildren of Science: Psychical Research and Parapsychology in Germany, c. 1870–1939*. Wellcome Series in the History of Medicine 88. Amsterdam: Rodopi, 2009.

Wong, Lucian. "Against Vaiṣṇava Deviance: Brāhmaṇical and Bhadralok Alliance in Bengal." *Religions* 9, no. 2 (2018): 1–19.

Wong, Lucian, and Ferdinando Sardella. "Vaiṣṇavism in Colonial Bengal: Beyond the Hindu Renaissance." In *The Legacy of Vaiṣṇavism in Colonial Bengal*, edited by Ferdinando Sardella and Lucian Wong, 1–14. Abingdon: Routledge, 2020.

Yelle, Robert A. *Explaining Mantras: Ritual, Rhetoric, and the Dream of a Natural Language in Hindu Tantra*. New York: Routledge, 2003.

Yelle, Robert A. *The Language of Disenchantment: Protestant Literalism and Colonial Discourse in British India*. New York: Oxford University Press, 2013.

Zander, Helmut. *"Europäische" Religionsgeschichte: Religiöse Zugehörigkeit durch Entscheidung—Konsequenzen im interkulturellen Vergleich*. Berlin: De Gruyter, 2015.

Zastoupil, Lynn. *Rammohun Roy and the Making of Victorian Britain*. New York: Palgrave Macmillan, 2010.

Zavos, John. *The Emergence of Hindu Nationalism in India*. New Delhi: Oxford University Press, 2000.

Index

Figures are indicated by *f* following the page number

Abhinavagupta, 150
Absolute, 151, 177–78
Adam, William, 85–86
Adhi Bhoutic Theosophical Society, 110
Ādi Brāhma Samāj, 90, 93, 152–53, 173
Advaita Vedanta, 77, 177, 183, 234
Adyar, 39, 69, 246
Agamas Research Society/Āgamānusandhana Samiti, 221, 225, 227, 246
Agamavagish, Krishnananda, 53
agency, 6, 20, 31, 213, 243–44, 248
Akbar, 50
alchemy, 39, 188, 231, 234
Alivardi Khan, 49
All India Cow Conferences Association, 227
Alter, Joseph S., 96
Amṛta Bāzār Patrikā (newspaper), 141, 246
Ānandamaṭh, 194–95, 250
Anglo-Vedic School, 61
animal magnetism. *See* mesmerism
Anquetil-Duperron, Abraham Hyacinthe, 41, 99
anti-colonialism, 31–32, 141–42, 144, 156, 163, 166–67, 190, 195, 242, 246, 247. *See also* nationalism
Anuśīlan Samiti, 195, 197–98, 246
Arya (journal), 117
Arya Gazette, 154
Ārya Samāj, 34, 39–40, 64, 69–70, 82–83, 102, 112, 116–17, 129, 154, 176–77, 180, 246
Aryan civilization
  Dayananda Sarasvati, 82
  Lectures on the Origin and Growth of Religion as Illustrated by the Religions of India, 75
  Müller's research, 75, 126, 208
  orientalist scholarship, 74
  Pramathanath Mukhopadhyay, 211
  Rammohan Roy, 82
  reform movement, 34, 84, 162
  religion, 243, 249
  Shivachandra, 187
  spiritual culture, 126
  Theosophical Society, 69, 73, 82, 94–95
  Theosophy, 69–73
  Vedic literature, 76
Aryan wisdom
  ancient initiation rituals, 55
  Aryan Brahmanism, 48
  Aurobindo Ghosh, 211
  Bengali Tantrikas, 240–41
  Dayananda Sarasvati, 83
  Indian emergence, 74
  Indian religion, 42
  Kalpa (journal), 60–61
  mind/matter relationship, 126
  Olcott speech, 92
  revivalism, 59–60, 153
  sanātana dharma, 58–60, 175, 245
  science, 60
  Tantra, 47
  Tantratattva, 185–86
  Theosophists, 35, 39, 58
  Theosophy, 246
  Vedic School of Bengal, 61
  Western science, 60, 95
Aryas, 83–84, 91, 156–57, 162, 243
Asad, Talal, 25
asceticism, 105, 151, 194, 196, 210–11
Asiatic Researches (journal), 66
Asiatic Society of Bengal, 108
Asprem, Egil, 41
Astral Light, 106
astral projection, 107–8
astrology, 39, 62, 174, 231
atheism, 40, 86, 107, 133

Avalon, Arthur
  Bengali intervention, 8, 38, 63, 228, 242
  collaborators, 220, 233
  colonialism, 54
  Cousins, 224
  esotericism, 213
  Mahānirvāṇa Tantra, 150
  publications, 5–6, 226–27
  scholarship, 33–34
  Serpent Power, The, 52
  Shivachandra, 33, 163, 184, 250
  Tantra, 36, 49, 240–41, 242
  Tantratattva, 174
  Varendra Research Society, 222
  World Soul, 101
  See also Woodroffe, John
Avalon, Ellen. *See* Woodroffe, Ellen

BADPS (Indian Society for the Propagation of Aryan Dharma), 156–57, 163, 187
Bagchi, Samarendranath, 164, 215, 217, 222
Bagha Jatin, 198–99, 207
Bahadur, Kumar Binaykrishna Dev, 132
Baier, Karl, 20, 22, 31, 41, 43–44, 97
Ballantyne, Tony, 16, 19, 108
Banaras Hindu University, 159, 227
"Bande Mātaram," 73, 193–94, 196, 207
Bandyopadhyay, Brajendranath, 61
Bandyopadhyay, Haranchandra, 61
Bandyopadhyay, Navinkrishna, 110
Bandyopadhyay, Panchkari, 181, 218, 239–40
Bandyopadhyay, Surendranath, 92, 117, 191–93
Banerjea, Reverend, 127
Banerjee, Milinda, 25–26, 74
Banerji, Sures Chandra, 6, 66
Baṅgabāsī (journal), 156, 157, 199–200
Baṅgamahilā (journal), 132
Baṅgīya Sāhitya Pariṣat· (literary society), 131–32, 135
Banner of Light (journal), 126
Barnāśram dharmma, 230
Basu, Amritalal, 217
Basu, Bamandas, 117, 120–22
Basu, Rajnarayan, 88, 90, 111, 132, 149–50, 152–53, 155, 180, 187, 189, 195, 197, 243, 250
Basu, Shyamacharan, 116
Basu, Srishchandra, 109, 116–19, 229, 247, 249
Batabyal, Umeshchandra, 132, 153
Bauls, 11, 35, 53, 165–66, 171, 185–86, 251
Bayly, Christopher, 21
Beames, John, 132
Bedbyās, 200–203, 246, 251
Benares, 35, 243, 246
Bengal, 14, 34–35, 48–49, 53, 84, 89–90, 108, 124, 132–33, 189*f*, 190, 198, 243. *See also* Bengali intervention
Bengalee (newspaper), 191
Bengali intervention
  Avalon publications, 8, 38, 63, 228, 242
  Baradakanta Majumdar, 7, 34, 38, 56, 229
  chakras, 34, 123
  dharma, 54
  failure of, 229
  global Tantra, 6–7
  Hinduism, 40, 54
  Kumarkhali network, 165
  kundalini, 34
  Nadiya and adjacent districts, 9*f*
  national education, 36
  Sanskrit culture, 52
  Shakta poetry, 53–54, 242
  Shivachandra, 12–13, 54
  Tantra, 33–34, 43, 110, 112, 162, 247
  Tantrik Occultism, 7, 229–30
  Theosophical Society, 8, 39–40
  Theosophy, 243
  Treatise on the Yoga Philosophy, 105
  "Truth-Seeker" article, 44
  Woodroffe, 13, 243
  yoga, 48, 122–23
Bengali School, 163, 177–78
Bengali Tantrikas, 36, 38, 46, 240–41, 243
Bengali Theosophical Society for the Promotion of the Meaning of the Eternal Aryan Dharma, The, 57–58
Bengali Vaishnavism, 15
Bengal National College, 207–8
Bengal Theosophical Society, 61, 93, 129, 158
Bergunder, Michael, 16, 21–22, 26, 250
Berhampore, 50, 89, 91, 110–12, 144, 172, 243

Besant, Annie, 39, 59, 118, 159, 191, 224–25, 227, 247. *See also* Theosophical Society
Bevir, Mark, 31
Bhabha, Homi, 27
bhadralok (English-educated middle class). *See* English education
Bhagavadgītā, 44, 85, 139
bhakti, 11, 53, 141–42, 145, 173
Bhāratbarṣīẏa Arya Dharma Pracāriṇī Sabhā, 156, 249
Bhārat Dharma Mahāmaṇḍal, 157–58, 221, 249
Bharati, Agehananda, 5
Bharati, Hariharananda, 152
Bhatia, Varuni, 95, 141, 161–62
Bhattacharya, Chandrakumar, 165, 168
Bhattacharya, Kamalakanta, 53–54, 172
Bhattacharya, Kunjabihari, 113–14
Bhattacharya, Raghunandan, 50, 151, 214
Bhuluyababa (Kalidas Gosh), 218
black magic, 4–5, 34, 46–47, 112, 113–14
black Tantras, 45
Blavatsky, Helena Petrovna
  Bombay arrival, 70
  Calcutta arrival, 93
  chakras, 106
  death of, 81–82
  Hatha Yoga, 106, 115
  Isis Unveiled, 105
  Key to Theosophy, 59–60
  and Lévi, 40
  materialism, 148
  Müller research, 77
  Pyarichand Mitra, 127–28
  racial stereotypes, 248
  Raja Yoga, 106–7
  relocation to Adyar, 71
  Secret Doctrine, 47, 160, 224
  Spiritualism, 112
  supernaturalism rejection, 103
  Tantra ceremonies, 114
  translations, 45, 59
  "Voice of the Silence, The," 224–25
  "Yoga Vidya," 102
  See also Theosophical Society
Blount, Norman, 220, 226
Boirac, Émile, 234
Bombay, 70
Bordeaux, Joel, 15, 54
Bose, Jagadish, 234
Bose, Jagadishchandra, 188
Bose, Nandal, 226
Brāhma Samaj, 34, 69, 84–88, 116, 129, 151–53, 172–73, 176, 246
brahmabidyā, 57, 60, 82, 170–71, 248
Brahman, 58, 59, 62, 79, 128, 131, 140, 152, 177, 181–182, 184–185, 202, 204, 206, 232
Brahmanism
  Aryan culture, 48
  entanglement, 85
  Hatha Yoga, 232
  magnetism, 100
  Mahānirvāṇa Tantra, 152
  meditation, 99
  mesmerism, 61
  Navadvip as center of learning, 50
  nondualism, 62
  orthodoxy, 249
  purity, 52
  Rammohan Roy, 86
  Report on the Anti-Partition and Swadeshi Movement in Bengal, 198
  science/religion debate, 86
  Shishirkumar Ghosh, 143
  Srishchandra Basu, 116–17
  Tantra, 48, 50, 118, 140, 242
  Tantratattva, 181
  Unitarianism, 89
  See also Hinduism
Brahmoism, 15, 142, 173–74
Brahmos
  Brāhma dharmma, 155
  Calcutta Unitarian Committee, 85
  Dayananda, 83
  decline of, 128
  education activity, 103
  foreigners, 181
  gurus, 180
  Hindu Mela, 189
  Indian Mirror (newspaper), 90–91
  Interpreter (journal), 129
  Mahānirvāṇa Tantra, 177, 180–81
  monotheism, 181
  nationalism, 83–84, 187
  Panchkari Bandyopadhyay, 240

Brahmos (*cont.*)
rationalism, 173
sanātana dharma, 129
Shashadhar Tarkacuramani, 200
Shishirkumar Ghosh, 141
Shivachandra, 176–77, 180
Tantra, 111
Theosophical Society, 91, 243
Theosophists, 128–29
Theosophy, 247
Unitarianism, 89
See also reform movement
Britain, 16. *See also* colonialism; English education
Brooks, Douglas Renfrew, 66
Buddha, 59, 138
Buddhism, 23, 25, 57, 66, 127, 214, 240
"Buddhist Catechism," 57
Bulwer-Lytton, Edward, 98

Calcutta, 34–35, 91–93, 95–96, 243, 246
Calcutta Mathematical Society, 239
Calcutta Psycho-Religious Society, 132, 135–36
Calcutta Review (newspaper), 121–22
Calcutta Unitarian Committee, 85
capitalism, 17, 36
Carbonari, 250
castes, 2, 50, 74, 83–84, 129, 149, 160–61, 167, 204. *See also* reform movement
Catechism of Hindu Dharma, 118
Catechism of Hinduism, 118
Catholicism, 36, 41, 64, 238–39
Chaitanya, 9–10, 50, 83, 141–42, 146, 150, 173
Chajes, Julie, 22
Chakladar, Kashinath, 165, 213
Chakrabarti, Kunal, 49
Chakrabarty, Dipesh, 25, 27, 29
Chakravarti, Bholanath, 172
Chakravarti, Kshetrapal, 131–37, 228, 243
chakras, 34, 43, 48, 52, 106–8, 121–23, 228
six-chakra system, 136, 144–45, 178
Chambers, William, 168
chastity, 130
Chatterjee, Ratneswar, 144–45
Chattopadhyay, Bankimchandra, 13–14, 73, 156–57, 193–96, 200, 222, 250
Chattopadhyay, Bhudhar, 13–14, 200–202
Chattopadhyay, Jagadishchandra, 234
Chattopadhyay, Mohinimohan, 93
Chattopadhyay, Nalinimohan, 236
Chaudhuri, Ray Jatindranath, 160
Chaudhuri, Saratchandra, 218
child marriage, 154, 199, 202
Chirol, Valentine, 193
Christianity
anti-Christian attitude, 79
anticlericalism, 247
asceticism, 105
attacks on, 45, 157
Baradakanta Majumdar, 57
Basu critique, 120
English education, 168
esotericism, 23
Freemasonry, 118
idolatry, 176
meditation, 97
missionaries, 72
muscular Christianity, 16
New Dispensation Church, 88
racism, 247–48
Rise of the Christian Power in India, 120
secularism, 237–38
Society for the Education and Liberations of the Women of India, 130
Tantra, 162, 225, 240
Theosophy, or Psychological Religion, 78–80
Woodroffe, 237
See also individual denominations
Christian Science, 4, 16, 234–35
Church of England, 88
Colebrooke, Henry Thomas, 42, 59, 66–67, 249
colonialism
agency, 6, 213, 244
Avalon publications, 54
Besant, 247
bhadralok (English-educated middle class), 49, 95
as "civilizing mission," 15
English education, 63–64
Eurocentrism, 6
global religious history, 26–28
Hinduism, 14
ISOA (Indian Society of Oriental Art), 224

local rivalries, 186
Müller lectures, 76
Orientalism, 30
race and caste in India, 74
religion and esotericism, 25
Shivachandra, 250
Tantra, 54, 242
Tantra Shastra, 63
Theosophical Society, 29–32, 95
universal brotherhood, 247
Woodroffe critique, 63
comparative religion. *See* religious studies
comparativism. *See* religious studies
Confucianism, 240
Congress Party, 192
Conrad, Sebastian, 19, 21, 23, 244
Constant, Alphonse-Louis. *See* Éliphas Lévi.
contact zones, 20
Conze, Edward, 66
Coomaraswamy, Ananda, 223–24
Cossim Bazar, 227
Cousins, James, 224–25
Cousins, Margaret, 224
Cowell, Edward Byles, 59
Crookes, William, 98
Crossley, Pamela, 18

Dacca Theosophical Society, 113
Dall, Charles, 87, 103
Darbhanga, 227, 249
Darwin, Charles, 41, 209–10
Das, Rahul Peter, 251
Das Gupta, Shashibhusan, 6, 36, 66
Datt, Hirendranath, 132
Datt, Rameshchandra, 132
Davis, Andrew Jackson, 126
Dawn (magazine), 207
Dawn Society, 207
De Michelis, Elizabeth, 7–8, 96–98
Derozio, Henry Louis Vivian, 86
Deussen, Paul, 61
Dev, Binaykrishna, 132
Devi Bhāgavata, 50, 177
Devi, Jayakali, 217, 220
Devi, Svarnakumari, 93, 166
dharma
BADPS (Indian Society for the Propagation of Aryan Dharma), 156–57
Bengali intervention, 54
Bengal Theosophical Society for the Promotion of the Meaning of the Eternal Aryan Dharma, 158
Dharma Maṇḍalī, 202
Explanation of Dharma, 200–207
Hindu dharma, 72
"Hindu Dharma Is Entirely Liberal," 129
Hinduism, 118
religion, 26, 39, 153
revivalism, 13
sanātana dharma, 10
secrecy, 62, 175, 251
Tantra, 49, 146
Tantrik Occultism, 7
Theosophists, 39
Dnyaneshvari, 43–44
dualism, 225, 230
Dublin University Magazine, 43–44
Durga, 49, 59, 174, 193, 227
Duval, Valentine, 168

Egypt, 54–55, 240, 250
Ehrlich, Joshua, 15, 54–55
Eichhorn, Johann Gottfried, 67
electricity, 7, 44, 61, 157, 201, 203, 208, 232, 248
Eliade, Mircea, 5, 65–66
Emerson, Ralph Waldo, 86
Encausse, Gérard. *See* Papus
English education
Bad Aryan (B.A.), 211, 249
bhadralok (English-educated middle class), 49, 95, 151–52, 189, 243
colonialism, 63–64
criticism of, 12, 94
Hindu Mela, 188–89
Indian Universities Commission, 207
national education, 236, 245
revivalism, 14
science, 62
Shashadhar Tarkacuramani, 203–7, 211
Shivachandra, 11, 35, 163, 167–69, 185–86, 199, 211, 249–50
Tantra, 62, 230
Theosophical Society denunciation of, 34
women's place in society, 129–30

Enlightenment, 7–8
Ennemoser, Joseph, 99
entanglement
  agency, 20, 213
  Bengal centers of learning, 243
  Brāhma Samaj, 84
  Brahmanism, 85
  esotericism, 67, 72
  global religious history, 19, 67, 242
  global Tantra, 25, 186
  modernity, 23, 244
  reform movement, 88
  science and esotericism, 41
  Tantra, 4, 25, 214
  Theosophical Society, 34
  Theosophy and orientalist scholarship, 69
  universal religion, 88
  yoga, 98
Esdaile, James, 125
esotericism
  Avalon, 213
  emergence of, 245
  empty signifier, 26
  Enlightenment, 7
  entanglement, 67, 72
  Esoteric Science and Philosophy of the Tantras, The, 117
  Freemasonry, 100
  Gandhi, Mahatma, 247
  global religious history, 16
  Gnosticism, 100
  Hinduism, 23, 67, 96
  industrialization, 7–8
  initiation, 67–68
  magic, 41
  mesmerism, 101
  modernity, 7–8, 23, 32
  non-Western actors, 32
  orientalist scholarship, 65–68, 248–49
  related groups, 39
  religion, 21–23, 25, 237, 246
  science, 23, 41, 245
  secrecy, 67–68, 251
  Tantrik Occultism, 7, 64
  Theosophical Society, 38, 60
  transgression of religion/science boundaries, 23
  Woodroffe, 213
  yoga, 96–98
  See also Spiritualism; Tantra; Theosophy; Western esotericism
Eßbach, Wolfgang, 21
Eurocentrism, 3–4, 6, 18, 27–28, 247. *See also* English education; Western esotericism
Evola, Julius, 6

Faivre, Antoine, 98
Farquhar, John Nicol, 39
femininity. *See* women
Fischer-Tiné, Harald, 18–19, 28, 32, 84
Fisher, Elaine, 23
Fitzgerald, Timothy, 27
five Ms, 150, 222
Flood, Gavin, 1, 6, 66
foreigners, 181
Fox sisters, 143
France, 29, 89, 99, 227–28
Freemasonry, 39, 46, 89, 99, 100–101, 118, 146, 148, 250
Free Religious Association, 88

Gandhi, Mahatma, 39, 247
Ganeri, Jonardon, 50, 68
Ganesh & Co., 8, 226–27
Gangopadhyay, Ardhendrakumar (O.C. Ganguly), 213–15
Gangopadhyay, Danbari, 172, 217
Gangopadhyay, Dinanath, 110
Garland of Letters, The, 215, 233
Gaudiya Vaishnavism, 53, 150
Gauramma, 220
Gehrmann, Susanne, 28
Gheraṇḍa Saṁhitā, 117
Ghobrial, John-Paul, 26
Ghosh, Abhishek, 6, 8, 15
Ghosh, Atalbihari, 54, 163, 207, 217, 220–21, 226–27, 250
Ghosh, Aurobindo, 97, 166, 191, 195–97, 207, 211
Ghosh, Barindrakumar, 195, 197
Ghosh, Hemanta, 141
Ghosh, Hemendraprasad, 217
Gosh, Kalidas. *See* Bhuluyababa
Ghosh, Shishirkumar, 35, 89, 141–44, 147, 162, 173, 186, 230–31, 243

Gibbon, 87
Giles, Alfred E., 126
Gītāñjali, 171
Gokhale, Gopal Krishna, 191
global exchanges, 2, 21, 24, 27, 32–33, 54, 65, 85, 211, 245
globalization, 2–3
global religious history, 4, 16, 18–19, 21–28, 32–33, 67, 242, 244–45, 247, 251. *See also* religious studies
Gnosticism, 66–67, 100, 248, 250
goddess worship, 2, 49, 53–54, 169, 171–72, 181–82, 192–95, 197–98, 205
Goodrick-Clarke, Nicholas, 22
Gordon, William and Alice, 91
Görres, Joseph, 99
Gosvami, Bijaykrishna, 10–11, 88, 172–73, 186, 199, 207
Gosvami, Debendranath, 57
Gosvami, Madangopal, 172
Goudriaan, Teun, 66, 101, 151
Grant, Kenneth, 6
Great Liberation, The, 63, 101, 227–28, 238
Green, Nile, 23, 31–32
Gregory, William, 161
Gupta, Sanjukta, 151
Gupta, Swarupa, 84
gurus, 52, 68, 147, 179, 243. *See also* initiation
gymnasium, 187, 195–96

Haeckel, Ernst, 41, 234
Hammer, Olav, 22
Hanegraaff, Wouter, 28–29, 32
Harder, Hans, 194
Harinath, Kangal, 10, 35, 165–66, 185–87, 196, 222–23
Hatcher, Brian, 13–14, 16, 85, 87, 104, 243, 246
Hatha Yoga. *See* yoga
Hauer, Jakob Wilhelm, 5
Havell, Ernest Binfield, 215, 220, 223, 226
Hegel, Georg Wilhelm Friedrich 208, 210–11
Hermann, Adrian, 20, 25, 246
Hermetic Order of the Golden Dawn, 106, 114
Hermetism, 22, 29, 39, 101, 248
Hindu College, 86
Hinduism
  Bengali intervention, 40, 54
  Brāhma Samaj, 84
  Brahmanism, 42, 180
  Catechism of Hinduism, 118
  Catholicism, 64, 238–39
  Central Hindu College, 118
  colonialism period, 14, 16
  Educated Women of India, The, 214
  esotericism, 23, 67, 96
  Hindu dharma, 72, 199
  Hindu Spiritual Magazine, 112
  magnetism, 157
  meditation, 76
  nationalism, 21
  orientalist scholarship, 74
  orthodoxy, 156–58, 238
  Partition of Bengal, 190
  "Physical Errors of Hinduism," 121–22
  Pramathanath Mukhopadhyay, 209
  reform movement, 7, 82–83, 87
  revivalism, 13, 15, 21, 159, 229
  Sarvamaṅgalā Sabhā, 10, 245
  science, 22–23, 62, 92, 157, 200
  secrecy, 60
  "Superiority of Hinduism, The," 111
  Swadeshi movement, 190
  Tantrik Occultism, 7
  Vedas, 40, 85
  See also Tantra; yoga
Hindu Mela, 93, 156, 188–89, 194, 196, 223
Hindu Realism, 234
Hindu Spiritual Magazine, 112, 142–46, 221, 246
Hock, Klaus, 20
Hodgson, Brian Houghton, 67
homeophathy, 113
Hossain, Mir Mosharraf, 166
Hume, Allan Octavian, 70, 191–92, 227
Hume, David, 87
Hume, Florence, 227
Husayn Shah, 50
Huxley, Thomas Henry, 41, 209, 234
hypnotism, 105, 133, 232, 236

Idealism, 208–210, 233
idolatry, 173, 176, 181

imperialism, 25, 27–28, 32, 248
India
  All India Cow Conferences Association, 227
  anti-colonialism, 31–32
  Aryan wisdom, 42
  and Egypt, 54–55
  femininity, 73, 76
  independence, 83
  India, What Can It Teach Us?, 75–76
  India: Her cult and Education, 208
  Indian Association, 88–89, 92
  Is India Civilized?, 235, 237
  as locus of Aryan wisdom, 39
  modernity, 23
  Modern Religious Movements in India (1915), 39
  National Council of Education, 207, 236
  national education, 36, 211
  reform movement, 16
  ruling history, 48–49
  self-fulfillment, 208–9
  self-rule, 195, 247
  Spiritualism, 126
  Theosophical Society relocation, 4, 33–34
  Theosophy, or Psychological Religion, 79–80
  Universities Act (1904), 207
  See also colonialism; Hinduism
Indian education, 15
Indian Girls' Free High School, 117
Indian League, 141
Indian Mirror (newspaper), 90–91, 102–3, 166, 246
Indian National Association. *See* Indian National Congress (INC)
Indian National Conference, 153–54
Indian National Congress (INC), 39, 88, 191–92, 227
Indian National Society, 117
Indian Reform Association, 88
Indian Research Society, 239
Indian Society for the Propagation of Aryan Dharma. *See* BADPS
Indian Society of Oriental Art (ISOA), 215, 223, 226
Indian Universities Commission, 207
Indo-European language, 73–76
initiation
  Atalbihari friends, 220
  Baradakanta Majumdar, 55
  esotericism, 67–68
  Gauramma, 220
  gurus, 11, 162, 169, 180, 186, 251
  Moeller into Vaishnavism, 226
  occultism, 71
  Spiritualism, 38–39
  into Tantra, 11, 60, 65, 140, 145, 147, 162, 170
  Theosophy, 39, 162
  Woodroffe, 213, 220
Inner Life, The, 228–29
Interpreter (journal), 129
Isis Unveiled, 105
Islam, 45, 53, 66, 119, 190. *See also* Muslims

Jackson, Carl T., 85
Jadavpur University, 208
Jahangir, 50
James, William, 234
Jesus Christ, 57, 59, 83, 85, 100, 144, 237–38
Jones, William, 59, 73–74, 214
Josephson-Storm, Jason Ananda, 42, 77
Journal of the Royal Asiatic Society, 250
Judge, William Quan, 30, 38
Jung, Carl Gustav, 5
Jung-Stilling, Johann Heinrich, 99

Kabbalah, 39, 67, 99
Kabyaratna, Durganath, 57
Kabyatirtha, Gishpati, 192
Kali, 49, 53, 193–95, 237
Kali Yuga, 139, 151, 155, 178–79, 184. *See also* Tantra
Kalpa (journal), 57–59, 57–62, 110, 230, 246–47
Kalpaka (journal), 144
Kant, Immanuel, 61, 76, 210
karma, 110, 113, 139, 184, 194, 230
Kartābhajā, 173
Kashi Tattva Lodge, 159
Kashmir Shaivism, 150
Kaula, 10, 50–51, 66, 150, 151, 169, 177, 233
Kerner, Justinus, 99
Kingsford, Anna, 224

Kingsford, Douglas, 197
Kleine, Christoph, 26
Kluge, Carl Alexander Ferdinand, 99
Kollmar-Paulenz, Karénina, 17
Komlosy, Andrea, 19
Konarak, 215, 216*f*, 218, 226
Kopf, David, 85, 173
Koschorke, Klaus, 246
Krämer, Hans Martin, 22
Kripal, Jeffrey, 5
Krishna, 59
Krishnagar, 9*f*, 48, 198, 243
Krishnagar College, 55–56
Krishnamurti, 227
Kulārṇava Tantra, 11, 52, 150, 155, 162, 177, 180, 232, 263, 291, 293
Kullukabhatta, 50
Kumarkhali, 12, 35, 164–67, 196, 243–44
kundalini, 7, 9, 34, 217, 228, 231
Kundalini Yoga, 43, 46, 48, 50–51, 54, 106, 108, 121, 185

Laclau, Ernesto, 25–26
Lacordaire, Henri, 100
Lahore Government College, 116
Lal, Vinay, 32
Lalon Fakir (Lalon Shah), 10, 11, 53, 166–67
Latent Light Culture, 142, 144
Laws of Manu, 155, 161
Leadbeater, Charles Webster, 227–29
Le Bon, Gustave, 234
left-hand Tantrics, 10, 46, 52, 101, 250, 283
Lévi, Éliphas, 40–41, 67, 98
Lévi, Sylvain, 5, 228
Leyden, John, 66
Light (journal), 142
Light of Asia, 119
Light of the East: A Hindu Magazine Devoted to Aryan Philosophy, Religion and Occultism, 137–41, 246
Liotard, L., 132
Liu, Lydia, 32–33
Locke, John, 86
Lodge, Oliver, 234
Lord Carmichael, 223
Lord Curzon, 189, 207
Lord Dalhousie, 125
Lord Gauranga, 142–43
Lord Hardinge, 190
Lord Kitchener, 223
Lord Lytton, 189
Lord Ripon, 191–92
Lorea, Carola Erika, 251
Lubelsky, Isaac, 31

magic, 39, 40–41, 99, 243
magnetism, 7, 41, 46, 61, 71, 99–100, 133, 147, 157, 201, 208, 232, 248
Mahabharati, Dharmananda, 144–45, 147, 150, 163, 221
Mahānirvāṇa Tantra, 8, 11, 35, 126, 128, 136, 144, 155, 162, 177–78, 180–81
Mahatma letters, 30, 115, 143
Maitra, Akshaykumar, 10, 166, 192, 221–23, 227
Majumdar, Ambika, 192
Majumdar, Baradakanta
  Barnāśram dharmma, 230
  Bengali intervention, 7, 34, 38, 56, 229
  castes, 160, 204
  on Catholicism, 239
  duality/nonduality, 230
  Eastern vs. Western culture, 60–61, 250
  Freemasonry, 250
  Hatha Yoga, 232
  Indian occult science, 34
  initiation, 55, 60
  Kalpa (journal), 57–59, 230
  Krishnachandra Ray, 49
  occultism, 47
  Principles of Tantra, 101, 229–30, 232, 237
  Raja Yoga, 232
  revivalism, 161–62
  sanātana dharma, 160–61
  science and Tantra, 54
  Shivachandra, 11, 163, 183, 250
  spiritual culture, 230–31, 233
  Swadeshi movement, 192
  Tantrasāra, 53
  "Tantric Philosophy," 47
  Tantrik Occultism, 43, 46, 52, 56, 66, 73, 231
  as Theosophist, 55–57, 170–71, 229, 232, 243
  Yiśukhriṣṭa, 57
  See also Tantra

Majumdar, Bholanath, 218
Majumdar, Jnanendralal, 239
Majumdar, Kangal. *See* Kangal Harinath
Majumdar, Pratapchandra, 88, 90, 92
Malabari, Behramji, 77
Malkani, G. R., 234
Manning, Patrick, 18
mantras, 1, 50, 52, 106–7, 208
Manusmṛti, 50
Martinism, 99
Masson-Oursel, Paul, 5, 228
materialism, 38–39, 41–42, 47, 60, 62, 89, 131, 140, 148, 183–84, 233, 243
Matter, Jacques, 67, 100, 249
Maturin, Charles, 72
Mavalankar, Damodar K., 109–10
Mazlish, Bruce, 18
McCutcheon, Russell, 27
McDaniel, June, 6, 9, 12–13, 229
meditation, 43–44, 76, 97, 99, 104, 113, 144, 169, 201
mediumship, 38, 71, 115, 133–34
Meerut Theosophical Society, 105
Mesmer, Franz Anton, 98
mesmerism
  Anquetil-Duperron, 41, 99
  astral projection, 108
  Brajendranath Bandyopadhyay article, 61
  esotericism, 101
  Hermetism, 101
  vs. Indian occultism, 47
  mantras, 106
  Mesmerism in India, 125
  Neo-Platonic concepts, 101
  Neo-Vedantic occultism, 97
  occultism, 40, 107, 251
  Olcott speech, 92, 106
  Raja Yoga, 106
  religion, 99
  Spiritualism, 125
  Unitarianism, 89
  Western esotericism, 34
  yoga, 41, 107, 108, 137
  "Yoga Vidya," 98
Mill, John Stuart, 92, 160
Milton, John, 93
missionaries, 39, 45, 63, 72, 83, 156–57, 176
Mission School of Lahore, 116
Mitra, Adharchandra, 139
Mitra, Pyarichand, 35, 89, 91–93, 125–31, 141, 143, 243, 249
Mitra, Rajendralal, 43, 108, 127
mobility, 19, 23, 244–45
modernity
  Bengali intervention, 13
  corrupting power of, 238
  English education, 206
  entanglements, 23, 244
  esotericism, 7–8, 23, 32
  Eurocentrism, 27–28
  global religious history, 23–24
  vs. occultism, 65
  orthodoxy, 238
  reform movement, 14, 64, 245
  religion, 16, 37, 243
  revivalism, 159
  Shivachandra, 14–15, 23, 171
  Swadeshi movement, 192
  Tantra, 11–12
  Theosophical Society, 92
Modern Postural Yoga, 96–97
Moeller, Hjalmar Ponten, 226
Mohammed, 83, 138
Monism, 225, 233, 234. *See also* non-dualism
Monotheism, 83, 87, 181
Moses, 83
Mousseaux, Roger Gougenot des, 98
Mukherjee, Jotindra Nath, 198
Mukhopadhyay, Bhudev, 156, 160, 200
Mukhopadhyay, Jatindranath. *See* Bagha Jatin
Mukhopadhyay, Kaliprasanna, 110–12
Mukhopadhyay, Madangopal, 218
Mukhopadhyay, Pramathanath, 8, 12, 36, 163, 183, 187, 207–12, 218, 233–36, 238–39, 244, 249–50
Mukhopadhyay, Satishchandra, 207, 208
Mukhopadhyay, Sirishchandra, 137
Müller, Friedrich Max
  Aryan civilization, 75, 126, 208
  brahmabidyā, 170
  castes, 160
  Chips from a German Workshop, 75–76
  India, What Can It Teach Us?, 75–76

Indo-European language, 75
Introduction to the Science of Religion, 75
Keshabchandra Sen and, 88
Olcott, 78, 80–82
orientalist scholarship, 244, 249
Protestantism, 79–80
religion origin, 42
Sacred Books of the East, 77, 81, 118
Six Systems of Indian Philosophy, 118
Tantra, 10, 248
Theosophical Society, 74, 77–78, 80
Theosophy, or Psychological Religion, 78–80
Theosophy and orientalist scholarship, 69
translations, 61
Upanishads, 85
Muslims, 56, 151, 166, 190, 194–95
Mustafi, Nagendrabala, 129–30
Muzaffarpur bombing, 197–98
mysticism, 44, 96, 101, 209

Nababharat press, 174
Nababidhān, 90, 152–53, 192
Nadiya district, 9f, 12, 15, 48, 251
Nanak, 83, 146
Nandy, Ashis, 32
Nandy, Mahindrachandra, 227
Sen, Narendranath, 90, 93–96, 125, 136, 166, 192
Naths, 44, 66, 104, 240, 261
National Council of Education, 207
national education, 64, 211, 213, 233, 236
nationalism
Aryas, 84
Aurobindo Ghosh, 196
Bamandas Basu, 120
Bloodthirsty Mother, 197–98
Brahmos, 83–84, 187
Dawn (magazine), 207
education, 245
gymnasium, 195–96
Hinduism, 21
Hindu Mela, 93, 156
Indian education, 15
Indian League, 141
Jagadishchandra Bose, 188
mobility, 245
Narendranath Sen, 90
National Congress, 160
negotiation of, 16
Pramathanath Mukhopadhyay, 187, 211
Rajnarayan Basu, 111
revivalism and, 14
revolutionaries, 197–98
Sarvamaṅgalā Sabhā, 207
science, 15, 36, 207
secret societies, 196–98
shakti, 196–98
Shaktism, 193, 246
Shivachandra, 36, 186–87, 242, 244
spiritual culture, 230
Srishchandra Basu, 117
Swadeshi movement, 36, 188–92
Tantra, 96, 187, 198–99, 207, 230, 244
Woodroffe, 187
Navadvip, 9f, 11, 15, 35, 48, 50, 53, 155–156, 168–69, 243
Neo-Tantra, 2, 17
New Age spirituality, 1, 4, 5
New Bengal School, 223
New Dispensation Church, 88, 155
New Logic, 50, 169, 171
New Platonists, 126
New Thought, 4, 16, 35, 97, 124, 135, 137, 143, 234–35, 243, 246
nondualism, 62, 177, 182, 184, 186, 208, 230, 234. See also Monism
non-Western actors, 31–32
nyāsa, 1, 50

O'Brien, Patrick, 18
occultism
astral projection, 107–8
Catholicism, 238
electricity, 248
emergence of, 67
France, 89
Freemasonry, 101
global occult, 23
hypnotism, 236
Indian, 47, 64, 68
Jesus Christ, 100
kundalini, 9
Lévi, Éliphas, 40, 98
Light of the East: A Hindu Magazine Devoted to Aryan Philosophy, Religion and Occultism, 137

occultism (*cont.*)
magic, 243
magnetism, 248
mesmerism, 40, 107, 251
vs. modernity, 65
Neo-Vedantic occultism, 97
New Age spirituality, 4
Occult Science: The Science of Breath, 105
orientalist scholarship, 248
religion and science, 36
Tantra, 8, 46, 68, 122, 213, 248
Theosophy, 229
Woodroffe, 238–39
yoga, 34, 65–66, 96–97, 101–3, 127, 243
See also esotericism; Spiritualism; Tantrik Occultism
Olcott, Henry Steel
Aryan civilization, 73
astral projection, 107–8
Bad Aryan (B.A.), 211, 249
Baradakanta Majumdar, 57
BDM (Bhārat Dharma Mahāmaṇḍal), 159, 249
Bombay arrival, 70
"Buddhist Catechism," 57
Calcutta arrival, 91–92, 95–96, 246
Indian Mirror (newspaper), 90–91
mesmerism, 92, 106, 125
Müller, 78, 80–82
Pyarichand Mitra, 127–28
relocation to Adyar, 34, 71, 89–90
Śiva Saṁhitā, 116
Tantras translations, 45
Theosophical Society, 34, 38, 89–90
translations, 59
yoga, 102, 104, 108, 117
Old, Walter Gorn, 135
Om: A Treatise on Vedantic Raj Yoga, 106–9
Orientalism, 29–31, 247, 251
orientalist scholarship
ambiguous role of, 248–49
Aryan civilization, 74
Avalon, 63, 228
Bengal, 48, 243
bhadralok (English-educated middle class), 245
esotericism, 65–68, 248–49
Eurocentrism, 247
global religious history, 247
India and Egypt, 55
Indo-European language, 73–74
left-hand Tantrics, 250
magnetism, 100
Müller, 244, 249
Navadvip district, 15
occultism, 248
reject Aryan wisdom, 39
religion, 71, 249
Shaktism, 13
Tantra, 242
Tantrik Occultism, 248
Theosophical Society, 12, 71
Theosophy, 69, 73–74
yoga, 96
orthodoxy, 12, 149, 152, 156–58, 172, 178, 188, 200, 226, 238, 243, 245, 249
Osho movement, 1–2
Osterhammel, Jürgen, 21, 23
Oupnek'hat, 44, 99. *See also* Upanishads

Padoux, André, 1, 6, 66
Pal, Bipinchandra, 125, 158–59, 172, 191, 200, 217, 220, 222
Pal, Vasantakumar, 164–65, 214–15
Pandit (journal), 108
pandits, 11, 15, 48, 50
Panini Office, 117–18
Papus, 29
Parliament of the World's Religions, 88, 97, 138
Partition of Bengal, 189*f*
Partridge, Christopher, 30
Passavant, Johann Carl, 99
Patanjali, 44, 105, 108, 127, 138, 172
Paul, Navinchandra, 104–5
Paul, St, 60
Pavy, Frederick William, 161
Pebbles, James Martin, 126, 142
periodicals, 246
Phikir Cāṁder Dal, 166
philosophy, 225, 249
Philosophy and Science of Vedantic Raja Yoga, The, 109
"Philosophy of the Tantras," 139
Pioneer (newspaper), 70

Plato, 60
Plotinus, 60
Positive Sciences of the Ancient Hindus, 234
Positivism, 124, 210
postcolonialism, 16, 27–28, 30, 247
postmodernism, 2, 27
Prakash, Gyan, 15, 188
pranayama, 105–106, 113, 115, 147, 232
Prārthanā Samāj, 153
Principles of Tantra (Avalon), 8, 12–13, 63–64, 101, 163, 228–30, 232, 237, 240
Protestantism, 63–64, 72, 79–80, 83, 238–39
psychical research, 30, 98, 143
psychology, 61, 92, 98, 108, 132, 203, 209
Blavatsky's psychological science, 105
Müller's Psychological Religion, 78–81
"Psychology of Buddhist Aryans," 127
"Psychology of the Aryas," 126
Tantra as psychological science, 146, 225, 235
Puranas, 11, 49, 59, 67, 177
Purnananda Giri, 52
Putnam, Lara, 245
Puységur, Marquis de, 99

race, 74, 160, 236–37, 247
racism, 30, 74, 247–48
Radha, 54, 173
Rai, Lala Lajpat, 154, 158, 191
Raja Yoga. *See* yoga
Rajshahi Harmony Theosophical Society, 110
Ramakrishna, 54, 172, 181
Ramanuja, 230–31
Roy, Rammohan, 52–53, 82, 85–86, 151–52, 155, 177, 180–82, 187, 240, 249
Ramprasad, 10–11, 53, 105–6, 121, 171, 176, 178, 221. *See* shakta poetry
Ramram Swami, 169
Ranade, Mahadev Govind, 153
Randeria, Shalini, 23
rationalism, 27, 173, 179
Ravenshaw, Edward Cockburn, 250
Ray, Dinendrakumar, 166
Ray, Krishnachandra, 10, 49, 50, 54–55, 101, 172, 240, 249
Ray, Prafullachandra, 188
Ray, Pramathabhushan Deva, 55–56
Ray, Saratkumar, 221
Ray, Shankarnath, 239
Ray, Shyamashankar, 89, 93
Raychaudhuri, Tapan, 13–14, 21, 199–200
reformers, 5, 7, 12, 82–83, 148
reformism, 12–13, 15–16, 34–35, 69, 82, 95, 152–55, 174, 246. *See also* reform movement
reform movement
  Ārya Samāj, 176
  Aryan civilization, 84, 162
  Aryas, 83–84, 162
  Brāhma Samaj, 69, 129, 153, 176
  Brahmoism, 174
  Brahmos, 87, 111–12, 152, 154–55
  castes, 83–84, 120, 129, 131, 153–54, 156
  child marriage, 154
  entanglement, 88–89
  female education reform, 120, 153–54
  Indian Reform Association, 88
  Krishnagar College, 55
  Kshetrapal Chakravarti, 132, 136–37
  Kulārṇava and, 52
  Mahānirvāṇa Tantra, 151–52
  modernity, 14, 64, 245
  orthodoxy, 152, 155, 245
  Pramathabhushan Deva Ray, 56
  Pyarichand Mitra, 128–31
  Rajnarayan Basu, 152–53
  "Revival and Reform," 153
  vs. revivalism, 35, 148, 152–55, 161
  sanātana dharma, 155, 159
  Shivachandra denunciation, 163, 176
  Shivanath Shastri., 155–56
  social reform, 95, 130
  Society for the Acquisition of General Knowledge, 86–87
  Spiritualism, 35, 40, 130
  Tantra, 7, 12, 39, 130, 155, 187, 242
  Tattvabodhini Sabhā, 155
  Theosophical Society, 34–35, 69, 82, 89, 95, 174
  Theosophy, 200, 245
  Unitarianism, 87
  widow remarriage, 151, 153, 156
  women's place in society, 83, 130–31, 154
  Young Bengal, 86–87

Regardie, Israel, 6
Reichenbach, Karl von, 98
Rele, Vasant G., 121
religion
  Aryan origin of, 34, 42, 243, 249
comparativism, 26, 86, 88, 251
  dharma, 26, 39, 153
  Eurocentrism, 28
  Free Religious Association, 88
  Indo-European language, 74
  Introduction to the Science of Religion, 75
  Lectures on the Origin and Growth of Religion as Illustrated by the Religions of India, 75
  magnetism, 41, 99
  modernity, 16, 37, 243
  Muslim/Hindu relations, 245
  national education, 236
  orientalist scholarship, 71, 249
  Osho-Rajneesh movement, 2–3
  Partition of Bengal, 189–90
  reform movement, 14
  scholarship of, 17
  science, 22, 36, 69, 249
  Theosophy, 92
  Theosophy, or Psychological Religion, 78–80
  twin birth of religion and esotericism, 250
  Unitarianism impact, 85
  universal brotherhood, 59–60, 89
  "What is the Bengali word for religion?," 153
  World's Parliament of Religions, 88, 138
  yoga, 237
  See also esotericism; global religious history; *individual denominations*; Tantra; Theosophical Society
religious studies
comparativism, 26, 71, 77, 86, 88, 251
emergence of comparative religion, 74, 86
Eurocentrism and postcolonialism, 27–28
global history, 3–4, 16–17
Theosophy, 21, 42, 71, 77, 74
revivalism
  Aryan wisdom, 59-60, 153
  Bankimchandra Chattopadhyay, 200
  Baradakanta Majumdar, 161
  Bengal Theosophical Society for the Promotion of the Meaning of the Eternal Aryan Dharma, 158
  Bijaykrishna Gosvami, 173
  Cousins, 224
  dharma, 13
  hidden secrets, 250–51
  Hindu dharma, 59
  Hinduism, 13, 15, 21, 159, 229
  Lala Lajpat Rai, 191
  Mahānirvāṇa Tantra, 149–52
  modernity, 159
  nationalism, 14
  orthodoxy, 149, 226
  vs. reformism, 35, 148, 152–55, 161
  "Revival and Reform," 153
  rise of, 128
  sanātana dharma, 58–59, 149
  Shakta poetry, 54
  Shashadhar Tarkacuramani, 200
  Srishchandra Basu, 118
  Strube, 15–16
  Tantra, 226
  Theosophists, 249
  Theosophy, 158–62, 200
  Vaishnavism, 162, 246
revolutionaries, 197–99, 242, 250
Richardson, David Lester, 55
Ripon College, 61, 207
rishis, 34, 61
ritual, 52–53, 63, 134–35, 179, 238, 250
Rosicrucianism, 39, 46–47, 99, 250
Rothenstein, William, 223–24
Rothstein, Mikael, 22
Rudbøg, Tim, 22

sabhās, 10, 156, 172, 243
Sachsenmaier, Dominic, 18
Sacred Books of the East, 77, 81, 118
Sacred Books of the Hindus, 117–18, 120
sādhana, 11, 66, 113, 134, 144, 145, 146, 175, 177, 179–86, 201, 205, 206, 208, 211, 226, 230, 234–35, 237–38, 240
Sādhāran Brāhma Samāj, 88, 90, 116, 173, 188
samādhi, 108, 122
sanātana dharma
  Aryan wisdom, 58–60, 175, 245

asceticism, 194
Aurobindo Ghosh, 196
Baradakanta Majumdar, 160
BDM (Bhārat Dharma Mahāmaṇḍal), 158
Brahmos, 129
Eternal Principles of Sadhana, or The Secrets of Tantra, The, 145–46
Explanation of Dharma, 201
Kali Yuga, 155, 178
Mahānirvāṇa Tantra, 150, 155
reform movement, 155, 159
Shivachandra, 10–11, 163, 171, 175, 178, 185–86
Spiritualism, 131
Tantra, 35, 48, 155–58, 163, 208, 248
Tantratattva, 174–75
Theosophists, 249
Theosophy as, 62, 130
Vedic dharma, 36
"What is the Bengali word for religion?," 153
See also revivalism
Sand, Reenberg Erik, 22
Sanderson, Alexis, 48–49, 66
Sanskrit, 11, 50, 52, 58, 75, 117, 168, 213–15, 222
Sarasvati, Dayananda
Anglo-Vedic School, 61
Ārya Samāj, 39–40, 82–83, 176–77, 180
attacks Tantras, 45
caste reform, 83–84
Hinduism, 63
Keshabchandra Sen, 88
Light of the Meaning of Truth, The, 45
reform movement, 82–83
Srishchandra Basu, 117
Tantra, 77
Theosophical Society, 34, 70, 103–4, 107
"Truth-Seeker" article, 44–45
yoga, 44, 110
"Yoga Vidya," 102, 104
Saraswati, Atalananda. *See* Atalbihari Ghosh
Sarbadhikary, Sukanya, 251
Sardella, Ferdinando, 14, 54
Sarkar, Akshaychandra, 200
Sarkar, Sumit 191–92
Sartori, Andrew, 6, 12, 186, 208
Sarvamaṅgalā Sabhā, 10, 36, 170–74, 188–89, 199, 207, 212, 217, 245
Sarvamangala temple, 218, 219*f*
Schopenhauer, Arthur, 138
Schrader, Friedrich Otto, 228
science
Aryan wisdom, 60, 95
bijñān (Bengali), 58, 163, 182–184, 203
English education, 62
esotericism, 23, 41, 245
Hinduism, 22–23, 62, 92, 157, 200
Indian rishis, 34
magic as, 40–41
magnetism, 99
materialism, 41, 47, 183–84
nationalism, 15, 36, 207
nineteenth century, 22
Prafullachandra Ray, 188
sādhana, 11, 182–84
Science of Breath and the Philosophy of the Tattvas, The, 106
Shivachandra, 36, 175, 179, 183, 188, 199
spiritual science, 36, 199–208, 249
Tantrik Occultism, 7
Theosophists" denunciation, 58–59
Western science as adversary and authority, 61–62
See also religion; Tantra; yoga
Seal, Brajendranath, 234
séance, 125, 133, 141, 143
secrecy, 60, 62, 65, 67–68, 139–40, 162, 175, 185, 250–51. *See also* initiation
Secret Doctrine, 47, 160, 224
secret societies, 196–98
secularism, 237–38
self-fulfillment, 208–9
Sen, Amiya P., 14, 21, 159
Sen, Jaladhar, 166–67, 192, 214, 221–23
Sen, Keshabchandra, 87–88, 90, 92, 103, 152–53, 155, 173, 192
Sen, Krishnabihari, 90–91
Sen, Krishnaprasanna, 156–57
Sen, Rakhalchandra, 57, 61, 129
Sen, Ramkamal, 90
Serpent Power, The, 52, 101, 228–29
sexuality, 1, 2, 247, 291

sexual relations, 2, 15, 150–51, 184–85, 231
Shah Jahan, 50
Shaiva Age, 48
Shaiva-Shakta traditions, 10, 15, 48–49, 152
Shaiva Siddhanta, 50
Shakespeare, 93
Shakta poetry, 53–54, 170–72, 178, 186, 234, 242, 251. *See also* Ramprasad
shakti, 2, 7, 196–98, 201, 208, 236
Shaktism, 9, 11, 13, 193, 205, 212, 236, 246
Shakti Tattva, 184–85
Shankara, 59, 61, 230–31
Shastri, Govindaram, 108
Shastri, Haridev, 214–15, 217–18, 220, 222, 227
Shintoism, 240
Shiromani, Ragunatha, 50
Shiva, 2, 46, 184–85, 250
Shastri, Shivanath, 88, 90, 92, 116, 125, 155–56, 173
Shom, Bipinbihari, 121–22
Shri Vidya, 50
Shri Yantra, 250
siddhi, 2, 65, 98, 101, 119, 134, 140, 175, 179–80, 182–184, 186, 222
Singh, Kameshwar, 221
Singh, Rameshwar, 157–59, 163, 221
Singleton, Mark, 97
Sinnet, Alfred Percy, 70
Sister Nivedita, 195, 224
Śiva Saṁhitā, 108, 116
smārta, 51–52, 150–51
Smith, Adam, 86
smriti, 59, 128, 174
Snell, Merwin-Marie, 138
social reform, 95, 130, 141
Society for Exercise, 195
Society for Psychical Research, 30, 98
Society for the Acquisition of General Knowledge, 86–87, 89
Society for the Education and Liberations of the Women of India, 130
somnambulism, 99–100, 137
South Asian religion, 1–3, 21, 245
Spencer, Herbert, 41, 92, 147, 161, 209, 235
Spinoza, 210
spiritual culture, 230–31
Spiritualism
  Banner of Light (journal), 126
  Blavatsky, 112
  emergence of, 35, 67
  esotericism, 229
  Fox family, 143
  Hindu Spiritual Magazine, 142
  initiation, 38–39
  intellectual exchange, 246
  Kaula, 233
  Kshetrapal Chakravarti, 134–35, 243
  Light (journal), 142
  mesmerism, 125
  New Age spirituality, 4
  New Thought, 35, 124
  occultism, 98, 127
  Peebles, 142
  Pyarichand Mitra, 35, 125, 243
  reform movement, 35, 40, 130
  sanātana dharma, 131
  séance, 125
  Shishirkumar Ghosh, 35, 141–44, 243
  Society for Psychical Research, 30
  Spiritualist (journal), 127
  Srishchandra Basu, 116
  Stray Thoughts on Spiritualism, 126, 128
  Tantra, 46, 136
  Theosophical Society, 38, 40, 107
  Transcendentalism, 35, 124
  Unitarianism, 89
  United States, 126
  Wallace, 41
  Woodroffe, 235
  yoga, 97–98
  See also Theosophy
spiritual science, 36, 199–208, 249
Spiritual Stray Leaves, The, 125–26
Sri Chaitanya Yoga Sadhan Somaj, 132–33
Srimati Gouramba Garu. *See* Gauramma
Srinivas, Tulasi, 2–3
Stevens, John A., 89
Stewart, Tony K., 251
Stuckrad, Kocku von, 41–42
Subrahmanyam, Sanjay, 23, 30–31
Swadeshi movement, 36, 89, 187–95, 198–99, 207, 246
Swami Abhedananda, 172

Swami Krishnananda, 172
Swami Prajnanananda, 174
Swami Pratyagatmananda Saraswati. *See* Pramathanath Mukhopadhyay
Swami Sachchidananda, 112, 147–48, 163
Swami Sadananda, 218
Swami, Shri Sabhapati, 106, 107–10, 117
Swami Sachchidananda, 145–48
Swami Vivekananda, 13–14, 97, 195, 198
Swedenborg, Emanuel, 97, 119
Swedenborgianism, 99
Sykes, William Henry, 67

Tagore, Abanindranath, 215, 223–24, 226
Tagore, Debendranath, 87–88, 93, 111, 116, 155, 165, 172–73
Tagore, Dvarkanath, 85, 87, 165
Tagore, Dvijendranath, 93
Tagore, Gaganendranath, 215, 223
Tagore, Rabindranath, 87, 93, 132, 165–66, 193, 223–24, 228
Tagore, Yatindramohan, 91, 93, 142
Tantra
  Agamas Research Society, 225, 246
  Akshaykumar Maitra, 223
  all-comprehensiveness, 237
  "Anatomy of the Tantras, The," 120
  anti-colonialism, 242
  Aryan wisdom, 47
  attacks on, 45
  Avalon publications, 36
  BADPS (Indian Society for the Propagation of Aryan Dharma), 187
  Bamandas Basu, 120–22
  Baradakanta Majumdar, 8, 42–43, 46–47, 57, 61, 106, 109, 244, 248
  Bengal, 49
  Bengali Tantrikas, 46
  as black magic, 4–5, 34, 45, 46–47, 225
  Brahmanism, 48, 50, 118, 140, 242
  Brahmos, 111
  castes, 50
  Catholicism, 64, 238
  Christianity, 162, 225, 240
  colonialism, 54, 242
  controversies over, 43
  Cousins, 224–25
  Dayananda rejection of, 83
  debates about, 109
  as debauchery and perversity, 45–47
  denounced scriptures, 10
  dharma, 49, 146
  diffusion of, 240–41
  English education, 62, 230
  entanglement, 25, 186
  esotericism, 3–4, 11, 38, 67, 113, 187, 237–41, 248, 250
  Esoteric Science and Philosophy of the Tantras, The, 116–17
  Eternal Principles of Sadhana, or The Secrets of Tantra, The, 145
  false gurus, 147
  female worship, 133–34
  five Ms, 150, 222
  Freemasonry, 46, 146, 148
  global reach, 1, 6–7, 20, 242–43
  global religious history, 4, 21
  Gnosticism, 248
  Hatha Yoga, 104
  Hermetic Order of the Golden Dawn and, 114
  Hermetism, 248
  Hinduism, 15, 63, 144, 245
  householders, 151
  hypnotism, 133
  Indian Society of Oriental Art (ISOA), 224
  Kali Yuga, 11, 43, 146, 150, 162, 170, 230, 249
  Kalpa (journal), 61–62
  Kshetrapal Chakravarti, 131–37
  Kulārṇava Tantras, 11, 52
  Kundalini Yoga, 50–51
  left-hand Tantrics, 10, 52, 101, 250
  Mahānirvāṇa Tantra, 11, 35, 126, 128, 144, 149–52, 162, 178
  mantras, 50
  vs. materialism, 42, 140
  modernity, 11
  Müller research, 10, 77, 248
  mysticism, 101
  Naths worship, 240
  national education, 36, 213
  nationalism, 96, 187, 198–99, 207, 230, 244
  necromancy, 112

Tantra (*cont.*)
negative view of, 223
New Age spirituality, 4–5
new religious movements, 16
nineteenth century developments, 17
occultism, 8, 46, 68, 122, 213, 248
"On the Early Tantras of the Hindus," 136–37
orientalist scholarship, 242
orthodoxy, 12, 155
Panchkari Bandyopadhyay, 240
personal magnetism, 147
philosophy, 225
"Philosophy of the Tantras," 139
"Physical Errors of Hinduism," 122
Pramathanath Mukhopadhyay, 208, 210–11, 244, 249
Principles of Tantra, 63–64, 101, 229
Protestantism, 63–64
public education, 187
Puranas, 49
Pyarichand Mitra, 249
Rajnarayan Basu, 155, 180, 187
Rammohan Roy, 155, 180–82, 187, 240
reform movement, 7, 12, 39, 130, 155, 187, 242
religion origin, 42, 249
"Religious Aspects of the Early Tantras, The," 131, 228
revivalism, 226
rituals, 50, 134–35
as root of Aryan traditions, 48, 111, 155–58, 163, 208, 248
sanātana dharma, 35
as science, 96, 111–12, 136, 187, 208, 225, 231
science/religion debate, 71, 124, 136
secrecy, 65, 139–40
sexual relations, 2, 134
South Asian religion, 1–3, 245
Spiritualism, 35, 136
Srishchandra Basu, 249
superstition and degeneracy, 45
Swadeshi movement, 187
Tantra of the Great Liberation, The (1913), 8
"Tantras and Their Teachings, The," 111
"Tantras and the Religion of the Shaktas, The," 239
Tantra Shastra, 63
"Tantras of Buddhism, The," 113
Tantratattva, 174–78
"Tantric and Puranic Ideas of the Deity, The," 110
"Tantric Philosophy," 47
"Theory and Practice of Tantra," 112, 146
Theosophical Society, 71
Theosophy, 48, 242
translations of, 45
Universal Worship, 148
Upanishads, 140
Vaishnavism, 140
Varendra Research Society, 56, 222, 246
Vedas, 11, 40, 43, 45–46, 48–50, 68, 249
Woodroffe, 64, 213, 217, 226–27, 244
yoga, 2, 62, 106, 112, 215
See also Avalon, Arthur; Bengali intervention; initiation; Tantrik occultism; yoga
Tantraratna (Panda), Jatindranath, 218
Tantrasāra, 53, 111, 162, 178
Tantratattva, 8, 11, 17, 36, 163, 169, 174–75, 178, 181, 185–86, 192, 213, 238–39
Tantrik Occultism, 7, 43, 46–47, 52, 56, 64–66, 73, 229–31, 248
Tantrik Texts, 221, 228
Tarakhepa (Manimohan Gosvami), 218
Tarakhepa (Tarapada Banerjee), 199
Tarapith, 171–72, 178, 199
Tarkalankar, Chandrakanta, 48
Tarkacuramani, Shashadhar, 10, 36, 48, 156–57, 159–60, 163, 171–72, 187, 199–208, 211, 249
Tattvabodhinī Sabhā, 52, 111, 155
Tatya, Tukaram, 108
Taylor, Kathleen, 6, 8, 64–65, 164, 178, 207, 215, 217, 220, 220–21, 227, 229
terrorism, 190, 197–98
Theosophical Society
Ārya Samāj, 34, 102
admiration for India, 29
agency of non-Western members, 31, 248
anti-Christian attitude, 79
anti-colonialism, 31–32

Aryan civilization, 69, 73, 82, 94–95
Aryan wisdom, 59–60
Aryas, 84, 91, 243
Baradakanta as member, 56–57, 243
Besant, 39, 59
Brāhma Samaj, 84–85
Brahmos, 91, 243
Catholicism, 41
colonialism, 29–32, 95
conflict among, 30
Cousins, 224
Dayananda, 82–83, 103–4, 107
education of Hindu boys, 93
entanglement, 34, 89
esotericism, 38, 60, 114–15
Esoteric Science and Philosophy of the Tantras, The, 117
established, 38
founding, 4
France, 29, 227–28
global religious history, 21, 33
as global religious movement, 3
Hatha Yoga, 34, 104, 135, 232
Hindu nationalism, 21
Hindu revivalism, 35
Hume, Allan Octavian, 191–92
Indian Mirror (newspaper), 90–91
Indian relocation, 4, 33–34
influence of, 21
intercultural transfer, 20
Kalpa (journal), 57–59
Kashi Tattva Lodge, 159
Kumarkhali, 12, 243–44
Kundalini Yoga, 48
lines of communication, 242–43
Mahatma letters, 30
missionaries, 72
mobility, 244–45
modernity, 92
Modern Religious Movements in India (1915), 39
Müller research, 74–83
Navadvip, 243
non-Western actors, 22
occultists, 29
Orientalism, 30–31
orientalist scholarship, 12, 71
pranayama, 105
Pyarichand Mitra, 127
racism, 30
Raja Yoga, 232
Rajnarayan Basu, 243
Rameshwar Singh, 221
reformism, 34–35, 69, 82, 89, 95, 174, 246
religion origin, 42
relocation to Adyar, 39, 43, 69, 71, 127, 244
revision of rules, 70–71
Sachchidananda Swami, 146
school for Hindu boys, 57
Schrader as librarian, 228
science, 41
Science of Breath and the Philosophy of the Tattvas, The, 106
Shishirkumar Ghosh, 141
Spiritualism, 35, 40, 107
Srimat Sachchidananda Swami, 145
Srishchandra Basu, 116
stated purposes of, 58
Swadeshi movement, 192
Tantrik Occultism, 248
translations among, 35
universal brotherhood, 70–71, 94, 237
Vedavyasa Press, 200
Western esotericism, 21–22, 28–29
Woodroffe, 226–29
yoga, 31, 34, 101–4, 107
Young Bengal, 89
Young Men's Indian Association, 224
See also Avalon, Arthur; Bengali intervention; Blavatsky, Helena Petrovna; Olcott, Henry Steel; Tantra
Theosophist, The (journal), 7, 33, 40–44, 46, 52–53, 70–72, 82, 98, 105–6, 227–28, 246–47
Theosophists, 55–57, 98, 125, 128–29, 131, 161, 170–71, 229, 232, 245–46, 249
Theosophy
anti-colonialism, 247
Aryan civilization, 69–73
Aryan wisdom, 58, 246
Bengali intervention, 243
brahmabidyā, 170–71, 248
Brahmos, 247
emergence of, 67

Theosophy (*cont.*)
global religious history, 245
initiation, 39, 162
Kshetrapal Chakravarti, 135
Mahatma letters, 143
occultism, 229
orientalist scholarship, 69, 73–74
Pyarichand Mitra, 128
race, 247
reform movement, 200, 245
revivalism, 158–62, 200
rivalries, 229
sanātana dharma, 62, 130
as science, 93
as scientific basis of religion, 92, 96
secrecy, 162
Shishirkumar Ghosh, 143
Spiritualism, 124, 225
Srishchandra Basu, 247
Tantra, 48, 242
Theosophy, or Psychological Religion, 78–80
Unitarianism, 89
universal brotherhood, 59–60, 248
Western esotericism, 245
yoga, 128
Zoroastrianism, 71
See also Tantra; Theosophical Society
Thoreau, Henry David, 86, 97
Tibetan Buddhism, 67
Tibetan language, 222
Tilak, Bal Gangadhar, 191
Tisdall, James, 215
Transcendentalism, 16, 35, 86, 124, 243, 246
translations, 32–33, 35, 45, 58, 61
T.S., 111–13, 145, 150
Tweed, Thomas A., 25

Unitarianism, 85–89, 243, 246
United States, 89, 126, 130
universal brotherhood, 59–60, 70–71, 89, 94, 236–37, 247–49
Universities Act (1904), 207
Upadhyaya, Gangesha, 171
Upanishads, 41, 44, 59, 66–67, 74–75, 77–80, 85, 87, 99, 111, 140, 155
Urban, Hugh, 2–9, 151–52, 178, 187, 251

Vaishnavism
asceticism, 194
Bengali intervention, 9
Bijaykrishna Gosvami, 173
Dharmananda Mahabharati, 145
gurus, 180
Kshetrapal Chakravarti and, 133
Moeller initiation, 226
revivalism, 162, 246
Sachchidananda Swami, 147–48
secrecy, 251
Shakta poetry, 53, 170, 172, 186
Shishirkumar Ghosh, 141–43
Shivachandra, 11, 163
Tantra, 113, 140
vāmācāra. *See* left-hand Tantrics
Vamakhepa, 171–72, 178, 199, 218
van der Veer, Peter, 16, 23, 31, 247
Varendra Research Society, 10, 56, 166, 212, 221–22, 227, 246
Vaughan, Thomas, 44
Vedantabagish, Kalibar, 172
Vedanta Math, 172, 174
Vedantism, 126, 184
Vedas, 10, 40, 42, 46, 59, 61, 74, 76–80, 83–85, 117, 129, 156–57, 160–61, 184. *See also* Tantra
Vedavyasa Press, 200
Vedic School of Bengal, 61
Vidyalankara, Ramatoshana, 52
Vidyarnava, Shivachandra Bhattacharya
Akshaykumar Maitra, 222
anti-colonialism, 163
antidolatry, 181
anti-reformist reformism, 11
Aryan civilization, 187
Atalbihari, 220, 250
Avalon publications, 33, 36, 163, 184, 230
Bagha Jatin, 198
Baradakanta Majumdar, 11, 163, 183, 250
Baul circle, 35
Baul poetry, 185–86
Bengali intervention, 54
Bengali School, 163, 177–78
bhadralok (English-educated middle class), 186

Bloodthirsty Mother, 192–93
brahmabidyā, 171
Brahmos, 176–77, 180
caste hierarchies, 167
colonialism, 250
corpse meditation, 169
Danbari Gangopadhyay, 172
death of, 217
English education refusal, 11, 35–36, 163, 167–69, 185–86, 211
Gaṅgeś (play), 171
goddess worship, 169, 171–72, 181–82
Guruism, 179
guru initiation, 169
Hinduism renaissance, 14
Jaladhar Sen, 166–67, 222–23
Kali Yuga, 179
Kangal Harinath, 166
Kaula, 10, 169, 177
Kumarkhali, 164–67
Kundalini Yoga, 185
modernity, 14–15, 23, 171
nationalism, 36, 186–87, 242, 244
nondualism, 182, 184, 186, 208
orientalist scholarship, 12
orthodoxy and, 172
Panchkari Bandyopadhyay, 181, 239–40
pandits, 11, 48
pictured, 164*f*
Pīṭhmālā, 170
Pramathanath Mukhopadhyay, 12, 163, 183, 207–8, 211, 250
Principles of Tantra, 228
Puranas, 11, 177
Rameshwar Singh, 221
Rammohan Roy, 176–77, 178
Rāslīlā (play), 170
rationalism, 179
reform movement denunciation, 163, 176
rituals, 179
sādhana, 186
sanātana dharma, 10–11, 163, 171, 175, 178, 185–86
Sanskrit education, 11, 168
Sarvamaṅgalā Sabhā, 170–74
science, 36, 175, 179, 183, 188, 199
sexual relations, 184–85
Shakta poetry, 251
Shashadhar Tarkacuramani, 10, 171, 199, 203, 206
song writing, 165
Swadeshi movement, 192–93, 199
Tantra, 12, 162–63, 169, 175, 248–49
Tantratattva, 11, 17, 36, 163, 169, 174–78, 185–86, 192
Vaishnavism, 163
Vamakhepa, 171–72, 178
Varendra Research Society, 188, 222
Vedantism, 184
See also Woodroffe, John
Vidyasagar, Ishvarchandra, 87, 167–68
Vidyasagar, Jivananda, 168
Vishnu, 46, 237
Viswanathan, Gauri, 31, 168, 247
Vitalism, 234
Vivekananda Society, 236
Voltaire, 86

Wallace, Alfred Russel, 41
Weiss, Richard, 13
Wenzlhuemer, Roland, 18–19, 244
Western civilization, 60, 62, 249. *See also* English education
Western esotericism, 16, 21–22, 28–30, 34, 245, 247, 250
Westernization, 23
Western science, 131, 232, 234
White, David Gordon, 1, 5, 6, 12, 66
widow remarriage, 151, 153, 156
Wilder, Alexander, 60
Williams, Monier, 10, 43, 101
Wilson, Horace Hayman, 10, 59, 63, 67, 250
Windischmann, Karl Joseph, 100
Winternitz, Moriz, 239
women
Baṅgamahilā (journal), 132
femininity, 1, 73, 76
Haridev Shastri, 214
Indian Girls' Free High School, 117
Kangal, 166
Ladies' Theosophical Society, 93
Mahānirvāṇa Tantra, 128
place in society, 129–30
revivalism, 149
Sādhāran Brāhma Samāj, 173, 188

women (*cont.*)
sexual relations, 184
Society for the Acquisition of General Knowledge, 86
Society for the Education and Liberations of the Women of India, 130
Tantra, 133–34
widow remarriage, 151, 153, 156
See also reform movement
Wong, Lucian, 14, 54
Woodroffe, Ellen, 8, 217, 226–27
Woodroffe, James Tisdall, 5, 227
Woodroffe, John
All India Cow Conferences Association, 227
Atalbihari, 207, 220, 226
Bengali intervention, 13, 243
biography, 5
Bipinchandra Pal, 164–65
Catholicism, 36
as chief justice, 214
Christianity, 237
Christian Science, 234–35
colonialism, 63
death of, 226
esotericism, 213
France Tantra lectures, 227–28
funeral for Shivachandra, 217–18
Garland of Letters, The, 215, 233
Haridev Shastri, 214–15, 227
Hirendranath, 132
Indian collaborators, 6, 8
Indian Society of Oriental Art (ISOA), 215, 223
Is India Civilized?, 235, 237
Jnanendralal Majumdar, 239
Konarak photo, 215, 216*f*, 218, 226
modernity, 23
National Council of Education, 236
national education, 36
nationalism, 187
New Thought, 234–35
occultism, 238–39
Panchkari Bandyopadhyay, 240
Pramathanath Mukhopadhyay, 8, 36, 207, 233–35, 249
on Protestantism, 239
Rothenstein, 223–24
Sachchidananda Swami, 112
Sanskrit, 213–15, 222
Seed of Race, The, 236–37
Shaktism, 246
Shivachandra, 8, 11, 13, 163, 166–67, 183, 213–15, 217–18, 220, 235, 249–50
Tantra, 64, 213, 217, 226–27, 244
Tantratattva, 213
Tantric yoga, 215
Tantrik Texts, 221
Theosophical Society, 8, 226–29
Tibetan language, 222
Varendra Research Society, 222
Vitalism, 234
Vivekananda Society, 236
World as Power, The, 233–35
World Soul, 101
See also Avalon, Arthur

yantras, 1, 51, 174, 181, 208
Yelle, Robert, 28, 63, 208
yoga
Bamandas Basu, 122
Baradakanta Majumdar, 232
Bengali intervention, 48, 122–23
black and white magic, 114
Brahma Yoga, 113
esotericism, 38, 97–98
false gurus, 179
Gheraṇḍa Saṁhitā, 117
Hatha Yoga, 7, 34, 104–9, 115, 119, 135–36, 139, 232
Hinduism, 96
as hypnotism, 105, 232
Imitation of Sreekrishna, The, 137
Indian Mirror (newspaper), 102–3
initiation, 60
Islam, 119
"Karma Yoga," 139
Kshetrapal Chakravarti, 133
Kundalini Yoga, 43, 106, 185, 231
Lectures on Hindu Religion, Philosophy and Yoga, 135
Mantra Yoga, 113
meditation, 43–44, 104
mesmerism, 41, 107, 108, 137
microcosm/macrocosm, 101
Modern Postural Yoga, 96–97

nondualism, 234
Olcott, 108
Patanjali, 172
psychic faculties, 98
Raja Yoga, 7, 34, 97, 104, 106–9, 136, 232
religion, 237
samādhi, 122
as science, 62, 102, 105, 122
Science of Breath and the Philosophy of the Tattvas, The, 106
secrecy, 185, 250
self-mesmerization, 108, 119
sexual relations, 15
siddhi, 98, 101, 119
six-chakra system, 136, 178
somnambulism, 137
Spiritualism, 97
Srishchandra Basu, 118–19
Theosophical Society, 31, 101–2, 107, 114–15
Theosophists, 131
Theosophy, 98, 128
Treatise on the Yoga Philosophy, 104–5
varieties, 7–8
Yoga in Modern India, 96
Yoga Philosophy, The, 108
Yoga Shastras, The, 44, 138
Yoga Sūtra, 98, 108, 127
"Yoga Vidya," 98–99, 102, 104–5, 107
Yogi and His Message, The, 144
Yogini Tantra, 50–51
See also occultism; Tantra
Yorke, Gerald J., 6
Young Bengal, 86–87, 89, 130
Young Men's Indian Association, 224
Yugāntar, 197–98, 218, 246

Zander, Helmut, 21
Zimmer, Heinrich, 5
Zoroastrianism, 71